England's Landscape

The West Midlands

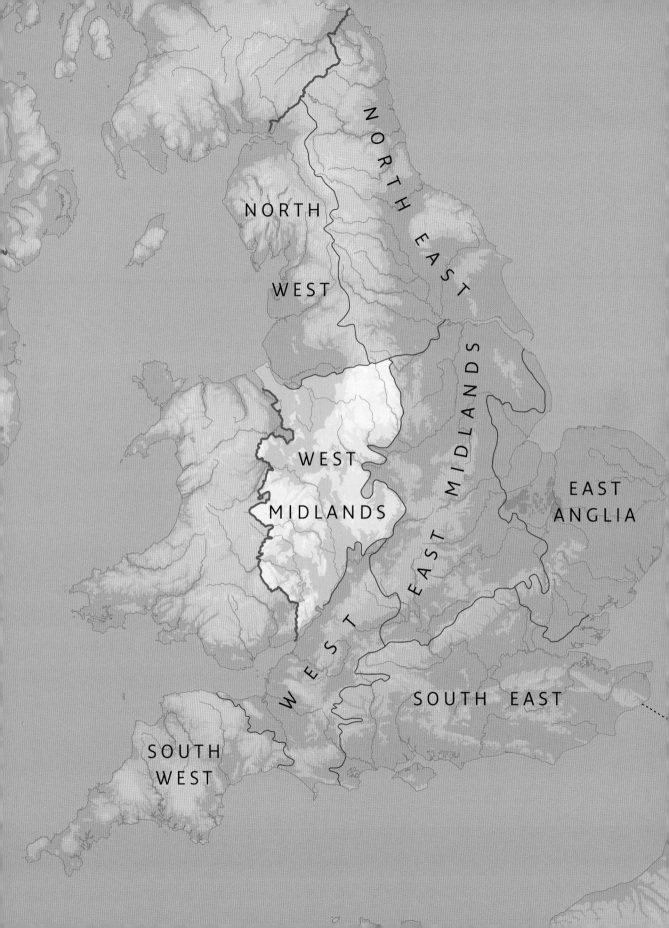

NORTH
WEST

NORTH EAST

WEST
MIDLANDS

EAST MIDLANDS

EAST
ANGLIA

WEST

SOUTH EAST

SOUTH
WEST

Collins

England's Landscape

The West Midlands

DELLA HOOKE

SERIES EDITOR NEIL COSSONS

ENGLISH HERITAGE

First published in 2006 by Collins, an imprint of
HarperCollins*Publishers*
77–85 Fulham Palace Road, London W6 8JB

www.collins.co.uk

10 9 8 7 6 5 4 3 2
10 09 08 07

ISBN 0 00 715575 1
EAN 9 78 0 00 715575 0

British Library Cataloguing in Publication Data
A CIP catalogue record for this book is available from the
British Library.

Map on previous page:
The regions: the red lines bound the general area covered by
each volume.

ACKNOWLEDGEMENTS

SERIES EDITOR
Sir Neil Cossons OBE
Chairman, English Heritage
President, Royal Geographical Society
The series editor would like to acknowledge the contribution of
the following people:

EDITORIAL BOARD:
Professor David Cannadine
*Queen Elizabeth the Queen Mother Professor of British History,
University of London*

Professor Barry Cunliffe
Professor of European Archaeology, University of Oxford

Professor Richard Lawton
*Professor Emeritus, Department of Geography, University of
Liverpool*

Professor Brian K Roberts
Professor Emeritus, Department of Geography, University of Durham

ENGLISH HERITAGE EXECUTIVE EDITORS:
Dr Paul Barnwell, *Head of Medieval and Later Rural Research*
Dr Martin Cherry, *Former Chief Buildings Historian*
Humphrey Welfare, *Northern Territory Director*
Graham Fairclough, *Head of Characterisation*

ENGLISH HERITAGE PROJECT MANAGERS:
Val Horsler, *former Head of Publishing*
Adele Campbell, *Commercial Publishing Manager*

All new ground and air photography was taken specifically for
this series. Thanks to: Damian Grady, Senior Investigator of
English Heritage Aerial Survey and Investigation Team, and to
the photographic and dark-room teams in Swindon; Steve Cole,
Head of Photography, and the staff of the English Heritage
Photography team. Archive material from the National
Monuments Record was researched by the Enquiry and
Research Services teams led by Alyson Rogers (Buildings) and
Lindsay Jones (Archaeology/Air Photos). Graphics lists were
managed by John Vallender and Bernard Thomason. Graphics
were produced under the management of Rob Read of 3's
Company (Consultancy) Ltd by Drew Smith. All other images
were researched by Jo Walton and Julia Harris-Voss.

Publisher & Commissioning Editor: Myles Archibald
Production Director: Graham Cook
Edited by Rowan Whimster
Designed by D & N Publishing, Hungerford, Berkshire
Indexed by Della Hooke

Printed in Italy by LEGO SpA, Vicenza

Contents

Foreword

The landscape of England evokes intense passion and profound emotion. This most loved of places, the inspiration for generations of writers, poets and artists, is at once both the source of the nation's infatuation and the setting for grievous misunderstanding. For people who visit, the views of England offer some of their most lasting images. For exiles abroad, the memory of the English landscape sustains their beliefs and desire for a homecoming.

But for those who live in England the obsession is double edged. On the one hand we cherish the unchanging atmosphere of a familiar place, and on the other make impossible demands of it, believing that it will always accommodate, always forgive. Only in the last half century or so have we started to recognise the extreme fragility of all that we value in the English landscape, to appreciate that it is not only the metaphor for who we are as a people but that it represents one of our most vivid contributions to a wider culture. At last we are beginning to realise that a deeper understanding of its subtle appeal and elusive character is the key to a thoughtful approach to its future.

The unique character of England's landscape derives from many things. But nowhere is the impact of human intervention absent. If geology and topography set the scene, it is the implacable persistence of generations who since the end of the Ice Age have sought to live in and off this place that has created the singular qualities of the landscape we have today. Not, of course, that the landscape before people was in any sense a static thing; on the contrary, the environment untouched by mankind was and is a dynamic and constantly changing synthesis. Every layer of that complex progression can still be found somewhere, making its own peculiar contribution to the distinctiveness of today's England. It is a compelling narrative. Through this series of regional studies our distinguished contributors – as authors and editors – have distilled something of what has created today's England, in order to decode that narrative.

Unique is an overused term. But it has a special resonance for the landscape of England, both urban and rural. What we hope readers of this series will begin to feel is the nature of the qualities that define the English landscape. Much of that landscape has of course been inherited from cultures overseas as conquest and migration brought here peoples who have progressively occupied and settled Britain. They created what might be called our shared landscapes, defined as much by what links them to the wider world as through any intrinsically native characteristics. The peoples whose common bonds stretched along the Atlantic seaboard have left a legacy in Cornwall more akin to parts of north-west France or Spain than to anywhere else in England. There are Roman roads and cities and medieval field systems that have their closest parallels in the European plains from whence they derived. Great abbeys and monasteries reflected in their art and architecture, their commerce and industry, a culture whose momentum lay outside these islands. And when disaster came it was a pan-European epidemic, the Black Death, that took away between a third and a half of the people. England's are not the only deserted medieval villages.

And yet, paradoxically, much of what today we would recognise as the quintessential England is only some two or three centuries old. Parliamentary enclosure, especially of the English lowlands, was itself a reaction to an even greater economic force – industrialisation, and the urbanisation that went with it. It has given us a rural landscape that epitomises the essence of Englishness in the minds of many. The fields and hedgerows surrounding the nucleated villages of the pre-existing medieval landscape are of course quite new when set against the timescale of human occupation. Indeed, when the first railways came through there remained, here and there, open fields where the rows of new hawthorn hedges were still feeble whips scribing lines across a thousand years of feudal landscape.

As Britain emerged to become the world's first industrial nation its astonishing transformation was at its most visible in the landscape, something new, indigenous and without precedent. It fuelled the debate on the picturesque and the sublime and was a source of wonder to those who visited from overseas. But in its urban and industrial excesses it soon came to be detested, by aesthetes, social commentators and a burgeoning class opposed to the horrors of industrial capitalism. What was perhaps the most decisive contribution of Britain to the human race provoked a powerful counteraction reflected in the writings of Ruskin, Morris, Octavia Hill and the Webbs. It was this anguish that a century ago energised the spirit of conservation in a growing band of people determined to capture what was left of the pre-industrial rural scene.

Today the landscape of England is, as ever, undergoing immense change. But, unlike the centuries just past, that change once again draws its energy and inspiration from forces overseas. A new form of global economy, North American in flavour, concept and style carries all before it. The implications for the long-term future of the landscape and the people who live in it are difficult to predict. The out-of-town shopping mall, the great encampments of distribution warehouses crouching like so many armadillos across the rural shires, the growth of exurbia – that mixed-use land between city and country that owes nothing to either – are all manifestations of these new economic forces. Like the changes that have gone before they have become the subject of intense debate and the source of worrying uncertainty. But what is clear is that a deeper understanding of the landscape, in all its manifestations, offers a means of managing change in a conscious and thoughtful manner.

This was the inspiration that led to this new regional landscape series. To understand the language of landscape, to be able to interpret the way in which people make places, offers insights and enjoyment beyond the ordinary. It enables us to experience that most neglected of human emotions, a sense of place. These books set out to reveal the values that underwrite our sense of place, by offering an insight into how the landscape of England came to be the way it is. If understanding is the key to valuing and valuing is the key to caring then these books may help to ensure that we can understand and enjoy the best of what we have and that when we make our own contribution to change it will not only reinforce that essential distinctiveness but improve the quality of life of those who live there.

Neil Cossons

1

England's Western Frontier

THE PERSONALITY OF THE REGION

The West Midlands has countryside of great diversity. From its northern limits along the banks of the Mersey to its southernmost extremity at the mouth of the Severn it has been a frontier zone for more than 4,000 years. To its west lie the uplands that were to take political form in the principality of Wales, to its east the gentler lowlands of central and eastern England. At its modern heart lie the great industrial conurbations of Birmingham, Wolverhampton and Coventry, while to the south and west lie some of England's most open and picturesque rural countryside. Little more than 180km from north to south, and 100km wide, its towns, villages and countryside nevertheless bear witness to every stage in the extraordinary story of human settlement and enterprise that has shaped and given inestimable richness to the landscape, which is today home to more than 6 million people.

This region is not one around which simple hard boundaries can be drawn. Many of the physical landscapes of which it is composed bear strong relationships to regions beyond its borders. The Peak District is, for instance, the southern part of the great Pennine spine that divides Lancashire from Yorkshire; the hills of Herefordshire and Shropshire are in many ways outliers of the Welsh mountains to the west. The area also includes three major drainage basins that connect it to other parts of the country – that of the Severn and Avon draining south-westwards towards the Bristol Channel, that of the Trent running north-eastwards towards the Humber estuary and the North Sea, and the third draining northwards by the Dee and the Weaver to the Mersey (Fig. 1.1). This outward-looking view is frequently mirrored in the region's human history, as will be shown more fully in the chapters that follow.

Throughout prehistory and into the period of Roman rule, the West Midlands was a frontier zone whose strongest links were with tribal cultures centred on and beyond its fringes. In the early medieval period the south-western parts of the area remained subdivided between separate small kingdoms that were only gradually brought under the domination of Mercia. Even after the Norman Conquest in 1066 the western part of the region remained a contested zone between the English and the Welsh, in which the newly-arrived Norman leaders enjoyed a considerable degree of administrative freedom from central royal control.

What, therefore, makes this disputed land a coherent region in its own right? Over the past half century historical geographers have made repeated attempts to subdivide England into distinctive landscape regions. Amongst the earliest and most successful were the maps, based upon the statistical evidence found within Domesday Book, that were produced by Professor Clifford Darby and his colleagues.[1] In parallel, the agricultural historian Joan Thirsk has identified historic farming regions: apart from the fells and moorland of the Peak District, virtually all of our own West Midlands falls into her 'pastoral vale lands', although she classifies south-central Herefordshire as 'arable vale lands', in other words,

Fig. 1.1 The topography of the region.

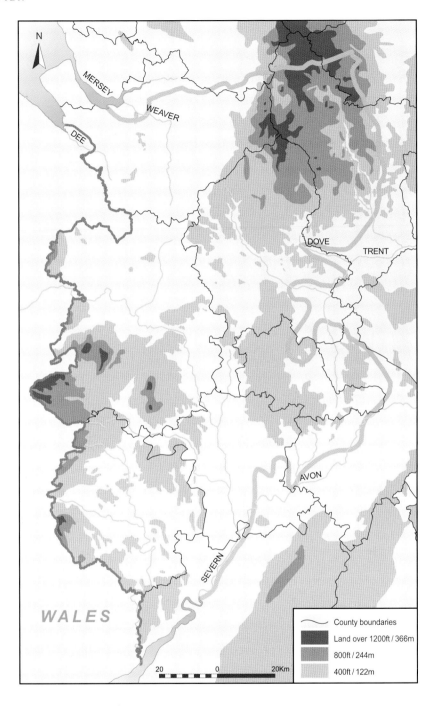

'champion' country.[2] Oliver Rackham, by contrast, has identified rather more generalised regions, distinguishing particularly between 'ancient' and 'planned' countrysides.[3] More recently still, the Countryside Agency has mapped what it describes as 'countryside character regions', which take into consideration all the different aspects of the present-day landscape – not only its geology and soils, but its vegetation cover, historic settlement patterns and contemporary land use (Fig. 1.2).[4] Developing the archaeological and historical themes, English Heritage has initiated a new programme of Historical Landscape Characterisation that recognises landscape evolution, as wrought by man, as a

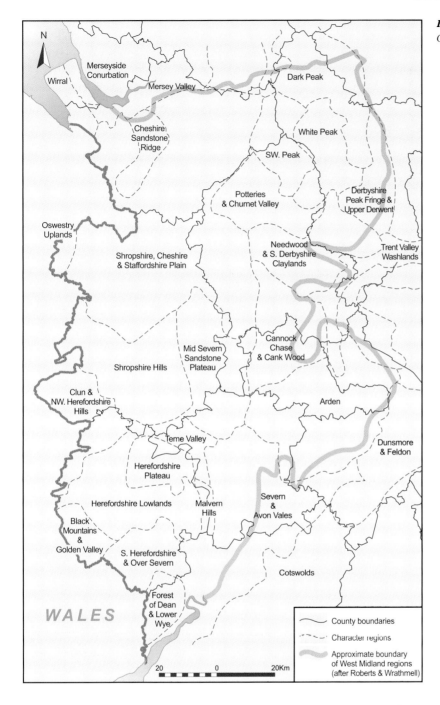

Fig. 1.2 Character regions (after Countryside Commission & English Nature).

N

Merseyside Conurbation

Wirral

Mersey Valley

Dark Peak

Cheshire Sandstone Ridge

White Peak

SW. Peak

Derbyshire Peak Fringe & Upper Derwent

Oswestry Uplands

Potteries & Churnet Valley

Shropshire, Cheshire & Staffordshire Plain

Needwood & S. Derbyshire Claylands

Trent Valley Washlands

Mid Severn Sandstone Plateau

Cannock Chase & Cank Wood

Shropshire Hills

Clun & NW. Herefordshire Hills

Arden

Teme Valley

Dunsmore & Feldon

Herefordshire Plateau

Herefordshire Lowlands

Malvern Hills

Severn & Avon Vales

Black Mountains & Golden Valley

S. Herefordshire & Over Severn

Cotswolds

Forest of Dean & Lower Wye

WALES

County boundaries

Character regions

Approximate boundary of West Midland regions (after Roberts & Wrathmell)

20   0   20Km

key factor influencing today's landscape. What each of these approaches has in common is a recognition that the present landscape is the product of thousands of years of historical evolution.

In setting the boundaries for this present book one further crucial source of help has been the *Atlas of Rural Settlement in England* created by the historical geographers Brian Roberts and Stuart Wrathmell.[5] Based upon a detailed study of 19th-century settlement maps and other sources of evidence, the atlas identifies a 'northern and western province', the southern part of which is the subject of this volume (*see* map p.2). The West Midlands also lies within

Rackham's 'ancient countryside', apart from the southern Pennines and south Shropshire hills that form part of his 'highland zone'. According to Rackham, this kind of landscape is characterised by a dispersed pattern of hamlets, small towns and ancient isolated farms linked by numerous winding roads that pass through a countryside containing many small woods or patches of heathland, old pollard trees and ancient hedges and many ponds. The highland zone, on the other hand, is distinguished by 'moors, dales, ancient oakwoods, and a mountain way of life'.[6]

The southern and eastern boundary of the region clearly marks an ancient historical divide, because it separated the areas of irregular field systems and largely dispersed settlement patterns found in the borderlands and western midlands from the 'classical' regions of medieval open field farming that occur to the south-east. Much of the latter had been cleared for agriculture by an early date, as witnessed by a concentration of Iron Age and Roman sites and a corresponding scarcity of woodland. By the late 16th and early 17th centuries they had become dominated by nucleated settlement and a mixed farming regime based on corn and stock. They are also characterised by concentrations of deserted villages, and include large areas of land that were enclosed by private and parliamentary act. These form part of Rackham's 'planned countryside' of nucleated villages and late-established farms, connected and divided by the straight roads and modern hedges of enclosure. However, Rackham's simple distinction masks the fact that planning in these kinds of regions was not limited to later historical periods. Equally, just as much change occurred over time in the 'ancient' regions that were not as static as has sometimes been assumed.

Roberts and Wrathmell's study reveals how, by the mid-19th century, much of the West Midlands was characterised by a highly dispersed pattern of settlement, a feature still perpetuated today in rural areas despite subsequent development. There is, however, a danger in defining the region solely in these terms. For example, the south-eastern border tends to follow the boundary between the more acid soils found on the Mercia Mudstones to the north-west and the limey soils of the Lias clays and Oolitic limestones to the south-east. These limey soils supported the nucleated villages and open fields of medieval times. Yet it is clear that medieval estates in south-east Worcestershire and south Warwickshire were closely linked in an established pattern of resource management to the more wooded regions to the north and that this may represent a system of interdependence already established by the Iron Age. At Shottery in the central Avon valley, for instance, an estate in an area of intensive agricultural exploitation was associated with other estates at Nuthurst in Arden and woodland in north Worcestershire perhaps as early as the late 7th or early 8th century. In the Domesday Book of 1086, Tanworth in Arden was similarly a dependent manor of the royal vill of Brailes, located some 40km away in the Feldon in the south of the county. The exchange of woodland resources and the products of intensive agriculture fused these complementary regions together in a way that lasted throughout the historical period. A boundary driven between them is, in many ways, an historical aberration.

There has always been a considerable variation in settlement density across the region. In the 19th century the Cheshire plain was an area of relatively high density with small villages and hamlets scattered across a drift-covered plain, often, in the past, with their own irregular open field systems – including small areas of former townfield that have given rise to distinctive enclosure patterns. Densities were slightly lower in the Wirral and over the plains of Shropshire and mid Staffordshire. These plains were areas of dispersed settlement and extensive tracts of old enclosures but with woodland and commons intermixed (often with common-edge settlements of small farmhouses and cottages) and with nucleated villages present in limited numbers. Further south and west, the area between the Wye and Teme also tended to be relatively heavily populated.

By comparison with other parts of the region, this is still a complex landscape in which upland escarpments separate intervening clay vales that are drained by rivers like the Wye, Lugg, Arrow and Teme and their various tributaries. Although there are scattered market towns across the region, villages are thin on the ground and the settlement pattern is made up of carpets of small hamlets and dispersed farmsteads set in intricate, anciently enclosed landscapes that still carry much timber. In the 19th century, there were lower densities in the Clun area of south-west Shropshire, the Severn valley of Worcestershire and the Forest of Dean, but few areas were as empty as the southern extension of the Pennines in north Derbyshire.

The population of the coalfield areas was increasing before the end of the 19th century and these subsequently expanded and spread across the countryside around. Indeed, few areas have lost settlements since the 19th century – most have grown and often coalesced. There have also been other changes in population levels. The Clun Forest area of south-west Shropshire is now the least populated part of the region, followed by south-east Shropshire, west Herefordshire and parts of west Derbyshire. The Wirral today, on the other hand, is an area of dense population around the focus of Birkenhead. The North Staffordshire Coalfield area and the central West Midland conurbation of Wolverhampton and Birmingham, with its outlier around Coventry, stand out as areas of particularly high population density with over 750 people per square kilometre (*see* Chapter 7, Fig. 7.49).

The purpose of this book is to explore the historical evolution of the West Midlands province and to see how this explains its characteristic landscape. In general, the landscape of the more remote prehistoric and Roman periods is hidden from easy view, obscured (but not necessarily destroyed) by subsequent development. When detailed written documents start to appear in the early medieval period they reveal landscape regions with which we are still familiar, although the individual features of which they were composed may be very different to those found in later periods. Although they are still recognisable, many of the elements of the Norman and medieval landscape survive today only as fragments or relics of their former selves – whether buildings such as castles, manor houses, abbeys or churches, or more extensive features of land use such as forests and parks.

As we begin our journey of exploration we have to remember that much of what we see today represents the cumulative activity of the last five hundred years or so of human settlement and, in some parts of the region, the even more dramatic changes wrought in the two hundred years since the Agricultural Revolution and the dawn of the Industrial Revolution. In general, however, the West Midlands remains an ancient landscape, one of adaptation rather than sudden change, and its evolution can still be read in the present-day countryside.

More detailed local studies suggest, however, that the real picture is more complicated, and that in some areas a combination of ancient and planned landscapes can be identified side by side. Some local landscapes may be 'old' in that they preserve ancient features and monuments from a wide range of periods. Others, by contrast, have been subject to many periods of 'survey planning', whether this occurred during prehistoric times, in the early medieval period, as a result of 17th- and 18th-century 'improvement', or through later enclosure, often involving entirely new field layouts and new settlements. From the earliest periods, land tenure played a particularly important role in determining the degree of continuity or change – either through the individual medieval manor or township, or in later periods through the landed estates of the gentry. In general, however, the West Midlands is a region in which the basic pattern of field boundaries and routeways evolved gradually. Arable farming was only moderately intensive and there was only limited agricultural change in the Middle Ages or post-medieval period.[7]

A LAND OF CONTRASTS

Let us turn now to a more detailed portrayal of the region's many diverse faces. In the north, the Dark Peak is a landscape that is at once exhilarating in its wide sweeping views yet often forbidding; dramatic on occasions but monotonous on others, its distances a challenge to walkers and travellers of any description (Fig. 1.3). Here, Millstone Grit and shales cap the underlying Carboniferous Limestone and support wild moorlands of blanket peat, heather and rough molinia grassland that extend unbroken for miles in parts of north Derbyshire. Hallam Moors straddle the boundary between Derbyshire and South Yorkshire to the west of Sheffield, but the most extensive areas of flat, unbroken moorland lie further to the north-west in the heart of the High Peak. Edale Moor reaches up to 636m on Kinder Scout (Fig. 1.1), while northwards across the desolate Snake Pass the moors rise once again to Bleaklow (628m). Along their edges, however, the high moors are dissected by streams issuing out of the moorland bogs, flowing fast in deep cloughs that carry a vegetation of dwarf shrubs, especially bilberry and heather; some may be wooded, particularly in the east of the region, unlike the land above. Every now and then, a low edge of dark gritstone accentuates the steep upper slopes of these valleys in stark contrast to the flat moorland plateaux. Stanage Edge, for instance, runs for several kilometres along the western brink of Hallam Moor above Hathersage, rising to 447m in High Neb. Further to the south, Curbar and Baslow Edges define the western brink of Big Moor in the region of the East Moors, while on the south-western fringe of the Peak District the Roaches form a high edge to the west of the Buxton–Leek road, the ragged teeth of Ramshaw Rocks overlooking the route.

Much of this is an empty land of far-distant, open vistas, although the wooded cloughs present a different, more enclosed landscape. The blanket peats began to form in some areas as early as the Mesolithic period (*c.* 5000 BC), possibly with the onset of increased precipitation, but formed much later in others (*see* Chapter 2). Although there was some settlement of the Peak District uplands in Bronze Age times, the gritstone moorlands remained thinly settled throughout Roman and medieval times, providing mainly seasonal pasture. After the Norman Conquest a considerable part of the region fell under forest law as the Forest of the High Peak. Subsequently, small-scale quarrying was extended and packhorse routes threaded across the moorlands. Settlement nevertheless remained sparse, with dispersed stone farmsteads and hamlets set within their inbye land (improved land and enclosed pasture close to the farm) that was often enclosed only in the 18th century. Today, the construction of reservoirs to serve the urban conurbations of central England has brought a new type of feature to the region.

To the west and east, coal-bearing strata outcrop to the north of Stoke and to the north-east of Derby. The York, Derby and Nottinghamshire coalfield lies

Fig. 1.3 A view in the Dark Peak region of Derbyshire, largely an area of Millstone Grit and shales.

largely outside the region of this volume, but in the 18th and 19th centuries the North Staffordshire Coalfield became an industrial area celebrated for its pottery manufacture.

Within the south-western and south-eastern arcs of the dark Millstone Grit and shales, Carboniferous Limestone comes to the surface and is threaded with intrusive metal-bearing lodes. Deep dales were sometimes formed by the collapse of the cave systems with which the limestone is riddled – rivers frequently plunge underground down 'swallow holes' in the summer season. This karst landscape consists of thin soils that were once intermittently wooded but today bear a thin, turf grassland vegetation. Bare grey-white crags often outcrop along the dale sides, as in Dovedale (Fig. 1.4), producing a landscape sometimes referred to as the 'White Peak' in contrast to that of the darker gritstones. This was a landscape that was attractive to farmers from the Neolithic period onwards, and it is today characterised by the surviving remnants of early field systems and particular kinds of later field patterns. Mining, too, especially for lead and silver, was established by Roman times and continued to play a dominant role in the region's economic prosperity. The area is far more heavily settled than the gritstone moorlands and is characterised by nucleated villages and small towns set amidst fields bounded by walls of distinctive grey-white limestone.

Uplands are also characteristic of much of the Welsh borderland in the counties of Shropshire and Herefordshire. The border itself tends to run close to the eastern edge of the high land in north Shropshire, with the highest summits lying a few kilometres within Wales, but further to the south there is much upland country within Shropshire itself, with the Clun Hills filling the south-western corner of the county. Elsewhere, sporadic outcrops of harder rocks form isolated blocks or longer upland ridges to the west of the Worcestershire–Staffordshire borders, such as the Malverns and the Wrekin. In Shropshire, a series of ridges run roughly NNE–SSW across the southern part of the county; these include the Clees, Wenlock Edge, Long Mynd, Stiperstones, Corndon Hill and Long Mountain. Each upland massif has its own individual character much influenced by the underlying geology. Between these ranges are flat-bottomed steep-sided valleys of pasture and arable farmland that contain most of the scattered settlements and villages.

In a journey across southern Shropshire, beginning near the south-eastern border and moving north-westwards, these upland massifs would be consecutively encountered – it is a journey, across the grain of the country, that was almost impossible to make in historic times and is still difficult now. The Clees are two steeply rising masses of Carboniferous rocks that include Millstone Grit and Coal Measures capped with the resistant dolerite or basalt that produces their flat-topped appearance. Rising to more than 530m, they are the highest hills in Shropshire. Titterstone Clee, on the south, is not only pock-marked with collapsed bell

Fig. 1.4 Dovedale in the White Peak of Derbyshire, a gash in the Carboniferous Limestone that may be the result of a collapsed cave system.

Fig. 1.5 Wenlock Edge, Shropshire,
an escarpment marked by a line of
ancient woodland.

pits along its southern flank, the results of coal mining, but the basalt has been
extensively quarried for roadstone, resulting in the virtual destruction of the Iron
Age fort on its summit, once the largest fort in Shropshire. Settlements of miners
and quarrymen, who often combined these tasks with smallholding, extend over
the lower commons and along the Cleobury Mortimer to Ludlow road. Brown
Clee, to the north, has also been quarried but on its summit the earthworks of the
great hillfort of Abdon Burf survive and the remnants of two others are situated on
its slopes. Brown Clee for a time lay under forest law and the parishes around
enjoyed shared grazing rights on the hill, their stock driven along a network of drifts
or straker ways towards the summit. Today a wide area of open moorland survives
above Abdon although the eastern flanks of the hill have been forested.

Corvedale, its farmlands drained by the River Corve, separates the Clees from
the long spine of Silurian Limestone that forms the escarpment of Wenlock Edge.
An almost unbroken stretch of ancient or replanted woodland is a distinctive
feature along its north-west-facing scarp (Fig. 1.5), which extends for some
25km from south-west to north-east until it terminates near the town of Much
Wenlock. In the Middle Ages this woodland formed part of Long Forest.
Although the limestone has been quarried for building material and for a variety
of industrial uses that include agricultural lime, cement, and smelting flux for
iron making, industry is not obtrusive in the area.

The narrow Ape Dale, drained by a series of brooks that include the Byne
Brook, separates Wenlock Edge from the Stretton Hills and the hill commons of
Caer Caradoc Hill, another summit of Precambrian volcanic rock that bears an
impressive Iron Age hillfort. Only a narrow faulted trough divides these hills
from the dominant mass of the Long Mynd, another smooth-topped plateau
of similar rock. The massif is deeply cut by narrow V-shaped valleys like that of
Carding Mill above Church Stretton, but on the summit there are many
kilometres of bleak featureless, often heather-covered, moorland.

Fig. 1.6 The central Shropshire hills near Pontesford, seen from the northern end of the Stiperstones.

West of the Long Mynd, the land remains generally high and beyond the narrow valley of the East Onny runs the ridge of the Stiperstones, the most pronounced ridge of all, formed of hard quartzite. Bare tor-like crags crown the summit and this is some of the wildest land in the county. Although a forest for a time in the Middle Ages, the top of the ridge is almost bare of vegetation and littered with scree. Deposits of lead and silver have been worked in the area, giving rise to squatters' communities on the commons and, near Snailbeach, the desolation of 19th-century lead mining. But there are pockets of land that offer a hidden and quite different landscape – like the pastures known as The Hollies on Lordshill, with their twisted and ancient remnants of an old holly forest and panoramic views northwards over the little detached pointed summit of Pontesford Hill (Fig. 1.6). Beyond the West Onny, the steep summit of Corndon Hill, with its many Bronze Age cairns, lies within Wales but the county then reaches out to include the ridge running north-eastwards from it, into which is tucked the stone circle of Mitchell's Fold, and sends a claim out into the plain of the Camlad beyond to take in the area around Chirbury. Indeed, further ridges rise westwards as the border runs along Long Mountain. Offa's Dyke, the great Mercian defensive earthwork, ran even further to the west at this point.

The south-western corner of Shropshire enfolds a further upland area, but one where the hills that drain eastwards via the River Clun and its tributaries are carved out of sandstones and shales. The River Teme marks its southern edge. In the medieval period this formed part of the Marcher lordship or Barony of Clun and was known as Clun Forest, a sparsely populated region administered from Clun Castle from the mid-12th century until 1549. Under such jurisdiction, Norman lords enjoyed considerable independence providing they policed the buffer zone between England and Wales. The region was too remote and vulnerable, however, to support the new town that was laid out here on the north bank of the river. By the end of the 19th century Clun remained no more than a small market town with about 1,000 inhabitants, at the heart of a poor district comprising much hilly land. Extensive enclosures of the open sheepwalks were made in 1845 and 1847 and a landscape of gentle, domed hills bearing tiny brown-green fields and pastures that now reach on to the hilltops melts 'imperceptibly into Wales' (Fig. 1.7). There is some rough pasture left, mostly on the hilltops above the secret valleys below that are hidden by patches of deciduous woodland. There are stands of dense coniferous forest plantations as

Fig. 1.7 *A rural view in the Clun Forest*.

well, especially where they form a barrier-band across the entrance to the area, extending from Bishop's Castle to the River Teme, and this 'lost' region was well described by Housman when he wrote:

> *Clunton and Clunbury,*
> *Clungunford and Clun,*
> *Are the quietest places*
> *Under the sun.*[8]

The western boundary region of Herefordshire also runs close to the edge of the Welsh mountains, leaving the Radnor Forest and the more southerly upland moorlands around Glascwm to lie within Wales. In the south-west of the county, to the south-east of Hay-on-Wye, the boundary follows the crest of the easternmost ridge of the Black Mountains (Fig. 1.8). Ewyas, from the Welsh 'sheep district', was the name of the region to the east where a series of NW–SE ridges of Old Red Sandstone separate isolated vales drained by the deeply incised valleys of the Olchon Brook, River Monnow, Escley Brook, and River Dore (the latter known as the Golden Valley). This remained a Welsh commote until it was siezed by the Normans, sometime after 1086, and controlled as two lordships from the castles of Ewyas Lacy and Ewyas Harold. Only the highest border uplands remain today as open moorland or unfenced sheep pasture, but this contributes significantly to the character of the region.

The border region has a long history as a frontier zone. The upland areas are thick with Iron Age fortified sites, but in the early medieval period this is where Anglo-Saxon rule met British opposition. Two major post-Roman linear dykes run close to the Welsh–English boundary – Wat's Dyke in Cheshire and Shropshire, and Offa's Dyke through Cheshire, Shropshire and Herefordshire – while a shorter dyke known as the Rowe Ditch runs N–S and cuts across the Arrow valley in Herefordshire. Years of Welsh raiding continued to devastate the borderland and some of the earliest castles in England (then simple motte-and-bailey features) were raised at Hereford, Ewyas and Richard's Castle by followers of Edward the Confessor. At the time of the Norman Conquest, southern Herefordshire still formed part of the Welsh districts of Ewyas and Archenfield (presumably as client kingdoms) and enjoyed a measure of independence, but constant raiding and

rebellion elsewhere led to the construction of dozens of mottes and later stone castles across the region. In spite of these early political difficulties, the region is fertile and settlement is scattered across the whole of the three western counties, largely producing a pattern of dispersed farmsteads, hamlets and small villages. Medieval field systems were generally irregular with many, scattered patches of open field surrounded by enclosed fields, woodland or open common, and the hills continued to provide valuable sheepwalks.

The southern part of Herefordshire also includes much hilly ground and there are moderate uplands, too, in the east of Herefordshire, for here sandstone ridges give rise to a rolling topography to the east of the River Wye and again in the north-east of the county. The south-eastern Herefordshire uplands rise further in the Forest of Dean, lying mostly within Gloucestershire. The land is not high, reaching only 237m in the north near Drybrook. Coal Measure rocks overlying Carboniferous Limestone have given rise to nutrient-poor soils that have remained well wooded to the present day in spite of the early exploitation of iron and coal resources, although much of this woodland has been replanted (*see* Chapters 5 and 7).

The upland regions of south Staffordshire, north Worcestershire and north-western Warwickshire are seldom as impressive as those of the Peak District or the Welsh borderland. They are lower and less of an impediment to development.

Fig. 1.8 The easternmost ridge of the Black Mountains, the border between England and Wales.

Fig. 1.9 The central Herefordshire plain. *Hay Bluff and the Black Mountains are visible in the distance.*

A plateau region generally above 121m in height extends southwards from the Trent valley in Staffordshire into north Worcestershire where its south-western rim rises to a height of over 243m, reaching 335m in the Clent-Lickey ridge. It is mostly composed of infertile drift-covered Coal Measure rocks or Bunter Pebble Beds, and coal-bearing seams occur along its western edge. A further drift-covered area of Coal Measures forms the east Warwickshire plateau, rarely above 183m in height, and here again coal-bearing strata outcrop along the north-eastern edge; both the South Staffordshire and East Warwickshire coalfields are uplifted horsts (blocks) separated by a lower-lying graben (trenches) floored with clay strata. The presence of accessible coal spurred industrial development in both these coalfield regions in the 19th century and the former gave rise to the well-known 'Black Country' conurbation.

Although the upland areas produce some of the most impressive landscapes to be found within the West Midland region, the lowland plains cover a wider area. These are usually floored with Mercia Mudstone that tends to give rise to rather heavy, slightly acidic soils and this rock type is found below almost the whole of the Cheshire lowland and the northern plain of Shropshire, the central lowland of Staffordshire into Derbyshire and across mid-Worcestershire and north-west Warwickshire. In Cheshire, the clays are overlain by a thick layer of glacial deposits. More fertile sandstones outcrop in the southern part of the northern plain of Shropshire and the central plain of Herefordshire (Fig. 1.9) and, although heavy, the soils of the Lower Lias clays of south-eastern Worcestershire and southern Warwickshire are also potentially more fertile than the mudstones.

All the clay lowlands supported historically a landscape of mixed farming with outlying farms, villages and hamlets distributed across the region. Some of the plain areas were afforested in Norman times, as in mid-Cheshire and mid-Worcestershire, but most of the forest areas tended to be enclosed by late medieval times. In Cheshire, north Shropshire and north-west Staffordshire, the plain has a lush pastoral character and ridge and furrow shows where former arable fields were enclosed as pasture in the late medieval and post-medieval periods. The monotony of the plain, especially in Cheshire, is occasionally broken by wooded sandstone ridges. In Worcestershire, the plain is drained by tributaries of the River Severn, including its major tributary the Avon, and the vale areas have been noted in the past for their flood-meadow pastures, their high yields of corn and their orchards. The Severn is the longest river flowing through the region. Rising in the mountains of west Wales on the flanks of Plynlimon it flows at first north-eastwards towards the Dee. The upper Severn was, however, 'captured' by the middle Severn and flows south-eastwards across the Shropshire plain before cutting southwards through the Severn Gorge at Ironbridge to continue on its course through Worcestershire towards Gloucestershire, the Severn estuary and the sea. For centuries it was a corridor for both imports and exports; river vessels plied their trade as far inland as Shrewsbury when the river flow allowed – even as far as Welshpool in times of flood – goods often being transferred from larger to smaller vessels at Gloucester or Bewdley. The areas of Lias clays to the south-east, in both Worcestershire and Warwickshire, were intensively cultivated until the period of Tudor enclosure and are again characterised by deserted villages that show the relict ridge and furrow of former open arable fields.

In general, lowland areas have historically been much more heavily settled than the uplands, although subsequent land use, or the lack of it, has often led to better survival of early settlement features in the more sparsely settled uplands, thus often presenting a distorted and misleading picture of the real pattern of settlement activity. Only recently has aerial photography begun to redress the balance by hinting at the earlier settlement layers that have been subsequently hidden below the fields and farmsteads of the lowlands. Apart from the obvious landscape contrasts arising from very different rock types and soils, farming systems that have developed to make use of the available resources have added their effect. One of the main differences between lowland and upland regions is the nature of field boundaries, for whereas boundaries on the latter made use of local stone, in the lowlands fields were almost always hedged and there are, indeed, many miles of surviving ancient hedgerow in parts of the region.

Outside the industrial conurbations, the lowland countryside is mostly one of rural farmland although there are areas in which ancient woodland or more modern plantation woodland is a prominent and characteristic feature. The most extensive woodlands are those of Dean and Wyre, both ancient forest areas that were put to heavy industrial usage. The Forest of Wyre straddles the border between Worcestershire and Shropshire and, although less extensive than Dean (4km E–W and 2–3km N–S), has a greater surviving area of ancient semi-natural woodland. Ancient or replanted woodland also survives in some other former forest areas like that of the former Deerfold and Bringewood Forest areas of north Herefordshire, parts of Needwood in Staffordshire, and along Wenlock Edge and in the Ironbridge Gorge region of Shropshire. But modern forestry plantations have, for the most part, replaced the old woodlands of Cannock Chase in Staffordshire and Delamere Forest in Cheshire (*see* Chapter 5).

Later in this book we will look in closer detail at the evolution of the rural landscape (*see* Chapter 5), but industry and mining, too, have had a marked effect upon regional landscapes. In some regions, early industry has left only relict features in an otherwise rural farming landscape, but in others early industry expanded after the Industrial Revolution, with much greater effect. Although heavy industries have since dwindled or disappeared, to be replaced by lighter manufacturing or service industries, the already extensive conurbations have continued to expand. The Mersey region, in the north-west, lies outside the West Midlands, but development in the Staffordshire Potteries, the Black Country and, to a lesser extent, the South Shropshire Coalfield/Coalbrookdale area has given rise to vast built-up areas in which originally separate village or town centres have become linked in an amorphous mass. Birmingham, too, fills a substantial part of the 'West Midlands' county area, spreading eastwards to Solihull and Sutton Coldfield and sending tentacles out towards Coventry beyond.

While this book is intended to cover the general evolution of the West Midland landscape, it can only hint at the depth of historical interest there is in virtually every square kilometre of town and countryside. The term 'landscape' is derived from the Dutch *landskep* and originally implied not so much what was seen but the way in which the landscape was represented – how the view was perceived, as by the eye of a painter. Indeed, the 18th-century devotees of the 'Picturesque' movement would carry a glass prism known as a 'Claude glass' through which to view the scene and only those educated in a very specialised field of lore would have been able to interpret all the classical symbolism involved. Today we might find this attitude pretentious, but there is no doubt that to understand the landscape is to see it with fresh eyes. More information is being discovered all the time, whether through archaeology – either by excavation or field survey – or by historical research. Geographical Information Systems (GIS) are also providing new ways to record, compare and present data. Air photography can capture regional distinctiveness expressed in field and settlement patterns over entire regions and bring them to a wider audience.[9] Few can claim to be completely knowledgeable about even one of the regions covered in this series of books, and the more one delves the more one finds there is to learn.

NOTES

1   For this region, *see* Darby & Terrett 1978; Darby & Maxwell 1962; Darby 1977.

2   Thirsk 1987, 39, map IV.

3   Rackham 1986, 3–5, fig 1.3.

4   Countryside Commission and English Nature 1997.

5   Roberts & Wrathmell 2000; 2002, 10, fig 1.4.

6   Rackham 1986, 4–5.

7   Williamson 1998, 14–15, 18, fig 3.

8   A E Housman, from *A Shropshire Lad*, 1896.

9   *England: The Photographic Atlas*, Get Mapping.com 2001.

2

Landscape and Life in the Prehistoric and Roman Periods

THE FIRST SETTLERS

Our evidence for the earliest presence of people in the West Midlands is still very sketchy. Apart from scattered finds of implements, Palaeolithic sites with good assemblages of tools are known only on the edge of, or just outside, the region – in caves in the Permian limestone of Creswell Crags in Derbyshire, and from King Arthur's Cave in Herefordshire. Human occupation at Creswell Crags, which includes several cave complexes, began in earlier Palaeolithic times, but the glacial ice sheets reached their maximum southerly extent some 20,000 years ago, covering the area. In the later Devensian stages, when the ice began to recede, much larger Upper Palaeolithic assemblages of horse, reindeer, red deer and hyena bones were deposited in Robin Hood's Cave and Mother Grundy's Parlour and the groups of early hunting people who used the caves on an intermittent basis have left behind them many kinds of tools, including a rib bone with a horse's head engraved on it. Recently, Cresswell Crags has also revealed the earliest example of Palaeolithic cave art ever found in Britain, in the form of engravings of ibex, horse, bison and birds carved onto the rock surfaces about 12,000 years ago.

King Arthur's Cave overlooks the River Wye near Symond's Yat in the south-western corner of the region and was first excavated in 1871. Here, too, there is extensive evidence of Upper Palaeolithic and Mesolithic occupation, both in the form of flint and bone artefacts and the bones of extinct animals such as the mammoth, woolly rhinoceros, hyena, giant Irish deer and cave bear. The cave was used between about 10,000 and 8000 BC, possibly as a base-camp, by hunter-gatherer communities.

During the advance of the ice sheets, southern and eastern Britain would have been tundra – treeless moorland – but, with the withdrawal of the ice, trees began to re-colonise the region. Birch, aspen and sallow appear first in the pollen record, followed about 8500 BC by pine and then, in succession, oak and alder, lime and some species of elm; then holly, ash, beech, hornbeam and maple.[1] During this time the West Midlands lay on the western fringe of a province where lime was the commonest tree although woods were, as now, a patchwork of tree communities containing trees at all stages of growth and decline. The idea of this ancient wildwood as an impenetrable 'forest' has, however, been challenged, and it has been argued that the woodland of this period was, in fact, relatively open – grazed heavily by herbivores such as red and roe deer, elk, horse, wild cattle and wild pig[2] – or damaged by fire, storm and drought.[3] The older notion of a central midland region characterised by unbroken forest has, therefore, to be rejected, and a landscape of mixed vegetation is likely to have been present, with denser woodland in the more inaccessible places. Where the natural woodland was open, it could be more easily cleared for crop growing by Neolithic farmers and tree growth inhibited by their grazing stock. These same early settlers may also have taken the branches and leaves of some tree species for fodder, a use which was probably a factor in the rapid decline of the lime.

Peat and mineral soil profiles suggest that the preceding Mesolithic inhabitants, who depended mainly upon hunting, deliberately burnt the vegetation to create glades of new grass growth to which animals would be attracted. Mesolithic occupation has been identified in the region by the identification of lithic assemblages – collections of their characteristic small tools, which tend to occur in regional clusters. Their implements are commonly found, for instance, on hill scarps or spurs above 335m in the South Pennines that would have afforded commanding views over the small valleys that dissect the plateau. Caves in limestone areas have also produced Mesolithic material, but additional finds made during the excavation of later settlement sites across the region show that Mesolithic activity was widespread. Well-drained, elevated locations in close proximity to water sources seem to have been visited regularly, like some sites on the south Staffordshire plateau (such as a small rock shelter near Rugeley or scattered sites near Sutton Coldfield).

A LANDSCAPE OF MONUMENTS

By Neolithic and Early Bronze Age times, between 4000 and 2000 BC, woodland clearance was well advanced. Most of the evidence for human activity during this period comes from burial and ritual monuments, which appear to look outwards towards other cultural regions for their inspiration, reinforcing the impression of the West Midlands as having something of the character of a frontier zone. Although they are not on the scale of those of Wessex, clusters of Neolithic and early Bronze Age ritual monuments have been found in various places, although they survive best on the uplands that fringe the region. As well as burial mounds of different kinds, they include standing stones, henges and stone circles. Arthur's Stone, on Merbach Hill at the head of the Golden Valley, near Dorstone in the Welsh borders, is a Neolithic burial chamber whose passages and chambers would originally have been covered with earth, but whose enormous capstone of local limestone now lies exposed to the elements. Another intact long barrow lies near by and the area appears to have been a focus of Neolithic funerary activity; there were others in the same region. The barrows belong to the Severn-Cotswold group of chambered long barrows, a type found as far south-west as the Mendips but which spills over into south Wales and the Black Mountains.

While these large chambered mounds were the burial places of the community, henges and stone circles represent the ritual meeting places of the living. On the siltstone and sandstone range that forms the Corndon and Stapeley Hills on the Montgomery–Shropshire border stands the remains of a stone circle known as Mitchell's Fold (Fig. 2.1). It was erected some time around 2000–1400 BC and 14 of its original 30 or so stones still stand in a circle about 27m in diameter. Only 2km to the north, Hoarstone Circle consists of 37 smaller stones of local dolerite arranged in a more oval arrangement 20–23m in diameter and with a single stone at the centre. This second monument stands in a lower position than the Mitchell's Fold circle and three significant gaps in its circumference align on prominent features on the surrounding skyline – Bromlow Common, Stiperstones and Corndon Hill.[4] Less than a kilometre south of Mitchell's Fold there was once a third stone circle, now destroyed, known as the Whetstones. Although we can only guess at their original purpose, all three of these small circles apparently served family groups and lay amidst clusters of burial mounds and standing stones.

Fig. 2.1 Mitchell's Fold stone circle, located on a col between Corndon and Stapeley Hills near Chirbury, south-west Shropshire.

Just to the south, at Hyssington over the modern Welsh border, was an important axe factory based on a local outcrop of picrite, a crystalline rock much favoured by early tool manufacturers. It has been suggested that the route over Stapeley Hill formed a Bronze Age trackway later to be known as *Yr Hen Ffordd* ('the old road') that gave its name to the hamlet of Hemford, and there are burial mounds along its route. Another trackway that may have been used by Bronze Age Irish axe-traders was the *Ffordd Saeson* near Oswestry that linked Anglesey with the Severn valley.[5] From concentrations of flint and stone artefacts it has also been postulated that a long-distance routeway leading across south Shropshire from the Kerry Hills in the west to the River Severn near Bewdley may also have been used by late Neolithic and Bronze Age traders carrying battle-axes and axe-hammers.[6]

On the other side of the region, in the Peak District, the sequence of prehistoric activity is similar. At Ballidon, in Derbyshire, lies the large multi-phased Neolithic mound of Minninglow. Containing several chambers, it is sited on one of the highest hills along the spine of the limestone plateau: 'the monument appears to sit above the world, from where the living and the dead alike could survey the extensive panorama'.[7] Another smaller chambered site at Five Wells is sited above the precipitous northern edge of Taddington Moor, from where it offers wide views over the broad shelves flanking the Wye gorge, an area that may have been one of the most favourable in the whole region for Neolithic grazing.[8] These tombs represent a different group to those of the west of the region and the earliest are generally round in shape. They too, however, represent ritual burial places used by successive generations of the local community.

As well as funerary monuments, the later Neolithic and Early Bronze Age people of the White Peak area of Derbyshire constructed circular embanked henge monuments that seem to have served as the ritual centres for communities established over a wide area. Arbor Low, one of the finest surviving examples, is an egg-shaped monument that comprises a circle of stones set within an encircling bank and ditch about 40m in diameter (Fig. 2.2). It is noted for the fact that today all the stones lie flat upon the ground. They were, however, originally set in holes in the limestone bedrock but these were too shallow to prevent their eventual fall. Inside the encircling bank and stone circle was a smaller setting of stones known as a cove, which apparently faced the maximum midsummer setting of the moon and may possibly have been associated with burial. Interrupting the main banked and ditched circuit of the henge were two entrance causeways, one on its northern side and another to the south from which the single earthen bank of an avenue curved away in the direction of Gib Hill, a huge long mound that began as a long barrow but has later round barrows superimposed.[9] Further to the north-west, to the north-east of Buxton, another henge, known as the Bull Ring, has lost its stones although the bank and ditch are still in good condition.

The Neolithic burial mounds of Derbyshire are restricted to the limestone plateau and may represent the seasonal meeting places of groups occupying 'home bases' in the surrounding valleys that provided better winter shelter. Until their populations grew, and they needed more land for cultivation, the earlier Neolithic communities of the area probably used the upland plateau for grazing. Most of the larger barrows and the later henge monuments constructed on the watersheds (apart from the Bull Ring henge and Pea Low barrow which still lie between agricultural zones) were perhaps in neutral locations suitable for 'inter-group' meetings or in disputed 'boundary' or seasonally-used zones.[10] Neolithic peoples were probably fairly mobile, coming together at seasonal gatherings when communal social and ritual ceremonies were likely to have been carried out. A large enclosure at Gardom's Edge above Baslow, for example, may be the equivalent of the causewayed enclosures that were the focus of contemporary social gatherings throughout many parts of southern England.

Neolithic and Early Bronze Age settlement sites are rarely found, although pottery and a hearth on the hill known as the Roveries near Lydham in Shropshire appear to be evidence of occupation, while another Neolithic settlement is attested below later occupation levels at Weeping Cross, near Stafford. Concentrations of flint assemblages around Clunbury in Shropshire similarly suggest the presence of permanent settlements or temporary camps, as does a Neolithic site identified at

Fig. 2.2 Arbor Low, *a Neolithic henge in the White Peak of Derbyshire.*

***Fig. 2.3 Cairns on the summit of
the Stiperstones:*** *the largest cairn is seen
in the foreground to the left of the track and is
21m in diameter and 1.8m high. Beyond is the
natural tor with a rock formation known as
the Devil's Chair.*

Lismore Fields, on the west side of Buxton in the Derbyshire Peak District. This
latter settlement lay in the upper Wye valley basin, then heavily wooded but
sheltered, and its occupants, probably predominantly pastoralists, may have
exploited the gritstone and limestone uplands for summer grazing and
agriculture, and the higher gritstone areas for hunting.[11]

Other types of feature surviving from this period are mounds of burnt pebbles
and charcoal found close to streams. Their use has been much debated, but it
seems likely that the heated pebbles had been cast into pits of water and the
resulting hot water used either to cook meat or to produce steam for a type of
Bronze Age 'sauna' or sweat lodge – a kind of ritual cleansing. Many such
mounds have been located on the Birmingham plateau, suggesting a substantial
population presence even in marginal areas.

By the later Bronze Age (1500–700 BC), societies were far more sedentary,
although farming was usually strongly pastoral. Both the Welsh borderland and
the Peak District are areas that have concentrations of round barrow mounds,
not all confined to the burial of a single individual. The construction of barrows
at particular points in the landscape may reflect territorial claims to the
traditional use of land strengthened by the presence of the ancestors. At this
stage, greater attention was given to the burial of the individual than in the earlier
communal mounds, although only a selected few – warriors, group
representatives or priests – may have received such burial. In Shropshire, a
notable string of cairns lines the prominent ridge of the Stiperstones (Fig. 2.3),
but similar barrows are common throughout the hillier regions of the county; in
Herefordshire, they are most frequent in the south-west and north-west of the
county. Many may have stood in boundary locations rather than in central places,
and in the Peak District they often became grouped to form large cemeteries, as
on Stanton Moor where there are also larger ring banks and stone circles, such as
that now known as Nine Ladies (Fig. 2.4).

The limestone uplands of the White Peak in north Staffordshire and western
Derbyshire are, indeed, littered with tumuli, ranging from the large multi-phased
Neolithic mound of Minninglow to the dozens of small Bronze Age barrows. At
Arbor Low, a round barrow built over the bank of the henge may represent the
claim of a new ruling elite to the traditional meeting place of the Neolithic
community (similar barrows overlay the long barrow at nearby Gib Hill).

Fig. 2.4 Nine Ladies stone circle,
Stanton Moor, Derbyshire.

Whereas the henges were often half-hidden from general view by the lie of the land, often on cols but apparently associated with trackways, the barrows were meant to be seen from afar and in some parts of the White Peak, especially, almost every hillock seems to be surmounted by a burial mound. Many barrows were located on the spinal ridge of the limestone plateau, perhaps reinforcing claims to land.[12]

Round barrows are also common on the eastern gritstone moors of the Peak District and may have been built first for the founder members of families or kin-groups, perhaps again asserting their right to land. The settlements they served, with their accompanying field systems, are now being identified, especially on the high shelves overlooking the Derwent valley to the south of Hathersage, mostly at an altitude of 250–350m and located on areas that then, before peat accumulation, enjoyed lighter sandy soils.[13] Sometimes it was pre-existing clearance cairns that were subsequently used for burial, but here each community appears to have constructed its own barrows and small stone circles, as on the Shropshire border. Such upland settlement may have continued into the late Iron Age, despite deteriorating climatic conditions.

While upstanding monuments have survived best on uncultivated uplands they do not form the complete picture. It is clear that only remnants of the pre-Roman landscape survive as visible features today. Although some prehistoric features have been removed by subsequent activity others lie buried beneath the landscapes of later periods. Air photography is helping to rediscover these fragile landscapes. It has increasingly indicated lowland sites along the gravel floors of the region's main river valleys, especially along the Severn in Worcestershire and Shropshire. In Wessex, causewayed enclosures represent one kind of ritual meeting place constructed in the Neolithic period but fewer are known outside that region. A possible example may lie at Walston, near Oswestry (*see also*, Gardom's Edge, above). At Strefford, 4km north of Craven Arms, a crop-mark enclosure bears some resemblance to a ritual henge monument in association with pits that seem to mark the upright timbers of a ceremonial avenue leading into it. Around are several ring ditches, the remains of round barrows of early Bronze Age date, indicating an important ritual and funerary centre in use between four and five thousand years ago.[14] Other henge monuments are also now being identified in valley regions, especially in Worcestershire along the Severn and Avon valleys, again suggesting a link between such monuments and major rivers. Crop-mark ring ditches, usually 10–50m in diameter, are also common along the Severn gravels and in the valleys of north Herefordshire, where they often occur in groups.

While ritual deposits in watery locations are not strongly in evidence in the West Midlands, and the tidal surge of the Severn may have carried away any votive offerings in the lower parts of this river, a few are known – no fewer than three late Bronze Age swords have been found close to the river channel of the Severn in Shropshire, two of them in the Ironbridge gorge. A Bronze Age dagger discovered in a formerly waterlogged area at Admarsh, Eardisland, in the Arrow valley of northern Herefordshire, certainly appears to have been a votive offering, for the piece is unfinished and the blade had been deliberately bent.[15] Sharpstone Hill in Shropshire, on the other hand, has produced evidence of offerings made in an upland location.

THE IRON AGE LANDSCAPE

The crop marks of enclosed settlements, many likely to be of Iron Age date, also appear in valley locations as well as on hill slopes – more than 700 had been located by 1993, notably in the upper Severn valley, and others are continually being found. They are often associated with trackways, field boundaries and other enclosures and paddocks – the component elements of small defended farmsteads. Although these lowland field systems appear now only as crop marks, others can be discerned as slight earthworks on hill commons, often most easily detected by air photography. On the Long Mynd, in Shropshire, a series of so-called 'Celtic fields' accessed by a double lynchet trackway overlooks the Onny valley above Plowden (Fig. 2.5). The field system here may have come into being in the Bronze Age when conditions were warmer and drier and allowed the cultivation of crops on what was later pastoral land.

Throughout large parts of England, evidence of coaxial field systems (fields and boundaries laid out upon a common axis) can be found fossilised in patterns of hedge lines and trackways that perhaps date from the late Bronze Age. These systems involve rectilinear divisions in association with long parallel boundaries that often seem to have followed the line of drove roads, which appear to link areas offering different but complementary resources – marginal grazing, croplands and river valley pastures. While systems of this kind are best known on Dartmoor or in parts of East Anglia, hints of similar patterns have been identified around Pembridge in western Herefordshire, where they are over-run by the later Rowe Ditch (Fig. 2.6). There is also strong evidence of roughly parallel, but undated, drove roads linking the Warwickshire Arden with the more intensively cropped areas of the Warwickshire Avon and Feldon.

By the late Bronze Age and Iron Age (800 BC–AD 43), larger enclosed or fortified centres were beginning to be constructed in the region, many in upland locations. Hillforts are particularly numerous in Herefordshire and on the south Shropshire hills although they continue along the mid-Cheshire ridge and are found

Fig. 2.5 A 'Celtic' field system on the Long Mynd of Shropshire above Plowden.

Fig. 2.6 Remnants of a probable coaxial field system pre-dating the Rowe Ditch near Pembridge in western Herefordshire.

*Fig. 2.7 **Iron Age hillforts** in the region.*

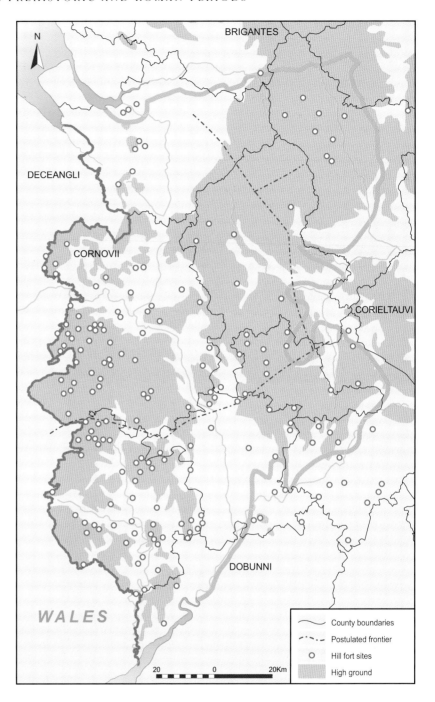

throughout the region (Fig. 2.7). Not only do they vary enormously in size and layout but they may also have served widely differing functions. Some may have been no more than simple pastoral enclosures, such as the Stitt Hill enclosure on an outlying plateau of the Long Mynd or Caer Din Ring on the upland plateau of the Clun Forest, both in Shropshire.[16] At the latter, deliberately constructed outworks may have been used to funnel cattle towards a gap in the enclosure. Climatic deterioration during the Iron Age may have led to increased pastoral activity at the expense of crop cultivation, especially on the higher marginal land, although cultivation seems to have been extended in many lowland areas.

Other hilltop enclosures were more impressive and many were undoubtedly defended settlements. Their positions gave them command over wide areas of the surrounding lowlands. Some, like the Breidden just over the Welsh border, have produced little evidence of continuous occupation and may have been used only seasonally or in times of threatened strife. Others, such as Croft Ambrey or Old Oswestry, seem to have been crammed with buildings and to have been virtually proto-towns. If Bronze Age barrows represent the activities of individual small communities, the hillforts seem to have served much larger groups as tribal areas coalesced and centred upon a more limited number of defended centres. While some seem to have been constructed in boundary or frontier regions, others are likely to have served as 'central places' within well-defined local territories. Beneath the hilltop enclosures, farming was carried out from scattered farmsteads, which probably housed extended family groups; dwellings were constructed of local materials, usually cob or timber walling with roofs of thatch, and were almost invariably round. Increasingly, these are being detected by aerial photography.

Fig. 2.8 Caer Caradoc, an Iron Age hillfort near Church Stretton, Shropshire.

The largest numbers of these defended centres occur throughout the Welsh borderland and excavation has revealed how frequently their portals and guard chambers were altered in the later Iron Age to create impressive entrances displaying the status of their builders. That there are more defended centres in the western part of the region rather than to the east may simply indicate that 'tribal' divisions were smaller and more numerous there. By the late Iron Age it becomes possible to identify tribal 'kingdoms' and cultural groupings by name, although the heart of the West Midland region seems to have remained a frontier area where a number of such 'kingdoms' met. Alongside a confederacy of smaller tribal units, the Cornovii appear to have held much of the northern borderland, while the Silures possessed land to the south-west and the Dobunni land to the south-east. Similarities in the form of their pottery vessels has, however, been used to define a single 'Western Marches hill-fort culture' throughout the areas of Herefordshire, Shropshire and southern Cheshire, a region in which (as we have seen) hillforts were particularly common. North-eastwards, the Brigantes probably held sway over at least the Dark Peak of northern Derbyshire, and the territory of the Corieltauvi (formerly referred to as the Coritani) seems to have extended across Derbyshire into eastern Staffordshire. Lead ingots manufactured in Derbyshire at a later date – under Roman rule – also refer to what may have been a minor tribe based in the Derwent valley of Derbyshire known as the Lutudare(n)ses.[17]

Most hillforts occupied prominent positions on defensible sites. Caer Caradoc, Shropshire (Fig. 2.8), is one of the most spectacular, crowning an outcrop of hard Cambrian rock at a height of 459m, while Old Oswestry, in the same county, is a multiple-ditched fort with complex entrance works which are

Fig. 2.9 Old Oswestry, *an elaborately defended multi-ditched Iron Age hillfort in Shropshire.*

perhaps the most elaborate of any in Britain (Fig. 2.9). The defences were added to a Bronze Age settlement and developed in successive stages from about 700 BC until some time before the Roman conquest.[18] But even more dramatic is British Camp on the crest of the Malvern Hills (Fig. 2.10). It lies at 338m above sea level and was constructed in two stages: first, a small oval hillfort with a ditch and rampart surrounding the main summit and enclosing 3ha and, second, an expanded rampart enclosing 13.5ha and the spurs to the south and north-east of the original site. As many as 118 hut circles have been identified within the interior and the extension incorporated a possible spring as a source of water.[19] The steep slope of the land does much to strengthen its defences, and a thousand years later a Norman ringwork was constructed at the highest point within the hillfort, perhaps to serve as a hunting lodge within the Forest of Malvern or as a symbol of Norman control (*see* Chapter 4). Although British Camp may only have been occupied on a seasonal basis, it looks out strategically across the Worcestershire plain to the east and much of Herefordshire to the west. Together with Midsummer Hill, a little further to the south, it may have stood on a defended boundary between the Herefordshire tribe, perhaps a branch of the Silures, and the Dobunni to the east. The line is apparently continued northwards by other hillforts at Berrow Green, Woodbury Hill, Stagborough, Trimpley, Arley and Kinver. Other hillforts, from Kinver through Wychbury Hill and Harborough Hill in Blakedown, to Bury Ditches in Wythall, are strung out along the uplands of the north Worcestershire border, probably then already a frontier region on the fringe of Dobunnic lands to the south.

Although few would question the defensive strength of hillforts such as British Camp, their purpose has been the subject of much discussion. Originally viewed merely as heavily defended hilltop refuges, many are now thought to have also acted as tribal centres for trade, commerce and ritual, whose elaborate entrance gateways and associated gatehouses were constantly remodelled to both impress visitors and deter attackers. In general, multiple-ditched forts with their elaborate entrance works, such as Bury Ditches 5km south of Bishops Castle, Shropshire, are later in date than the simpler enclosures.

In pastoral upland regions, hillforts may also have acted as nodal points from which valley resources could be controlled and integrated with upland grazing. Such a scenario would help to explain the frequency with which hillforts appear in the borderland and in other hilly regions like the south Staffordshire plateau, where Castle Hills, Walsall, and Castle Ring near Cannock Wood dominate regions that were used for seasonal grazing and possibly for intercommoning by different tribal groups.

Fig. 2.10 British Camp on the Malvern Hills.

Tribal societies, however, were not dependent only upon the rearing of livestock for even in the Welsh borderland the hillforts were surrounded by lowland farms for which many served as foci. At Croft Ambrey in Herefordshire the heavily defended summit plateau was filled after about 250 BC with granaries that were used for the storage of corn, implying that this large fort served as a gathering point for its surrounding territory. Earlier, until about 300 BC, an annexe outside the main enclosure had contained a ritual site where ceremonies left quantities of charcoal, ash, burnt bone and broken pottery. Some of the pottery had been brought in from the Malvern Hills area to the south-east.

Above all, hillforts seem to represent centres intended to control resources and trade, undoubtedly implying other functions based upon ritual, status and the need for defence, and they became increasingly sophisticated in the borderland over time. In addition to such items as metalwork and pottery (especially Malvernian ware), salt was one of the most important items to be traded and briquetage – the coarse vessels used to convey the salt – shows how salt was obtained from the inland salt-producing centres of Droitwich and Nantwich. The latter supplied the tribes of the Welsh borderland, but places in Dobunnic territory drew their salt from Droitwich after the 4th century BC (an area also characterised by the presence of iron currency bars). This is perhaps indicating the emergence of more centralised tribal loyalties.

The eastern tribes may have been more centrally organised than those in the Borders: Hanbury in Worcestershire, for example, appears to have served a considerable area that may tentatively be identified with a later known folk region.[20] Further north, hillforts are found in north-western Derbyshire but some, like Fin Cop, already constructed in the late Bronze Age, appear to have been no more than temporary refuges. If north Derbyshire was part of Brigantian territory, it seems to have been organised without the need for major hillfort centres. Mam Tor, on a prominent hill above Chapel-en-le-Frith, had been abandoned by the 4th century BC and of the eight or so hillforts recognised in the Peak District, most have only a single rampart of bank and ditch.

THE CELTIC YEAR

While trade played a major role in the region's economy, and warfare or cattle raiding may have, on occasions, involved the younger males, everyday life for most undoubtedly revolved around the farming year. Agricultural practices were closely linked to the seasons, all closely related to special ritual periods among Celtic peoples.[21] In the Celtic world, Imbolc, a feast subsequently associated with Brighid and placed in the Roman calendar as February 1st, was when the ewes are said to have begun to lactate, but Beltane, a festival which became attached to May 1st, was a festival of purification and the protection of stock and home by fire. By the time of the spring equinox, domestic stock were giving birth, while manuring, ploughing and the sowing of spring cereals was probably already completed.

During the spring and summer, stock had to be excluded from crop-growing areas and was moved away, once crops were up, to summer pastures in river valleys or on upland commons. Farming tasks throughout the summer included caring for the sheep and cattle and keeping crops free of weeds. Cattle were being mated around the time of the summer solstice, the beginning of Lughnasa (August 1st). This marked the onset of the harvest after which cattle, sheep and pigs could be turned out onto the fields. The autumn equinox marked a focal point in the year marked by some of the most important rituals. Among the Celts, Samhain (November 1st) marked not only the end of summer but the ending of all things – leaves were falling from the trees signalling the onset of winter and death, although for the time being food was plentiful. At this time, with the prospect of the barren winter months ahead, the Celts turned to their gods and to their ancestral spirits; the gates between this world and the next were open and the gods might readily accept any sacrifices made to them.

After the autumn equinox, sheep and pigs were mated but the pigs were taken to seasonal pastures, seeking acorns in the woods; sheep and cattle, too, were moved to winter pastures although in some regions they might still have been folded nightly on the harvested fields, contributing valuable manure to fields due to be planted in the spring. Autumn-sown cereal crops were planted and natural resources such as nuts, berries and fungi collected; woodland might be coppiced. After the winter solstice animals probably stayed close to the settlement. Horses were probably managed as semi-feral herds, rounded up in about September and the young horses captured for training, being kept mainly for chariotry and riding in the Iron Age. Animal husbandry would have involved considerable movement across the landscape – some hillforts' outworks may have served as stock enclosures when herds were gathered together and many of the trackways and roads still in use in the West Midlands have originated as droveways linking pastures used at different periods of the year (*see* above).

THE IMPACT OF ROME: NEW TOWNS AND ROADS

The leaders of the Roman Empire had to prove themselves by their military might and one way of achieving renown was to push back the Empire's boundaries. It was this that brought Julius Caesar to the shores of Britain on a reconnaissance trip in the 1st century BC and led the Emperor Claudius to send an enlarged army under the command of Aulus Plautius back to conquer the land in AD 43. Claudius himself came over for a short time and perhaps led his armies into battle. Client kingships were established, strengthening the trading ties that had already been established, and the independence of such kingships thus curtailed. Dominance by the Romans after the middle of the 1st century AD, after initial upheavals, undoubtedly instigated a period of greater peace and prosperity. Forts were established as military bases and new roads were constructed to link these and new urban centres, helping to maintain a viable economy and centralised control. That part of Britain held by the Romans – Britannia – was divided into *Britannia Superior* in the south (focused upon London) and *Britannia Inferior* in the north, focused upon York. The divide ran through the midland region, probably influenced by the old tribal boundaries of the Iron Age, with *Britannia Superior* probably incorporating the tribal territories of the Cornovii and the Dobunni, *Britannia Inferior* those of the Brigantes and Corieltauvi. *Britannia Superior* was further divided in the

Fig. 2.11 The site and remains of **Viroconium Cornoviorum,** *Wroxeter Roman town.*

early 4th century and the western section, *Britannia Prima*, with its capital at Cirencester, extended north-westwards as far as the Wirral.

Among the military centres, *Deva* (Chester) was known to the British as *Caerlegion* because it was maintained as a major legionary fortress. It controlled the main access route into north Wales along the coastal plain and a crossing point at the head of the navigable tidal section of the Dee. Both the fort and its surrounding civil settlement were to be walled, parts of the Roman town wall surviving in the lower part of the medieval wall just to the east of the Northgate. An amphitheatre was built just outside the town in the 1st century and this was later replaced by another enormous stone building with timber seating. This was the biggest amphitheatre to be built in Roman Britain, perhaps to mark the town out as the intended northern capital.[22] Other towns developed in the region, often near early forts located in strategic positions on the military road network, as at Littlechester in Derbyshire. Towns were also provided close to native centres as a means of spreading Roman cultural values; the formal market basilica, the bath house and forum laid out within a grid of streets became a feature in such centres as Wroxeter, *Viroconium Cornoviorum*, the focus of the Celtic tribe of the Cornovii (Fig. 2.11). A legionary fortress was established here at an early date but prosperity came from the town's position on a major routeway close to the frontier with Wales. Civil settlements, or *vici*, developed close to the main forts and served as minor administrative centres, as at Rocester in eastern Staffordshire. But peace came at a price: if the British were willing to adopt the Roman standard of living – the ceremonial toga when occasion demanded, and Roman styles of food and cooking – they also had to pay high taxes to Rome. There were, of course, difficult periods with threats of external attack but these were probably felt less in the West Midlands, well away from the coasts.

A system of military roads was laid out that was to influence communication links for succeeding centuries. Two of the earliest routes were the Fosse Way, running from south-west to north-east across southern Warwickshire, and Watling Street, running north-westwards from the Thames estuary (Fig. 2.12). The latter had initially played an important role in the army's advance towards the lands of the Cornovii and remained a link from Colchester and, later, London to the tribe's provincial capital at Wroxeter. Crossing it, a road from the West Country to Yorkshire joined with the Ryknild Street (from Bourton and Alcester) at Metchley near Birmingham and ran on through *Letocetum* (Wall) towards *Derventio* (Littlechester near Derby) and Doncaster. From Littlechester another road ran north-westwards across northern Staffordshire to *Aquae Arnemetiae*, the spa at Buxton, and on to Manchester and beyond. Other routes included one that

Fig. 2.12 The Roman Watling Street near Stretton, Staffordshire. *Roman* Pennocrucium *stood near here.*

Fig. 2.13 Roman towns and the main Roman roads of the region.

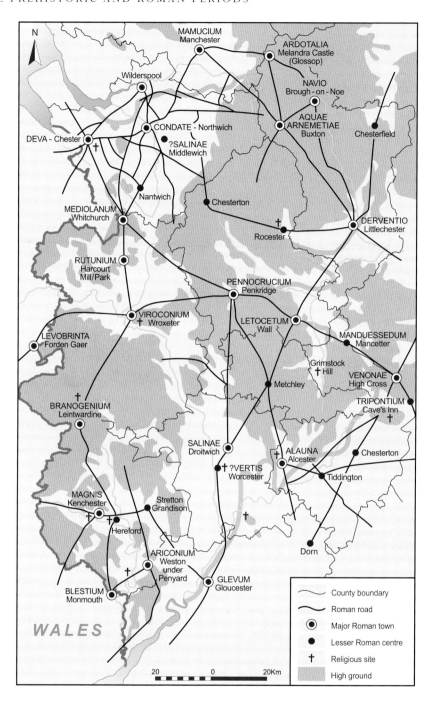

connected Alcester to Droitwich before continuing northwards to Greensforge and *Pennocrucium* (Penkridge), another that linked Metchley to Penkridge, *Mediolanum* (Whitchurch) and *Deva* (Chester), and a third road through the Welsh orders to *Magnis* (Kenchester), *Branogenium* (Leintwardine), Wroxeter, Whitchurch, Middlewich and Northwich (Fig. 2.13). These provided what amounted to a grid of NE–SW and SE–NW routes across the region, to which many other minor local roads would have connected.

NEW GODS AND OLD

The Romanised population of Britain worshipped a wide range of gods, many of whom represented a fusion of Classical and native Celtic deities. The full distribution of ritual sites across the region is far from known but *Aquae Arnemetiae* (Buxton) developed around a Romano-Celtic cult that was centred on natural hot and cold springs dedicated to the Celtic goddess Arnemetia. Lead-lined baths, red plaster and Roman building remains were found in the 18th century near St Anne's Well. *Deva*, the site of a legionary fortress at what is now Chester, also takes its name from a Celtic goddess associated with the river name and a rock-carving of Minerva has been found in a quarry to the south of the river, representing a Roman adaptation of the Celtic deity, while another altar dedicated by the legions in AD 154 appears to equate Jupiter with a Celtic god Taranis. At Baughton, just over 1km from the town, an altar dedicated to the 'nymphs and fountains' was also erected by one of the legions at the source of the piped water supply to the fortress.

At other sites in the West Midlands we see the same story of religious innovation and adaptation: Roman gods, especially popular with the army, became linked to local Celtic deities. At Wroxeter in Shropshire, a Classical temple was dedicated to either Venus or the Celtic horse goddess Epona before going out of use in the 4th century, perhaps in the face of Christianity. The first ritual activity at Grimstock Hill near Coleshill in Warwickshire was focused upon a pit that was later enclosed by a wooden rectangular temple in the 2nd century, later replaced by a stone building. In the early 4th century a bath building was added, but religious activity again seems to have ceased after the mid-4th century. This complex may have been dedicated to Mars, applied to an anonymous Celtic god with similar attributes.[23] A small temple at Orton's Pasture, Rocester, in Staffordshire, lay close to the Roman fort complex and again included a simple rectangular shrine or temple, although this time activity seems to have been confined chiefly to the 2nd-century military occupation of the fort. In Herefordshire, an altar dedicated to the god Jupiter has been found associated with a possible *mansio* at Leintwardine. There may also have been a 1st-century shrine at Wall, where carved heads, some horned, have been found in the bathhouse. The human head was regarded by many Celtic peoples as having supernatural powers and in the Dark Peak area of Derbyshire a collection of seven undated stone heads from around Glossop, and another from Castleton, suggest a local cult centre. Horns, like those depicted on some of the heads at Wall, possibly represented sexual vigour combined with military aggression and were especially popular among the Brigantes to the north.[24]

To the west of the Severn (another river that bore the name of a goddess, Sabrina), a new temple complex was laid out at Lydney as late as the 4th century AD, developed as a healing sanctuary dedicated to the god Nodens. Several altars have also been found in Herefordshire and there were sanctuaries at Croft Ambrey and Donnington in Herefordshire and probably also at Bury Walls in Shropshire and other locations. Several of these were on the sites of Iron Age hillforts, and it may also be significant that a prehistoric barrow was included within a temporary Roman marching camp at Bromfield in Shropshire. Lindow Man, a sacrificial 'victim' found buried in a peat bog near Wilmslow in Cheshire, also seems to represent continuing Celtic tradition, for radiocarbon dating suggests that his ritual death took place early in the Roman period.

Christianity was adopted by the Roman Empire in the early 4th century and a large building found at Wroxeter may have been a church.[25] To the Romans, this was at first just another mystery cult but it offered the prospect of ever-lasting life, whatever persecution might be suffered on earth. The British had difficulty in abandoning their old gods but, as the official religion of the Empire, Christianity inevitably gained ground, especially amongst the elites, and was, perhaps, deeply entrenched and well organised by the end of the period.

NEW INDUSTRIES AND MARKETS

Industry and commerce flourished in the Romanised West Midlands. For the first time, pottery manufacturing was now carried out on a large scale from regional centres, including the production of domestic ware and glass from the Malvern potteries and mortaria and tiles from kilns in the Nuneaton area of northern Warwickshire. To serve the new markets of the region, other potteries were established at Wilderspool in Cheshire, at Wroxeter and near Whitchurch and Clun in Shropshire, at Stoke and near Bishop's Offley in north-west Staffordshire, near Leominster, Lingen and Leintwardine in north-west Herefordshire and near Ledbury in the south-east of the county, and in various locations in the Severn valley of Worcestershire. Lead and silver were mined in Derbyshire, centred upon a lost *Lutudarum* near Wirksworth, and lead in south-west Shropshire and near Chester in Cheshire. Salt production continued at Droitwich, probably known to the Romans as *Salinae*. Middlewich, the other salt-producing centre in Cheshire, may have borne the same Roman name.[26] Late Roman lead pans show that salt was also being produced at Northwich and Shavington (Nantwich) in Cheshire, possibly under the control of the newly-arrived Christian Church. Further north, Wilderspool, on the Mersey, was a centre for pottery manufacture, iron smelting and smithing, bronze and lead working and glass making, while glass working, enamelling and bronze working were carried out alongside ceramic manufacture at Wroxeter. Ironworking sites were not uncommon and their remains have been found at many locations across the region, especially near Worcester and Ross. In the latter area, the dialect word *scowles* may refer to overgrown broken ground produced by ancient iron-ore workings.

Unlike the Cotswolds, the heartland of *Britannia Prima*, the West Midlands was never a favoured place for investment in costly villas by leading members of society. In time, however, the traditional native round timber house was often replaced by a more 'modern' rectangular building, complete, sometimes, with under-floor heating, painted wall plaster and a tiled roof. A site recently excavated at Throckmorton in Worcestershire shows this sequence well, and along the Arrow valley of Warwickshire in the hinterland of Roman Alcester several settlements have produced evidence of floor tesserae, roof tiles and, occasionally, fragments of painted plaster, associated with what were otherwise ordinary small farms. These would have stood within a relatively open landscape of enclosed fields bounded by hedges, ditches, or both. Around Wroxeter and elsewhere, most of the native farmsteads scattered across the countryside continued as more traditional survivals of Iron Age farms, a change in lifestyle indicated only by an abundance of mass-produced pottery and utensils.

Sophisticated villa complexes like those found in the Cotswolds are virtually unknown in the region, although a number of small villas are known around *Deva*. At Eaton by Tarporley, for example, an initially timber-built house was reconstructed in stone in a modest winged-corridor style with wall paintings, a bath-suite, mosaics and hypocausts. This may have been the home of a local aristocratic family and was well sited as the focus of an estate practising both crop growing and stock rearing. Rather more of the contemporary settlements in Shropshire may, perhaps, be regarded as villas. They spread across the northern lowland plains and the southern valleys of the county but rather fewer have been found in Herefordshire.

Currently, only seven Roman villas are known within Staffordshire, although crop marks have revealed traces of both native farmsteads and extensive field systems, especially in the vicinity of Wall and along the terraces of the Trent and Tame. In Warwickshire, most villas lay in the richer, southern parts of the county or in the vicinity of Alcester and Chesterton, again a minority (only 20 or so known to date) among numerous lower-status rural settlements, many of which show continuity of occupation from the Iron Age. In Worcestershire, too, a small group of villas has been found in the fertile Vale of Evesham and possibly two near the salt-producing centre of Droitwich.

At some sites, continuity of occupation can be demonstrated from late Iron Age times on villa sites as on native farmsteads. Such evidence is found at two locations near Lyonshall in Herefordshire and at Hales in west Staffordshire where four round huts were to be replaced by a corridor villa in the early 2nd century. The continuation of native styles in the region suggests that a foreign administration had been superimposed upon a society that, initially at least, retained many of its old traditions, although agriculture was probably becoming more intensive and more land was brought into cultivation. Indeed, increased alluviation in some river valleys at this time is probably the direct result of extended ploughing and increased woodland clearance.

The rise of urban centres created new markets for agricultural surplus, while the taxes that were imposed to support the army and the administration led to a more complex economic system. Although agriculture was probably extended to new areas during this period, Romano-British field systems have usually been

lost beneath later cultivation systems and can only be detected by air photography or from the scatter of pottery fragments associated with manuring of the fields. Native field systems, however, are clearly attested in the White Peak of Derbyshire to the east of Buxton where the land remained under pasture and where nearly 40 contemporary settlement sites have been identified. Almost all of them were situated above the best agricultural land and their farmers may have also been part-time prospectors for lead.

At Carsington, a richer settlement may perhaps be regarded as a 'villa' and has been suggested as a candidate for the lost *Lutudarum*. At Hopton and in the Dove and Wye valleys, farming settlements are distributed on average at half-mile intervals and two distinct

Fig. 2.14 A Romano-British settlement and field system on *Chee Tor in the Derbyshire White Peak.*

forms of field can be recognised – small rectangular enclosures near the settlement and 'long fields' abutting onto these. The former may have been stock corrals and the latter arable fields. The best preserved settlements lie on marginal land close to the 305m contour, like those at Chee Tor in Blackwell (Fig. 2.14) and Cow Low in Green Fairfield above the Wye, the latter with a well-preserved system of square-shaped fields and lynchets, Rainster Rocks in Brassington, and Brushfield Hough. At Roystone Grange in Ballidon, the land seems to have been laid out as two separate ovals, one without internal walling and one of about 30ha with long but subdivided strip-shaped fields for the cultivation of cash crops, tilled using the big coulter plough. The settlement, made up of a number of dwellings built in the lee of Roystone rocks, may have supported some 30 to 50 people who depended upon the marketing of wool and lead. Parts of the undivided enclosure close to the settlement may have been used as infield where the stock would be kept during the winter months, fertilising the ground. In summer, the sheep and cattle would be grazed on the open pastures – the commons – beyond.

The overall density of settlement in some parts of the region is still uncertain. While some areas appear to have supported increasingly large populations, the area centred upon Knutsford in Cheshire, for instance, has so far remained empty of settlement evidence, to the extent that it has been interpreted as 'a large expanse of uncleared and uncultivable forest', probably maintained to supply fuel to the industries of Wilderspool and Middlewich. It was also the presence of plentiful woodland fuel supplies, together with suitable local clays, that attracted the Roman pottery and tile industries to the Warwickshire Arden.

The way in which the Roman towns met their end is still the subject of discussion. At *Viroconium* (Wroxeter), a tombstone in memory of one, Cunorix, an Irishman, erected *c.* 475, could have been that of a late Roman military commander, perhaps brought in to defend the town. Native-style timber buildings were erected over the rubble of the Roman buildings in the 5th century but a 6th-century resurgence led to the construction of other buildings of considerable size and status.[27] *Viroconium*, like so many other Roman towns, died during the 7th century. It appears to have lost its economic *raison-d'être* and its power base although it may have retained a quasi-military function for a time. During this same post-Roman period, some earlier hillforts may have been reoccupied, for there are signs that the Breiddin was used as a temporary refuge. Wat's Dyke may also have been constructed at this time to protect the Chester area and seems to suggest mistrust between the northern Cornovii and those occupying territory to the west.[28] The break with Roman Britain was not a sudden one, and sub-Roman buildings also overlie a Roman villa at Whitley Grange near Hanwood near Wroxeter. Roman cultural influences in the region nevertheless seem to have diminished rapidly in the 5th century. At Wall, Kenchester, Alcester, Worcester and perhaps Leintwardine we see the same repeated story of decay and partial abandonment, although the Roman salt industry continued at Droitwich and Nantwich.

The lasting features of Roman occupation were the towns and the military roads – both totally new introductions to the country. Although the actual buildings fell into disuse, few towns ultimately lost their role as urban foci controlling the surrounding countryside. This may have been because many were deliberately redeveloped later as centres in an attempt to emulate the Romans' economic capability or because they were seen as fulfilling a role as bases of power and culture. The Christian Church, in particular, seems to have chosen Roman sites for the latter reason although it is not known how far Roman Christianity survived to influence this (*see* Chapter 3). Even where urban sites failed, as at Wroxeter, other central places were to emerge near by.

NOTES

1   Rackham 1996, 27.
2   Vera 2000, 376–8.
3   Kirby 2005.
4   Watson & Musson 1993, 20–1.
5   Rowley 1972, 31.
6   Chitty 1963.
7   Barnatt 1998, 102.
8   Ibid, 102–3.
9   Barnatt & Smith 2004, 28.
10   Barnatt 1996, 6–6.
11   Barnatt & Smith 2004, 15.
12   Barnatt 1996, 69.
13   Barnatt & Smith 1997, 23–7, figs 6 and 7.
14   Watson & Musson 1993, 15.
15   White, P 2003, 35–7.
16   Watson & Musson 1993, 24–5.
17   Rivet & Smith 1979, 403.
18   Watson & Musson 1993, 30–1.
19   Bowden 2000, 13–14.
20   Hooke 1985a, 80, fig 21.
21   Cunliffe 2000, 58, 77.
22   Ainsworth & Wilmott 2005.
23   Magilton forthcoming.
24   Green 1993, 63.
25   White & Barker 2002, 107–8.
26   Rivet & Smith 1979, 451.
27   White & Barker 2002, 106.
28   White, R 2003, 4.

3

The Early Medieval Landscape

TERRITORIES AND FOCAL REGIONS IN EARLY MEDIEVAL ENGLAND

As the Roman armies were withdrawn at the beginning of the 5th century to protect the heart of the Empire from barbarian attacks, petty princedoms emerged in many regions to fill the power vacuum. However, they were unable to keep invaders at bay, invaders that included Scots and Irish, plus Germanic tribes from the North and Baltic Sea coasts. Indeed, the latter may first have been deliberately employed to help keep out the former but arrived in ever-increasing numbers in the 5th and 6th centuries. Eventually Anglo-Saxon petty kingdoms were established and these coalesced into more stable kingdoms by the 7th century. Thus the Mercians spread their rule across the midland region from a homeland in the Trent valley, their name meaning 'dwellers on the march, borderers' (probably referring to the border between the Anglo-Saxons and the Welsh although that between the Mercians and the Northumbrians has alternatively been suggested). By the 8th century their sphere of influence extended westwards to the present border with Wales, northwards to a line running from the Mersey to the Humber, eastwards to the borders of the East Angles and south into the territory of the West Saxons. The southern and eastern kingdoms of the country were to owe them allegiance in the late 8th century. In the midlands, they had fully subsumed the *Pecsætan* tribal area of the Peak District by the 8th century and the sub-kingdoms of the *Magonsæte*, of the border region, and the *Hwicce*, whose kingdom was focused upon the Severn valley and north Cotswolds, by AD 800 (Fig. 3.1).

Historical documentation increases dramatically in the early medieval period, largely in the form of place-names and charters, although it is also possible to work back to this period from later evidence. Such sources, for the first time, provide evidence for territorial organisation – ranging from the 7th-century kingdoms down through the folk regions within them, culminating in the fragmentation which led first to the so-called 'multiple' or composite estates and then, within these, to the smaller Anglo-Saxon estates. In these we see the emergence of the township communities and proto-manors that were to be the building blocks of the ecclesiastical parishes with which we are familiar today.[1] At the beginning of the period, the region was still a meeting place of boundaries rather than a recognisable entity, although the Hwiccan and Magonsætan kingdoms were ultimately to be drawn into Mercia. In the 8th century the construction of Offa's Dyke may have been a statement of political power against the remaining Welsh kingdoms, particularly that of Powys. Shorter linear dykes, like the Rowe Ditch that cuts across the Arrow valley in north Herefordshire, were probably constructed in the so-far unravelled early period of British/Anglo-Saxon conflict.

It is also possible to see how some of the land units referred to here as 'folk regions', the building blocks of the kingdoms, appear to have been based upon the availability of complementary resources – centred upon a river valley area but

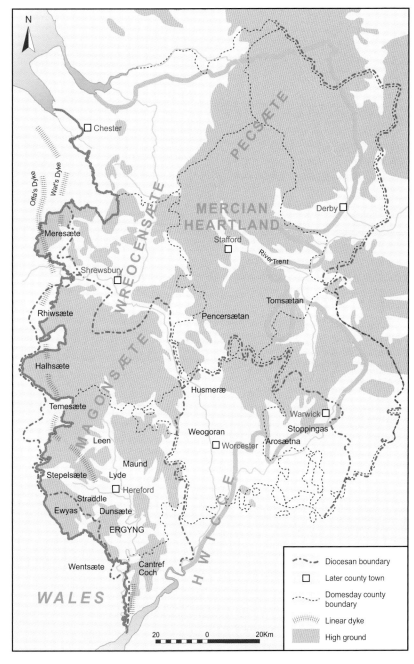

Fig. 3.1 The Anglo-Saxon kingdoms.

extending up into areas of seasonal pastures on hills or within wooded regions, areas which were often used increasingly for hunting as the Anglo-Saxon period progressed.[2] Within Worcestershire, the *Husmeræ* occupied a region extending from the Stour valley to the Clent Hills and the *Weogoran* occupied land either side of the River Severn, their focus Worcester, 'the *ceaster* (walled town) of the *Weogoran*'. In south Staffordshire, the *Pencersæte* occupied the Penk/Sowe valley corridor, their land extending from a focus near the former Roman *Pennocrucium* on the Penk to the marginal uplands of the south Staffordshire plateau and the Lickey Hills; while the *Tomsæte* occupied the Tame valley, with a territory which probably extended southwards along its headwaters, the Blythe, into the wooded region of north-west Warwickshire. In this county, the *Arosætna* probably occupied the Alne/Arrow valley to the north of Roman Alcester. Recently, Coplestone-Crow[3] has been able to identify some of the units within the Magonsætan kingdom in what is now Herefordshire, interestingly a territory that seems to have been much more fragmented than say, Warwickshire, just as it appears to have been in the late Iron Age. Northwards, the *Wreocensæte* occupied land around the Wrekin.

As estate fragmentation proceeded from about the 8th century onwards most of the new 'manors' that were being formed at this time lost access to the communal summer pastures of the larger folk regions. Occasionally links were partially retained, represented by estates granted together by charter and, later, those between capital manors and dependent berewicks; or between mother churches and dependent chapelries. These show, in particular, how estates in the Vale of Evesham and north Gloucestershire had links to the more wooded regions of central Worcestershire and the Malvern foothills, while the interrelationship of the Warwickshire Feldon and the more wooded Arden remained intact on many manors until well into the medieval period. The royal manor of Brailes, for instance, in the south of the county, still possessed the woodland manor of Tanworth in Arden in 1086 (which remained a detached part of the medieval hundred in which Brailes lay), providing access to both timber and pastures for livestock.

The ethnic origins of the region's people in this period still raise many questions. The native British may have continued to play a significant role in the region after the coming of the Anglo-Saxons and perhaps the division between the Christian and British-Roman world and that of the pagan Anglo-Saxon one became more pronounced in sub-Roman Britain. Initial studies of the DNA characteristics of the modern population cover only the north-east of the region. They indicate that there was a stronger Anglo-Saxon or Danish presence (the two cannot be genetically isolated) in what is today Derbyshire and eastern Staffordshire, an area known to have been heavily settled by the Danes.[4] However, a stronger British presence is suspected further to the west and south.

The population of the western districts of the region is likely to have remained largely British and tribal names containing the Old English term -sæte may, indeed, indicate people of a British origin.[5] The first king of the Magonsæte adopted the name Merewalh, which means 'illustrious Welshman'. In the case of the subsidiary territory of the *Stoppingas* of Wootton Wawen, however, we encounter a type of -*ingas* name that indicates land given to an Anglo-Saxon leader and his followers relatively early on in the period of Anglo-Saxon colonisation. Here one such group was apparently granted a block of land of about 50 hides across the headwaters of the River Alne in Warwickshire. But *who* gave this land unit – the British of the Alcester region or the Anglo-Saxons who seem to have preferred Bidford-on-Avon a few kilometres to the south? And why did the bulk of the population – if, indeed, large numbers of British survived – eventually aspire to identify itself with an immigrant culture?

Although the kingdoms of the Hwicce and the Magonsæte were drawn into Mercia, a dynasty of Welsh kings ruled throughout the 6th and early 7th centuries in Ergyng (southern Herefordshire) and actively fought against the Saxons (a battle at Hereford is recorded in 760). Here, Welsh control was only lost after the mid-9th century but the kingdom had its own bishops and only in the mid-10th century was the boundary to the south of Hereford fixed by Athelstan along the River Wye, putting the eastern part of the earlier territory under English control. Originally the kingdom had probably included lands on both sides of the Wye, its eastern boundary perhaps marked by the 11th-century boundary of the diocese of Hereford, which followed the River Severn and the Malvern Hills. It was only a remnant of this territory, between the rivers Monnow and Wye, which was to bear the name Archenfield, although the name is derived from the Roman centre of *Ariconium* (in Weston-under-Penyard, east of the Wye).[6] Archenfield remained subject to Welsh law and custom under English overlordship until after the Norman Conquest. Ewyas, in the south-west, remained a Welsh district until after the Norman Conquest.

Across the region, extensive woodlands such as those of Morfe, Kinver, Lyme and Arden were to retain their British names: Kinver *Cynibre* and Brewood *Brewde* contain the British *bre* meaning 'hill' and Arden the British *ardu* meaning 'high or steep'; Lyme may be derived from *lemo*- 'elm' but a Latin term *limes* implying 'a boundary zone' seems more plausible,[7] and Morfe may be derived from *maerdref* indicating 'reeve's or mayor's hamlet'. The Old Welsh word for 'wood', *cēd*, is found in various names such as Cheadle and Pencoyd. Other British hill names include those with *penn* 'head', like Penn near Wolverhampton, and *barr* 'top, summit', as in Great Barr, Birmingham. Many British river names were also taken into common usage and most of these names seem to have been adopted into English speech before the end of the 7th century.

At the very tip of the Wirral, Wallasey (*weala* + *eg*) meant 'Welshmen's island', and Liscard in Wallasey, 'hall on the rock', may point to a former British court site; another *walh*- name ('Welshman, foreigner') is Walton further along the Mersey to the east. *Cumbre* also means 'Welshman' and is found in the names Comberbach and Combermere. British place-names survive in concentrations along the south-western border of Cheshire at locations such as Barhill (*barr*) and Crewe (*cryw* 'basket', hence 'wickerwork weir'). Other examples are Eccleston (*ecles* 'church'), Ince ('the island') and Bryn (*bryn* 'hill').

In Shropshire, Wroxeter and Wrekin are survivals of Romano-British names. In the former, the Old English *ceaster* has been added to the British place-name that may have meant 'place associated with a man named *Virico*', perhaps transferred from the Wrekin hillfort. A substantial number of Shropshire's rivers also bear pre-English names, including the Clun, Cound, Roden, Perry, Severn, Teme and Tern, together with numerous stream names near the western and southern boundaries of the county. Shropshire also provides several *walh-* names, mostly enclaves in rich riverine areas such as Walcot near Shrewsbury, Walcot near Clun, another Walton in the south of the county and a Walford on the Perry in the basin of the middle Severn. Wenlock may contain the Welsh *gwyn* 'white', perhaps referring to the limestone escarpment of Wenlock Edge, while names with Mynd and *crug* also contain Welsh words for 'mountain'.[8]

As might be expected, surviving British names are more abundant in Herefordshire: Welsh districts survived in the south of the county until the Norman Conquest. Of the district names, Ewyas is 'sheep district', Ergyng (Archenfield) is derived from the Romano-British *Ariconium* (above) and, in the north, Leen is 'district of streams'. Pre-English names for rivers abound, like those of the Teme, Humber, Lugg, Wye, Leadon, Glynch, Frome, Gamber, Dore, Dulas, Monnow and Olchon, and British hill names include Pencoyd. The British *tre*, meaning 'farmstead', is common across the southern part of the country although there are fewer *walh-* names (this is not surprising if the majority of the population regarded themselves as of Welsh stock and would hardly have referred to themselves as 'foreigners'). Walford ('Welshman's ford'), was the name given to a ford across the Wye in the south of the county and to another across a brook in Letton in the upper Teme valley in the north. In addition, there are also names incorporating the Welsh term for a church (*llan*) and names like Foy, St Weonards, Sellack and Cloddock, which refer to British saints.

Walh- names, usually associated with, and close to, estate centres, are more common in the east of the region and represent the presence of Welsh-speaking communities amongst the dominant 'Anglo-Saxon' population. They include Waltons near Eccleshall and Penkridge in Staffordshire, both centres with strong British associations: the former as the site of a British Christian community and the latter as the focus of the Pencersætan folk territory that succeeded the Roman *Pennocrucium* and eventually became an Anglo-Saxon royal vill. Names of this kind sometimes occur in pairs: there are, for instance, two Walton settlements associated with Wellesbourne in Warwickshire, another Anglo-Saxon royal vill. These *walh* settlements may have represented more servile communities serving the estate, their lowly status causing them to remain relatively self-contained.[9]

Fig. 3.2 Offa's Dyke to the north of Knighton.

The existence of such names implies that most of the population had by the 8th century, at least, adopted an Anglo-Saxon identity and was by then speaking Old English, the language of the Anglo-Saxons. How this came about is not known, but it seems unlikely that the British population had been entirely wiped out and it may have taken several hundred years for the British language to be virtually replaced by Old English; a change undoubtedly encouraged by the new leaders for language can be a powerful ethnic tool. As the ascendancy of Mercia began to transform a fragmented frontier region into a recognisable political entity, relations with the Welsh, at least those of the kingdom of Powys, seem to have deteriorated and this may be why Offa's Dyke was constructed along the Welsh border.[10] Some Welsh kingdoms formed alliances with the Anglo-Saxons but the Welsh of Powys appear to have renewed their raids across the border. Even earlier, they may have been attacking far into Staffordshire and there is an account, written long after the actual event which may have taken place in the mid-7th century, of an attack on Lichfield (and its church) by the British leader Cynddylan, who was subsequently killed. Offa's was the grandest of a series of dykes, most much shorter but all likely to date from the post-Roman period, and it is still clearly visible in the landscape as it follows the brows of hills and ridges overlooking the former Welsh kingdoms to the west (Fig. 3.2).

Within the Anglo-Saxon kingdoms, central places can be identified with a degree of confidence. Economic and power bases must have been shaken up drastically by the withdrawal of Roman power: towns had been displaying a drop in prosperity from at least the 3rd century but their centrality seems to have been taken over in many instances by the newly arrived Church – *Viroconium* has the minster church of Wroxeter close by, Alcester (Roman *Alauna*) was probably the 'celebrated place called Alne' where an ecclesiastical council was held in 709; Worcester became the seat of the bishops of the Hwicce. Timber halls, which seem to indicate Anglo-Saxon palaces, have been recorded from the air as crop-mark sites at Hatton Rock in Hampton Lucy (either a royal or episcopal palace) and Long Itchington in Warwickshire, and at Frogmore in Atcham in Shropshire (Fig. 3.3). The site of Offa's reputed palace in Marden, Herefordshire, has not yet been located but two 8th-century mills that were probably associated with it have been found beside the River Lugg near Marden church. Many of the central places that can be identified were royal vills or the sites of early minster foundations (*see* below), the latter serving their respective *parochiae* carved, often, from identifiable folk regions. The early minsters are most easily identified in the Hwiccan kingdom where records were maintained by the Church of Worcester.

There are, however, a number of unanswered problems that remain fundamental to an understanding of what happened in this period. Estimates of population numbers at present remain little more than intelligent guesses and the possibility of a reduction in numbers in the earlier part of the Anglo-Saxon period remains likely but unproven. Environmental evidence for land use in the midland region is still limited. Is there any firm evidence for economic collapse, as has previously been supposed, after the Roman withdrawal in the 5th and 6th centuries? The area of land under crops may well have receded with the withdrawal of the Roman army and the apparent demise of the towns. An increase in pasture, more clearly apparent over the chalklands of southern England, may, however, simply reflect a return to native methods of farming. It has been argued that the evidence for general woodland regeneration at this time is patchy outside northern England, where climatic deterioration may have been a contributory factor.[11]

The distribution of the Old English *leah* term seems to indicate wooded regions, although this woodland should probably be envisaged as wood-pasture or secondary woodland, the kind of open woodland now favoured by specialists as the most likely type of natural ancient woodland present in prehistoric and later England.[12] Only when animal grazing is prevented, at least temporarily, can trees regenerate with ease to form dense woodland. There are reasons for the

Fig. 3.3 Timber halls at Frogmore, Atcham, in Shropshire.

increasing protection of woodland in later Anglo-Saxon times connected with the growing interest in hunting displayed by Anglo-Saxon kings, but a wood-pasture type of vegetation (grazed open woodland) appears to have been typical of certain regions well before it is confirmed by later pre-Conquest sources. Had this been present since prehistoric times or was there a period of woodland regeneration in the so-called 'Dark Ages'? Although environmentalists have found little evidence of land abandonment in the immediate post-Roman period in southern England, pollen analysis on the site of Metchley Roman fort in Birmingham suggests that occupation here may rapidly have given way to increased woodland, and there was also a similar reduction in land use in the Stafford area to the north. This may, however, imply nothing more than a retraction in regions that were less well suited to cultivation and a return to the exploitation of more sustainable resources such as wood-pasture.

ECCLESIASTICAL DEVELOPMENT AND THE ROLE OF LANDOWNERSHIP

Early medieval minster churches were normally established in royal vills or at other established estate centres like the *Leonis monasterium* founded at Leominster, whose Welsh name is *Llanllieni* 'church in the district of streams'. It was founded by Merewalh to serve the former British polity of Leen but he may have been re-endowing a pre-existing British minster. It is unclear how far Christianity, established in British territories, continued to influence later arrangements, but Leominster is not the only contender for an existence as a British ecclesiastical centre. According to Bede, a synod of the British church was held at Chester in about AD 600, and it is likely that Roman Christianity had survived there. When Chester was attacked between 613 and 616 by Northumbrian forces under Æthelfrith, a host of 'monks' from the British monastery of Bangor-is-y-coed who had come to pray for victory are said to have been slaughtered. The significance of such a victory is that it would have separated the Welsh from their British compatriots to the north, but Chester was to rise again as an ecclesiastical focus in the 11th century.

Other British Christian communities or churches are indicated by *ecles* place-names and these include Ecleston on the Roman road leading south from Chester, which may have served as the 6th-century mother church for the fortress at *Deva* (Chester); Eccleshall in Staffordshire; Eccles House in Chapel-en-le-Frith and Eccles House in Hope, both in Derbyshire; Eccleswall [Court] in Linton-by-Ross and Eccles Green in Norton Canon, Herefordshire; Exhall near Coventry and Exhall near Alcester, both in Warwickshire. Landican in the Wirral seems to be the **lann* (British 'church', becoming Welsh *llan*) of an unknown British saint, Tegan. Within the Magonsætan kingdom, in what is now Herefordshire, there are considerable numbers of churches dedicated to British saints. Dewchurch (*Lann Deui*), for instance, is dedicated to St Dewi. Around *Aricionium* there are several dedications to St Dyfrig, claimed to have been the first bishop of Llandaff. Llanfrother in Hentland parish may be the site of his earliest monastery (rather than Hentland in Goodrich where there was another early church), later linked to the church of Hentland in a combined dedication to St Teilo his successor, as at the church of Llanwarne.[13] There were other early dedications to this saint at St Devereux and Lower Buckenhill in Woolhope. Other early Herefordshire *llan* names referring to such British saints include *Lann Timoi*, now Foy (St Moi), Llancillo (St Tyssilio, the premier saint of Powys), Llangunville Farm in Llanrothal (St Cynfall), Lann Erbdil (later Madley, St Erbdil) and several others. Dedications to known or obscure British saints and 'other **lann/lann* names' lie mostly in the southern part of the county where the British Church retained control into the 10th century (Fig. 3.4) – Archenfield had its own Welsh bishop,

Cyfeiliog, in 914 when he was captured by the Vikings and both Ewyas and Archenfield remained within a Welsh diocese long after this (Archenfield until 1131 and Ewyas until 1852). The location of some British monasteries and churches can be identified from the 12th-century *Liber Landavensis, Book of Llandâf*, but not all are certain. Between the Wye and Severn in Gloucestershire, also Welsh territory, the church of Lancaut was dedicated to St Cewydd in about AD 700 and that of St Briavels to St Brioc or Brieuc.

Although the dedications to British saints at Chester (St Brigit) and at the end of the Wirral are unlikely to be early, they clearly recognise the importance of a Celtic past in the region. Beyond the Welsh areas are isolated dedications to other British saints. The church at Cressage, near Wroxeter, was originally dedicated to St Samson, a 6th-century Welsh saint who may have visited the area. An Irish anchorite and saint, St Modwen, allegedly had a religious house at Burton upon Trent in the 7th century and when she died she was buried on Andredesy Island, her remains later enshrined within the abbey founded close by in 1004. Another British saint, St Barlok, had connections with Norbury in Derbyshire. Isolated dedications like this may have arisen much later, however, perhaps as late as the 12th century when the cult of saints and relic-hunting was most popular.

The conversion of the Anglo-Saxon kingdom of the Hwicce, the adjacent kingdom to the east, is never recorded and it is entirely possible that both this kingdom and that of the Magonsæte in the border country were areas of British Christianity long before the conversion of the Anglo-Saxons. It has been argued, for example, that St Helen's played a role as the late Roman or British Church at the focus and foundation of Worcester's ecclesiastical power.[14] An origin as a British *clas* church (one held by a religious community) has also been claimed for St Michael's at Lichfield, and for the churches at Hereford, Leominster and Much Wenlock, and Christianity seems to have been well established in the Welsh borderland by the 6th century. Similar claims have been made for Baschurch in Shropshire, which appears to have been *Eglwysseu Bassa*, apparently referring to a cluster of churches, perhaps as early as the 9th century.[15] Pagan Anglo-Saxon cemeteries and burials certainly appear to diminish in number towards the west. The true picture, however, may still be incomplete.

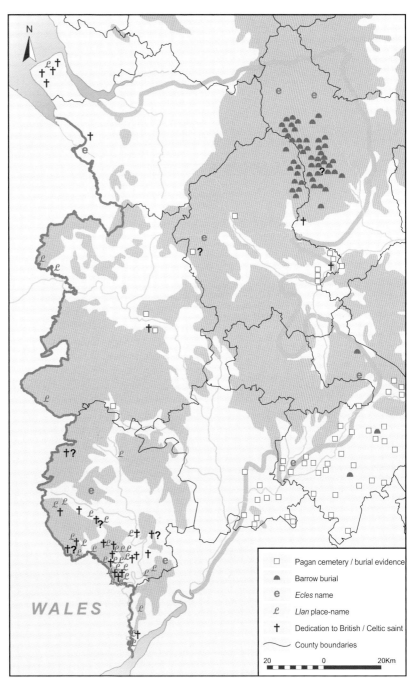

Fig. 3.4 Pagan Anglo-Saxon cemeteries and British Christianity.

The Anglo-Saxons, when they arrived, were pagan, and early burials of the later 5th or early 6th centuries are virtually confined to the east of the region (Fig. 3.4). A concentration of barrow burials on the limestones of the Peak District, often as secondary interments in earlier barrows, seems to represent a fashion of burial that remained current until the late 6th or early 7th centuries in the region of the *Pecsæte*, perhaps a deliberate expression of pagan identity in the face of a rival faith (although a mixed pagan–Christian rite may also be implied as many bodies were placed in grave-pits that were cut west–east).[16] It has been suggested that these burials may represent a new elite of Anglian stock who had imposed themselves upon existing farming communities, possibly attracted by the lead mines of the area.

Very few Anglo-Saxon burials have been found in the west of the region. The most secure contender is a late (possibly mid-7th to mid-8th century) cemetery of maybe 35 burials on the site of a late Iron Age farmstead enclosure at Bromfield in Shropshire, although here the orientation of the graves and the paucity of grave-goods may suggest Christian influence, albeit with occasional acknowledgements to pagan rites in the inclusion of a few brooches, beads, knives and a fragment of an iron buckle. Other post-Roman burials are known from Dewsall and Ashgrove in Marden in Herefordshire and from Much Wenlock and Wroxeter in Shropshire, but again they lack grave-goods and some have roughly E–W oriented graves that suggest Christianity (the name Dewsall suggests a dedication to a British saint, St Dewi). The Much Wenlock burial consisted of three bodies oriented NE–SW, for which radiocarbon dates of the 3rd–5th centuries and the 5th–6th centuries have been obtained.

Isolated finds of brooches, a single bead and an urn sherd show the presence of Anglo-Saxons in Cheshire but no actual pagan burials have been discovered. While *hlaw* (Old English 'mound, hill') place-names in the region (for example Purslow, Beslow and Longslow in Shropshire) are likely to indicate the presence of often artificial mounds there is little proof that these were necessarily used for burial rather than to symbolise meeting places, perhaps continuing the symbolism of claims to land practised by earlier societies. Nevertheless, the presence of *hlaw* names beyond the known range of pagan burial suggests that the picture may yet be incomplete and the recent discovery of a middle Saxon pottery sherd within a ring-ditch at Sutton in Herefordshire confirms that this is so.

Pagan place-names may indicate areas where Anglo-Saxon pagan belief lingered, for example where names commemorate Anglo-Saxon gods such as Woden, as in Wednesbury and Wednesfield, on the south Staffordshire plateau, or Wensley (*Wodnesleie* 1086) in Derbyshire. Even if Christianity was already strong in the west, there are hints of an earlier Romano-British paganism surviving in the region, not as an organised pre-Christian faith, but probably as superstition only partly subsumed into Christian ritual. Many aspects of pre-Christian belief were common across Europe and Romano-British and Anglo-Saxon paganism can be difficult to disentangle, but the strength of its survival is reflected in a continuous series of edicts (orders) issued by the Christian Church throughout the early medieval period forbidding worship at pagan shrines, particularly the practice of making offerings at trees, springs or stones.

Holy wells, often associated with healing, still abound in the borderland, where many of them are associated with Christian saints, rededicated as sources of pure water for baptism or healing. St Bride's Well at St Briavels in the Forest of Dean may represent the transference of the deity from the Celtic goddess Brighid to St Brighid (Brigit) who died about 524 and was the abbess of a convent in Kildare, Ireland. Several other springs in Herefordshire and Shropshire were named as 'Lady Wells', probably indicating a dedication to the Virgin Mary.[17] In the borderland, too, ancient yews are frequent in churchyards, several of them much older than the churches they overlook and perhaps accommodated from more ancient veneration. Their association with regeneration may have made them acceptable to the Roman Christian Church. At Claverley, Shropshire, a large yew may have been associated with a Romano-British burial site before the construction of the Norman church, and other ancient yews are found beside early churches at Much Marcle in Herefordshire (Fig. 3.5) and Church Preen in Shropshire. At Hope Bagot, Herefordshire, a much-decayed old yew still grows over a spring close to the Norman church, representing a combination of two kinds of ancient cult feature.

Like the tradition observed in the borderland and found sporadically across the rest of the country, churchyard yews of considerable age are found at Doveridge and Darley Dale in Derbyshire. Holy wells, all early and apparently embodying a Celtic tradition, are also found in more central and eastern parts of the West Midlands, including Uttoxeter, Lichfield (where there are several, including St Mary's, St Chad's, a possible example beneath the chapel of St Peter in the cathedral, and springs at St Michael's), Shrewsbury St Chad's, and St Osburg's Pool at Coventry that lay beside the first minster but had vanished by the 16th century. It has been claimed that dedications to the Christian saint St Bartholomew, 'the caster out of devils', indicate places where the Church had to attempt to dispel pre-Christian belief and such sites certainly appear to increase in the West Midlands, especially in the counties of Worcestershire, Staffordshire and Cheshire.

After the conversion of the Anglo-Saxon rulers, the Roman Church gained ascendancy over the British Church and other early minsters were founded across the region. The picture is clearest in the Hwiccan kingdom because the records of Worcester monastery, which had taken over many of the earliest minsters, were produced in the scriptorium there and managed to survive the Danish invasions of the 9th century (Fig. 3.6). Elsewhere, identification is more difficult although some important mother churches may have been established relatively early, like the *monasterium* of Much Wenlock in Shropshire. Arguments have been presented for the minster status of churches such as Bromfield and Morville, also in Shropshire, or Farndon in Cheshire. In this region, Lichfield, Hereford and Worcester were chosen by Archbishop Theodore as diocesan centres in the late 7th century, the first for the Mercians, and the others for the Magonsæte and the Hwicce. Chad, who was appointed as bishop to the Mercians at their appointed see of Lichfield, had been trained within the British Church and Worcester's role as the seat of the bishopric of the Hwicce may have been based upon the earlier prominence of St Helen's church in the immediate post-Roman period (*see* above).

The earliest minsters did not always survive, especially those like Bredon or Fladbury in Worcestershire that were subsumed into the Church of Worcester. Some were 'family minsters', established by the Anglo-Saxon aristocracy, and other early minsters were established on royal estates, as at Winchcombe in the north Gloucestershire Cotswolds, a favoured vill of the Mercian kings by the 9th century. Repton was the foremost ecclesiastical centre of Anglo-Saxon Derbyshire and the burial place of several Mercian kings, but Wirksworth had close associations with the Northumbrian Church; the abbey here held shares in the valuable lead mines of the region, granted to them by the Mercian kings.

Decorated crosses, probably marking the sites of early open-air preaching places, are also a feature of early Christianity in the West Midlands. Their different styles of decoration indicate that one school of carvers was active in the Peak District of central Mercia in the late 8th and early 9th centuries, and another, represented by crosses at Sandbach in Cheshire, in the mid-9th century. The Peak District crosses include angels on the cross heads and plant-scrolls distinguished by tightly scrolled, almost leafless branches, and one has to imagine them perhaps plastered, painted and decorated with glass to represent fine jewels. At Wirksworth, in Derbyshire, a 9th-century pre-Viking carved stone shows no fewer than eight religious scenes; this appears to have been part of the

Fig. 3.5 Ancient churchyard yew, Much Marcle, Herefordshire.

Fig. 3.6 Known early and later pre-Conquest minsters in the region.
The map shows only recorded pre-Conquest minsters and is likely to be incomplete. Major churches recorded in Domesday Book are also shown (see Blair 1985).

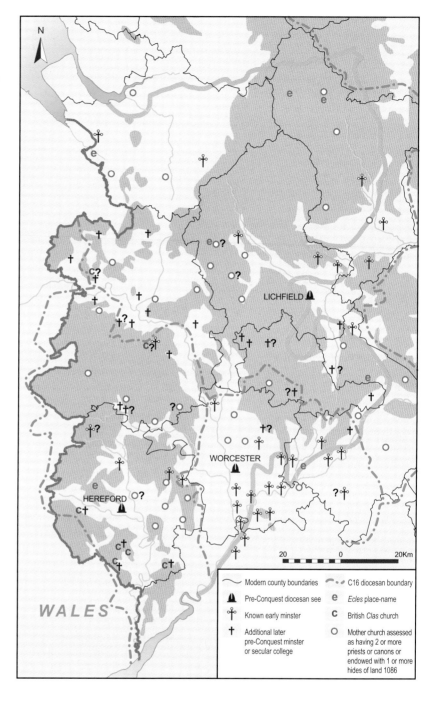

sarcophagus of an important saint. Remnants of other carved crosses have been found at Hope, Chapel-en-le-Frith, Eyam, Taddington and Darley Dale in the north-west of the county, and further south at Bakewell, Bradbourne, Norbury, Checkley and Brailsford (that at Bradbourne was re-erected after attempts had been made to destroy it at the time of the Reformation). At Eyam, the most complete of these depicts the Virgin and Child and a profusion of angels. Others in Staffordshire are found at Ilam, Leek, Eccleshall, Chebsey and Rolleston, with another at Wolverhampton. The cross at Leek depicts in its interlace ornament a 'Staffordshire knot', and the tall sandstone column from Wolverhampton, with acanthus ornament typical of a southern English school of sculpture (Fig. 3.7), may be based upon a Roman column from Wroxeter or Wall. Further fragments of crosses in the Hereford and Gloucester region represent a 9th-century west Mercian group that includes examples from Acton Beauchamp, Newent and Cropthorne in the Worcestershire Vale of Evesham. Many of these depict strange animals, such as the bird, lion and possible goat found within the large scrolls of the Acton Beauchamp cross, the long-legged creature with a cat-like face on a long neck on that from Newent and, on the Cropthorne cross, the 'dragonesque creature with the head, claws, and wings of a bird and a tail terminating in a large leaf ', birds with hooked beaks; a beast with 'a long tongue protruding from its mouth and looped round its foreleg'; and another 'having a protruding tongue tied in a Stafford knot' (Fig. 3.8).[18] A later group of Anglo-Danish crosses, probably of the 11th century, is found around Macclesfield in Cheshire, extending into north Staffordshire and Derbyshire. A once brightly painted carving of an angel on an 8th-century limestone panel, recently unearthed at Lichfield Cathedral, may have formed part of the shrine of St Chad, an integral part of the Saxon church that lies under the present cathedral.

Church building had also been going on apace after the 9th and 10th centuries as lords established new churches upon their manors within the minster *parochiae*. Many early churches were of timber but most were later rebuilt in stone, although this generally did not happen until after the Norman Conquest. Anglo-Saxon fabric can be identified in only a small number of the region's churches, including some of the more important minster churches like Wootton Wawen and Wroxeter or those associated with other central places like Atcham (near an Anglo-Saxon palace site) (Fig. 3.9). At Wootton Wawen, the lower part of the tower survives from the early cruciform church, with all four arches leading to the nave, chancel and transepts still clearly visible. At Much Wenlock, only the foundations of the early church have been found, beneath the later crossing, while at Hereford a fragment of an early church has been incorporated into the later south wall of the Bishop's Cloister of the cathedral. Many of the other churches with early fabric are found along the Welsh borderland, perhaps because churches here have often been less subject to rebuilding.

Like the Anglo-Saxons before them, the Vikings had also been pagan when they arrived, but it was a condition of Alfred's treaty with Guthrum in about 880 that the Danish leader be baptised. The division of the country under this treaty left

Fig. 3.7 The Wolverhampton cross, *perhaps based upon a Roman column from Wroxeter or Wall and likely to date from the 9th or 10th century.*

Fig. 3.8 The 9th-century Anglo-Saxon *cross head at Cropthorne, Worcestershire, showing its mythical creatures.*

Fig. 3.9 Atcham church, dedicated to St Eata, a companion of St Aidan, has some Anglo-Saxon fabric and there are probably reused Roman stones at the base of the walls.

the Danes in possession of the entire area north of the Watling Street, although Alfred's daughter Æthelflæd was able to push back the frontier after 917. As a result of this, the Danish states south of the Humber were amalgamated into the West Saxon kingdom, despite the fact that the districts of the five boroughs, including Derby, remained substantially Danish in character. The lasting legacy was the introduction of Danish words and place-names into the east of the region. Further settlement by Norwegian Vikings brought a later stratum of Scandinavian place-names to the Wirral and adjacent parts of Cheshire. Among these, Thingwall represents the site of a meeting-place or *þing* and Great and Little Meols take their name from Old Norse *melr* meaning a sand-bank or sand dune.

Some of the early minsters were to be re-endowed in the period of Benedictine reform in the 10th century, among them Pershore, Evesham, Coventry and Burton upon Trent. A Mercian noblewoman, Wulfrun, may also have been refounding an earlier monastery when she endowed Wolverhampton minster in 994. Other religious houses at Much Wenlock, Coventry and Leominster were also re-endowed in the mid-11th century by Leofric, Earl of Mercia.

THE EARLY MEDIEVAL LANDSCAPE

Although population densities remain unknown, it is possible to postulate some tentative models of how early medieval rural settlement was organised in the West Midlands. At the beginning of the period the whole region seems to have been dominated by a pattern of dispersed farmsteads, but by the late 8th or 9th century settlement becomes increasingly concentrated around the new estate nuclei in the more heavily populated areas of intensive crop-growing. The area in which nucleation was dominant tends to coincide with that of the densest concentration of Romano-British farmsteads, especially in the valley lowlands.

The dating of settlements rests very much upon pottery evidence – something that is in short supply in the region. The commercial potteries of Roman Britain failed at the end of the 4th century and, after that, recourse was made more and more to wooden vessels and basketware for domestic use. The Anglo-Saxons did make use of a fibrous ware that does not survive well and is usually only found during excavations, but even then it was not plentiful in this region until much later (finer pottery is limited to a small number of high-status sites before it begins to be made again in some of region's towns around the 9th century). Relatively few early Anglo-Saxon settlement sites have been identified and still fewer excavated – they have sometimes been revealed as crop marks where the cellars of what have been termed 'sunken-featured' buildings (often used as weaving sheds) show up from the air as dark circular patches. At Catholme, in the Trent valley in Staffordshire, a series of farmsteads was continually rebuilt over a period of some 400 years; they lay immediately to the north-east of an earlier Romano-British site.[19] Most settlements of this period were, however, small scale and subject to shift and have proved very difficult to locate.

Despite a serious shortage of reliable dating evidence, nucleation seems on the whole to have been a gradual process, with isolated settlements still being recorded near estate boundaries in Worcestershire's Vale of Evesham in the 11th century (settlements which had entirely disappeared by later medieval times).[20] Nucleation also seems to have occurred hand in hand with the introduction of open-field farming. The spread of open-field agriculture was a feature right across Europe at this time and must reflect a change in landholding rights. It seems to have begun on the demesne (the lord's) lands of the multiple estates, usually those held by the Crown or by the Church, where groups of bond tenants supported the central vill, their land held in subdivided quillets (strips). Perhaps it was this kind of land management that was deliberately adopted on the new 'manors' as the great estates fragmented, each 'manor' supported by its own patch of demesne land. In much of the region, including the borderland, these 'manors' were tiny and numerous; the area was also to be characterised in later medieval times by parishes with numerous patches of open-field land, usually associated with the early manorial foci or hamlet centres. Some of these open-field cores may have been farmed as 'infield', kept permanently under cultivation by the liberal use of animal manure, while patches of 'outfield' could be ploughed as required. As the estates became socially and economically viable communities, with their own land and clearly defined boundaries, they are often referred to as townships.

Only in relatively densely populated areas did the open fields become extensive, or evolve as a result of subsequent reorganisation, perhaps many centuries later, into systems closer to the standard three- or four-field medieval pattern that characterises the south and east midlands. Although the concentration of people in a central focus of settlement might aid the sharing of ploughs, especially where soils were suitable for ploughing only over a very short period, and provide equal access to shared fields, this kind of development was by no means as universal in this region as in the areas of intense crop cultivation to the east and south.

Where charters are available, they start to reveal the finer details of the Anglo-Saxon economy and land use – they allow the reconstruction, for instance, of the saltways that radiated out from Droitwich.[21] Much of this is evidence is derived from accompanying boundary clauses that provide a kind of 'word-map' of the countryside, and in turn allow regional patterns of land use to be confirmed.[22] These include the areas of intensive crop-growing where fields – probably by the end of the period open fields – already extended as far as estate boundaries, with furrows marked out by the plough dividing them from the lands of neighbouring settlements (Fig. 3.10).[23] In general, however, these intensively cultivated areas lie beyond the borders of the West Midlands region.

Fig. 3.10 Early medieval landscapes: part of the Vale of Evesham (now in Worcestershire), an area of intensive cultivation (after Hooke 1985).

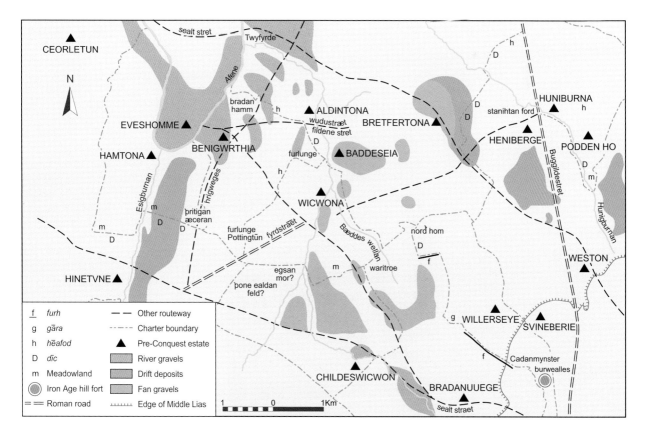

Fig. 3.11 View across the Vale of Evesham from Saintbury on the Cotswold scarp.

In south-east Worcestershire, the Vale of Evesham was one such area (Fig. 3.11). A fertile region drained by the River Avon, it supported several rich monasteries and there are many charters that reveal it as a well-settled area with extensive field systems to the south of the river and rich waterside meadows.[24] More typical is that part of central Worcestershire (Fig. 3.12) where the charter bounds show that there were pockets of open field around settlements, but also fields enclosed by hedgerows, with pockets of woodland surviving along estate boundaries (Fig. 3.13).[25] Although ploughlands where the oxen turned are recorded on the southern boundary of Himbleton in the late 9th century and headlands along the northern boundary of Bredicot in the 10th, the majority of boundary landmarks consist of crofts (enclosed fields), hedges, meadows and patches of woodland, suggesting a mosaic of managed countryside. One of the crofts in Huddington, 7km east of Worcester, was used for the cultivation of barley, but the mention of cattle sheds indicates a mixed farming economy. The woods of the area were frequented by deer and one named hedge was intended to control the native roe deer. The land seems, in general, to have been less well drained than it is today with patches of marshland and more extensive areas of fen, especially in the heart of *Fleferð*, a district of the mid-Worcestershire plain whose name incorporated the Old Englsh *fyrð*, meaning 'land covered with brushwood'. This kind of closely farmed, but not everywhere intensively cropped, countryside was probably characteristic, too, of much of the border country.

More remote areas, again with many ancient hedgerows, but with less

Fig. 3.12 View across central Worcestershire showing a landscape of hedged fields and copses.

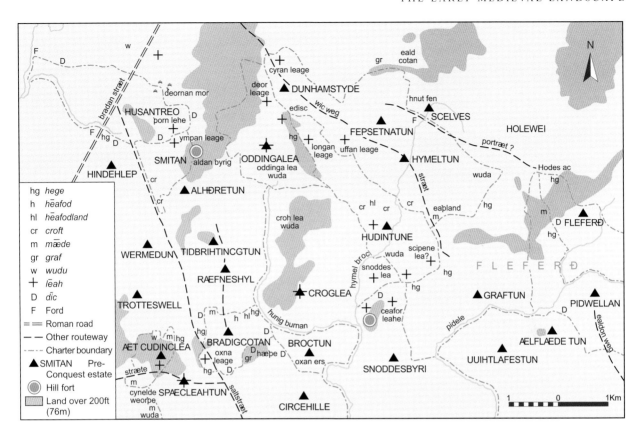

Fig. 3.13 Mid-Worcestershire: *a developing region (after Hooke 1985).*

cropped land and probably with a more dispersed settlement pattern, were found in wooded countryside, as in the Worcestershire region to the west of the Severn, where more of the land seems to have been set aside for hunting and for game reserves.[26] The area below the Malverns, where the flat west Worcestershire plain lies today under farmland, had become forest by the time of the Domesday Book in 1086, but the earlier charters record game reserves, with boundaries sometimes intended to keep out wolves, interspersed with areas of marshland, woodland and farmland (Fig. 3.14). Pigs are mentioned on several occasions and there were sometimes disputes over swine-pasture. The Crown reserved the right to the surplus swine mast (acorns, beech nuts etc) at Ombersley in Worcestershire, allegedly in the 8th century, but the bishop and clergy of Worcester successfully prevented the royal swine-reeve from extending his wood-pasture rights at Leigh Sinton in Malvern Forest in 825. In 855 the community was released from pasturing the king's swine at Bentley, an estate to the north of the Teme.

Warwickshire charters reveal a similar progression from the intensively cultivated regions in the south of the county, the Feldon or 'open land', to the more sparsely settled and more heavily wooded areas to the north.[27] Where boundary clauses are numerous, as in the central part of the Avon valley, a clear picture is presented of estates practising mixed farming – keeping plough oxen and sheep and growing corn, barley and beans – with meadows beside the rivers and with mills and river fisheries. Within Arden, to the north, charters with boundary clauses are fewer but there are glimpses of the patches of woodland that characterised this region, like the 'old wood' (Mockley Wood) in Ullenhall, 'the white wood' (later known as Monwode Lea 'the common wood') in Arley and 'the ferny wood' in Oldberrow, with the occasional farmstead such as 'Wyn's farmstead' (Old English 'worð') lying close to an estate boundary. The more

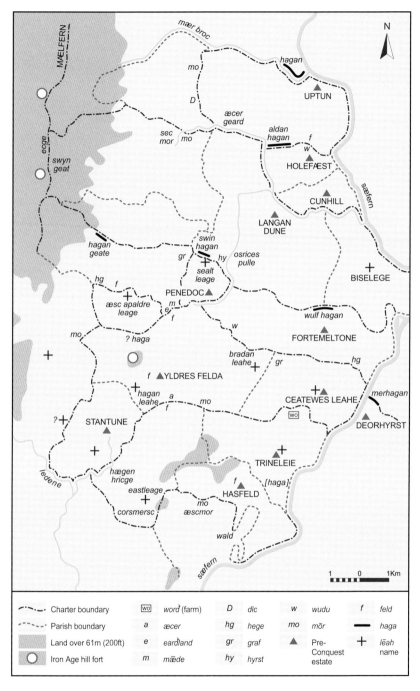

MAELFERN

mær broc

mo

hagan

D

æcer geard

UPTUN

sec mor mo

aldan hagan

f w

ecge

swyn geat

HOLEFÆST

sæfern

CUNHILL

LANGAN DUNE

swin hagan

hagan geate

gr hy osrices pulle

sealt leage

BISELEGE

hg f

PENEDOC

æsc apaldre leage

e m f

? haga

wulf hagan

mo

FORTEMELTONE

bradan leahe gr hg

w

f YLDRES FELDA

hagan leahe a f mo

CEATEWES LEAHE

merhagan

wo

DEORHYRST

? STANTUNE

TRINELEIE

hægen hricge

[haga]

eastleage f

HASFELD

ledene

corsmersc

mo æscmor

wald

sæfern

1   0   1Km

Fig. 3.14 West of Severn: *below the Malverns.*

Legend:

- Charter boundary
- Parish boundary
- Land over 61m (200ft)
- Iron Age hill fort

wo	*word* (farm)	
a	*æcer*	
e	*eardland*	
m	*mæde*	

D	*dīc*
hg	*hege*
gr	*graf*
hy	*hyrst*

w	*wudu*
mo	*mōr*
▲	Pre-Conquest estate

f	*feld*
—	*haga*
+	*lēah* name

limited data available for Warwickshire can, however, be supplemented, as elsewhere, by place-name evidence, which confirms the clear regional patterns of land use that were already present in this period.[28]

Unfortunately, charters with boundary clauses are not abundant across the whole region. They provide the richest data for Worcestershire where many estates were held by the Church of Worcester, but very few survive for Herefordshire and Shropshire. Two important groups of charters, those relating to Wolverhampton minster and a Burton Abbey group, also survive for Staffordshire.[29] A 10th-century charter boundary of Marchington and an 11th-century boundary clause of Rolleston show the estates extending into the woodlands of Needwood. Wooded countryside is also represented by landmarks in other charters: a *haga*, or game enclosure, is noted, for example, on the boundary of Hatherton, which lay within the later Forest of Cannock, while there was 'the wallowing-place of the hart' and a 'hunter's track' on the boundary of Pelsall in the same forest, with swine pastures in other parts of the area. At Barr Beacon, a high point on the south Staffordshire plateau, a 10th-century charter records *þone ealda ad* 'the old beacon site', while a burial place for thieves is captured a century later as a landmark on the boundary of Rolleston as 'the thorn where the thieves lie'. This execution site stood close to a routeway that forded the river here, and routeways are particularly prominent in Staffordshire charters. Many church records for eastern parts of England were undoubtedly destroyed during the Danish attacks in the 9th century and only a few charters with boundary clauses survive for Derbyshire. Swine are again mentioned in connection with a gritstone ridge that marked the southern boundary of Birchover on Stanton Moor.

Another, even earlier, series of charters were recorded in the 12th-century *Liber Landavensis*, *Book of Llandâf*, dating from the late 6th to the 9th century. While most concern places in Wales some cover the south-western area which lay within the Welsh kingdom of Ergyng.[30] Although these bounds do refer to topographical features (especially streams), woods, and even earthworks, identification of the individual land units remains difficult. References to a 'great wood' at Llandinabo (?Harewood) and woods at Llancillo on the north bank of the Monnow and beside the River Gamber, the last two areas not well wooded today, seem to indicate a rather more wooded environment in these areas in the early medieval period.

What is revealed by the early documents and place-names is that this was, by the early medieval period, a full countryside, liberally dotted with settlements and farms so that very few parts of the region could be considered truly remote. The natural landscape of hill and valley, stream and marsh was still of fundamental importance and large areas of waste and semi-wilderness survived, as woodland, moorland and undrained marsh, but there were few areas untouched or unaltered by the hand of man. The woodland and waste might still await future colonisation but was managed for timber or pastured by livestock; even in the most remote recesses the deer and wild boar were not safe from controlled hunting by man. In most areas the picture is one of farms, fields and interconnected roads, with few communities more than a kilometre or so away from a neighbour. What is more, the regions that can be identified through the early medieval documents are still apparent in today's landscape, despite the changes that have occurred over the succeeding thousand years.

URBAN CENTRES IN THE EARLY MEDIEVAL PERIOD

Many of the early towns of the West Midland region had developed as defended urban centres. One of the earliest, Hereford, probably began as an ecclesiastical centre in the late 7th century but the defences appear to have been built before those of any other midland *burh*, first constructed in gravel and clay in the mid-9th century only to be strengthened later in the century by a timber-laced rampart and subsequently by a stone revetment wall in the early 10th century.[31] Tamworth was the most important royal Mercian vill in the 8th century when Offa had a palace there and it may also have been already defended before it became a centre for the reconquest of the Danelaw under Alfred's daughter Æthelflæd. But the defended towns were also meant to develop as economic centres, with good roads serving a market for the surrounding countryside.[32] With her husband Æthelred, ealdorman of Mercia, Æthelflæd fortified Worcester in the late 9th century, ordering that the *burh* should be built 'for the protection of all the people', and they shared market dues with the Church of Worcester. Later they established burhs at Shrewsbury and Chester (907), the latter possibly threatened by Norwegian settlers in the Wirral, and refortified Hereford and Worcester (910). After her husband's death Æthelflæd went on to build fortresses at or near Bridgnorth (*Cwatbrycge*) on the Severn (912), Stafford (913), Warwick (914), and 'Eddisbury' in Cheshire (914), the last, established either in the Iron Age hillfort of Castle Ditch near Delamere or at Edisbury in Rainow near Macclesfield, failing to become a town. Other burhs were established further north at Runcorn, Thelwall and Manchester and, finally, in 920, at Bakewell.

Both Stafford and Shrewsbury made use of the defence offered by marshland and a river meander, Shrewsbury on the Severn (Fig. 3.15) and Stafford on the Sow. The burhs, defended against the Welsh or the Vikings, are likely to have made a considerable impression on the landscape of early and late medieval England. Apart from the burhs, it has been claimed that minster foundations were the nearest things to urban sites in early Anglo-Saxon England and many, indeed, gave rise to towns close to their precincts.[33] The great minsters stood out as virtually the only stone buildings in a landscape where other buildings were small and constructed out of timber and thatch. Their buildings not only expressed the power of God on earth but also, perhaps just as consciously, the role of the Church itself.

The boundaries of the midland counties with which we are familiar today are not ancient and were drawn up around the newly established burhs, like Stafford,

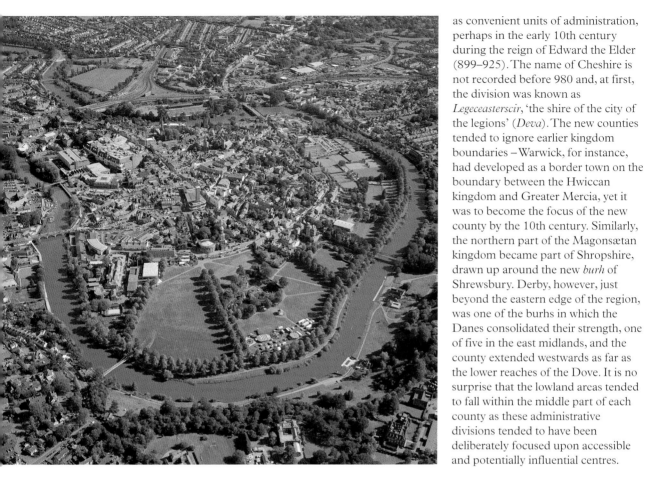

as convenient units of administration, perhaps in the early 10th century during the reign of Edward the Elder (899–925). The name of Cheshire is not recorded before 980 and, at first, the division was known as *Legeceasterscir*, 'the shire of the city of the legions' (*Deva*). The new counties tended to ignore earlier kingdom boundaries – Warwick, for instance, had developed as a border town on the boundary between the Hwiccan kingdom and Greater Mercia, yet it was to become the focus of the new county by the 10th century. Similarly, the northern part of the Magonsætan kingdom became part of Shropshire, drawn up around the new *burh* of Shrewsbury. Derby, however, just beyond the eastern edge of the region, was one of the burhs in which the Danes consolidated their strength, one of five in the east midlands, and the county extended westwards as far as the lower reaches of the Dove. It is no surprise that the lowland areas tended to fall within the middle part of each county as these administrative divisions tended to have been deliberately focused upon accessible and potentially influential centres.

Fig. 3.15 Shrewsbury. *The Anglo-Saxon* burh *was constructed within a meander of the River Severn and a castle defended access via the narrow neck of land to the north-east after the Norman Conquest (top left of photograph).*

NOTES

1   Hooke 1998a, chs 3 and 4.
2   Hooke 1985a, 82, fig. 22.
3   Coplestone-Crow 1989.
4   Weale *et al.* 2002; Capelli *et al.* 2003.
5   Higham 1993, 89, fig 3.6.
6   Coplestone-Crow 1989, 2–5, map 2.
7   Coates 2004.
8   Gelling 1992, 53–71, figs 29–34.
9   Hooke 2002, 68.
10 Hill & Worthington 2003, 113–14.
11 Dark 2000, 132–53.
12 Hooke 1989, 120–2; Wager 1998, 154–7; Vera 2000, 376–8.
13 Coplestone-Crow 1989, 92, 100, 136.
14 Bassett 1992, 29–35.
15 Gelling 1990, 30–1.
16 Some burials in the region cannot be dated with certainty and a full gazetteer is given in Barnatt 1996, 57–61.
17 Rattue 1995, 173–9.
18 Romilly Allen in *VCH Worcestershire II*, 1906, 183.
19 Losco-Bradley & Kinsley 2002.
20 Hooke 1985b, 135–8.
21 Hooke 1998a, 8.
22 Hooke 1981a; 1983; 1990; 1999.
23 Hooke 1985a, ch 6, 190–226, fig 43.
24 Ibid, 213–22.
25 Ibid, 238–42.
26 Hooke 1989, 126, fig 6.
27 Hooke 1996; 1999.
28 Hooke 1996, 102–4, fig 3.
29 Hooke 1983.
30 *Book of Llan Dâv*, ed Gwenogvryn Evans 1893, 1979 edition.
31 Baker 2003, who notes that dating at present rests upon imprecise ceramic evidence.
32 Hooke 1980.
33 Blair 1988, 47–50.

4

From the Norman Conquest to *c*. 1500

Estate management policies had begun to transform the landscape of England before the arrival of the Normans, especially in the heavily cultivated zones – villages set amidst open fields were already a feature in many regions, often now clustered around a church, and these continued to grow. The open fields were extended as the population continued to expand, but some contraction is evident in the early 14th century, especially in the more marginal lands, and the Black Death of 1348 (and subsequent plagues) accelerated this dramatically. New farmsteads were also spreading into more marginal areas. Although the area under forest law was extended, development continued in wooded areas and over upland wastes: the 13th century, in particular, was a period in which much assarting (woodland clearance) and enclosure took place. Under the Normans, symbols of seigneurial power and control were made deliberately more obvious in the landscape: castles and fortified manor houses, many stone-built, signified status and authority over the surrounding landscape and its people and often new villages or towns grew up around them; newly founded abbeys similarly manipulated local resources in a way that made a significant mark upon the landscape.

THE NORMAN CONQUEST AND THE EVIDENCE OF DOMESDAY BOOK

Castles were a prominent feature of Norman seigneurial control, graphically conveying the role of lordship within the landscape. Many survive today as no more than grassy tumps, but they were used initially as defended centres from which to wield control over newly conquered territories or, as in the Welsh areas of the borderland, as the first step towards extending Norman control. The earliest castles usually consisted of an earthen motte, probably with a timber shell keep, and a defended bailey that held storehouses, barracks and other important structures. The border country remained prone to attacks from the Welsh who, indeed, held the initiative until the early 1060s under the leadership of Gruffydd ap Rhydderch and, after his death, of Gruffydd ap Llewellyn. Even before the Norman Conquest, Edward the Confessor, who had been raised in Normandy, had introduced Norman lords into positions of power in the borderland, including Osbern who had established the lordship of Ewyas Harold in the Black Mountains and built one of the first castles in England (Fig. 4.1).[1] Another was built at Richard's Castle, to the south of Ludlow, and Ralph, Edward's nephew, built himself a castle at Hereford. Cheshire, too, had been largely outside royal control before the Conquest, held by the head of the most powerful noble house in England, Leofric of Mercia; Leofric's grandson, Earl Edwin, reigned supreme across the north midlands at the time of the Conquest.

Fig. 4.1 An early castle: Ewyas Harold, Herefordshire.

William's efforts to re-establish royal control across the country were sometimes, as in Cheshire, Staffordshire and Derbyshire, accompanied by the harrying of the countryside, and castles were also raised to quell any possible rebellion: he raised a castle at Warwick in *c.* 1068, at Stafford in 1070 (probably at Broad Eye on the north-western side of the town), at Chester in 1071 and at Shrewsbury before 1086 (probably that which had already been besieged by the Welsh in 1069). Castles were not only defensive strongholds but provided the first and most significant bases for active military operations against enemy forces. In Herefordshire, Domesday Book records the castleries – areas of jurisdiction – associated with the castle at Clifford on the Wye held by Ralph de Tosny, that at Ewyas Harold held by Roger de Lacy, inheriting from his father Walter, and that at Wigmore held by Ralph de Mortimer. In Shropshire, Helgot had a castle on land he held from Earl Roger at Holdgate; another of the Earl's tenants had built a castle at Oswestry. In Staffordshire, Henry de Ferrers threw up a castle at Tutbury soon after the Conquest to serve as the administrative centre of his estates, most of which lay in Derbyshire. By 1086 it had attracted a community of tradesmen in the borough at its foot; there was a market, and the town was to continue to serve as the administrative centre of the Honour. Others castles were soon constructed by other leading Norman families both as defensive and administrative centres. At Bridgnorth, Robert de Belleme moved the people of Quatford to a site in a more commanding position overlooking the Severn and his castle there was under construction by the 1080s.[2]

Domesday Book shows how individual Norman lords were already in 1086 building up their 'empires' of great estates spread across the countryside. In the midland core region, the Crown had tended to retain estates in the more wooded parts of the countryside, perhaps already betraying the interest Norman kings showed in hunting, although in Herefordshire William also continued to hold the royal centre of Leominster, reputedly the seat of the earlier King Merewalh of the Magonsæte, and royal estates were scattered across the northern part of the county. In most counties, the Church had been the main beneficiary of land grants over the centuries and the bishop and clergy of the various dioceses had to be counted amongst the greatest landowners, often enjoying the most fertile areas. The Bishop and canons of Hereford held estates across central Herefordshire, the Church of Worcester vast estates across Worcestershire and Warwickshire, the Bishop of Chester (and Lichfield) estates, some based upon Eccleshall and Lichfield, in Staffordshire and others in Cheshire with a few more in Derbyshire. The diocesan centres were not the only ones holding great estates, for in Worcestershire the abbeys of Evesham and Pershore held much land, although the latter had had many of its estates taken away and given to the Church of Westminster by Edward the Confessor and William the Conqueror before 1086. In Shropshire, the Church of St Mildburh at Much Wenlock, re-founded as an abbey by Earl Roger, held many of the estates of the earlier foundation. But secular Norman lords were already powerful. Earl Roger held most of Shropshire as well as land in Staffordshire, Henry de Ferrers was strong in Staffordshire and Derbyshire, and many other such Norman landowners can be traced through the great Domesday Book record.

In the extent of its coverage, Domesday Book is unique for the period and remains the envy of all other countries in Europe. It provides a view of the English countryside at the time of the Norman Conquest that is unrivalled in its detail. Based upon a number of separate regional compilations, a final text was drawn up as Great Domesday Book by scribes at Winchester, providing the new ruler with a list of landholders and sources of revenue. In the Domesday economy 'the plough was king' and the density of plough teams recorded across the region can help to indicate the areas of greatest arable potential. In general, densities are far higher to the south-east of our region – in south-east Worcestershire, southern Warwickshire and Gloucestershire (where they might reach more than 1.7 per sq km, 4.5 per square mile). These were the regions that had already been intensively exploited in the Roman period and where intensive crop cultivation continued into medieval times, associated with settlement nucleation and the strong development of open-field farming. Densities were also high across central and eastern Herefordshire. Although the continuation here of a more dispersed settlement pattern may have augmented the number of teams kept, the region was also well populated and the eastern plain, in particular, characterised by fertile loam soils. Most of Worcestershire, apart from the higher land of the north-east, was also well settled and cultivated. The north-east had lower densities of plough teams but, at 0.4 – 1.0 per sq km (1 – 2.5 per square mile), remained on a par with the lowland areas of the region's more northern counties: eastern and central Shropshire, the Wirral and west Cheshire, western and eastern Staffordshire and southern Derbyshire. Much of western Herefordshire had recently been wasted by Welsh attacks but it is unlikely that the hill lands would in any case have been as prosperous as the lowlands, and northwards across the region plough-team densities were much lower in upland areas such as the Cannock plateau and north Staffordshire, eastern Cheshire and the Dark Peak area of north-western Derbyshire, falling to below 0.2 teams per sq km (0.5 per square mile) (Fig. 4.2).

Woodland and wood-pasture was a valued resource and was generally abundant across the region. It has been estimated that Worcestershire was 40 per cent wooded at the time of the Domesday survey, surpassed only by the Weald of south-eastern England and Gloucestershire west of the River Severn.[3] Staffordshire was 32 per cent woodland, Cheshire 27 per cent, Derbyshire 26 per cent and Warwickshire 19 per cent (mostly in the north, within that part of the county discussed in this volume). Only Shropshire appears low, with only 8 per cent woodland. However, the Domesday folios do not mention the royal forests that later extended across the southern half of the county and it is possible that the Domesday entries omit any woodland already 'in the king's hands', as in some other areas elsewhere in the country. Certainly, King Edward hunted from Shrewsbury and the number of 'hays' that were recorded – places for capturing deer – suggest that much more woodland was present than was actually recorded.[4]

Domesday Book also records a number of special economic assets within the region. In Worcestershire, the salt industry of Droitwich continued to flourish. Leaden vats (evaporation trays) for the industry were made at Northwick, possibly using lead transported up the River Severn from southern Gloucestershire.[5] In Cheshire, the industry was concentrated around the 'wiches' of Nantwich, Middlewich and Northwich. Equally outstanding was the lead-mining industry of

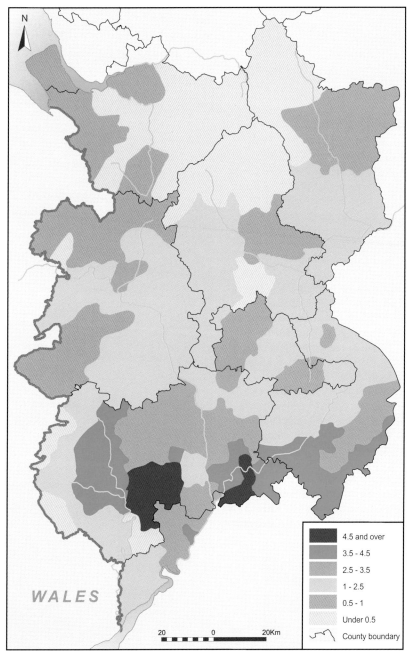

Derbyshire, a source of regional wealth since prehistoric times. This was concentrated mainly within the manors of Wirksworth, Ashford, Bakewell, Crich and Shuckstonefield, and Matlock Bridge, strung out along the eastern margins of the Peak District between Hope and Wirksworth.[6] With a combined render (payment) from five other royal manors (Darley, Matlock Bridge, Wirksworth, Ashbourne and Parwich) of £40 of pure silver, this too is likely to have been obtained from the lead mines. Renders of iron in the city of Gloucester and at Alvington on the Severn estuary probably reflect ironworking within the Forest of Dean, although this is not mentioned specifically in Domesday Book. Smiths were obviously active across the region for the renders consisted of iron and rods of iron, to make nails for the king's ships. Water-mills were by now frequent along all major and minor rivers and streams, and eels were often noted as a render from the mill pond. River fisheries, too, are often recorded. In Gloucestershire, the fisheries along the Severn and Wye, which were earlier recorded in pre-Conquest charters, continued to be important, but others are also recorded in Herefordshire along the Wye, Lugg and Teme; in Shropshire along the Severn, Perry, Roden and Tern; in Worcestershire, along the Severn and its tributaries the Teme, Stour and Avon; in Cheshire along the Dee, Gowy and Weaver; and in Derbyshire along the Trent and Derwent. While meadow is usually included within Domesday statistics, references to pasture or to domestic stock are rare in the final Great Domesday compilation.

Fig. 4.2 Domesday plough-team densities (*after Darby*).

MOTTES AND CASTLES AFTER DOMESDAY

For the sheer concentration of mottes, few regions can equal the Welsh borderland, which was now to become known as the Welsh Marches, where several hundred motte and bailey castles reflect the westward expansion of the Normans into Welsh territory and the troubled conditions which persisted there in the first few centuries after the Norman Conquest (Figs 4.3 and 4.5a). Here the castle was an instrument of domination and of efforts to strengthen the hold of the Marcher lords in a frontier region. These Marcher lords enjoyed a degree of autonomy unmatched in the rest of England. In return for keeping the Welsh at bay they enjoyed the right to exercise their own judicial powers, establish boroughs and forts, and to wage 'private war'. But the concept of communal responsibility to defend the locality still underlay the feudalism and personal ambition of the Middle Ages. A castle would defend its territory, sometimes an extensive castlery or honour, rather than the artificial unit of the county, and armies would be raised locally. Some early castles are better described as ringworks, the encircling bank made up of material thrown inwards from the surrounding ditch (an example can be seen at Heath Farm, Amaston, in Shropshire).[7]

Three great border territories were focused upon Chester, Shrewsbury and Hereford. Shrewsbury, located within a meander of the River Severn, had 250 inhabited houses and five churches by 1066 although after Welsh raids 50 of the houses stood vacant in 1086 and a further 51 had been destroyed to make way for the castle that guarded the narrow neck of the river loop and the landward approach to the town (*see* Fig. 3.15). A network of minor castles was also established and there were outposts within Wales at Rhuddlan and near Montgomery, the latter erected by Roger de Montgomery, Earl of Shrewsbury. William Fitz Osbern, the Earl of Hereford, defended the Wye basin with castles at Wigmore, Clifford and Ewyas Harold, raiding into Wales and establishing the lordship of Striguil around Chepstow. Wigmore became the centre of Ralph de Mortimer, one of the strongest border lords. Many of the early castles were rebuilt in stone in the 12th and 13th centuries, first with a shell or tower keep, while later stone curtain walls with additional towers were often added around the bailey.

The earliest stone castles tended to have square or rectangular keeps like those which still stand at Tamworth in Staffordshire, Goodrich (Fig. 4.4) and Clifford in Herefordshire or Clun in Shropshire, all probably dating from the 12th century.

Fig. 4.3 A well-preserved motte-and-bailey castle at More near Bishops Castle *in the Welsh borderland.*

Fig. 4.4 Goodrich Castle, southern Herefordshire.

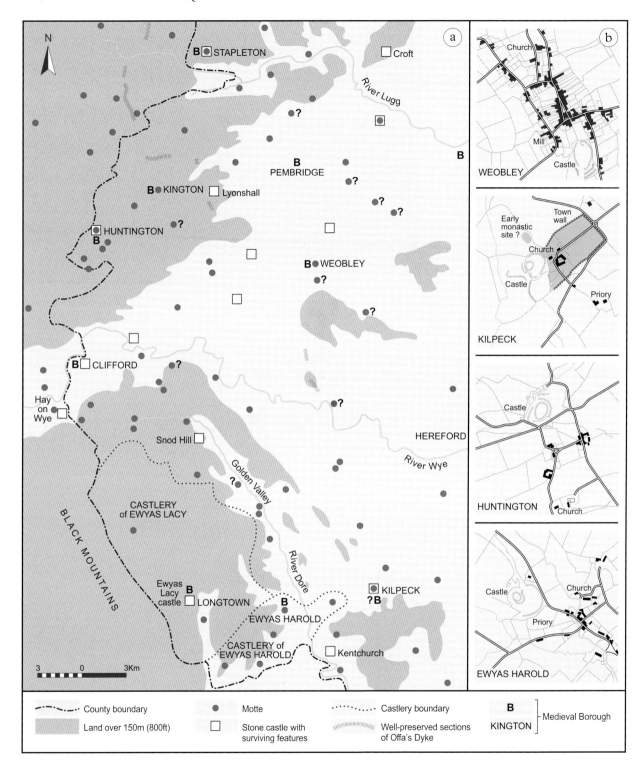

a

N

B⊡ STAPLETON

☐ Croft

River Lugg

?

⊙

B

B
PEMBRIDGE

?

B● KINGTON   ☐ Lyonshall

?

?

?

⊡ HUNTINGTON

B

?

☐

B● WEOBLEY

?

☐

?

B☐ CLIFFORD

?

?

Hay
on
Wye
☐

Snod Hill ☐

HEREFORD

River Wye

Golden Valley

?

BLACK MOUNTAINS

CASTLERY
of EWYAS LACY

River Dore

⊡ KILPECK

Ewyas
Lacy
castle B
☐ LONGTOWN

B
EWYAS HAROLD

?B

CASTLERY of
EWYAS HAROLD

☐ Kentchurch

3   0   3Km

b

Church

Mill

Castle

WEOBLEY

Town
wall

Early
monastic
site ?

Church

Castle

Priory

KILPECK

Castle

Church

HUNTINGTON

Castle

Church

Priory

EWYAS HAROLD

—··—··— County boundary   ● Motte   ············ Castlery boundary   **B** ⎤
                                                                                              ⎬ Medieval Borough
▒ Land over 150m (800ft)   ☐ Stone castle with   ▨▨▨ Well-preserved sections   KINGTON ⎦
                                 surviving features   of Offa's Dyke

By the 13th century, castles began to be more regular in plan, often with a strong gatehouse to control entry, but their military function declined in the 14th century and more comfortable fortified manor houses began to take their place. Strictly speaking, permission from the king had to be sought to build a castle, but it was only after *c.* 1200 that a licence to crenellate became essential. In subsequent centuries, many of the early mottes fell out of use and were simply abandoned, but others that served higher-ranking officials and families were refortified and rebuilt to current fashion. Villages and towns were often established below castle sites, protected by seigneurial power. The castles had been strategically placed in terms of their defensive capability, and while some of their settlements managed to become successful market centres, others dwindled as their castles were abandoned, often because their location failed to sustain them.

Fig. 4.6 Clun Castle, south-west Shropshire, *showing the remains of its medieval pleasure grounds; the remains of water features can be seen in the meadows below the castle.*

The castle at Clun had originated as a motte-and-bailey castle perhaps as early as the late 11th century, but had been rebuilt in stone by the FitzAlans, lords of Clun and Oswestry, at the end of the 12th century after the battle of Radnor during which Prince Rhys is said to have reduced its predecessor to ashes. The castle controlled access to the rich midland plains through the Clun valley and controlled the movement of flocks and herds along the Clun–Clee Ridgeway: tolls could be exacted and a town was established. The new castle was to be more than a military stronghold for its grounds included a medieval 'pleasance', or pleasure garden, and fishponds (Fig. 4.6). However, it had to withstand further attacks for it was captured and burnt by Llewelyn ap Iorworth in 1214, although when he came again in 1234 he was unable to take the castle and instead burnt the town and laid waste the surrounding district. Not surprisingly, the castle needed considerable repair according to a survey made in 1272. In such a vulnerable location, the town failed to prosper – a borough rental of 1300 shows that there were some 60 tenements lying empty and worth nothing.[8] The FitzAlans had abandoned the castle in the 1270s in favour of their main family seat at Arundel in Sussex, and it was attacked again by Owain Glyndwr in the early 1400s. Today the castle is ruinous and in the care of English Heritage, but its Great Tower still stands four storeys and 25m high above the moat. At Kilpeck in Herefordshire, a motte with the remains of a shell keep is associated with a 12th-century church, which contains some of the finest examples of the Herefordshire School of sculpture in the county; both the keep and the church may have been built by Hugh Forester, the descendant of the first Norman lord. The earthworks of a deserted walled town with a planned layout lie immediately to the north-east (Fig. 4.5b).

Castles in this area seem to have been genuinely fortified rather than just expressions of status and power, although the latter function was inevitably of major consideration. (Like so many others, the ringwork set within the Iron Age hillfort of British Camp on the highest point of the Malvern Hills could be seen, and was *meant* to be seen, for miles around.) The medieval period was one of considerable political intrigue, especially between rival claims to the throne of England or between the king and the barons. For example, Robert de Belleme, earl of Shrewsbury, rebelled against King Henry in 1102, while Hugh de Mortimer's uprising against Henry II in 1154–5 led to the destruction of his

OPPOSITE PAGE:

Fig. 4.5a Mottes in a section of the borderland.

Fig. 4.5b Selected border castles with their associated settlements.

WEOBLEY castle is a ringwork within a bailey dating from the late 11th century but with a later stone keep and curtain wall that were still standing in the 17th century. The borough is documented in 1255 and a pattern of burgage plots is clearly visible. KILPECK castle is a motte and bailey first documented in 1134 when Hugh Forester endowed his new priory near by (a possible early monastic site lay to the NE of the church). The castle later had a shell keep and three baileys. The present road pattern respects the layout of the former planned and walled medieval town and the church is a fine example of the 12th-century Hereford School of sculpture. There is now only a shrunken settlement at Kilpeck.

HUNTINGTON castle had a motte and two baileys with later stonework, but the associated borough, laid out by 1267, also failed to survive. EWYAS HAROLD was a very early pre-Conquest motte and bailey, with a later stone castle, and the first settlement grew up within the outer bailey. It was moved to a new site east of the Dulas brook when a Benedictine priory from Dulas was transferred here c. 1100. The town was a borough by 1300.

castle at Cleobury Mortimer and the capture by the king of that at Wigmore. Many new castles were also constructed during the anarchy of Stephen's reign (1135–54) and further acts of rebellion took place throughout the remainder of the 12th and early 13th centuries. Castles changed hands frequently in this climate of political intrigue, and the Welsh were ever ready to take advantage of moments of unrest or weakness to resist Norman aggression, making the borderland an especially vulnerable area.

Such turbulent politics combined with threats from Wales led to the destruction of several castles but, following Edward I's conquest of Wales in 1284, the borderland was for a time made relatively safe from immediate attack, although its earls remained immensely powerful and rebellious, and as late as 1400 the Welsh were once again rising up under the leadership of Owain Glyndwr. It is clear from a long catalogue of disturbance that the castles of the borderland were regularly used as military bases and were intended to be strong enough to resist long sieges. It was only with the introduction of the heavy cannon during the Wars of the Roses in the mid-15th century that some of the weaker castles began to become obsolete.

Several castles were nevertheless to remain in use much longer: Ludlow Castle (*see* Fig. 4.18) in Shropshire is a substantial building occupying a steep rocky promontory above the River Teme and overlooking the medieval borough. Its outer curtain wall, 2m thick and nearly 11m high, encloses an inner and outer bailey, the former – probably the original ringwork – enclosed within an inner curtain wall 2.4m thick. It appears to have changed hands several times between the de Lacys and the Mortimers during the 11th and 14th centuries, but was eventually badly damaged by the Lancastrians in 1459. In 1475 a Council of Wales and the Marches was established at the castle and from about 1501 it became the residence of the Lord President of Wales. It was then kept in good repair until 1689 when the position was abolished, after which it was allowed to decay until purchased by the Earl of Powys in 1811.[9] Yet it remains one of the most impressive medieval castles found in England. The fate of several other castles is discussed in Chapter 5.

In less troubled periods, lordly manor houses might retain elements of fortification but were able to become more comfortable homes, with large windows that would earlier have left them vulnerable to attack. These are manor houses that retain some of the outward characteristics of castles, but which instead of having a military purpose, were badges of lordship intended to convey the status of their owners. This response to more settled times is well illustrated by Acton Burnell and Stokesay (both in Shropshire), where the needs of defence play second fiddle to architectural sophistication and creature comforts. Robert Burnell, Edward I's secretary and chaplain, who later became Bishop of Bath and Wells, created a three-storey rectangular block with red sandstone walls more than 1.2m thick and with projecting angle towers at Acton Burnell, capable of defence but designed 'to appeal to the aesthetic sense' as well.[10] It is now a mere shell (Fig. 4.7). The associated borough, which had 36 burgesses in 1315, did not flourish. Stokesay (Fig. 4.8), an almost perfectly preserved example of a 13th-century fortified manor house (rather than a fortress), belonged to a rich medieval merchant, Lawrence of Ludlow.[11] Another example in the same spirit is Pembridge Castle near Welsh Newton in Herefordshire, which is a small border castle that has survived – greatly restored – as a private house; some of the fabric may pre-date 1200 but the semi-circular towers and gatehouse are of the 13th century.

Fig. 4.7 Acton Burnell 'castle', Shropshire.

Fig. 4.8 Stokesay Castle, Shropshire.

ABBEYS AND CHURCHES

As part of the Norman reform of the Church under Archbishop Lanfranc, who enforced an order that cathedrals should be moved from villages to towns, the diocesan centre of the see of Lichfield was transferred in 1075 from that relatively insignificant place to Chester. But only 27 years later it was shifted again to Coventry where the new Benedictine priory, established by Earl Leofric and Countess Godiva in 1043, was wealthy and prospering. Lichfield was only recognised again as a cathedral in 1228 and even then the diocese was to be known as that of Coventry and Lichfield, with the monks of Coventry and the canons of Lichfield sharing the right to elect the bishop. It was not until Coventry priory was dissolved at the Reformation that Lichfield became the only chapter once more, although in 1541 the northern part of the diocese was detached to form the new diocese of Chester.

Fig. 4.9 The remains of Much Wenlock Abbey, Shropshire. Here the estates of an early minster were granted to the French Cluniac order by Roger de Montgomery in the late 11th century.

Norman lordship in the borders strengthened ties with the abbeys of France: in the late 11th century the estates of the early medieval minster of Wenlock were granted to the French Cluniac order by Roger de Montgomery, dependent upon La Charité in France (Fig. 4.9). The new monks expediently 'discovered' the bones of the first abbess, St Mildburh, which they then laid out in a newly-built shrine. Those monastic cells that remained dependent upon a monastery in Normandy or elsewhere, often manned by foreign monks, were known as alien priories or cells and regarded as exploitative by local people; the financial arrangements of Wenlock, however, were also mistrusted by their parent order which, in 1279, dismissed the prior, John of Thefford. When war broke out with France in 1295, Wenlock became liable to severe taxation until it broke its links with La Charité and Cluny a hundred years later. At Tutbury in Staffordshire Henry de Ferrers brought monks from the abbey of St Pierre-sur-Dives in Normandy to establish an alien priory of Benedictine monks and here, again, alien status brought unpopularity with local people. By the late 14th century,

ABOVE: **Fig. 4.10 Kilpeck church, Herefordshire**, *a church in the 12th-century Romanesque style, with carvings on the church door.*

when the wars against France aroused strong feelings, foreign controlled monasteries only escaped suppression by becoming autonomous.

In the borders, especially, Norman power was expressed in church foundations – there are substantial numbers surviving – and lordly patronage led to the development of the Hereford and Dymock (or Bromyard) Schools of sculpture in the 12th century. In the former, the influence of the European Romanesque style was carried first to cathedral churches like Hereford and Gloucester, but was to be expressed subsequently in smaller Herefordshire churches such as Kilpeck (Fig. 4.10) and Shobdon, and in a few outside that county,[12] probably worked by travelling groups of sculptors. A product of lordly patronage, these churches were given the lavish decoration seen further afield in great churches like Reading or Sarum, including motifs derived from western France and Spain combined with more indigenous elements. Before the Reformation, every church would have been brightly painted with scenes from the Bible and the lives of the saints, augmenting the now half-understood symbolism of ornament sculpted in stone and wood. At Claverley in Shopshire, a long strip of wall painting of about 1200 shows a battle between knights on horseback that represents the Battle of the Virtues and the Vices. At Ripple, in Worcestershire, 15th-century misericords

RIGHT: **Fig. 4.11 Medieval misericords in the church at Ripple, Worcestershire**, *illustrating* The Labours of the Months: April – bird scaring.

(carvings on bench ends) depict the 'Labours of the Months' – delightful images of the farming year (Fig. 4.11). Not all Norman parish churches were as elaborate. Heath chapel in Shropshire, for instance, has been described as 'the perfect example of a small Norman church, now lying quite on its own in a field' (Fig. 4.12).[13] It was originally built on the Prior of Wenlock's estate to serve a community developing the upland margins, but was left stranded when arable cultivation ceased to be viable in the later Middle Ages.

Fig. 4.12 Heath chapel near Clee St Margaret, Shropshire, *a small Norman church left isolated after the desertion of the village near by.*

On the Continent, several new monastic orders were founded which attempted to regain the ethic of austerity, and they were also brought to England, like the small poverty-stricken cell of the Grandmontines at Craswall near Hay-on-Wye in Herefordshire. But the Cistercians, originally seeking out remote locations, had a greater effect upon the countryside. They accumulated large estates, often in hilly regions like the

Fig. 4.13 The Dore or Golden Valley, Herefordshire. The fertile setting for the Cistercian abbey founded here in 1147.

Staffordshire moorlands (the abbeys of Croxden, Dieulacres and Hulton) or at Abbey Dore in the Golden Valley (Fig. 4.13) on the western borders of Herefordshire, locations in which they could maintain the extensive sheep flocks that were to bring them wealth from wool production. In the Warwickshire Arden, the abbeys of Bordesley, Stoneleigh, Merevale and Combe kept some 20,000 sheep between them at the end of the 13th century, although the plateau area was not noted for the high quality of its wool. The Cistercians were sometimes accused of moving existing settlements, such as the villages of Musden and Rushton in Staffordshire, allegedly destroyed by Croxden Abbey, or Smite in Warwickshire – but here the monks of Combe Abbey probably shifted the villagers to their new town of Brinklow, better located for marketing on the Fosse Way itself (Fig. 4.14).

Fig. 4.14 Brinklow, Warwickshire, a new town established along the line of the Fosse Way, below the medieval motte and bailey castle, by the Cistercian monks of Combe Abbey.

The Cistercians were adept at draining the marshy low-lying regions and managing water resources: at Bordesley in Worcestershire, the complex system of fishponds they laid out along the River Arrow beside their abbey is still preserved. They also took the opportunity to enhance their revenues by assarting woodland, especially land that was free from manorial restrictions;[14] among those known to have done this were Stoneleigh in Warwickshire and Dieulacres in Staffordshire. In Shropshire, Wenlock Priory was actively assarting in the forests of Shirlett, Wrekin and Clee, and in this county many of the later foundations, like Buildwas (Savigniac) and the Augustinian houses of Haughmond, Lilleshall and Wombridge, were in undeveloped well-wooded locations where they were able to prosper because of their expansionist policies.[15] Chester Abbey, a Benedictine foundation, drew an income from sea fishing. Other foundations were active in early industrial development: the monks of Bordesley Abbey may have introduced needle making to the Arrow valley in the adjacent area of Warwickshire; in Cheshire, the canons at Norton Priory were skilled in tile making, those at Vale Royal Abbey in glass manufacture; the Staffordshire abbey of Hulton, in addition to a tannery, tile and pottery kilns, had coal mines; Buildwas Abbey and Wenlock Priory carried out ironworking on a small scale in the Shirlett Forest area in Shropshire, which was the precursor of later industrial development in the region.

Some foundations became extremely powerful and both Shrewsbury Abbey and Coventry Cathedral-priory were granted the privilege of being subject only to the pope, the abbot and prior attending Parliament in a capacity equal to that of baron of the realm. Coventry Cathedral-priory was to become the ninth richest monastery in England. In Worcestershire, in the medieval period, some 40 per cent of the county was owned by the Church of Worcester.

In Derbyshire, many distant abbeys and monasteries held granges, or farms, in the Dark and White Peak. Most of them were situated on the limestone between the rivers Dove and Wye where suitable sheep pasture was readily available (Fig. 4.15). Many were founded by the late 12th century deliberately to produce cash-crops for the parent institution to sell. The Cistercians had the greatest number of granges

Fig. 4.15 Granges in the White Peak with, right, map of the medieval landscape of Roystone Grange.

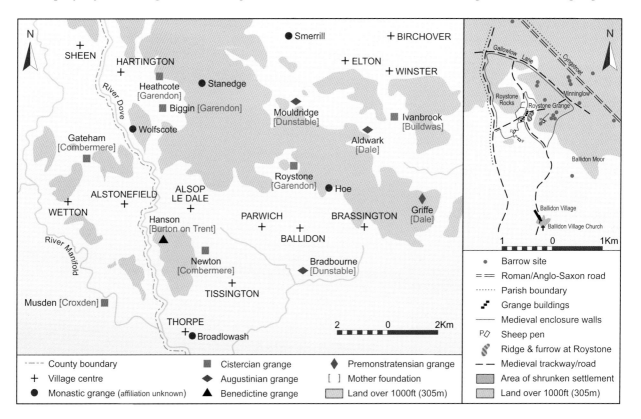

and were making a major contribution to wool production in medieval England, although they also reared cattle. The wool was exported to Flanders and elsewhere on the Continent and brought them enormous wealth. Granges would have had one or more large barns and other ancillary buildings, perhaps with a chapel attached. Sometimes the remains of these survive as earthworks, perhaps incorporating fishponds and a mill: some of the best surviving earthworks in this area are found at Mouldridge in Brassington and Cotesfield in Hartington, Derbyshire, where linear enclosures and the ruins of buildings survive, and also at Smerrill Grange near Elton, situated overlooking the deep gorge that runs down to Middleton-by-Youlgreave. In this region of the White Peak, granges were held by the abbeys of Buildwas (Shropshire), Burton (Staffordshire), Combermere (Cheshire), Garendon and Leicester (Leicestershire), Merevale (Warwickshire), Roche (Yorkshire), Dale and Darley (Derbyshire) and Dunstable Priory (Bedfordshire).

Because granges made such an impact upon the landscape, it is worth examining one in a little detail. Roystone Grange, originally known as Revestones, was one of the granges of the abbey of Garendon (Fig. 4.16). It lay beside a trackway known as Gallowlow Lane that ran on north-westwards over the high moors towards other Garendon granges at Biggin and Heathcote and may have been used to reach the market founded at Hartington in 1200. Garendon was one of England's earliest Cistercian monasteries and began exporting wool to Flanders in 1225. Its grange at Roystone covered only limited acreage with pasture for 300 sheep, but it also possessed the right to pasture stock on Ballidon Common and the abbey was later to acquire further land at Biggin and Heathcote near Hartington. The buildings of the grange at Roystone are known only from earthworks and the footings of walls, but it has been possible to reconstruct its layout by intensive fieldwork (Fig. 4.15).[16]

Fig. 4.16 View over the Derbyshire grange of Roystone, *showing the present-day farm; only the foundations remain of the medieval grange.*

The grange lay in a hollow, close to the available water supply in the climatic optimum of the 12th century. A few small enclosed crofts stood in the valley behind it, but the hills to either side lay in one great enclosure bounded on the north-east by Gallowlow Lane and on the south-east by the boundary of the earlier Romano-British farmstead that it superseded. Although traces of ridge and furrow survive in the field overlooking the grange, the field layout shows little capacity for crop growing and this was predominantly a sheep ranch, the paddocks near the grange being for the control of stock, which probably included a few cattle as well as sheep. The remainder of the enclosed grange was used for infield grazing, and driving walls leading up to a number of sheep pens have been identified. Above lay the open sheepwalks of short turf downland, with occasional prehistoric barrows surviving on the hilltops. Farm work was carried out by lay brothers, but additional labour probably came from the neighbouring village of Ballidon to the south-east, now a shrunken settlement set amidst the ridge and furrow of its former fields.[17] Musden Grange, near Rushley in Staffordshire, also has settlement earthworks surviving. The grange was based upon a gift made by Bertram of Verdun in *c.* 1179 to the Cistercian abbey of Croxden, but land was acquired gradually over time.[18] The main settlement earthworks, representing the grange farmhouse, lie on steeply sloping ground at the north-eastern corner of a 240ha block of land overlooking the River Manifold. A limited area of arable land has left ridge and furrow in the valley; woodland clothed – and, on the north, still clothes – the steep valley sides. Banks through the woodland suggest a former droveway linking the valley and upper pastures, for above, on the limestone grassland, were again the sheepwalks; a rectangular enclosure, now within later fields, is probably a place where the flocks were gathered in medieval times.

Some foundations, however, were never adequately endowed and struggled to survive from the outset, while others, despite rich endowments and further bequests, experienced difficulties over later centuries. Their abbots and abbesses, priors and prioresses, were not necessarily the most able financial managers and even the best had to contend with periodic problems brought on by such inescapable events as the Black Death, floods and droughts, cattle disease or failed harvests; others had to meet heavy taxation demands or financial demands upon their hospitality from travellers or visiting officials. The possession of relics such as those of St Wærburh, kept at Chester; those of the murdered St Ethelbert, king of East Anglia, at Hereford; St Oswald, the martyred king of Northumbria, at Oswestry; St Bettelin at Ilam and St Audrey at Stone might, however, bring them lucrative returns from visiting pilgrims. Lichfield had the relics of no fewer than three saints – St Cedd (died 664), St Owen (died *c.* 670) and St Chad (died 672). The latter was the first bishop of Lichfield and his remains were probably housed in the sanctuary beyond the high altar – together with some of the relics of Hedda, abbot of Peterborough, who was martyred in 870 by the Danes.

The perceived wealth of some establishments was to be their undoing, for when Henry VIII wished to augment his personal revenues he was to turn his attention to a Church that had continually opposed his personal desires. The fact that he was able to demolish the accepted ecclesiastical system so thoroughly is little short of astonishing, but he had the backing of the new Protestant movement and the ambitions of a growing merchant class. As ever, there were plenty ready to benefit from the acquisition of princely favours in the shape of lands and building sites (for the grand buildings rapidly became sources of building materials, a use encouraged to prevent any possible future restoration) and the land market opened up. The impact on the landscape of this huge change in the pattern of ownership is examined in Chapter 6. All the 848 religious houses existing in 1534 were dissolved and their inmates dispossessed; over two-thirds of the houses have now vanished completely, at least above ground. Only a handful of monastic churches bought by local communities (for example Malvern) were spared. In many cases they survive in truncated form, as in the case of Abbey Dore in Herefordshire and Pershore in Worcestershire, where the magnificent chancels survive but the naves have vanished.

TOWNS AND MARKETS

Some of the established monasteries had already become active in controlling trade and marketing by the 11th century, encouraging towns to grow up at their gates to generate revenue from commerce and market tolls. In the Avon valley of Worcestershire, the abbeys of Pershore and Evesham developed market towns in this way; the former had also established Broadway as a market on an important saltway by the 12th century. Abbot Nicholas is accredited with making the borough at Burton in the late 12th century, laying out a new street that was completed by the next abbot (William) between 1200 and 1214; Burton's Abbot Richard also made a borough at Abbot's Bromley in 1222. The Bishop of Lichfield and Chester laid out a newly planned town around the cathedral at Lichfield in the mid-12th century and his Eccleshall manor was recognised as a borough in 1199. Wolverhampton was to acquire its market *c.* 1180 and the Dean granted his burgesses privileges similar to those of Stafford in 1263.

In the border country, Marcher lords such as the Mortimers enjoyed unrivalled freedom and were soon establishing, below their castles, small Anglo-

Norman boroughs to control trade. Here the inhabitants, brought in both from the local countryside and abroad, enjoyed privileges of marketing. Control over the Welsh Marches was also marked by the creation of new Anglo-Norman towns in the late 11th and early 12th centuries, as at Brecon, Builth and Hay, which were created as the Welsh kingdom of Brycheiniog was overrun. Later, lesser lords were also establishing boroughs, as at Weobley in Herefordshire where the de Lacys incorporated an open market square into their new town.

Closer to the Welsh border, in the commote of Ewyas, a motte-and-bailey castle belonging to Roger de Lacy at the time of the Domesday survey stood above the Olchon Brook at Pont Hendre but was seized by the Welsh in 1146 after which, in the late 12th century, the de Lacys seems to have replaced the original castle by a new circular keep in their new borough of Ewyas Lacy, later to be known as Longtown (Fig. 4.17), to control the route from Hay-on-Wye to Abergavenny.[19]

Prior to the Black Death in the 14th century, both rural and urban populations were increasing. It is estimated that some 10 per cent lived in towns in the 11th century but that by 1300 the number had increased to 20 per cent.[20] A new period of civic pride was being instigated. In the 12th century, markets were being licensed in many such centres and both ecclesiastical and secular lords were seeing these as a means of increasing their revenues. New towns were deliberately laid out in the 12th and 13th centuries to cash in on this trend, like Ludlow in Shropshire, some of whose burgage plots were laid out before 1186, Henley-in-Arden (Warwickshire) founded by Peter de Montfort in 1220, or Knutsford (Cheshire) established in the 1290s. All of these new towns deliberately included formal street layouts with space for markets. Some were later to achieve borough status, and as commercial centres they became natural magnets for specialist craftsmen.

Not all new town creations were successful, especially those in the more remote corners of the borderland: Ploughfield in Shropshire, a borough in 1233, is no more than a hamlet today. Similarly, little is left of Richard's Castle, near Ludlow, which had 103 burgesses in 1304, except the deep lanes and footpaths that lead to its now overgrown mound, a church and a few farms. At Caus in Westbury, on the foothills of Long Mountain, the earthworks of a massively fortified town and castle established by Roger FitzCorbet in 1198 can still be seen, as can those of Huntingdon in Herefordshire.[21] Kilpeck, too, established at the foot of the castle

Fig. 4.17 Longtown in Ewyas, Herefordshire: a new borough established by the de Lacys to control the route from Hay-on-Wye to Abergavenny. The original motte and bailey castle built before 1086 can be seen, tree covered, near the bottom of this view while the Lacy's new castle stands within the town mid-centre.

Fig. 4.18 View over Ludlow town, *showing the castle on its south-western side. The Clee Hills can be seen in the background.*

Fig. 4.19 Ludlow: the planned medieval town *(after Lilley 2002, 143). The castle was built in the late 11th century, probably by Roger de Lacy, as a fortress on the Welsh border, and completed in about 1130 with a four-storey keep on the south side of the inner bailey facing the town. New buildings were added in the late 13th/early 14th century under Mortimer possession. The castle was remodelled after being damaged in the Wars of the Roses and became the residence of the Lord President of Wales c. 1501–1689, and the administrative centre for Wales and the Marches, with the Judges' Lodgings completed at the present entrance c. 1581. The defences were dismantled after the Civil War.*

The first town was created by the de Lacys in the 11th century and probably lay along Old Street on a north–south routeway leading down to the river Teme, but the de Lacys laid out a new town to the east of the castle in the late 12th century. This included the main commercial centre of the High Street extending eastwards from the castle gate – terraced shops at the eastern end have replaced temporary market booths – and parallel roads leading south (Broad Street and Mill Street) with narrow back lanes to provide access and permit the subdivision of plots. St Lawrence's church (1300–1500) stands in its own plot to the north. The town prospered throughout the Middle Ages, with growing suburbs, but many of the medieval timber-framed houses have been encased in brick to give the appearance of a late 18th-century Georgian town.

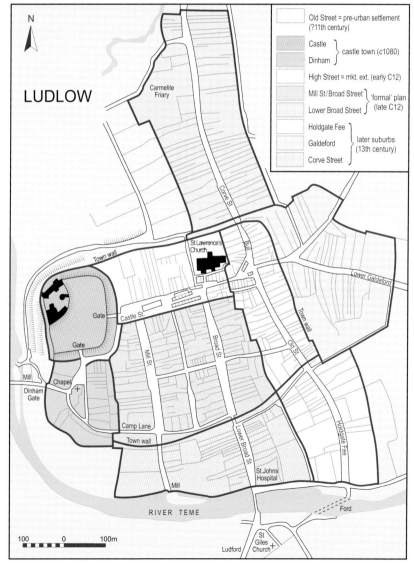

built by the fitz Normans after the Conquest, faded away in the Middle Ages to leave only the earthwork remains of the rectangular defended settlement that was the former 'borough' (*see* Fig. 4.5b). Other towns that failed include Tintwhistle and Knutsford Booths in Cheshire, Clifton-on-Teme in Worcestershire (which became a free borough in 1270) and Lyonshall in Herefordshire, the latter only recently identified as a former town: more than 2ha of earthworks extend for over a kilometre from the southern part of the village towards the church.[22]

Most newly established towns were, however, to become the country towns of our present-day counties, continuing to prosper as administrative and market centres throughout medieval times. Ludlow itself was to become the finest of Shropshire's planned medieval towns, laid out on a rectilinear grid-iron plan in the early 12th century with a wide street that acted (and still acts, despite some infilling) as a market place, and a town wall (Figs 4.18 and 4.19). The church of St Lawrence, much rebuilt in the 15th century, is also cathedral-like in its dimensions. In the 13th century, the town's prosperity rested upon the wool and cloth industry but its function as a fashionable centre for the local gentry in the 18th and 19th centuries is reflected in a wealth of Georgian houses fronting the principal streets.[23] Further north, Shrewsbury was laid out afresh with a new market place and grid of streets in the 13th century and its woollen industry set it among the 12 richest towns in England in 1300.[24] Many of its later timber-framed buildings survive.

Many of the new towns were to be walled – not only to keep out unwanted intruders but also to show that these were specially privileged places, incidentally protecting their all-important marketing facilities. Chester, with wharves on the River Dee, was the largest town in the north-west of England. Although Chester lost houses between 1066 and 1086, it was exceedingly wealthy in the 12th and 13th centuries, prospering as a strategic centre well placed at the time of the Welsh wars. Its medieval walls, standing to a height of 4.5–7.5m, incorporated Roman foundations and were repaired in the 18th century after Parliamentarian attacks so that a wall-walk can still be made. Within the walls were several medieval religious foundations, including St Wærburh's Abbey, the town mill and the main commercial centre around the east gate. After Edward I's conquest of Wales, Chester's importance declined, further diminished by the silting up of the Dee estuary.

The great success story of the Middle Ages was Coventry in Warwickshire. Although its Benedictine abbey was not founded until 1043, there are hints of an earlier Christian establishment in the *ecles* place-name of Exhall, suggestive of an earlier British church in the vicinity. The building of its town wall was begun in the 1350s, with towers spaced at intervals. By the end of the 14th century it had become the fourth largest town in England after York, Bristol and London,[25] again prospering from the success of its wool trade, especially with Flanders. A new borough charter granted by Earl Ranulf II in the 1150s had included a clause granting newcomers freedom from paying tax during their first year in the town providing they built houses there, thus encouraging development, and the earls of Chester deliberately abandoned their castle in the middle of the town in the second half of the 12th century to make way for new property.[26] The success of Coventry's trade was, however, ultimately to lead to its decline, for the monopolies and power of the guilds became restrictive and forced entrepreneurs to move elsewhere.

FOREST, CHASE AND PARK

Large areas of the West Midlands had been relatively well wooded throughout early medieval times, valued for their timber resources and as wood-pasture. Some of these woodlands retained names that were at least partly British in origin (*see* Chapter 3). It certainly seems that many upland regions were also wooded and Lyme appears to have been the name given to at least the western edges of the Pennine-Peak massif, the steep escarpment which forms the boundary of lowland Cheshire and Lancashire. Today this is a region of wild upland moors and peat-bog, but in medieval times the valleys were full of oak-woods and records refer frequently to *Lima* or *Lyme* as a *nemus*, *boscus* or *foresta*, descriptions clearly referring to woodland.

Although such regions had been used for hunting in Anglo-Saxon times, the Norman kings rapidly placed many of them under rather stricter forest law. By the time of the Domesday survey in 1086 this new law protected the woodland or *vert* as cover for game and restricted clearance but, above all, it reserved the capture of the 'beasts of the forest' (the red and fallow deer, the roe deer, and the wild boar) to the king or his officials. Those who transgressed faced severe penalties that included blinding, castration, loss of limbs or death – there is actually a record of the decapitation of two poachers in the Peak Forest. In the borderland considerable wastage had taken place due to Welsh and Viking attacks, and hays, thickly scattered across the countryside, represented enclosures for controlling and capturing deer without the full formality of forest law – the forerunner of the later park, although forests were to be established across most of southern Shropshire. Domesday Book does not set out to make a comprehensive record of forest since it was already 'in the hands of the king' – there is no mention of forest in Derbyshire, for instance, and only one reference in Shropshire; in some other counties there is no full record. The forests, at first relatively limited in extent, encompassed both wooded and moorland areas but the former remained important sources for timber and wood-pasture, rights which could only be granted by the king.

The forests had been enormously extended under the early Norman kings (Fig. 4.20). Covering nearly a third of the country at their maximum extent under Henry II in the late 12th century, they had taken in more heavily settled areas with their villages and fields, thus causing increased resentment. Hunting was carried out on horseback with dogs and hawks, both practices already referred to in pre-Conquest charters and Domesday Book. By the end of the 12th century, a wide band of countryside on either side of the River Severn lay within forest: from the forests of Lythewood, Shirlett ('the shire forest'), Wyre and Malvern on the southern and western side to Mount Gilbert or Wrekin, Morfe, Kinver, Ombersley and Horewell on the northern and eastern side. In the Middle Ages, the Marcher lordship of Clun was also referred to as Clun Forest. Feckenham was the most thickly wooded part of Worcestershire; however, nearly all but the south-eastern section of the county – the Vale of Evesham – had also fallen under forest law. In the north-west of the county Wyre spilled over from south-eastern Shropshire and in the south-west lay Malvern Forest that extended southwards with Corse into west Gloucestershire. Dean lay further to the south. Most of southern Staffordshire, too, was so designated – the forests of Kinver and Brewood linking eastwards with the Forest of Cannock and the Ferrers 'Forest' of Needwood (administered as part of the Honour of Tutbury). Most of the Lyme region was taken into the forests of Macclesfield or Peak. In the centre of Cheshire, Delamere (Mara) and Mondrem formed one continuous forest and Wirral was added later. If the Warwickshire Arden was ever a royal forest, as seems to have been the case (a forester held Kenilworth in 1086), it did not hold this status for long, probably because of the influence of the earls of Warwick.[27] Henry had made some entirely new forests, too, like the short-lived New Forest to the east of Newcastle-under-Lyme in north Staffordshire which was in existence by 1166 but disafforested in 1204.[28]

Henry II was, however, already selling parts of his forests by the end of his reign to raise money, and Henry III was selling timber from the forests in large quantities in the mid-13th century. In the early part of his reign he had been forced to retract his father's forest boundaries if they went beyond the Crown's ancient demesne and both Horewell and Ombersley in Worcestershire were

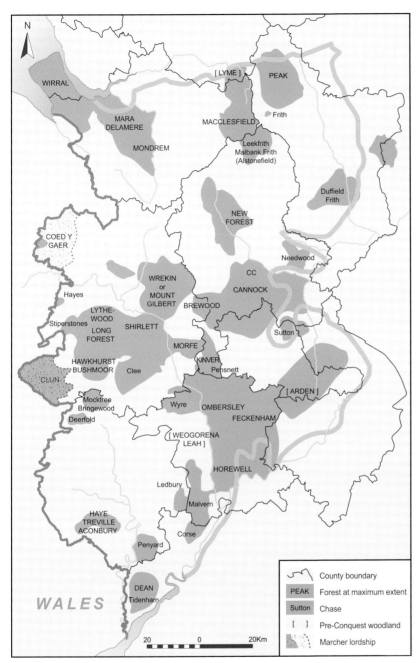

Fig. 4.20 Medieval forests at their maximum extent (13th century).
Forest law was introduced by the Norman kings but often affected areas that had already been used for hunting in Anglo-Saxon times (Hooke 1998c). Forests were extended by the Norman kings until opposition by the barons and the people forced the retraction of their boundaries in the late 13th century. Midland forests were numerous but generally limited in extent. Some lost forest status early (?Arden). Clun was administered as a marcher lordship. Divisions within a forest were often termed 'hays'. If part of a forest was granted into private ownership it became known as a chase, becoming subject to common law. These included the former forests of Malvern, Corse, Stiperstones and Clee, or enclaves within a forest such as Cannock Chase (CC), although some chases, like Duffield, were later to revert to the Crown.

Map legend:
- County boundary
- PEAK Forest at maximum extent
- Sutton Chase
- [ ] Pre-Conquest woodland
- Marcher lordship

20 0 20Km

disafforested in 1229. Finally, Edward I was forced to retract forest boundaries to their ancient cores in the late 1290s, with new perambulations confirmed in 1301. As they diminished in size, the kings' interest in hunting waned and many forests became regarded more as a source of funds, raised by the sale of timber and licences to assart, thus diminishing them further.

Some forests had been granted into private ownership at a very early date, thereby becoming known as chases. William I had given much of Peak Forest to William Peveril (*see* below), and by 1246 Wyre Forest on the Worcestershire-Shropshire border had become a chase of the Mortimers of Wigmore. Cannock Chase in Staffordshire was carved out of the royal forest of Cannock in 1189 by Richard I for the bishops of Lichfield, in return for money for a crusade, and

Bishop Meuland was granted the rights of free chase in 1290. On its south-eastern fringe, Sutton Chase was granted by Henry I to the earls of Warwick, and Pensnett, on the eastern side of Kinver Forest, became a chase of the barons of Dudley, the de Somerys, in the 13th century. A poem, recorded in the late 16th century but much older, tells the tale of the Tamworth tanner who allegedly met Edward IV when he was out hunting, probably on Sutton Chase:

> *In summer time, when leaves grow greene,*
> *And blossoms bedecke the tree,*
> *King Edward wolde a hunting ryde,*
> *Some pastime for to see.*
>
> *With hawke and hounde he made him bowne,*
> *With horne, and eke with bowe;*
> *To Drayton Basset he tooke his waye,*
> *With all his lordes a rowe.*[29]

Fig. 4.21 View within Peak Forest.

Malvern Chase in Worcestershire, with the adjoining area of Corse in Gloucestershire, was granted to Gilbert de Clare, Earl of Gloucester, in 1290 when he married the daughter of Edward I. On the other side of the Malverns lay the Bishop of Hereford's chase in south-east Herefordshire. In Derbyshire and north Staffordshire, a number of private chases were called 'friths', a name derived from the Old English *fyrð* meaning 'brushwood', but one that may have acquired a semi-legal implication, perhaps as land enclosed from the common waste (as in Wales where it became a common field-name). Malbank or Malbon Frith (the latter in Alstonefield) and Leekfrith were chases of the earls of Chester; Duffield and Hartington Frith chases of the earls of Lancaster (after 1266). Following political disruption or through inheritance, some of these chases, like Wyre, Malvern and Duffield, were to revert back into the hands of the Crown at a later date. The Ferrers' 'Forest' of Needwood thus became part of the possessions of John of Gaunt and the House of Lancaster.

The Peak Forest was, indeed, the wildest of the midland forests (Fig. 4.21). It was royal demesne at the time of Domesday Book but in 1068 much of the land in the Peak was granted by William I to William Peveril. When the Peveril estates were forfeited in 1155 (after allegations about the poisoning of the Earl of Chester) they passed back to the Crown, to be transferred in 1372 to the Duchy of Lancaster. The forest covered the whole north-western corner of the county, some 100 sq km, and was divided into three districts: Campana or 'open country' in the south and south-west, Longdendale in the north and north-west, and Hopedale in the east. The boundaries were marked by stone crosses, some of which still survive. Roughly at its centre was the forest hall, *camera in foresta regia Pecci*, now represented by Chamber Farm in Peak Forest parish, which once also had a chapel attached and a great pond (the chapel to be replaced by one near Bowden that gave rise to the place-name Chapel-en-le-Frith). The forest abounded with deer, so much so that, according to an account of Giraldus Cambrensis in *c.* 1154, men and dogs were trampled to death by fleeing deer.[30] Wild boar were among the game presented to the king at the time of his visit in 1235–6 (Wildboar Clough is the name of a valley near Axe Edge). In the mid-13th century, it is recorded that wolves killed sheep and a colt and wolf-hunters were employed in Campagna later in that century:

> *Each year, in March and September, they ought to go through the midst of the forest to set traps to take the wolves in the places where they had been found by the hounds; and if the scent was not good because of the upturned earth [disturbed by laying traps], then they should go at other times in the summer (as on St Barnabas' day, 11 June), when the wolves had whelps (*catulos*), to take and destroy them, but at no other times; and they might take with them a sworn servant to carry the traps (*ingenia*); they were to carry a bill-hook and spear, a hunting-knife at their belt, but neither bows nor arrows; and they were to have with them an unlawed [ie unmutilated] mastiff trained to the work. All this they were to do at their own charges, but they had no other duties to discharge in the forest.*[31]

Wolves were not confined to the Peak and were present in Cannock Forest in the 13th century, while over the Dark Peak moors deer, wild boar and wolves roamed freely until Tudor times. The wildness of the place was probably one of the factors that facilitated so much poaching in the forest, often by surrounding country gentlemen and the clergy. Pasture rights gave many people access to the forest although these rights, too, were abused, with a detrimental effect upon the forest vegetation. The queen kept a stud of 115 mares and their foals in Campana, 'to great injury of the forest', and there were vaccaries (cattle farms) for sheep and cattle. Temporary booths set up for the herdsmen gave rise to numerous place-names such as Nether Booth, Barbar Booth, Grindsbrook Booth, Ollerbrook Booth and Upper Booth around Edale. Monastic houses, often lying far afield, were also granted land within the forest, like Basingwerk Abbey in Flintshire that had a grange at Charlesworth in Glossop. A Commission was set up in 1526 to investigate overstocking within the forest and it was found that the number of herds had increased from two to five – some 903 beasts, with 4,000 sheep and 16 score *capilles* [*capellae* 'she-goats']. Although 18 score deer were observed by the commissioners, many were in such poor condition that they were unlikely to survive the winter, mainly due to the destruction of the pasture by sheep. By 1584 deer numbers had been reduced from 18 score to 5 score.[32] Such was the fate of most of the forests and the Peak was disafforested *c.* 1640.

   Within the remaining forests, money could also be made by issuing licences to impark or assart for farmland – a line of private parks were permitted in Long Forest in the 13th century, along the dip-slope of the Wenlock escarpment.[33] Such enclosures were to become significant features in the medieval landscape. The king maintained parks within some of his forests, as at Hanbury in Worcestershire within Feckenham Forest, where there was a *parcus ferarum*, 'park for wild animals', by 1086; castle owners, especially, were quick to follow his example, soon followed by lesser lords. Most licences for emparkment granted to his more affluent subjects lay on the margins of the royal forests. The majority of private medieval deer parks were licensed between the 12th and 14th centuries and often lay in the more remote parts of parishes as befitted hunting reserves. Like the king's parks, these were primarily intended to hold deer, a source of venison for the table, but rabbit warrens, also, were introduced and fishponds maintained, the park usually managed from a warrener's lodge. A ditch with an earthen bank topped by a palisade, known as a pale, usually marked the boundary of the park and, within it, groves of woodland were often protected from the deer as a source of timber. Indeed, some of the region's ancient woodland owes its survival to its having lain within such a park as at Whitfield (part of the earlier park of Treville), Moccas and Lyonshall in Herefordshire. Such limited areas were indeed used for hunting and were a source not only of venison and other game animals but provided a pastime for visiting guests. This did not always, however, have a happy outcome: Thomas Burdet, who had a park at Arrow near Alcester, Warwickshire, was upset by the killing of his favourite white buck by Edward IV 'passionately wishing the Hornes in his Belly that moved the king so to do', for which utterance he was convicted of high treason and executed[34] – this by the same king who is said to have rewarded the tanner of Tamworth (*see* above) with a park at Plumpton for entertaining him by his rudeness when he failed to recognise him.

In Cheshire, many parks lay in the wooded north of the county but only the king held a park within the heart of Macclesfield Forest – his 'wood of Wilwich' imparked early in the 13th century. Parks were liberally scattered across most of Staffordshire; a portion of the Forest of Cannock was granted to the Bishop of Lichfield and here the latter was licensed to impark in 1290. Whereas most of the Shropshire forests lay in the south of the county, most of the parks lay in the north, but there were fewer in Herefordshire, at least four made by the Bishop of Hereford in his own chase at the foot of the Malvern Hills. In Worcestershire, the king maintained five parks in the heart of the Forest of Feckenham, that at Hanbury having a fine fleet of large fishponds, managed from lodges situated on the ridge above (Fig. 4.22), but at least six other parks were also permitted. Parks were also thickly clustered across the Warwickshire Arden (Fig. 4.23). The largest, to the north of Warwick, was associated with the Earl of Warwick's castle, and others were established to the west of Kenilworth Castle, held by the Earl of

Fig. 4.22 Hanbury Park, Worcestershire.

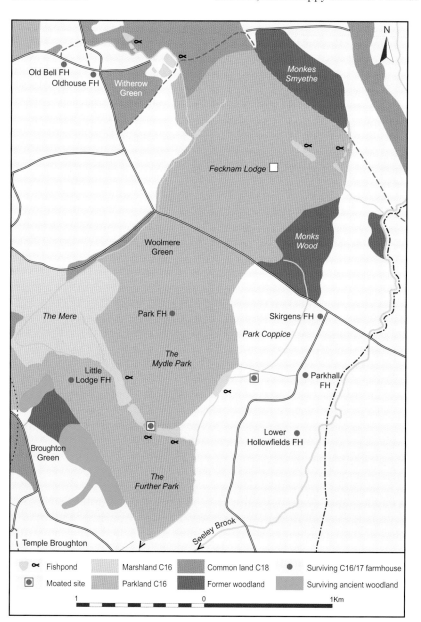

✖ Fishpond	Marshland C16	Common land C18	● Surviving C16/17 farmhouse	
▣ Moated site	Parkland C16	Former woodland	Surviving ancient woodland	

1   0   1Km

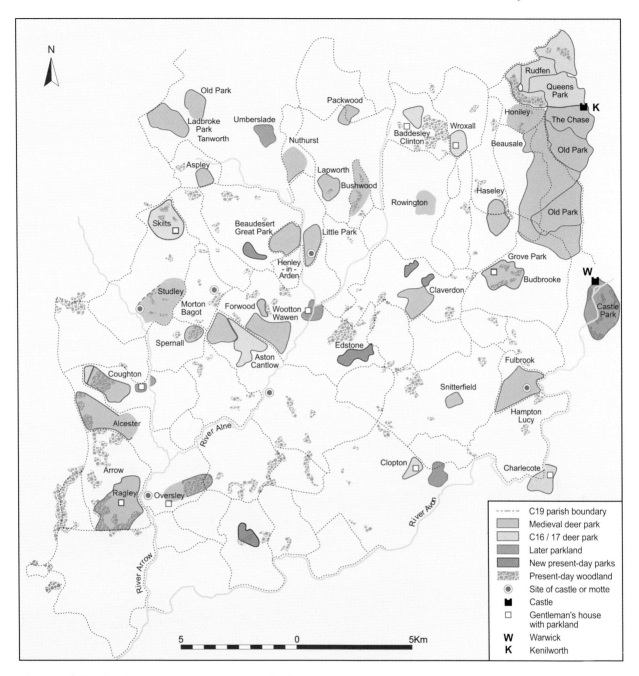

N

Old Park
Ladbroke
Park
Tanworth
Umberslade
Packwood
Nuthurst
Wroxall
Baddesley
Clinton
Honiley
Rudfen
Queens
Park
K
The Chase
Beausale
Old Park
Aspley
Lapworth
Bushwood
Rowington
Haseley
Old Park
Skilts
Beaudesert
Great Park
Little Park
Henley
- in -
Arden
Grove Park
Budbrooke
W
Studley
Morton
Bagot
Forwood
Wootton
Wawen
Claverdon
Castle
Park
Spernall
Aston
Cantlow
Edstone
Fulbrook
Coughton
Snitterfield
Hampton
Lucy
Alcester
River Alne
Arrow
Clopton
Charlecote
Ragley
Oversley
River Arrow
River Avon

– · – · – · –	C19 parish boundary
	Medieval deer park
	C16 / 17 deer park
	Later parkland
	New present-day parks
	Present-day woodland
⊙	Site of castle or motte
◼	Castle
☐	Gentleman's house with parkland
W	Warwick
K	Kenilworth

5   0   5Km

Fig 4.23 Medieval and later parks in the Warwickshire Arden. Permission to enclose a medieval hunting park had to be granted by the Crown and most were enclosed between 1200 and 1350 (Cantor 1982, 76). In Arden, a lord was generally allowed to make a park so long as sufficient common was left for his tenants and, in an area with considerable woodland and waste, this allowed many lords to acquire such a status symbol, imitating the castle parks at Kenilworth and Warwick. It was only later, in the 16th century, that the park became a pleasure ground around a mansion house and this idea was furthered by 18th-century landscape designers such as 'Capability' Brown, extending the tradition beyond the regions of the medieval parks (Hooke 1988).

Lancaster. The earliest references to a park at Kenilworth are during Henry II's reign, when the castle was in the king's hands, but by the 16th century these had been extended northwards and westwards and they almost joined Wedgnock Park belonging to the earls of Warwick (Fig. 4.24). Several smaller castles in this county, as at Aston Cantlow, Studley and Beaudesert on the southern fringes of Arden, also maintained their own parks. Only later was the park to change its function by becoming an ornamental feature around a great house.

Duffield was a smaller forest to the north of Derby, long in the hands of the Ferrers who administered it from their castle at Duffield until the reign of Henry VIII when their lands, too, were forfeited after the rebellion of Robert Earl Ferrers. The forest was then conferred upon the Earl of Lancaster and administered from Tutbury. Unlike the Peak Forest, where the stone-walled Campana was the only enclosure, Duffield contained as many as eight enclosed parks, the most important of them Ravensdale where there was a forest lodge for the whole forest (with its own chapel), and perhaps several large lakes. John of Gaunt sent hunting dogs for coursing in the park on several occasions in 1372. The pale surrounding this park is almost continuous today except where it has been destroyed in one part by quarrying, and the park also possesses what may be one of the few remaining examples of an actual deer-course. This was a long run for chasing deer in the ritualised way that replaced earlier hunting. Most deer-courses along fixed tracks in England date from after the early 16th century but that suggested at Ravensdale (Fig. 4.25) appears to be one of the earliest examples known, possibly going back to the late 14th century.[35]

Fig. 4.24 The deer parks of Kenilworth and Warwick *(reproduced from Dugdale 1656).*

Many parks were under agistment – licences granted to use the pastures of the launds (glades) and the forest wood-pasture resources. This use has a long history and there were already disputes over rights to mast (forage for pigs) before the Norman Conquest. The traditional rights of landowners and peasantry to pasture within the forests were generally respected in medieval times. Swine were usually only allowed in the forests during the pannage season (14 September to 18 November) when they sought out acorns and beechmast. Income was

Fig. 4.25 Medieval deer course in Ravensdale Park, Derbyshire.

also to be gained from granting licences for assarts (clearance). Many were made to ecclesiastical bodies and resulted in islands of clearance around small foundations, like the land of the nunneries of Henwood and Wroxall in the Warwickshire Arden. It was usually the weaker foundations that moved into the forests, but more distant foundations also received land – like Roche in Yorkshire, Welbeck in Nottinghamshire, Merevale in Warwickshire and St Mary, Leicester, which acquired rights in Peak Forest – establishing vaccaries (cattle farms) and gaining grazing for cattle, sheep and pigs.

Although the great Norman forests have gone, replaced mostly by farmland, there are a few places where one can gain an impression of what was once a familiar scene. Much of Peak Forest remains little altered as bleak moorland. Dean is still heavily wooded but most of this has been replanted after major clearances in the past; some of the most natural stands are found along the east bank of the Wye. Wyre, on the Worcestershire–Shropshire border, has more surviving ancient semi-natural woodland (*see* Fig. 5.37b). The area has a long history of coppice with standards management (standards are occasional individual tall trees, usually oaks, left

Fig. 4.26 Sherbrook valley, Cannock Chase.

standing). The oak timber was reserved for ship and house building and the coppiced underwood (also mostly oak) was used for firewood or small timber (such as hurdles) and later for charcoal (*see* Chapter 7). Indeed, it was the need for charcoal for iron smelting that probably ensured the forest's survival. There are many walks laid out through the forest and, despite much modern plantation forestry, many acres of old Wyre oak survive.

Two forests that have sadly changed their character due to modern softwood plantations are Delamere in Cheshire and Cannock Chase in Staffordshire, although in Delamere woodland had virtually disappeared by the 18th century (*see* Chapter 5). Yet a walk along the more open Sherbrook valley on Cannock Chase still gives an impression of old 'hunting' land (Fig. 4.26).

The brook is fringed with alder groves and the rising spurs covered with bracken; conifers generally recede into the distance and herds of deer frequently cross one's path. At the northern end of the valley, there is one magical place of surviving ancient woodland – the Brocton Oaks (Fig. 4.27). Here many venerable old trees survive – although some are in a state of advanced decay.

Most of the medieval deer parks were also enclosed for pasture in subsequent centuries but they have not all been lost. There are many stretches of park pale or the earthworks of former fishponds and warrens that can still be seen in the landscape. In later warrens, long earthen pillow mounds were often artificially raised to provide burrows for rabbits. At Wolseley Park

Fig. 4.27 Ancient oaks at Brocton, Cannock Chase.

on Cannock Chase a medieval deerleap or *saltatorium* has been restored where the fence is lower for a short distance. This type of feature allowed the deer access to the park but discouraged their escape. Sometimes ancient pollard trees have survived from such an environment. These were trees, usually oak and ash, which were cut off above the grazing line. The new timber, which the animals could not reach, was allowed to regrow until the next cutting some 20 or so years later. Treated in this way, a tree can live much longer than if it had been allowed to grow as a maiden without intervention.

There are, however, fewer surviving whole medieval parkland landscapes. One of the most rewarding to visit is Moccas Park in Herefordshire, now managed by English Nature (a permit is necessary). Although there is no documentary record for this having been a medieval park, it may have formed part of the 14th-century park of Dorstone.[36] The name is almost certainly a

Fig. 4.28 Ancient pollarded oaks in Moccas Park, Herefordshire.

corruption of Welsh *mochros*, 'moor or place of pigs', perhaps indicating an early wood-pasture usage. It occupies the north-east facing slope of Dorstone Hill, overlooking the River Wye. The park was managed for deer, cattle, horses and sheep by Sir George Cornewall after 1771 and was already famous for its oaks, which included the 'Moccas Oak' painted by Thomas Hearne. In 1876 this tree was completely hollow with a girth of about 10m. It has since been lost but there are others nearly as big which may date back as far as *c.* 1400, although most are younger – planted in the early 16th century or later.[37] The Revd Kilvert referred to these venerable trees as 'grey old men' (Fig. 4.28). Patches of ridge and furrow in Lower Park show periods of medieval cultivation; most of the veteran trees actually stand on or around the ridge and furrow and some probably began their lives as hedgerow trees. Moccas has been called 'a landscape of remarkable trees' and there are numerous superb specimens of oak, ash and sweet chestnut, especially in the Lower Park, and in the Upper Park, on the hill slope, are large-leaved limes, some pollarded, that may be 400 or more years old, ancient yews which may be relics of the former natural woodland cover, and sweet chestnuts and beech that were probably part of a designed landscape.

Sutton Park, near Birmingham, is a survival of part of the former chase held by the earls of Warwick, which was carved out of a royal forest. The park was sold to Bishop Veysey in 1528 but its timber was destroyed and the park turned over to pasture, some of it for the poor. When it passed to Sutton corporation, felling and the sale of timber continued, leaving most of the 850ha (2,100 acres) as open land. Holly was, however, a valuable fodder crop for all animals and the ancient holly woods survived in the east of the park, even when the other trees were exploited and destroyed. Tall old hollies are still found within their abraded wood banks in the park today although most of the area has an open heathland vegetation. There are other areas where an attempt has been made to recreate ancient woodland landscapes. Bringewood Chase in northern Herefordshire was the private chase of the Mortimer lords until 1461 when Edward Mortimer became Edward IV and it became a royal chase. The higher ground to the north of Richard's Castle – Haye Park Wood – has been replanted and is now part of the newly designated 'Mortimer Forest'. Bagot Forest in Staffordshire has also been replanted. Here the woodlands and ancient trees of Bagot's Park, an extension of Needwood, survived until 1933 when the timber was felled to alleviate death duties. During the Second World War the wood was sequestrated for ammunition storage and the park used for war-time arable production; the remainder was later sold, converting the wilderness into 'sterile barrenness' of conifer plantations.[38] Many of these are still under Forestry Commission control but management plans now allow for the return of oak.

FARMING SYSTEMS

As population increased in the early Middle Ages, the area of land under cultivation was extended. In regions of intensive crop cultivation, pasture was often in very short supply and had to be augmented by the very necessary fallow field maintained under the conventional 'midland system' and by carefully regulated meadow systems that allowed access to pasture after the gathering of the hay that was essential for winter fodder. But the main open-field areas of England lay outside this region. The White Peak appears to be one exception for here nucleated villages developed, set within extensive open fields, and a similar pattern developed in the Derwent valley. In most of the midland region, pasture was not scarce and a mixed farming economy was possible but crops were still cultivated in open fields. In less heavily populated areas, such as the Warwickshire Arden, much of Worcestershire or the border country, open fields were less developed but occurred in scattered patches around manorial nuclei and hamlets, and outlying pastures remained important for the rearing of domestic stock. In Cheshire and the borderland, in late medieval times, there were often dozens of scattered patches of open field in any one parish, often only 8–12ha each – some 40 patches were later recorded in Much Marcle and 46 in Marden in Herefordshire, for instance (*see* below), with extensive open fields occurring only in the more densely populated valley regions.

The arable was ploughed into long ridges separated by furrows that aided drainage, and a group of strips would often have formed a separate holding. In turn, both peasant and lord held holdings that were often scattered throughout

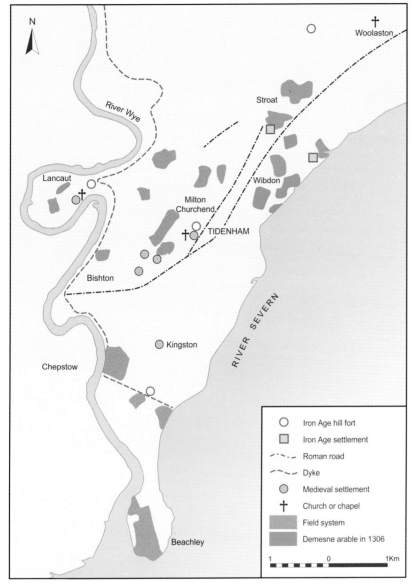

Fig. 4.29 Tidenham, Gloucestershire:
medieval settlement and field systems (after
Faith 1994).

the township. While the strips were under cultivation they were the sole responsibility of each tenant, but after the harvest these were thrown open to grazing by all. The extent of former open field, like the presence of the villages themselves, may have been underestimated in the west of the region, for recent studies in the Arrow valley of Herefordshire have identified both deserted village sites and the remains of their open field systems.[39] Outlying isolated farmsteads also seem to have been a feature of the settlement pattern, from the early medieval period at least; they were established beyond the village cores, and some may have continued in areas occupied since earlier times. Other farms, in addition to the monastic granges, were carved out of the Derbyshire moorlands.

A study of Tidenham, on the west bank of the Wye in Gloucestershire, has shown how the settlement centres within the early medieval manor developed under Norman lordship as resources were more intensively utilised.[40] The holdings of lords and peasants (the Domesday *villani* and the later customary tenants of the Middle Ages) may have been physically integrated in the same field system with places bearing *tūn* place-names (today usually giving names ending in '-ton') like Kingston, 'the [Mercian] king's *tūn*' (as opposed to the bishop's *tūn* in the diocese of Hereford) and Milton, 'the middle *tūn*', developing upon the demesne inland, land traditionally exempt from tax, that was found at each of these centres (Fig. 4.29). Thus, the peasant dwellings of the early medieval period developed after the Conquest into nucleated settlements with their own field systems. At Kingston, one settlement nucleus surrounded the 14th-century manor house at Beachley and another developed on the Gloucester to Chepstow road, while the holdings of the customary tenants at Bishton lay to the west of the village.

Another study has been made of Marden in Herefordshire, which took its name from an early medieval district name, Maund, a division within the Magonsætan kingdom, and remained a royal manor in 1086.[41] The southern part of this royal manor became the township of Sutton, an early medieval centre that probably developed on the already cultivated land around the Iron Age hillfort of Sutton Walls (Fig. 4.30). At Freens Court in Sutton St Michael a large timbered and stone range and an aisled barn, located initially by crop-mark evidence and now a scheduled ancient monument, have been dated to the 12th century; the barn probably held the grain collected in the royal manor.

Within the parish, it is possible to identify the scattered areas of open-field arable that were to be amalgamated through subsequent reclamation of the waste, probably in the late 11th and 12th centuries, leaving only green ways for later assarting. The intake of these then created a truly continuous arable tract. This is likely to have permitted the division of the arable into the three roughly equal-sized fields within which a regular three-course rotation could have operated; this appears to have been in place by the late 13th century.

In the northern part of the manor no such amalgamation occurred and settlements remained scattered with more irregular field systems, despite assarting in the period between *c.* 1250 and 1300. This irregular pattern may represent the earliest pattern found throughout the parish before change occurred in the south between the late 11th and early 13th centuries. Bond tenants and *villani* are likely to have lived in the hamlet clusters. The location of the dwellings of the medieval freeholders, however, remains uncertain and these may have been isolated farmsteads associated with compact holdings (as at Tanworth in Arden; *see* below). Medieval clusters in the north of the manor shrank after the Black Death leading to the amalgamation of many holdings, although new wayside and wasteside hamlets developed after the 16th century. This is an important model that might apply to much of the borderland (*see* Chapter 5).

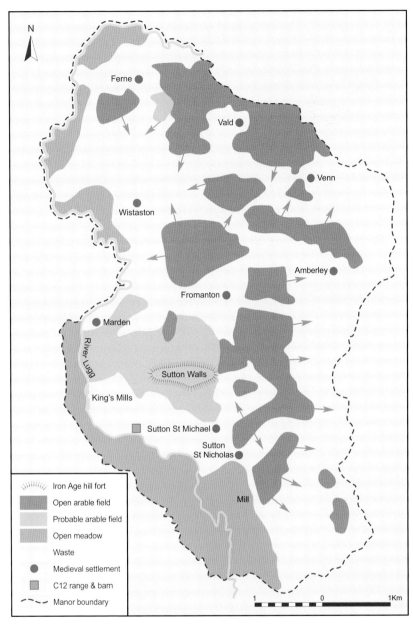

Fig. 4.30 Marden parish, Herefordshire, *the development of land use on the manor, showing probable 11th-century land use. The arrows indicate the direction of the expansion of arable land from the earliest open-field cores (after Sheppard 1979).*

It is often difficult to reconstruct medieval landscapes, but field-names frequently suggest the presence of earlier woodland and waste beyond the open fields. Although field-names seldom remained permanent except in tightly controlled open-field regimes, those recorded on historical maps can give some indication of past land use. Names like 'Old Field', 'lands' and 'furlong' may hint at early open-field cores, while more recently cleared land might show itself as former rough pasture ('Gorsey' or 'Gorstey Piece', 'Stoney') or as former woodland. In the region around the Ironbridge Gorge, it is clear from the incidence of names such as 'ridding' (from Old English **ryding* 'cleared land'), 'stocking' (from Old English **stoccing* 'piece of ground cleared of stumps') and 'wood' or names ending in '-ley' (from Old English *leah* 'wood, clearing, open woodland', *see* Chapter 3) that the region was subject to widespread assarting in medieval times (Fig. 4.31). This exercise can be repeated anywhere in the

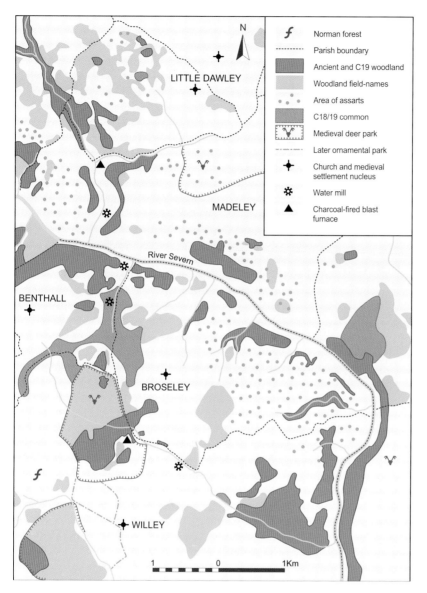

Key:
- ƒ — Norman forest
- - - - — Parish boundary
- Ancient and C19 woodland
- Woodland field-names
- Area of assarts
- C18/19 common
- Medieval deer park
- Later ornamental park
- ✚ Church and medieval settlement nucleus
- ✳ Water mill
- ▲ Charcoal-fired blast furnace

LITTLE DAWLEY

MADELEY

River Severn

BENTHALL

BROSELEY

ƒ

WILLEY

1   0   1Km

ABOVE: *Fig. 4.31 Medieval woodland in the Ironbridge region of Shropshire (from Hooke 1998b).*

region, especially when historical estate maps can be used to give an earlier coverage than the 19th-century tithe awards.

The northern areas of Worcestershire and Warwickshire were relatively sparsely populated at the time of the Norman Conquest with room for further colonisation. As new land was taken in from woodland and waste (assarting) it was often farmed from newly established farmsteads whose owners, often subject to only light manorial duties, held much of their land in one block, unlike the fragmented strip holdings of the manorial villagers. Some became relatively well off and the moats, which many of them created around their houses (Fig. 4.32), usually between the 12th and 14th centuries, were as much a sign of status as a fulfilment of purely functional requirements (draining the house site, helping to prevent fire or offering greater security), and many were also associated with fishponds. Tanworth in Arden (Fig. 4.33) contained perhaps as many as nine moated farmsteads, established often at the instigation of the lords of the manor, here the earls of Warwick, within woodland and heathland beyond the small core of open-field land. There were already a number of small hamlets or farms like Bedsworth and Cheswick that bore Old English names. Two small deer parks were established in the 14th century – Old Park and Ladbrook Park, and parts of

Fig. 4.32 A medieval moated site: Wike in Coughton, Warwickshire.

their earthen pales can still be identified. Patches of ancient woodland survive in the area, such as Mockley Wood near Tanworth in Arden (Fig. 4.34), but 'shaw' place-names (from Old English *sceaga* 'a strip of undergrowth or wood'), often recorded in the 12th–14th centuries, suggest other strips of woodland separating enclaves of clearance, perhaps implying a mixture of rough grassland and woodland over the drift-covered soils of the Arden plateau. Reconstruction of a strip of land along the Arrow valley of Warwickshire reveals a similar scatter of moated sites beyond the village cores, linked by a close network of roads. Moated sites are also particularly frequent in Cheshire where they mostly represent early manorial centres or, again, colonisation of the woodland in areas of clay subsoils. Some such later farmsteads were also to claim quasi-manorial status.

Before the Black Death in 1348–9, farming had been expanding across the region, helped by the warm, dry conditions of a climatic optimum. Most people lived in villages and hamlets, cultivating mainly cereals within an ordered manorial regime. Arable farming was labour intensive and ploughing was probably the most onerous task undertaken; domestic stock formed part of the

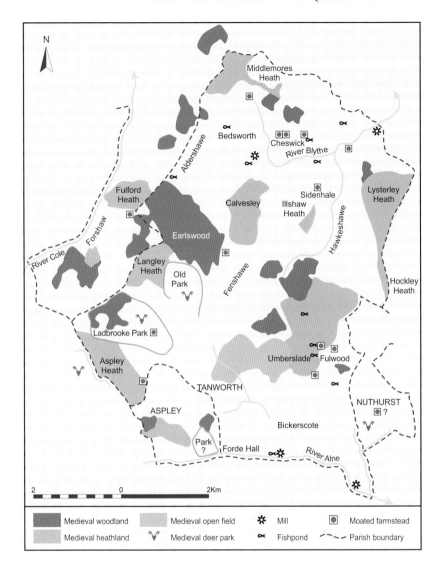

■ Medieval woodland	■ Medieval open field	✷ Mill	◉ Moated farmstead
■ Medieval heathland	🜨 Medieval deer park	⤬ Fishpond	‒ ‒ Parish boundary

ABOVE: *Fig. 4.33 Tanworth in Arden: a medieval landscape in the Arden region of Warwickshire.*

LEFT: *Fig. 4.34 Ancient Arden woodland: Mockley Wood near Tanworth in Arden.*

Fig. 4.35 Montford fish weir, Shropshire.

common herd and were under the care of a shepherd. Those occupying outlying farmsteads set within their own land usually enjoyed greater freedom, and pastoralism played a greater part in the farm economy. Partly under the impetus of the monasteries, sheep were the commonest animals kept, especially in western and northern regions. The hills of south Shropshire and north Herefordshire were a major source of wool for export from the 13th century, much of it traded through Ludlow. The English wool trade flourished through the 13th and 14th centuries, the wool being sold to the merchants of Flanders, Italy and elsewhere. Pigs were also reared, swineherds taking the herds into the woods in autumn to forage on acorns and beechmast. In Macclesfield Forest, vaccaries or cattle ranches had been established by 1360. Fishing continued in the region's rivers, and weirs consisting of stake fences to hold wicker baskets might be constructed across the channel or across specially made 'bylets', as at Montford in Shropshire (Fig. 4.35).[42]

The 14th century, however, brought a range of problems. There were deteriorating climatic conditions, calamitous harvest failures, and attacks of sheep murrain and cattle plague in 1315–22. The agricultural system could only just support the high levels of population that had developed in more favourable times, but few could foresee how these would be decimated by the Black Death a few years later. In 1348–9, a third of the population of Shropshire died within one year; 40 per cent of the clergy, ordered to remain at their posts, died in the midland dioceses. Although there were always peasants willing to take over the more favourable tenancies, especially within Arden and south Staffordshire, it became increasingly difficult to maintain the old manorial villein economy based upon intensive agriculture. The Black Death brought an abrupt halt to expansion of the arable and heavily disrupted the social and economic foundations of many village communities. A succession of waves of various epidemic diseases in effect dampened down the rural economy until well into the 15th and 16th centuries.

NOTES

1   Rowley 2001, 89–92.
2   Lilley 2002, 140.
3   Rackham 1996, 50–1.
4   Saunders 1978, 140.
5   Hooke 1981b; 1985a, 126.
6   Holly 1962, 323.
7   Watson & Musson 1993, 62.
8   Rowley 2001, 107–8.
9   Jackson 1988, 33–5.
10 Pevsner 1958, 22.
11 Rowley 2001, 98.
12 Thurlby 1999.
13 Pevsner 1958, 147.
14 Aston 1993, 118–29; Bond 2004, 87–92.
15 *VCH Shropshire IV* 1989, 44–5.
16 Hodges 1991, 98–106, 110, fig 74, 118, fig 81.
17 Ibid, 113–18
18 Cleverdon 1995, 30–6.
19 Shoesmith 1996, 167–74.
20 Dyer 1994, xv.
21 Rowley 2001, 99, 100–3.
22 White, P 2003, 49, fig 30.
23 Watson & Musson 1993, 91–3.
24 Ibid, 89–90.
25 Skipp 1979, 148.
26 Lilley 2002, 148, 153.
27 Hooke 1988, 51–3.
28 *VCH Staffordshire II* 1967, 348–9.
29 Percy 1996, 76.
30 Cox, in *VCH Derbyshire I* 1905, 400.
31 Ibid, 404, citing Forest Proceedings, Duchy of Lancaster, bundle I, Nos 3 and 11.
32 Ibid, 412, citing Duchy Surveys Commission no. 1285.
33 Rowley 2001, 141.
34 Dugdale 1656, 980.
35 Taylor 2004.
36 Whitehead 2000, 44.
37 Harding & Wall 2000, 15.
38 Ford 1999, 128–9.
39 White, P 2003, 49–51.
40 Faith 1994.
41 Sheppard 1979.
42 Watson & Musson 1993, 80.

5

The Last 500 years: the Development of the Rural Landscape

FARMING LANDSCAPES

After about 1500 the rural landscape of the West Midlands began to experience change to an ever-greater degree. The enclosure of arable strips had begun in the 14th and 15th centuries and was hastened by the after-effects of the Black Death. Regular three-field systems akin to the so-called 'midland system' seem to have been a feature of areas only where crop-growing was more intensive, population levels high and lordship strong, like southern Warwickshire – the so-called 'champion' regions. The vast amounts of subservient labour upon which manors in these areas had relied for their arable output were no longer available. Economic conditions also began to favour stock rearing – first sheep, then cattle – which led many manorial lords in the late Tudor period to consider laying their arable down to grass. Their land was thus divided into large hedged stock enclosures, for enclosure was a necessary prerequisite for market specialisation in livestock production. Cattle markets had been established in Birmingham, Stafford and other towns in the medieval period and, over much of the region, arable farming was already subordinate to livestock husbandry; this trend was merely intensified. Medieval parklands were also used more intensively after the 16th century and often divided into stock pastures. Enclosure was, however, eventually to affect all areas.

The late Tudor wave of enclosure had the greatest effect in the 'champion' corn-growing regions. In southern Warwickshire this resulted in a landscape mosaic of empty enclosed townships – in which the former village gave way to a single farm and where village lanes and footpaths largely disappeared – lying side by side with townships in which the village recovered after the Black Death and retained its open fields much longer. Village desertion was also a particular feature of the Lower Lias clays of central Worcestershire on the fringe of the region, although villages did not necessarily disappear suddenly or early and some have subsequently recovered to a certain degree. Although the West Midlands did not suffer quite so markedly as many other regions, desertion and shrinkage did occur throughout the area, especially in parts of Herefordshire, and many hamlets became single farms, their open fields turned over to enclosed fields of pasture (Fig. 5.1) as stock raising became more and more profitable.

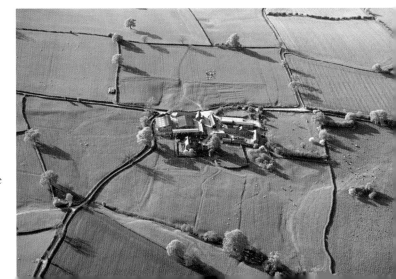

Fig. 5.1 Norton deserted medieval village, Shropshire.

In Tudor times, the old regulated manorial economy, already in retreat during the later medieval period, succumbed more rapidly to market forces and entrepreneurial initiative. The market for land became more fluid and new merchant families emerged to join the old landed dynasties. Henry VIII's dissolution of the monasteries in the 1530s and '40s had released an enormous amount of land onto the market and there was a growing middle and merchant class eager to acquire landed estates. James Leveson, for instance, a merchant of the staple (wool) from Wolverhampton, bought up manors in Shropshire that had formerly belonged to Lilleshall Abbey and Wenlock and Wombridge priories. The borders were often regarded as marginal to the main interests of many aristocratic families after the mid-16th century, providing new opportunities for merchants and lawyers keen to acquire land, many of whom were resident in the region and rather more commercially minded than their predecessors. The newly acquired land was farmed as part of large estates by tenant farmers. Many landowners attempted to convert such tenures into leaseholds or 'copyholds at will' that would permit rents to be periodically raised, and from the mid-16th century lords began to give shorter leases, often of 21 years (very different to the more secure traditional lease of three lives or 99 years).[1]

Enclosure was not always a sudden, planned process. In many areas it proceeded gradually through agreements between landholders – in general,

Fig. 5.2 Hedgerow with aratral curve.

enclosure here was a piecemeal affair, encouraged by the estate owner but largely carried out in the late medieval period by his tenants. Most estates were subdivided into tenant holdings and in this region these were often consolidated units at a relatively early date. Early piecemeal enclosure tended to preserve the outline of former open field strips and furlongs. Hedgerows today still often show the distinctive shape of an aratral curve – a backward-facing S shape – produced as the plough oxen made their way along the furrow to turn on the open-field headlands (Fig. 5.2), and sometimes the strips (or selions) can be traced through surviving ridge and furrow where the land has since remained unploughed (Fig. 5.3). Pockets of former open field can often be identified in the border counties, especially, from today's field patterns. Where hedgerows are ancient, they are often rich in colonising species like field maple, blackthorn and crab apple, which creep in to supplement the ubiquitous hawthorn.

In the White Peak of Derbyshire, villages usually lay amidst extensive open fields in medieval times, with the steep dale sides and upper land remaining open

Fig. 5.3 Ridge and furrow.

common waste. A particularly characteristic pattern of enclosed fields was
produced here as groups of strips in the open fields around the villages became
separated by stone walls that followed the former furlongs. Around Chelmorton
and Flagg the resulting long narrow fields extend for kilometres over the rolling
limestone landscape (Figs 5.4 and 5.5). Many are laid out at right angles to the
village street, the same width as the street frontage of a single farmstead. Such
enclosures were made by private agreement, usually in the 17th century, but in
some places enclosure began as early as the 14th century: with the sanction of the
manorial lord well over half of the open fields at Wardlow had been enclosed by
the time the earliest map was drawn in 1617.[2] The closes, as they are known, were

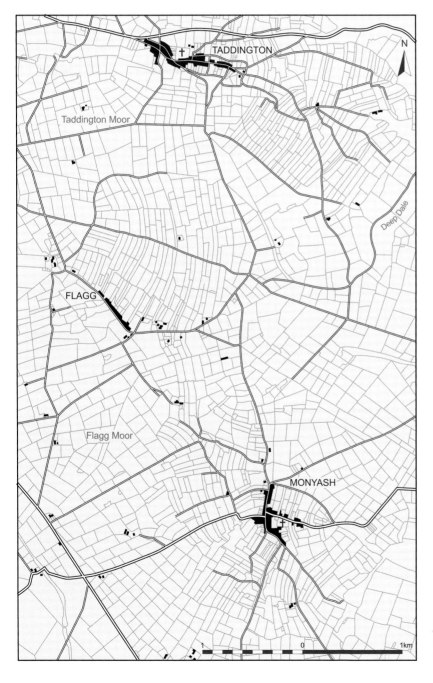

Fig. 5.4 *Field patterns in the*
Chelmorton–Flagg area of the
White Peak.

Fig. 5.5 Chelmorton–Flagg strip field patterns.

Fig. 5.6 Herefordshire orchards.

mainly for sheep rearing, still then the main source of wealth in the White Peak. They contrast markedly with the larger square-shaped enclosures of the granges, and with those fields created as the process of enclosure continued through the 18th and even into the 19th century. Villages remained nucleated and the area sits rather oddly within the region as a whole.

By the late 17th century, less than one-fifth of Shropshire was still open field and enclosure had been a long-drawn-out process; much of what remained was near towns where the landholding was complex. The gradual introduction of enclosure and related 'improvement' is also exemplified in Herefordshire. Noted in medieval times for its wool from the Golden Valley and for its wheat, by the 17th century it had grown famous for its hop fields and orchards (Fig. 5.6). In 1656 it was 'reputed the orchard of England'[3] and in 1788 it was stated that: 'Herefordshire has ever borne the name of the first cider county',[4] with apple cider and pear perry sold in London. Much of Herefordshire was a county of ancient enclosure and has been described as 'a richly varied landscape of cornfields, pasture, hop-fields, woodlands, parkland and hedgerows, scattered with small hamlets and threaded by deep lanes. This was an old enclosed county of modest properties, of minor gentry, smallholders and cottagers'.[5]

Although not recorded as well wooded in Domesday Book, the county has always been famous for its timber trees, especially its oaks. There had also been expansion onto the margins of the hill commons. Along the Olchon valley at the foot of the Black Mountains, for instance, ring-fenced holdings stand out clearly along the lower slopes of the hills (Fig. 5.7), farmed from the single farmsteads that cluster along the valley side. William Pitt, the agriculturist, writing on

Worcestershire in 1813, notes 'The greater part of this county is ancient enclosure, the fences being often full of timber trees, particularly elm, of which this county produces the finest in England ...'.[6] By the 17th century, enclosed farmland was more extensive than open-field land in the Welsh borderland. Land could also be taken in temporarily from the commons for crop cultivation. Robert Plot, the 17th-century antiquary, describes the 'brecks' in Staffordshire – temporary enclosures made on heathy lands for a period of five years or so for a rotation of rye, barley, pulse and oats. A similar system has been described at Sutton Coldfield in north Warwickshire in which the sandy soils of the Bunter Beds, normally waste, would be taken by householders in lots of 1 acre and cropped for five years before being thrown open again.[7]

*Fig. 5.7 **The Olchon valley in Herefordshire**, showing intakes on the lower slopes of the ridge.*

As the ethos of 'agricultural improvement' gained ground in the 17th and 18th centuries, larger-scale changes were put underway, producing much of the landscape we see today. More organised enclosure, simultaneously affecting whole blocks of land, required all proprietors to enter into an agreement, and throughout the 18th century enclosure under this method began to make more impression. Enclosed land was easier to control for livestock rearing, which played a major role in the region, but also allowed easier innovation in most branches of farming: by 1750 open-field cultivation had virtually disappeared in Shropshire and was much reduced in Herefordshire and Staffordshire. Enclosure of the early arable was not, however, the only way to obtain additional pasture for stock. In marginal areas, land could be drained or cleared of trees, while fields could be pushed up into the hill commons. Interest therefore turned towards the potential of the remaining areas of wetland, woodland and upland sheepwalks. In Shropshire, the fen-like Weald Moors, which had served as a summer grazing area for surrounding communities, were targeted by the Levesons, the major landowners in the area, with the reclamation of some 2,730 acres (1,100ha) by 1650. Such measures called for heavy investment and could only be carried out by rich landowners, but newly drained and enclosed land rapidly increased in value.

The influence of the great estates, which controlled much of the region's farmland, was enormous in this period. Many held land in this region and elsewhere. We have already encountered the FitzAlans, earls of Arundel, who had held one of the largest estates in Shropshire since the 12th century but in the 13th century also acquired extensive lands in southern England. Their Shropshire inheritance remained one of the four or five greatest landed estates in the county until the middle of the 17th century.[8] Many estates, however, had changed hands over the centuries: there had been a tendency for the larger landowners to withdraw from direct involvement in agriculture, especially when economic and political conditions had been unstable. Demesne profits had declined and much land was leased out, especially on the Arundel estates. Most 18th-century estate owners, however, were keen to maximise their profits and many were at the forefront of agricultural innovation. Only they had the money

Fig. 5.8 Fields produced by parliamentary enclosure in the Vale of Evesham, Worcestershire.

Bredon Hill rises in the near distance.

to carry out agricultural experimentation and to play an active role in the Agricultural Revolution that gained ground in the middle of the century. The speed of enclosure was, however, also affected by the attitudes of individual landowners, who generally favoured it; some, like the Craven estate owners of Shropshire, remained notoriously inactive.

Overall, this movement led to the widespread enclosure of the remaining open fields after the middle of the 18th century. No longer driven by the interests of animal husbandry, it was hastened now by the rising demand for corn during the Napoleonic Wars with France when corn prices rocketed. After the General Enclosure Act of 1836, bills for enclosure could be put before Parliament and, if awarded, commissioners and surveyors were appointed to carry out the plans. The landscapes that resulted from enclosure by consent were generally less rigidly geometric than those that resulted from parliamentary enclosure, which resulted in large straight-sided regular fields and often, too, new road layouts. These fields can frequently be detected on the modern map and in many areas dominate the present-day field pattern (Fig. 5.8). High grain prices also encouraged the ploughing of what had hitherto been considered marginal land and the remains of the straight, narrow ridge and furrow, characteristic of the ploughing-up campaigns of this time, can be seen in places high on the Shropshire hills.

This latest stage of organised enclosure affected what was left of the common wastes and led to the loss of much of the remaining woodland and most of the medieval upland sheepwalks of the West Midlands – the extent of the remaining 'semi-wilderness' was drastically reduced. In general, the agricultural writers of the day had little appreciation of 'wilderness' and bemoaned it as a lost opportunity. William Pitt had regarded Needwood as a waste ripe for development in 1796 when he estimated that 140,000 acres (57,000ha) of commons still existed in Staffordshire: although it might be 'wild and romantic ... its continuance in its present state is certainly indefensible', and he had the same opinion about Cannock Chase, which he felt should be turned over entirely to cultivation. Moorlands he specifically disliked, with their 'barbarous' stone walls in contrast to 'vastly more beautiful' quickset hedges, and he felt that as much land as possible should be ploughed up.[9] Francis Marston, a surveyor employed in 19 or 20 Shropshire enclosures, strongly considered that the side of Clunbury Hill and the whole top of the Long Mynd should be used for plantations to increase their utility and beauty.[10]

There was also a growing tendency to dislike squatters who were seen as able to live feckless lives upon the back of their 'free grazing' and the move towards the enclosure of the commons was driven as much by social motives as by economic ones. As one Worcestershire landowner stated in 1813 concerning the enclosure of 'barren waste land': 'The advantages are innumerable, to population as well as cultivation; and instead of a horde of pilferers, you obtain an useful race as well of mechanics as other labourers'.[11]

The production of lime to lower the acidity of the newly broken hill commons was a feature in parts of the Welsh border. New out- or high-barns were also constructed, sometimes remote from the farmhouse, as the last phases of enclosure took in the woods and rough grazings of the uplands (Fig. 5.9), as along the north side of Corvedale in Shropshire.[12] The woods themselves were often of greater value for their timber, as the Navy's need for new ships pushed timber prices upwards: it was noted in 1805 that 300 oaks had recently been felled on the slopes of Credenill near Hereford.[13]

Landowners had been able to take increased profits from their country estates in the 18th century and the 'nouveau riche' eager to move into this world had included industrialists, bankers, businessmen and slavers. 'Rack rents' that could be racked or raised each year became popular; tenant farmers, in any case, might be paying as much as a third of their farms' gross produce as rent, plus tithes to the Church and local taxes such as poor rates. With the Agricultural Revolution, great attention was paid to livestock breeding and grassland management. Some landlords did reinvest their profits, and improved stock housing was one feature: fold yards were set aside for fatstock and the intensive feeding of cattle was practised. Herefordshire bullocks were fed on hay, corn, oilcake and linseed and accommodated in special sheds after the 1770s.[14] Herefordshire cattle became famous throughout the world; improvement began in the early 18th century and by the 1850s first-class herds were found across the county and were being exhibited at Royal and other shows.

The more flexible agricultural practices fostered on the landed estates included convertible husbandry in which fertility was maintained by alternating grain and grass crops; 'ley farming' in which rotational grasses were laid down for a period of years before further ploughing (often termed convertible or 'up-and-down' husbandry), ensuring a mix of animal farming and crop production; and the introduction of new crops. Fodder crops such as clover and sainfoin made an appearance in the 18th century as nitrogen fixers, adding to soil fertility. The production of commercial crops such as barley for brewing began to increase. In many regions, there was a fall in the number of livestock kept by the middle of the 18th century as arable gave greater returns, and the distinction between 'woodland' and 'champion' regions was lessened.[15] From the middle of the 18th century, model farms were laid out and designs could be ordered from pattern books. On an estate, the 'home farm' could serve as a model for tenants, with superior outbuildings and equipment. Model and experimental farms were also being constructed – as at Sandwell, on the western outskirts of Birmingham, where the farm has recently been restored by Sandwell Borough Council, or the model dairy at Shugborough in Staffordshire. There was new equipment to accommodate, like threshing machines. Plans survive of James Loch's designs for Lilleshall Hill Farm in Shropshire (1818) and

Fig. 5.9 A high barn in the White Peak region of Derbyshire, sadly now ruinous. The barn had space for a cow byre and hay storage.

Beaudesert Home Farm in Staffordshire (1817), both of which show buildings ranged around a fold yard.[16] At Groundslow Field Farm, Tittensor, the land agent of the Trentham estate implemented an entirely new field layout in which 56 irregular fields were reduced to 15 straight-sided ones, each of 10–25 acres (4–10ha), between 1830 and 1843 and hedgerow removal was advocated at Stretton Hall in Penkridge in 1847.[17] Whole villages were on occasions laid out anew (*see* below).

Some estate farm buildings were carried to extremes in the attempt to create a rural arcadia – Robert Adam's dairy at Croome Court, Worcestershire, was designed in Greek neoclassical style in 1760–73. At Home Farm in Shugborough Park, Staffordshire, the seat of Thomas Anson, a great flood in 1795 provided the opportunity for new farm buildings designed by Samuel Wyatt. On the south side of a yard a range of buildings that included a brewhouse, a water corn mill and a malthouse faced stables and cowhouses on the north side; farrowing pens and stables enclosed the yard on the west and on the east stood the steward's house.[18] The Home Farm was intended for the maintenance of the Ansons, their staff and guests, and was staffed by 22 labourers in 1805 in addition to the steward and the man who managed the mill and malt house. Great quantities of ale, dairy products, bread flour, cereals and meat were produced. Similar farm buildings were laid out at Attingham Park in Shropshire in the 19th century, especially at Cronkhill.

By the 1860s, the large Staffordshire landowners had gained a reputation as the leaders in agricultural improvement: men like the 1st Lord Hatherton at Teddesley, near Penkridge, who drained and irrigated gravelly soils to grow wheat and barley or support cattle and sheep. He ran a free agricultural school on his estate for 300 boys and in 1845 helped to form the Cannock Agricultural Association for tenant farmers in the area.[19] Successful regional crops were further exploited. Worcestershire, like Herefordshire, was growing hops 'in great perfection' at the beginning of the 19th century,[20] especially along the valleys of the Severn and Teme, and the oast houses in which the hops were dried became a familiar sight in the countryside (Fig. 5.10). The county had been noted for fruit since medieval times (cherries were sold at Worcester market). Rich meadows and pastures along the Avon, Severn and Teme, enriched by the annual floods,

Fig. 5.10 Oasthouses, Herefordshire.

supported cattle and sheep, and market gardening was becoming established not only in the Vale of Evesham but to the north-east of Worcester. As new railways provided links to the rapidly growing midland towns, the cultivation of fruit growing and vegetables increased dramatically after about 1870. New specialist crops like strawberries, asparagus, outdoor rhubarb and early vegetables for salads found their place in the nation's diet.

THE TAMING OF THE LANDSCAPE

In Cheshire, open fields were irregular and of variable extent but townships often had but one single open field, often referred to as the town field, made up of a series of furlongs or flats – small clusters of strips.[21] As in Herefordshire, much of the open field had been enclosed by 1500. By the beginning of the 18th century the enclosed fields had sustained herds of dairy cattle for a long time and the county was renowned for its cheese. Virtually all 18th-century enclosure by private or by parliamentary action was concerned with 'waste' or common pasture beyond the open fields. Enclosures by private act around Delamere Forest began in 1767 with the enclosure of more than 400 acres (160ha) in Cuddington, followed by the enclosure of 1,700 acres (690ha) in Frodsham and Weaverham in 1780 and a further 1,100 acres (445ha) in Frodsham in 1797.[22] By that date, however, there was very little woodland left and most of the area was scrub, rough grassland and heath. There were many other enclosures in the district around but the forest itself was not enclosed until after an act of 1812: 8,750 acres (3,540ha) were allotted in 1816 with amendments being made until 1819. The land was, however, of little value and by the early 20th century much of it had reverted to woodland and plantations. Apart from an act covering some 6,000 acres (2,400ha) in Dodleston and part of neighbouring Flintshire, most awards elsewhere were of relatively small acreages and the 'tidying up' of hill, heath and mossland occurred over a period of time. In Malpas, Bunbury and Acton, in the south of the county, it took 11 separate acts between 1794 and 1864 to achieve this, the later ones dealing with fewer than 40 acres (16ha) each. In north Cheshire there were still substantial areas of unenclosed mossland surviving into the 19th century, but over much of the county enclosure over the centuries has produced a quiet 'tame' rural landscape.

Although open field was enclosed in Staffordshire in the 18th century, by far the greatest acreages involved woodland and heath: like the 2,206 acres (893ha) enclosed at Chedleton in 1737. In Leek, there were four successive enclosures: more than 3,000 acres (1,200ha) at Bradnop in 1769 and nearly 3,000 acres (1,200ha) at the Roaches or Hen Cloud, Lowe, Leek Frith and Tittesworth in 1811. In the area of the former Kinver forest, in the south-west of the county, over 1,000 acres (400ha) in Kinver and Compton were enclosed in 1774; a few years later Ashwood Hay and Wall Heath in Kingswinford (some 1,400 acres: 570ha) were enclosed and a further 1,300 acres (525ha) in the same parish in 1787. An act for the enclosure of Needwood extinguished common rights over 9,604 acres (3,887ha) in 1805 but the final allocation was not made until 1811. This was the time of inflated corn prices during the Napoleonic Wars and Needwood was converted from woodland to a largely open farmland landscape of regular fields and straight roads. Still, a central block of forest survived into the middle of the 19th century and new parks helped to preserve the early forest character, but only the northern edge of the forest gives any sense, today, of what it had once been like. Maer Heath near the Shropshire border was divided and allotted for enclosure by Josiah Wedgwood in 1810. The core area of Cannock Chase was the last woodland area to be affected by parliamentary act, enclosed after 1853 in a series of acts that covered Hammerwich (670 acres: 271ha), Burntwood (1,840 acres: 745ha), Cannock (nearly 3,000 acres: 1,200ha),

Fig. 5.11 Cannock Chase conifer plantations.

Norton Canes (880 acres: 356ha) and finally, in 1885, over 5,000 acres (2,000ha) at Rugeley. Today, this is largely a region of conifer plantations, with some more open areas of bracken-covered heathland (Figs 5.11 and 5.37c).

Large acreages were also enclosed by private act in the White Peak District of Derbyshire. In parishes like Monyash, the medieval open field had already been enclosed before Parliamentary enclosure but over 1,200 acres (485ha) of upper sheepwalks here were subdivided into large fields in the 1770s although in other parishes in the area field size was to vary considerably. Enclosure in Matlock in 1780 affected some 1,719 acres (695ha) and in Baslow and Bubnall, Curbar and Froggatt in Bakewell in 1826 nearly 4,000 acres (1,618ha). This stage of organised enclosure and its stupendous scale meant the virtual end of the open sheepwalks in the area. Instead, the straight walls, made up of obviously surveyed lengths, cut as grey-white lines across the landscape and still dominate it today. In the Dark Peak, Peak Forest had effectively ceased to exist by the late 17th century, but the freeholders' portions were not fully enclosed and the poor continued to use the open moorland as common pasture. However, nearly 2,000 acres (809ha) were enclosed in Whitfield in Glossop in 1810, followed by another 1,490 acres (602ha) in the same parish before 1830. Grouse shooting was a sport which increased in popularity in the second half of the 19th century and rendered access by the public to the remaining moorlands even more problematical.

In Shropshire, it was again the woods, hills and heathlands that were the subject of most of the 18th- and 19th-century enclosure acts, merely continuing a process that had begun much earlier, carried out by both landlord and tenant, including the squatters of industrial areas like the Clees. Even though Shropshire was already 'an area of old inclosure' at the end of the Middle Ages,[23] these later enclosures were widespread throughout the county, especially the Hine Heath district in the north-east, the Shirlett Forest area, and around Bridgnorth, Claverley and Quatford in the south-east. The upland area of the Long Mynd lost 4,000 acres (1,600ha) to enclosure at Stretton-en-le-Dale in 1788, some 1,788 acres (720ha) in Lydley and Cardington in Cardington and Church Stretton in 1814 and a further 1,022 acres

(414ha) of certain commons in Church Stretton, Wistanstow and Edgton in 1822. Although most of the enclosures carried out under the general acts of 1845 concerned only general 'tidying up', some areas were particularly affected, especially along the Welsh border from the Ellesmere/Oswestry district, the Worthen/Chirbury area, down to the Clun 'Forest' – over 20,000 acres (8,094ha) in the old Clun Forest area alone between 1845 and 1891. Enclosures by private act covered around 13,616 acres (5,510ha) around Clun between 1845 and 1854, including about 8,600 acres (3,480ha) in the core area of the forest by an act of

Fig. 5.12 Clun sheepwalks.

1837 awarded in 1847. Although most of the enclosures carried out under the general acts of 1845 concerned only general 'tidying up', in Clun Forest they covered 6,675 acres (2,701ha): land in Clunbury, on the Bettws Hills and in Llanfair Waterdine. Shropshire's final enclosure on the Llanfair Hills was as late as 1891. Here 1,634 acres (661ha) were enclosed with enormous straight-edged enclosure fields (Fig. 5.12) that contrast vividly with the irregular small ancient enclosure fields of the valleys. Elsewhere in Shropshire it is only the higher summits of ranges like the Long Mynd and the Stiperstones that remain open.

In Herefordshire, it was generally the earlier enclosures by private act that entailed relatively large acreages and these did include a substantial amount of open-field arable in spite of the amount already taken in by earlier enclosure. Over 2,000 acres (800ha) in Leintwardine, Burrington, Downton, Aston and Elton were enclosed in 1803 in the area of Bringewood Chase and the former Mocktree Forest, but the 1,410 acres (570ha) enclosed in Yarkhill, Weston Beggard, Dormington and Stoke Edith in 1804 included much former open-field arable, as did the 1,000 or so acres (400ha) enclosed in Much Marcle in 1797, the 2,000 acres (800ha) in Bodenham (1813) and the 3,638 acres (1,472ha) in Marden (1819). Most subsequent acts concerned areas of 100 acres (40ha) or less. They did, however, concern parishes scattered throughout the county. When this land is plotted in detail, it is clear that the late surviving open fields lay on the fertile plain of Hereford to the north and north-east of Hereford, land that was drained by the rivers Lugg and Frome, tributaries of the Wye. Much former common meadow was also enclosed along the rivers Lugg and Frome, water meadows that were particularly valued as seasonal pasture, enriched by successive annual floods (Fig. 5.13). Enclosure also affected the hill commons – not just the extensive upland commons along the Welsh border like Cusop Hill or

Fig. 5.13 Water meadows along the River Lugg in Herefordshire.

Urishay Common in Michaelchurch, Escley and Peterchurch and parts of Dorstone, but the smaller patches of common scattered across the county. The hill commons, especially those bordering the Golden Valley, had long been subject to piecemeal enclosure throughout the historical period and to squatter encroachment in later periods, and these were among the last big areas to be enclosed. Open sheepwalk commons remain a feature, however, of the eastern ranges of the Black Mountains, in particular the Black Hill and Black Darren range above the Olchon valley (Fig. 5.14).

The main areas of midland four-field open-field systems in Worcestershire, the Vale of Evesham and the Lias claylands, lay beyond the boundary of the region, as did the main areas of three-field, four-field and even multiple-field open-field systems in Warwickshire.[24] Some open field (mainly of three-field systems) was enclosed by private and parliamentary act in north Worcestershire and north Warwickshire but more enclosure affected non-arable land, especially in the areas around Worcestershire's Clent Hills or the Warwickshire Arden, like the 1,170 acres (470ha) enclosed in Hampton-in Arden in 1802. Over 300 enclosures by parliamentary act had been carried out by the end of the 18th century alone, and the results were as the great landowners had predicted: crop yields more than doubled; sheep produced twice as much meat and three times as much wool in value. By the end of the 18th century, 2½ million acres (800,000ha) of open field had been enclosed and a similar amount of common land brought into intensive cultivation, producing a landscape much as we see it today[25] – a patchwork of generally hawthorn-hedged fields that we have come to regard as the norm. However, not only the visible landscape was affected by enclosure, for a new social landscape evolved as people working the land moved out from the villages to outlying farms, leading to a change in village character that was to have later repercussions.

Fig. 5.14 Unenclosed sheepwalks on the Black Mountain range on the Powys/Herefordshire boundary.

LANDSCAPES OF LEISURE

One of the few non-utilitarian features that did meet with the approval of the 18th-century agricultural writers was the gentleman's park (Fig. 5.15). Although the medieval hunting parks had generally succumbed to enclosure, the desire to establish a park around a country house had gained ground since the 15th century and thus continued the tradition while extending it to regions beyond those with plentiful waste – often into the heart of the main crop-growing regions. In Herefordshire, at Foxley, Uvedale Price inherited an estate already 'improved' by his father and concentrated further upon picturesque landscaping in the 18th and early 19th centuries. Nathaniel Kent was commissioned to assist in the remodelling of the estate between 1770 and 1774 and a belt of encircling woodland was completed to create 'compositional coherence' (the house has disappeared but much of Price's planting survives). In Warwickshire, Murray extolled the fact that almost every nobleman and gentleman in the county had valuable timber on their estates, but the finest and best-grown oaks were on the property of Mr Dugdale at Merevale and on the estate of the Marquis of Hertford at Ragley.[26] Even aristocratic pastimes had an influence upon the landscape, for fox-hunting became immensely popular after the 18th century and coverts were planted to give cover to fox-earths and game birds. By Victorian times, extended house parties at country houses revolved around hunting, fishing and shooting. In the Dove valley, the Meynell hunt gained national repute, centred upon the Cavendish family's seat at Doveridge. The Albrighton, the North Staffordshire, the South Staffordshire and the Atherstone hunts had all been established by the mid-19th century although the Albrighton had late-18th-century origins. The preservation of the gritstone moors of the Dark Peak was ensured by their suitability as grouse moor, although there was continued conflict over public access.

Fig. 5.15 Charlecote deer park, Warwickshire, *still stocked with deer today.*

ESTATE REORGANISATION

Large estates were also being reorganised in the 19th century. In particular, the number of tenant farms was often reduced as amalgamation occurred. In Cheshire, there were 45 tenants on the Tollemache estate in 1846 but most of these tenancies were to be replaced after 1850 by a smaller number of new units. Smallholdings of 15 acres (6ha) or so, even if they formed no part of a larger estate, as at Malpas in Cheshire, were often forced out of business, while the remaining more active or efficient farmers rose up the social scale. In Cheshire, in 1871, the top 42 landowners, 0.17 per cent of the total number of owners of freehold property who owned more than 2,500 acres (1,000ha) each, accounted for no less than 43.7 per cent of the area of the county. The largest landowner in Cheshire in 1871 was John Tollemache of Peckforton, with 25,380 acres (10,270ha). The influence that estate structure was to have on the landscape has not always been fully appreciated. The great estate owners were not only at the forefront of enclosure, but their management procedures influenced the farmed landscape to a marked degree that can still be seen today. The Duke of Sutherland's estate in the early 19th century covered vast acreages of north-east Shropshire and the adjacent parts of Staffordshire and, between 1811 and 1822, many farmhouses and cottages were erected under the stewardship of their Scottish agent, James Loch, reflected in the plain neoclassical farmhouses still occupied today and the logically planned layout of their farmyards.[27]

The mid-19th century was something of a 'golden age' for farming. Dairying and cheese production was profitable, especially in Cheshire. The numbers of cattle doubled between 1830 and 1860 in Cheshire and fine new farmsteads were built on the Wilbraham and Tollemache estates in the south of the county.[28] However, prices, especially of cereals, fell disastrously in the 1870s, partly due to the importation of cheap grain from North America, Australia and New Zealand, and production dropped after a series of bad harvests between 1875 and 1878. The numbers employed in agriculture declined considerably between 1870 and 1914, labourers by 36 per cent. Although the First World War brought a brief period of prosperity for farmers when goods could not be easily imported, imports again pushed down prices between the wars and many workers left the land. Only the marketing of milk improved. Between the wars and after the Second World War many estates were broken up, country houses abandoned to dereliction and many traditional farm buildings utterly neglected. Small farms were amalgamated and farmer's co-operatives were better organised, but the increased use of machinery drove many agricultural labourers from the land.

Fig. 5.16 Surviving strip fields at Madley, Herefordshire.

SETTLEMENT PATTERNS

The irregular field systems of much of the region have given rise to a characteristic settlement and field pattern in which early manorial nuclei can be identified, often with their patches of townfield that were subsequently to be enclosed to give rise to patches of strip-like fields (Fig. 5.16). This pattern is repeated throughout the borderland and can clearly be identified on 19th-century tithe maps, with many hamlets also possessing associated areas of former open arable or even open strips at that date, although it is not always possible to detect whether the peripheral farmsteads were taking in land cleared of woodland, or were improved enclosures taken from common grazings bearing underwood, heath, moorland and marsh, or even former open field. The oldest elements of the landscape seem to have been the surviving blocks of ancient woodland, old hedgerows cut from woodlands and tracts of commonable waste, present here in greater profusion than to the south and east (Fig. 5.17).[29]

The Cheshire plain, this 'quietly undulating country, with many streams flowing gently in wide valleys',

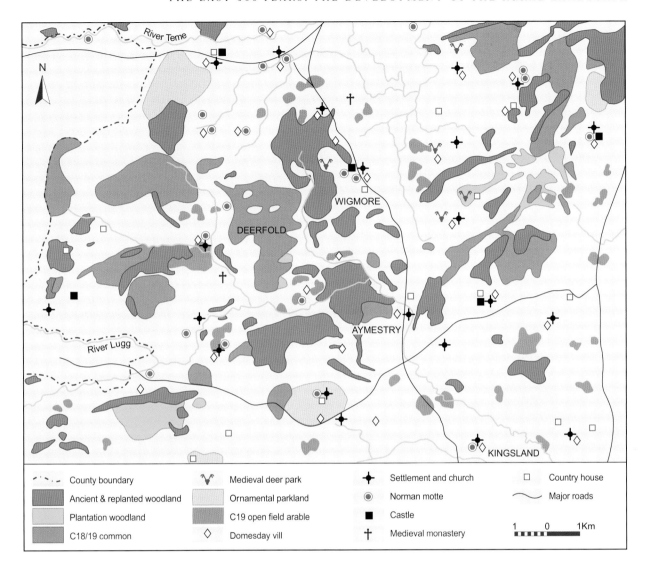

Fig. 5.17 *Nineteenth-century land use and surviving ancient woodland in north Herefordshire.*

has been characterised as a region of dispersed hamlets and farmsteads comprising 'parochial centres, some ancient, some more recent, with, traces of small areas of townfield in the form of distinctive enclosure patterns'.[30] Two- and three-field systems were practised but the open-field patches remained small, surrounded by old enclosures or enclosures from the common waste.[31] By contrast, the landscape between the Shropshire hills and the Severn plain is one of rapidly-changing contrasts, in which limited areas of open townfield were scattered amongst woodlands, open commons and extensive tracts of old enclosure. Settlement elements include very small villages with patches of former open field, isolated farmsteads and moated sites, hamlets often bearing the affix 'green' and parish churches, these standing solitary or in a hamlet.

Further into the heart of the West Midlands similar dispersed settlement elements are more plentiful and nucleations fewer. Diverse hamlets, many of them again including the word 'green' in their names, scatters of small farmsteads and cottages and some larger isolated moated farmsteads occupied an area in which common waste was more plentiful than woodland and patches of open field more restricted. The late medieval pattern of small, irregular, hedged fields has not been lost in the Warwickshire Arden, and the tree-lined hedges help to

Fig. 5.18 View over the Warwickshire Arden near Ullenhall.

preserve a 'bosky' appearance (Fig. 5.18). Such hedges are often very old and species-rich, set with trees such as oak and ash at regular intervals.

Further to the south, in the Wye–Teme area, settlement is very dispersed indeed and the only nucleations are either market towns or very small hamlets set in an anciently enclosed landscape that is still well wooded, although modern development is now blurring this traditional picture. Some of the outlying farms may represent an ancient settlement pattern that was not overwhelmed by village nucleation and even some of the village cores were to become reduced to the scale of hamlets or even to disappear altogether, often leaving little more than an isolated church. This area also contained greater expanses of open field that seem to have represented the end-result of aggregation from a succession of smaller townfield kernels already present by the late 11th century (*see* Chapter 4).[32] There was, however, considerable variation within the area, for open fields were more extensive along the Wye valley to the north of Hereford. The flatter plain of Hereford offers a quite different landscape to the rolling Herefordshire countryside seen from the Malvern ridge (Fig. 5.19). Here, vast numbers of small hamlets and farms set in the midst of enclosed landscapes and connected by an intricate network of roads and lanes reflect a complicated history of medieval settlement in a once-wooded landscape.

The squatter settlements that grew up along the edges of the commons, especially in mining districts (*see* Chapter 6), are a common characteristic of the west of the region, as around Bircher Common in Herefordshire, the Clees

OPPOSITE PAGE:

BOTTOM: *Fig. 5.21 Squatter settlement around the Clees.*

Fig. 5.19 View south-west over Herefordshire from the Malverns.

(Figs 5.20 and 5.21) and Farlow Common in Shropshire, and along the Wye in Walford and Whitchurch, Great and Little Doward. Some of the cottages in the latter area were occupied by nailers who used resources from the Forest of Dean. Many of the cottagers in these settlements combined mining, quarrying or nail making, for example, with small-scale crofting.

By the 17th century, towns revived to meet the increasing demands of a growing consumer society. Across the region, the small market towns formed the focus of local rural activities before the major improvements to communications carried out after the 18th century, and many held regular fairs. The county towns stood at the top of the hierarchy and in 1642 Neremiah Wharton, a roundhead sergeant, described Hereford as 'environed with a strong wall, better than I have seen before, with five gates and a strong bridge of six arches over the river, surpassing Worcester

Fig. 5.20 A cottage below Brown Clee *that probably began as a squatter's intake at the edge of the open common.*

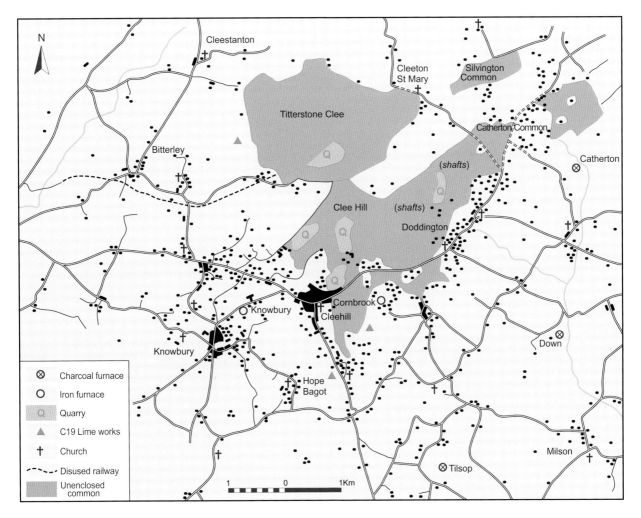

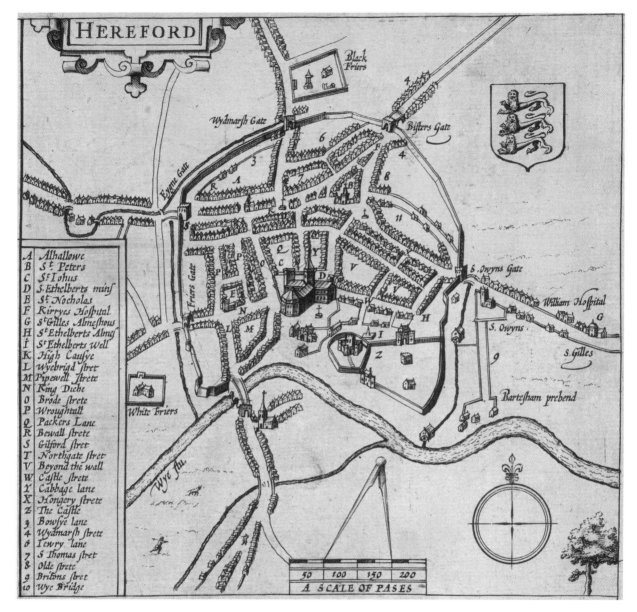

A	Alhallowe
B	St Peters
C	St Iohns
D	S. Ethelberts minf
E	St Nicholas
F	Kirryes Hospital
G	St Gilles Almeshous
H	St Ethelberts Almef
I	St Ethelberts Well
K	High Caufye
L	Wyebrigd ftrete
M	Pipewell ftrete
N	King Diche
O	Brode ftrete
P	Wroughtall
Q	Packers Lane
R	Bewall ftrete
S	Gilford ftret
T	Northgate ftret
V	Beyond the wall
W	Caftle ftrete
X	Cabbage lane
Y	Hongery ftrete
Z	The Caftle
3	Bowfye lane
4	Wydmarfh ftrete
6	Iewry lane
7	S. Thomas ftret
8	Olde ftrete
9	Britons ftret
10	Wye Bridge

Fig. 5.22 John Speed's view of Hereford, published in The Theatre of the Empire of Great Britaine *1611–12.*

(Fig. 5.22). In the city, there is the stateliest market place in the kingdom, built with columns, after the manner of the Exchange'. Ross, on the other hand, was described by William Cobbett in 1821 as 'an old-fashioned town, but … very beautifully situated'.[33] Like many of Herefordshire's towns it displayed its main function by its fine 17th-century market hall built of red sandstone (Fig. 5.23); many other market halls were timber-framed, such as those of Ledbury, Pembridge and Leominster (a centre for the wool trade and for glove making in the 16th century).

Of the smaller market towns, many had lost their function by the 16th century and even Chester, the largest medieval town in the north-west, suffered decline before its revival in the late 16th century, the gradual silting up of its estuary forcing shipping towards the quays of the Wirral. Macclesfield, also in Cheshire, was becoming a thriving industrial centre by the 16th century with its nascent cloth and button industries. From the 17th to the 19th century, the droving of cattle from Wales to London brought increased prosperity to some of the old market towns and there were flourishing cattle markets at, for instance, Hereford and Bromyard in Herefordshire or Rugby in Warwickshire, while Craven Arms and Kington, close to the Welsh border, were known for their sheep fairs. The main cattle markets, however, lay to the south-east in towns such as Northampton and Leicester.

Along the south-eastern margins of the region were a number of towns that had grown up as centres of exchange between more wooded pastoral regions and the intensive crop-growing regions to the south – towns like Stratford-upon-Avon and Alcester in Warwickshire or Pershore and Evesham in Worcestershire. Of those

Fig. 5.23 Market hall, Ross-on-Wye, Herefordshire.

market towns that survived, some, like Weobley in Herefordshire, noted for its ales in the mid-19th century but no longer for any market, have now diminished in importance. Some struggle to survive as economic centres for shopping and small-scale industry while others, like Leominster or Tenbury Wells, Oswestry and Whitchurch, retain more of their ancient function as regional centres, although Tenbury, like so many other rural towns, has recently lost its livestock market.

The 18th century saw the growth of many of the region's towns: in Worcestershire, Halesowen increased its population almost fivefold, and Evesham and Pershore were not far behind, the fairs at the former famous, according to Nash, 'for the sale of strong black horses'.[34] In the 18th century, a new craze for 'taking the waters' developed and towns with access to mineral springs rapidly began to exploit this trend. After George III sought a cure at Cheltenham in Gloucestershire in 1788, spas became very fashionable centres at which to holiday or to rent or buy a 'second home' town-house; ballrooms and boarding houses were built around the pools and baths. In Derbyshire, Buxton, known in Roman times for its thermal springs, revived the spa tradition and its fashionable Bath-inspired Crescent was begun in 1780 by the fifth Duke of Devonshire (Fig. 5.24). Matlock Bath grew up as a spa at the same time, about 1km from the old village, but gained in popularity after the opening of the railway line in 1849, and Bakewell enjoyed a short period as a spa around 1800 under the Duke of Rutland. The Victorians were particularly keen on 'taking the waters'. Droitwich in Worcestershire was able to benefit from its brine and its Brine Baths were opened in 1836, gaining a reputation for the alleviation of rheumatism. Malvern was praised for the purity of its springs on the Malvern Hills. The first three to be exploited were the Holy Well and St Anne's Well on the eastern flanks of the hills and the Chalybeate Spring near the church. Some places tried unsuccessfully to cash in on the fashion – even Dudley in the Black Country had its salt wells and baths, opened for the 1847 season.

COMMUNICATIONS

The market towns of the West Midlands were linked by roads of variable quality whose routes and connections to London were outlined by John Ogilby in his *Britannia* in 1675 (Fig. 5.25). It was a public duty to maintain public highways for travellers throughout historical times. During the whole of the post-Tudor period records are full of complaints about parishioners failing to keep through roads in good order. From medieval times until the 18th century, the work and expense involved in maintaining and repairing the roads was levied from the inhabitants of each village through which the roads passed.[35] These duties were enforced by common law and the local organisers were, until Tudor times, the medieval corporate units such as the Church, the manorial court, the guilds and borough corporations. In 1555 an Act of Parliament (the Statute for Mending of Highways) made provision for each parish to regularise its methods of highway maintenance and authorised the appointment of parish surveyors who were to exact an annual four days' labour and cartage service from local landowners and householders. From the end of the 17th century, a parish rate was levied to provide hired labour in place of unpaid service. Only in the 19th century did highways cease to be the responsibility of parochial officials and pass instead to the new district councils that were formed in 1894.

Local roads were not generally well maintained but most traffic was by horse, whether this involved packhorses or riders, and horses could cope with difficult conditions. Some were long distance routes, like those mapped by Ogilby or shown on the early county maps. The local pattern of routeways reflects settlement patterns and there were probably many more local tracks in use before the invention of tarmac, taking the shortest feasible route. The intricate pattern of tracks that developed in part of the Warwickshire Arden is fairly

OPPOSITE PAGE:
Fig. 5.24 The Crescent, Buxton, Derbyshire, begun in 1780 with the revival of the town as a spa.

Fig. 5.25 Early long-distance routeways including drove roads in the region.

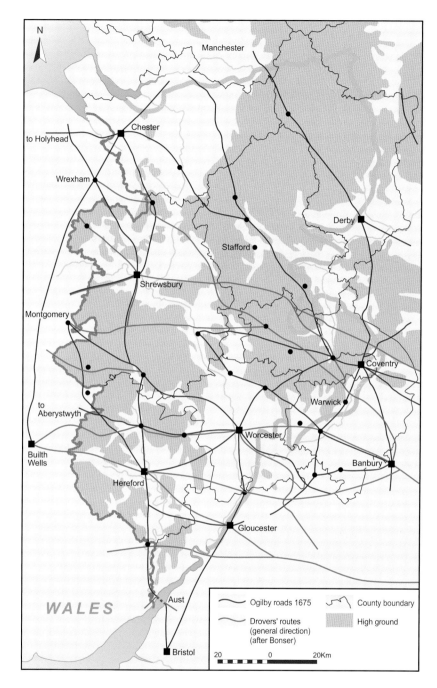

typical for a region of mainly dispersed settlements (Fig. 5.26). The state of the roads deteriorated through the 18th century and, as expanding industrial development required better transport and communications, turnpike trusts were set up to improve major roads, gates or toll-houses being set up at which the tolls could be collected. In Warwickshire, most turnpikes were established by parliamentary act in the mid-18th century on roads leading to London or linking market towns, with occasional toll-houses along their routes (Fig. 5.27). The improvements carried out greatly reduced journey times. A journey from Birmingham to London was reduced from three or four days to 15 hours by the end of the century. Carriers using broad-wheeled wagons began to replace

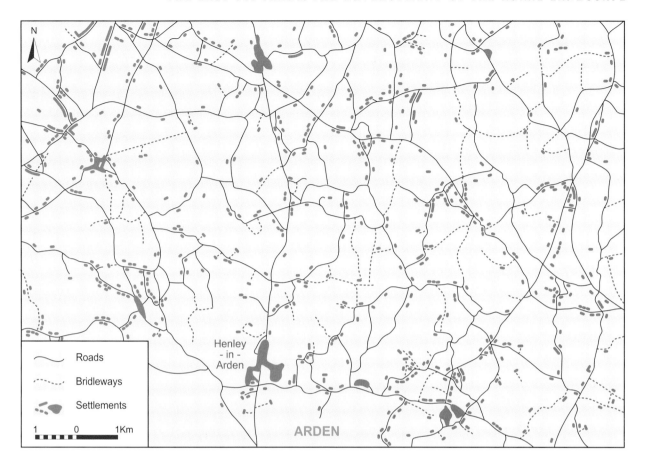

packhorses. After 1800, some entirely new roads were constructed, like the ones south of Ludlow in Shropshire that led to Tenbury and Leominster or those from Coalbrookdale to Wellington, Minsterley to Churchstoke, or Morville to Shipton, the latter providing a route from Bridgnorth to Ludlow that avoided the Clee Hills. Eventually, these roads would face competition from the railways and the last toll-gates in Shropshire were removed in 1883.

Fig. 5.26 Road and settlement patterns in the Warwickshire Arden.

Fig. 5.27 A toll-house on the turnpike road from Much Wenlock at Broseley, Shropshire.

After 1773 it became easier to change the route of a highway. Before this, a landowner had to issue a writ in the Court of Chancery in London, which empowered the sheriff of the county to convene a meeting of the freeholders of the hundred in which the proposed alteration lay. This was time consuming, cumbersome and expensive, but the law of 1773 enabled the turnpike trusts and private landowners to effect alteration with the agreement of only two magistrates (despite any opposition from tenants or labourers). At this time a number of roads were also moved to create or improve designed parklands, giving privacy and 'polite exclusion'.[36] At Charlecote in Warwickshire the former road to Wellesbourne passed through what is now a deserted medieval village within the parkland and was moved southwards outside the park. Other instances of road removal occurred at Studley in Warwickshire in 1821 at the time of the enclosure of the remaining commons and when Studley new 'Castle' was built in 1834, and similar changes occurred in many other locations.

Sometimes travellers came into conflict with other users of the roads. The mail coach from Brecon making its way to Hereford was once held up by a slow-moving herd of cattle being driven by the Welsh drovers from a small village north of Llandovery in Carmarthen towards London. This entailed a trek of 320km that would take 14 days, with the drovers ever aware of the need to reach the Monday morning market at Smithfield with beasts that had not been over-driven or rushed and had been able to enjoy good herbage along the route. The coach refused to stop and the driver lashed out with his whip in all directions, terrifying the cattle. For this, he was thrown into a ditch by the drovers who continued on through Hereford, Ledbury (there was a 'drovers' field' next to the Feathers Inn where they stayed), Little Malvern and Upton upon Severn. From here, the cattle swam across the River Severn and the journey continued by lane, avoiding as many toll-gates as possible, as far as St Albans and on to the Smithfield market.[37]

In addition to the Hereford to St Albans route, various other recognised drove routes crossed the borderland (*see* Fig. 5.25). One group ran through Oswestry and Bishop's Castle to join at Leebotwood before running due east through Wednesbury to meet the Welsh Road that ran south-east from Whitchurch and Wrexham to London. Others came in from Builth Wells, running through Bromyard, Worcester and Alcester to Buckingham and beyond. A more southerly route from Brecon ran eastwards to High Wycombe, but alternative routes can also be traced and many bore the name 'Welsh Road'. The passage of 800 cloven hooves would soon turn a road into a muddy quagmire, although the drovers also made use of grass-grown tracks over the hills to evade tolls and obtain softer going and grazing for their cattle.[38] Some rivers were forded or swum, like the Severn at Upton or the Avon at Offchurch.

CONTESTED LANDSCAPES

Throughout the 18th century, while many members of the gentry and nobility took their social responsibilities very seriously, feeling themselves responsible for government, law and justice, and, through trade and business, for the welfare of the country, the legal system reflected their own need to protect status and property.[39] Although society remained hierarchical and hanging and transportation were common sentences for even minor theft, some illegal acts were felt to be the 'natural right' of those who indulged in them, poaching among them. The rural labourer did not always accept the actions of his 'betters' without question.

A landscape that was affected by contested claims involving reactions against the established order was that of Cannock Chase in Staffordshire. When attempts were made to enclose parts of the Chase in the late 16th century, depriving commoners for a while of their traditional sheep pastures, riots broke out. The Catholic Paget family had recently taken over from the Protestant Astons, who had previously held the hereditary office of keeper of the game on the Chase, and rivalry existed between the two young heirs of each family as they came into their inheritances. In 1580 Thomas, Lord Paget, was imprisoned for recusancy (adhering to the Roman Catholic faith) and this provided the opportunity for the first riots. Paget had cleared woodland to provide charcoal for his ironworks but had initiated the practice of coppicing to ensure regrowth. This required that grazing animals should be excluded for a time, the woods being enclosed normally for a period of seven years. The rioters, all but two from Rugeley and Brereton and already offenders who were frequently cited at the manorial courts, caused a series of fires to destroy fences that were not otherwise broken down. Their acts culminated in fights between the rioters and the keepers that involved increasing violence; they were obviously expressing their personal dislike of Paget in their actions, and were not a little encouraged by his rival Walter Aston.[40] However, enclosures were not always carried out to protect woodland or gain land for agriculture, for large acreages in woodlands and uplands were again set aside as private hunting reserves and warrens. The extension of game laws in the mid-18th century increased the powers of local landowners and their bailiffs, and the extension of pheasant shooting certainly led to stricter control over public access to woods and fields; traps set to catch poachers could inflict horrific injuries.

Matters on Cannock Chase deteriorated further in the 18th century when the Earl of Uxbridge, inheriting the estates in 1743, attempted to extend his warrens at the expense of the remaining commons where sheep vied with the rabbits for pasture. His family had long claimed unrestricted right of common within the manors of Rugeley, Haywood, Longdon and Cannock, and the rather more dubious right to free chase and free warren over the whole of the Chase, much to the annoyance of neighbouring gentlefolk over whose lands they would follow the game. Poaching had never ceased, especially among the small communities of labourers, colliers and weavers: over a third of those caught came from the villages of Longdon and Rugeley and over two-thirds from within 5km of Beaudesert Park, the Paget family seat. Punishments included fines, prison (three months for a hare, a year plus the pillory for a deer)[41] or transportation; dogs (often lurchers) were frequently hung (there are 'hanging dog' woods in many of the region's forests); families, including the old and very young, were left destitute.

But many commoners believed that they had had common rights from time immemorial, including the 'rights to take game on the Chase by ancient custom'. In the winter of 1754, they attempted to assert their perceived rights, heralding their assault by a march of 200 men, carrying 'spades and clubs at the ready, broom and rushes in their hats', past Beaudesert Hall. In this 'rabbit riot', they filled in the burrows on five of the six Uxbridge warrens and killed 10,000–15,000 rabbits (with an estimated value of over £3,000). Their achievements were short-lived, however, for after resort to the law, justice declared in favour of the earl: the warrens were restocked and many cottages torn down. In fact, the Pagets' wishes were usually followed by the Justices of the Peace (who were in any case, their friends). Due punishment was felt essential to combat idleness and profligacy among the poor: 'The eighteenth-century gentry and aristocracy were deeply convinced that the national well-being demanded an industrious poor, and they denounced endlessly the "immoral economy" of the poacher'.[42] But the hunt, the chase and the shoot were also seen as the pursuits of country gentlemen, to be restricted to those possessing land, tokens of social position to be jealously safeguarded, game a currency not to be debased. The Marquess of Anglesey, inheriting the Paget estates in 1812, immediately began the practice of surrounding his preserves with mantraps and spring guns intended to kill and maim.

Poaching figures prominently in Quarter Sessions records from the late 16th to the 19th century and it was the game laws that caused the greatest friction between villagers and gentry. After 1831, taking game without a certificate resulted in a fine rather than transportation, and hunger remained the chief motive behind the crime. However, gamekeepers were still subjected to physical assault and there are many instances of well-known local 'professional' poachers who prided themselves on their skills. Most other rural crimes were associated with drunkenness and assault but in general villages were quiet places.

Until transport radically improved in the 19th century, rural life tended to be very parochial and most people played out their lives within narrowly defined landscapes. Although market days and hirings brought people into contact, there was often a degree of reluctance to admit outsiders into one's life – even if they only came from the next village. In 'closed' parishes where landownership was concentrated in the hands of one or two proprietors, the old hierarchies were slower to break down.[43] Industrialisation in the 19th century changed the situation considerably, encouraging migration and movement, especially by younger inhabitants of the countryside or the rural poor seeking a better life in the towns and one that offered greater social freedom. By the 1870s, some of the isolation and self-sufficiency of the village community was breaking down as more and more goods were produced in towns rather than by the village blacksmith. Although schools were provided, attendance in farming districts was often poor and children often had to make long journeys on foot in all weathers, sometimes for an education that reached only minimal standards. In the 19th century, most men and boys would still have been employed on the land while many girls went into domestic service as maidservants or worked on farms, helping with minding the poultry or in the dairy. Everyone lent a hand at harvest and haymaking and there were other rural activities that looked as far as the towns for help with particular seasonal activities – like market gardening, fruit picking and hop gathering in Herefordshire and Worcestershire. At such times, rural schools would close as children helped to augment their parents' income. Rural crafts were still in evidence in the 19th century, including milling, smithing and carpentry, weaving, shoemaking and tailoring, and there were often local specialities, like needle making in the Arrow valley of Warwickshire. Earnings were generally low and many of these trades were to diminish as industrial manufacturing took over later in the 19th century and as stricter regulations were brought in to curb child labour.

RURAL RITUAL: LANDSCAPES OF THE MIND

Traditional festivities, usually organised by the Church or Chapel, offered a welcome break to heavy farm work. In the White Peak area of Derbyshire there was a long-established tradition of dressing wells with flowers on Ascension Day. Allegedly an offertory following escape from the plague, this tradition may be older but was rare outside the area. The best-known festivals take place at Tissington, Ashbourne, Barlow, Buxton, Eyam, Tideswell, Wirksworth and Youlgreave but spill over into Endon in Staffordshire and have more recently been adopted elsewhere (Fig. 5.28). During Rogationtide – the four days between Easter and Ascension Day – many parishes would 'beat the bounds' to recognise their boundaries, with the parson reading from the bible at strategic points that often bore the name 'Gospel Oak'; boys would be beaten, bumped or ducked to impress the boundaries on their minds. Most such festivities involved feasting and 'church ales' – the church alehouse still stands at Colwall in Herefordshire (Fig. 5.29). Strangely, 'May singing' and 'garlanding' was not a prominent feature of most of our region outside Cheshire. In Warwickshire, however, Coventry had a maypole until 1591 and May gatherings were stopped at Henley-in-Arden in 1655 to deal with:

> *unlawful meetings of vain and idle persons ..., for erecting of maypoles and may-bushes, and for using of morris dances and other heathenish and unlawful customs the observation whereof tendeth to draw together a great concourse of loose people*[44]

Fig. 5.28 St Milburg's (Mildburh's)
Well: a well dressing at Much Wenlock in
honour of the former abbess of Wenlock Abbey.

At Boscobel in Staffordshire the future Charles II is said to have hidden from his
Parliamentarian pursuers in a giant oak tree after the Battle of Worcester in 1651,
although the present 'royal oak' is reputed to have been grown from an acorn
from the original tree. After the formal restoration of the monarchy, on 29 May
1660, Charles restored customs discredited by the Puritans and on this date, Oak
Apple Day, celebrations were grafted onto the old May traditions of fetching
home greenery: people wore oak sprigs and oak leaves were hung in houses, as at
Bromyard and Bosbury in Herefordshire well into the 1930s. In Ludlow and the
surrounding villages, people rallied to the Crown with the ringing of church bells
and a huge fire was kindled in Worcester Cathedral Close.

Fig. 5.29 Church ale house, Colwall.
Another has recently been restored at Areley
Kings, Worcestershire.

Summer festivals were given prominence in the border country and fairs were held in June and July. Midsummer fires were still lit in Herefordshire fields to 'bless the apples' in the 17th century, although associated revels had earlier been condemned by the Reformation Church for being 'in contempt of the Christian religion, and for upholding the old frantic superstitions of papistry' (the words of the newly installed Protestant clergy installed at Canterbury in 1561). Midsummer fires continued, too, on Cannock Chase. After the heavy labour of harvest, 'Harvest Home' was a period of thanksgiving and the Church very successfully took over traditional feasting with the institution of the harvest festival in the 19th century. In the autumn, Hallowtide involved the bringing of comfort to the souls of the dead by the ringing of church bells and, in some places, by prayers said over bonfires. In Warwickshire at Hallowe'en a burning bunch of straw was carried around a field and in Shropshire people ate 'soul cakes' on All Soul's Day to seek mercy for 'Christian soules'.

A unique festival now held in September is the Abbots Bromley Horn Dance (Fig. 5.30) but in the early 17th century this was an entertainment of the Christmas season and the date was probably changed when it was revived in the early 18th century, after a lapse of up to a hundred years.[45] It was perhaps associated with Staffordshire's Forest of Needwood and had earlier been called a hobby-horse dance. One set of antlers worn by the dancers has been reliably dated to the 11th century but belong to the reindeer, not native to England and more generally found in Scandinavia, and the date at which they were brought to England is not known. Originally, the dance may have been part of a north midland tradition of hobby-horse dances employed to raise money for parish funds, well attested in the early Tudor period. The 'horse' is still part of the Abbots Bromley Horn Dance but its meaning remains obscure.

The hobby-horse was also to become an integral part of many Morris dances before the 1630s. Morris dancing (Fig. 5.31) is an activity that became popular in the court of Elizabeth I and which developed into a number of separate regional traditions, including those of Wales and the Marches, Lancashire and Cheshire; it played an important role in the Christmas celebrations of the Welsh border in the 19th century. Mumming was another Christmas celebration, the players at Ross arriving with blackened faces to represent characters like Father

Fig. 5.30 Abbots Bromley Horn Dance.

Christmas, St George and the King of Egypt. The danger presented by masked revellers had led to a ban upon the practice in Chester in the 15th century but more ritualised mummer's plays have continued to the present day, many since the 17th century incorporating sword dances. In many places in Herefordshire Twelfth Night ended with a visit to a 'holy thorn', a variety of the common hawthorn, *Cretaegus monogyna* 'Biflora', which flowers both in winter and summer.[46] Numerous cuttings from the original thorn at Glastonbury were distributed around the country and the Revd Francis Kilvert notes how he went to Dolfach in the upper Wye valley in January 1878 to see the holy thorn blossoming there. Most of the best-known specimens are now gone but a descendant lives by a narrow lane at Little Birch in Herefordshire and another stands within railings at Appleton in Cheshire, here once adorned or 'bawned'

Fig. 5.31 Morris dancing: *today a part of many local folk festivals.*

with ribbons and garlands in early July. In most of these traditions, the Church was careful to play a significant role, if only to quench any idea of 'pre-Christian' superstition and to control rowdiness.

The influence of the established Church had long been strongly rooted in every facet of rural life and especially in the main events of life – birth, marriage and death – but Nonconformity was gathering strength in Victorian England and appealed to the mass of the population. This was often fought by the established Church that continued to preach that 'God, in his infinite wisdom, had appointed a place for every man, woman and child on this earth and it was their bounden duty to remain contentedly in their niches'. Even the seating arrangements within the parish church reflected social order with the families of the squire and clergymen sitting in special pews, segregated from the rank and file of the congregation.[47] 'Chapel', on the other hand, helped to break down individual isolation and loneliness, and was presented as a place of peace and brotherly love. There were many sects and some minor groups called forth a sharp emotional response against devilish practices. Dissenters other than Unitarians and Roman Catholics had been allowed to register their meeting-houses after the Toleration Act of 1689 but they were unpopular for a while after the Old Pretender's rebellion in 1715. Methodism, however, soon flourished, especially in the growing industrial areas where many new chapels were built. It was also popular among the mining communities of the countryside. The Methodists were not alone, however, for Anglican mission chapels were also built for the squatter communities on the fringes of the commons (*see* Chapter 6). The Methodists even took to the road in horse-drawn caravans at the end of the 19th century to reach rural communities in an evangalising mission.

Rural life often fell far short of the idyll extolled by poets and writers. Although poor, rural workers usually enjoyed better health than those living in the urban slums. Respiratory diseases and tuberculosis were, however, rife among the younger people while the old suffered from rheumatism; epidemic diseases such as smallpox, typhoid and diphtheria might break out and medical care was rudimentary in the 19th century. The establishment of cottage hospitals in the 1860s was a great step forward, offering patients an improved diet and rest. Vaccination against smallpox became available in the second half of the 19th century. Cottagers often lived in cramped conditions. It was the duty of the Overseers of the Poor to find housing for the needy of the parish – and in Morton Bagot in Warwickshire this often meant a room in a cottage constructed on the commons – but for the really destitute the workhouse was often the only answer, especially for the old if their sons and daughters were unable to help in their upkeep, because parish assistance was meagre. Many of these institutions were cruelly and rigidly run, with paupers and orphans kept half-starved and married couples separated in gaol-like conditions, many miles distant from their former homes and friends. Poor relief always carried with it a social stigma (Arnold Bennett describes fear of such a 'Bastille' in the Potteries in his novel *Clayhanger*).

THE POST-WAR DECADES

The two World Wars of the 20th century made relatively little lasting impression upon the rural landscape. In the First World War, practice trenches were dug in the Peak District and near Hereford the remains of a munitions compound can still be found in the grounds of a former country house.[48] Enemy bombs in the Second World War were mainly directed upon industrial towns like Coventry. A few airfields were later taken over by flying clubs or became sites of depots and industrial complexes but most other signs are hidden and subtle, and have to be sought out by military enthusiasts. The barracks used to house the armed forces (as on Cannock Chase) or their prisoners (as in Needwood) have long since gone; country houses that were requisitioned have either been restored or demolished (*see* Chapter 6). Concrete pillboxes were built along 'stop-lines' to halt the invading forces: a line of pillboxes followed the Dove valley to defend the main rail and road routes to the north and concrete gun emplacements survive on the Avon 'stop-line' at Eckington in Worcestershire and at Holt beside the River Severn in the same county, while the Shropshire Union Canal was to serve as an anti-tank ditch protected by other pillboxes. Often the activities of the armed forces were covert and little known: Wolverton Hall in Stoulton in the Vale of Evesham in Worcestershire was the local headquarters of the Auxiliaries. Hideouts in woods, farm buildings, cellars and even deserted badger setts were meant to house the secret army that was to be left behind to harry the Germans as and when they invaded.[49] Elsewhere, there were tunnel and cave systems in the sandstones of north-east Worcestershire, like the Rolls Royce shadow factory at Drakelow that produced aircraft engines. At Fauld, close to Hanbury in Staffordshire, an underground arms and bombs depot in old gypsum mines exploded in 1944 – in what was up until then the world's biggest man-made explosion – to swallow up a farm, farmland and many mine workers, and to leave an immense crater that is still visible today.

After the Second World War, England's rural landscapes came under increasing pressure. Government policy brought about major changes: influenced by a perceived need for greater self-sufficiency during and after two World Wars, the 1947 Agriculture Act revived farming by advocating guaranteed prices for produce. Grain yields rose and the nation was provided with cheap food. Increased mechanisation, a switch from spring- to autumn-grown cereals and the innovation of fast-working chemical pesticides and herbicides were the chief mechanisms of change. New crops like rape and flax were also increasingly cultivated, their unfamiliar colours an addition to the traditional scene (Fig. 5.32). In 1973, as England and Wales joined an enlarged European Community, further payments encouraged greater efficiency in farming and 'the river of change became a flood'.[50] Crop production, especially, continued to be highly profitable: more land was broken up for the plough and 'inconvenient' hedges removed. Livestock numbers also increased, although mixed farming became an anachronism – foodstuffs could be bought in and stock intensively reared.

All of this had a serious and deleterious impact on the historic landscape, especially the ploughing up of traditional pastureland for intensive grain production. In the West Midlands, however, the effects were less disastrous than on the chalk downs of southern England. Here the infertility of most of the remaining open upland commons helped to preserve them. However, hedgerow removal, favoured because it allowed easier use of modern machinery and prevented the sterilisation of potential arable land, led to serious loss of traditional boundaries in some areas, especially during the 1980s. The quickset hedgerows planted at the time of parliamentary enclosure were not habitat-rich,

Fig. 5.32 Crops such as rape, shown here, and flax bring new colours to the English countryside.

Fig. 5.33 Multi-species hedgerow, Great Alne, Warwickshire.

but the more ancient mixed hedgerows (Fig. 5.33) provide valuable wildlife corridors in what can otherwise be a rather sterile environment. Visually, they are one of the delights of the rural scene, often set with hedgerow trees, and an examination of historical maps reveals how great the loss has been, although fortunately it is now more strictly regulated by law.

Old herb-rich pastures were also destroyed – perhaps as much as 97 per cent of England's flower-rich lowland grassland disappeared between 1930 and the mid-1980s[51] – to be replaced by mono-species grasslands or arable. The maintenance of the surviving flood meadows has been another feature to disappear, mainly through the intensification of agriculture, especially arable farming, since the 1970s (Fig. 5.34).[52]

The spread of housing and industrial development has taken an immense toll of England's farmland since the end of the 19th century and in spite of protective 'green belts' around urban conurbations it continues today. Motorways and improved roads have sliced through the countryside, blighting wide areas not only visually but with unbroken levels of intrusive noise. The last areas of water meadow along river valleys have been used as transport corridors and many are still under threat. The bulk of the country's remaining Lammas meadows – meadows managed by a traditional allotment system – lie in the midland counties of Herefordshire, Gloucestershire and Worcestershire, including the 132ha of Lugg Meadow and the 109ha beside the Severn in Twyning.[53]

Fig. 5.34 Surviving flood meadows beside the River Severn.

There has also been a change in landownership. In 1911 only 13 per cent of holdings in England and Wales were in owner occupation and in Shropshire this proportion was around 10 per cent, covering only 8 per cent of the land. By 1979, 52 per cent of Shropshire farms, covering 42 per cent of the acreage, were wholly owned by their occupiers and a further 13 per cent mainly thus owned, backed up by beneficial government policies.[54] The picture is the same across the region. New farm buildings have also changed the face of many settlements – huge over-wintering barns for livestock, sometimes at a distance from the farmhouse, are far more intrusive, if more suitable, than the old buildings they have replaced. Many of the latter have been abandoned and have collapsed; others have been converted into housing.

Ironically, over-production within Europe was to become a problem in itself, not only because it was highly destructive of traditional landscapes but because it led to the production of surplus produce that cost vast amounts to store. This has caused many policies to be reconsidered – milk production quotas were introduced in 1984 to control production, arable land has been taken at least temporarily out of production in set-aside schemes, and there has been increasing emphasis upon less intensive and less chemical-dependent farming methods. Government-sponsored schemes to 'steward' the land in ways more sympathetic to natural habitats and the preservation of archaeological or historical features have been introduced and their effects can be seen in many areas. A report by the Countryside Agency in 2004 nevertheless identified large parts of the midland region as showing 'marked change inconsistent with countryside character'. The role of the countryside has, however, changed. Today few of the people who live there are directly concerned with the land and this is unlikely to alter.

More subtle changes have also had a destructive effect on regional character. Until recent times different styles of hedge laying lent a subtle character to local areas. In the West Midlands many hedges had been strong enough to keep in livestock, particularly bullocks: ditched on one side and taller than most other styles (up to 1.5m) they provided a thick brushy barrier on the field side to keep cattle from rubbing against the laid hedge and nibbling the new shoots at its base.

Fig. 5.35 Woodland below the Malverns in Herefordshire, much of it on ancient woodland sites.

Outside Derbyshire, they were also strengthened with twisted bindings (often of hazel or willow) along the top. Mechanical cutting has now abraded many of these distinctive characteristics.

Another, more natural, change has been the loss of the elm, once a common feature of the region's hedgerows. It was so much a part of the Warwickshire landscape that it has been called 'the Warwickshire weed'. It has always been subject to disease and the Dutch elm disease, a type of fungus that prevents the tree from maturing, was known before its worst outbreak in the late 1960s and '70s. A Forestry Commission survey estimated that 75 per cent of Worcestershire's elms and 64 per cent of those in Warwickshire had been affected by 1976, with a concentration of the disease in the Severn and Avon valleys. By November 1977 most elms had been lost in the central West Midlands, one of the worst affected areas.[55] The effect has been greatest in the open areas to the south-east of our region but everywhere the loss has altered the visual landscape.

Farming sits relatively easily within the region's landscape. In spite of hedgerow loss, the great prairie fields of eastern England have little place here and the lowland parts of the West Midlands remain a mosaic of medium-sized fields separated in most areas by mixed hedgerows. Herefordshire remains the most richly wooded county, even if the woods are a mere shadow of what once existed. Much of this is can still be classified as 'ancient woodland' (*see* Fig. 5.17) although this has been augmented by woods planted in late and post-medieval times.[56] In particular, the hill slopes overlooking the Lugg near Hope under Dinmore, the Olchon valley near Peterchurch, and the western slopes of the Malvern Hills carry a mosaic of ancient woods and pastures (Fig. 5.35).

Fig. 5.36 Bluebells in Bannam's Wood, Morton Bagot, in the Warwickshire Arden.

Once so well timbered, Worcestershire's ancient woodland survives best in the west of the county, especially within Wyre (Fig. 5.37b): although this woodland was disafforested by 1700 it survived as a major source of timber and bark used in tanning processes, managed by coppicing. Arden's woodland in Warwickshire, however, has been reduced to mere sporadic patches. They are, however, carpeted in spring with the native bluebell that is (combined with dog's mercury and wood anemone) one of the indicators of an ancient woodland site (Fig. 5.36). Nor are the other counties rich in woodland – Shropshire has its Wenlock Edge woodland and more along the Ironbridge Gorge but little else. In the west of the county, Cheshire has ancient woodland along the valleys of the River Weaver, Ash and Wych brooks and on the Peckforton Hills, with newer plantations in Delamere Forest, planted on what had become open heathland, and in the east of the county within what was once Macclesfield Forest. The cloughs in the north around Lyme Park may, however, represent survivals of ancient wood-pasture. Staffordshire still has woodland along the Churnet valley and the old northern edge of Needwood (Forest Banks), plus the plantations on Cannock Chase (Fig. 5.37c), while in Derbyshire woodland survives along the Derwent, with plantations in the upper Derwent and Goyt valley. Most of the woodland on the Dark Peak had been cleared by the 18th century and any woods there now are small and fragmented.

In Gloucestershire, the Forest of Dean extends north–south in an almost unbroken span for over 11km and east–west for 6km, although to the east of Coleford it now consists mostly of replanted woodland.

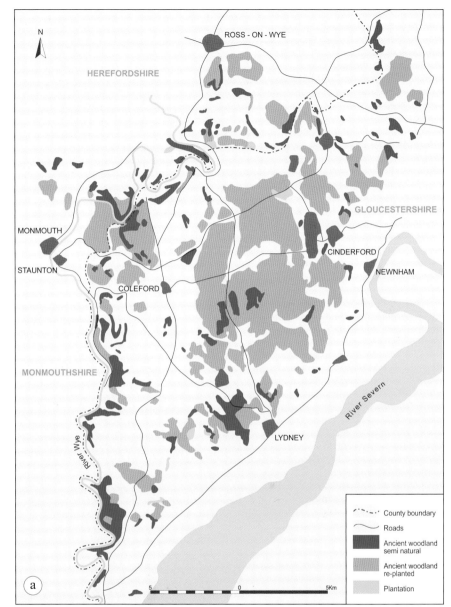

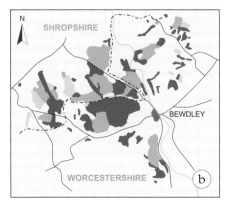

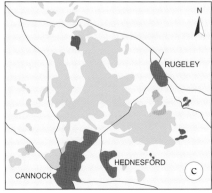

Fig. 5.37 The woodlands of a) Dean, b) Wyre and c) Cannock Chase.

Around Staunton, another pocket of woodland extends north–south for 5km to the east of the village and further woods lie to the south of Ross. Some of the best-preserved and least-disturbed stands of ancient woodland in Dean are found along the eastern bank of the Wye and in Old Park Wood west of Lydney (Fig. 5.37a).

Much of this region is an ancient landscape. Many settlements have occupied the same site for over a thousand years and the land around them has been cultivated for even longer, although the actual fields may have changed their form, their use and their boundaries over time. Some hamlets and villages have disappeared but in general the trend has been towards the infilling of the settlement pattern and the extension of farmland – a trend that has reached an unprecedented rate in recent decades. The patches of semi-wilderness that remain – woods, hills and moors – have become increasingly precious but the settled landscape also has a different kind of beauty. It is brimming with the evidence of how man has adapted it to provide for life and living over the centuries and this tale is told through the everyday features of house and field, tree and plant life, for every inch of the region is, to a greater or lesser extent, a man-made landscape.

NOTES

1   Stamper 1989, 25–6.
2   Barnatt & Smith 1997, 75.
3   Beale 1656, 1724 edn, 2.
4   Marshall, W 1789, II, 206, quoted in *VCH Herefordshire I* 1908, 427.
5   Daniels & Watkins 1994, 10.
6   Pitt 1813, 52.
7   Roberts 1973, 221; Plot 1686.
8   *VCH Shropshire IV* 1989, 77–8.
9   Palliser 1976, 127–8, citing Pitt 1796, 102–4.
10 Stamper 1989, 53.
11 Mr Darke of Bredon, quoted in Pitt 1813, 58.
12 Stamper 2003, WMRRFA, Seminar 6.
13 Ibid; Brayley & Britton 1805, 583.
14 Lake 1989, 104.
15 Yelling 1977, 185.
16 Lake 1989, 110–11; *VCH Staffordshire VI* 1979, 98–9.
17 *VCH Staffordshire VI* 1979, 100–2.
18 Ibid, 116.
19 Greenslade & Stuart 1984, 83.
20 Pitt 1813, 112.
21 Phillips & Phillips 2002, 52.
22 Enclosure acreages follow Tate & Turner 1978.
23 *VCH Shropshire IV* 1989, 171.
24 Roberts 1973, 204, fig 5.5.
25 Fleming & Gore 1979, 89.
26 Murray 1813, 140–3.
27 Stamper 2003, WMRRFA, Seminar 6; *VCH Shropshire IV* 1989, 185.
28 Lake 1989, 130–1.
29 Roberts & Wrathmell 2002, 169.
30 Trueman 1938, 88–9.
31 Roberts & Wrathmell 2000, 54, fig 48.
32 Sheppard 1979.
33 West & West 1985, 89, 91, quoting Wharton & Cobbett; Morris 1992, 31.
34 Nash 1781–2 cited in Lloyd 1993, 87.
35 West 1962, 157.
36 Williamson 1995, 104.
37 Saunders 1959, cited in Bonser 1970, 188–90.
38 Bonser 1970, 188.
39 Hay 1977, 189–91.
40 Harrison 1999.
41 Hay 1977, 236.
42 Ibid, 245.
43 Horn 1987, 1–18.
44 Easter Quarter Sessions Records, 1655, *Warwick County Records iii*, 271–2.
45 Hutton 1996, 90.
46 Palmer 2002, 200–1.
47 Horn 1987, 169.
48 Richardson & Musson 2004, 97.
49 Lowry & Wilks 2002, 14.
50 Quotation from M Cocker, 'The fall of the wild', *The Times*, 21 August 2004.
51 Fuller 1987.
52 White, P 2003, 83–4.
53 Brian 1993.
54 *VCH Shropshire IV* 1989, 156–7.
55 Wilkinson 1978, 144–5.
56 White, P 2003, 66.

6

Buildings in the Rural Landscape

FROM MEDIEVAL CASTLE TO RENAISSANCE PLEASURE PALACE

Historical events add their effects onto the landscape, both physically and by contributing to its cultural traditions. Sometimes the results are positive, as with the great 'Tudor rebuild' that changed the face of whole settlements, and sometimes destructive. Emblems of power were particularly vulnerable in times of political change. The Dissolution of the monasteries led to the destruction of the great abbeys in the 16th century while the Civil Wars of the mid-17th century led to the damage or loss of some great houses and most of the castles.

Royalist support was generally stronger in the Welsh border than in the midlands. In Cheshire, the market towns were generally for the Parliamentarians; the royal stronghold of Chester fell in 1646 and its walls were destroyed. There were sieges all across Shropshire, although none was a decisive battle of the wars. Shrewsbury castle was strengthened as one of the king's principal strongpoints, houses in its vicinity were demolished and the town walls patched up. The town fell in 1645, followed by Bridgnorth and, finally, Ludlow. The Royalists holding Goodrich Castle surrendered after a six-week siege in which the water supply was cut off, mines dug and the largest mortar in England, 'Roaring Meg', brought to bear on the keep: the roof was destroyed and the walls breached. Most castles had long ceased to be feudal strongholds and had been generally altered to provide more luxurious living accommodation. They were, however, frequently brought into use again at this time, a use that led to the destruction of many as the Parliamentarians gained control – including that at Bridgnorth, where the surviving keep, having defied attempts to destroy it, now stands at an incline of 15 degrees (Fig. 6.1). In Warwickshire, Warwick Castle is still today an impressive building, having easily withstood a half-hearted Royalist siege lasting 14 days and escaping further damage because Lord Brooke favoured the Parliamentarian cause.

Kenilworth, on the fringes of the Warwickshire Arden, illustrates the less happy fate of many such buildings. It was erected in the 12th century by Geoffrey de Clinton,

Fig. 6.1 Bridgnorth castle showing the keep after attempts by the Parliamentarians to destroy it in the Civil Wars.

Fig. 6.2 Kenilworth Castle, Warwickshire, *also rendered untenable by Cromwell's Parliamentary army.*

chamberlain to Henry I, and possessed an enormous keep built of the local sandstone (Fig. 6.2). An artificial mere some 800m long protected it on the south and west and a moat on the north and east. Because of its military strength it was taken over by Henry II during the rebellion of 1173–4 and maintained by future kings, John adding a curtain wall with towers. The hunting parks associated with the castle had been established by the reign of Henry II (*see* Figs 4.23 and 4.24). A period of neglect under Henry III left the great chamber roofless but the castle held out against the king in the baronial wars of 1266 and only surrendered under siege because of famine – the weak point of even the strongest castle – and resisted the king again for a time in 1322 during the rebellion of Earl Thomas of Lancaster. When owned by John of Gaunt, the father of Henry IV and a man of immense wealth, it was converted into a veritable palace and Henry VI sent 30 cannon for its defence during the Wars of the Roses. In a previous generation, Henry V had added a moated pleasure-house on the side of the mere called 'The Pleasaunce'. The poet, Thomas Elmham, tells us:

> There was there a fox-ridden place overgrown with briars and thorns. He
> removes these and cleanses the site so that wild creatures are driven off.
> Where it had been nasty now becomes peaceful marshland; the coarse ground
> is sweetened with running water and the site made nice.[1]

The 'pretty banqueting house of timber' was, however, dismantled by Henry VIII to provide material for lavish new buildings within the castle itself. When Elizabeth I granted the castle to her favourite, Robert Dudley, who she was to create Earl of Leicester, it reached the zenith of its period as a palace, with large windows let into the keep, a new gatehouse, pleasure grounds and a new block to replace Henry VIII's timbered range: fit for Elizabeth's visit in 1575. No longer a fortress, it had to be abandoned by King Charles at the beginning of the Civil Wars. The royal garrison was quickly withdrawn and the castle was occupied by the Parliamentarians. Like most other fortified sites, it was then deliberately rendered untenable by Oliver Cromwell in 1649 and only the living quarters spared. The keep was blown up and the outer walls breached, the mere drained. In the 18th century, the remaining buildings housed a colony of weavers but had reached their present state of ruin by the 19th century.

Dudley Castle was another that saw the transition from Norman motte to feudal stronghold (with a 14th-century keep) to Tudor mansion (Fig. 6.3). It stood at the focus of a medieval honour (a collection of estates) and a small priory subject to the castle had been founded close by in the 12th century. By 1221 the town of Dudley had developed as a 'seigneurial borough' around the castle, which dominated the town layout, and the de Someries obtained a licence for a market in 1261. In about 1550, the arch social climber John Dudley replaced the 14th-century hall with a grander great hall in Renaissance style. By this time Dudley had already acquired Warwick Castle, monastic land and manors on a grand scale and was eventually to become Earl of Warwick, Duke of Northumberland and Lord Protector of England until he made the mistake of raising a rebellion in favour of Lady Jane Grey. The earls of Dudley, however, still appointed the bailiffs that maintained law and order in the mid-19th century, thus retaining authority over the town.

Fig. 6.3 Dudley Castle: the original Norman motte can be seen to the left of the picture but the feudal stronghold of the de Someries eventually became the Tudor mansion of the Dudley family.

THE AGE OF THE COUNTRY HOUSE

Throughout the late and post-medieval period, the great country houses played a significant role in the English landscape – not only as the focus of the great landed estates which dominated much of the countryside but as the visual expression of the power, wealth and status of their owners (*see* Chapters 4 and 5). This power was based upon the ownership of land, for possession of a landed estate offered political clout and, generally, a reserve of capital; income was derived from tenants and their rents although, as we have seen, these traditional sources of wealth were supplemented and refreshed by the profits of royal service, war trade and commerce. The role of the country house in the local community cannot be overestimated. In earlier periods their owners dominated the economy of local regions, and in later historical times they not only influenced the way that much of the countryside was managed but they and their estates remained the main source of employment in rural areas. The income from the landed estate was not always sufficient to support the lifestyle it was meant to portray, however, and could be augmented by income from trade, commerce and government or royal service. While estates and country houses generally reflected the wealth of the more favoured ranks of society they were also prone to the vicissitudes of economic forces and political events.

Fig. 6.4 Lower Brockhampton, a fine late 14th-century timber-framed manor house in Herefordshire.

Although a number of great estates had been built up by those in tune with the political leadership of the country before and after the Norman Conquest, the houses of medieval landowners were in general relatively modest. Many were moated, although with a moat that was more an expression of status than defence. Lower Brockhampton at Bringsty in Herefordshire (Fig. 6.4) is a moated late 14th-century timber-framed house with a 15th-century gatehouse that melts delightfully but unobtrusively into the secluded valley in which it stands. Another fine house that was to escape much change is Haddon Hall near Bakewell in Derbyshire. It sits on a rocky outcrop overlooking the River Wye on a site occupied since the 11th century. Of local stone with a castellated frontage, the mainly 14th-century house escaped subsequent alteration. Although the gardens were remodelled in the 17th century, the house itself was deserted for the 200 years of the 18th and 19th centuries while its owners were residing at Belvoir Castle in Rutland.

The Dissolution of the monasteries by Henry VIII had released much land, which was rapidly acquired by those enjoying royal favour and holding high office. Frequently the great ecclesiastical buildings were treated as sources of stone to be sold – a deliberate attempt to prevent their re-use for religious purposes – but parts of their living quarters might escape destruction. Stoneleigh Abbey in north-west Warwickshire, for example, passed to the dukes of Suffolk in 1538. It was soon afterwards sold to the Leigh family and the remains of the Cistercian abbey survive within the largely Georgian house that the family subsequently built for themselves. At Much Wenlock, in Shropshire, the Norman infirmary of the Cluniac priory and the range added to it in the late 15th century were similarly used as the basis of a house that is still surrounded by the dramatic ruins of the abbey. Little Malvern Court in Worcestershire includes the 15th-century prior's open hall of a Benedictine monastery, while the monastic buildings of Flaxley Abbey in Gloucestershire form part of a house that was extended in the mid-17th century and restored later in the 18th.

In the 16th century, the country house became, more than ever before, a badge of status and affluence. As a consequence, a wave of spectacular houses, resplendent with turrets, tall chimneys and acres of glass – mini-palaces in fact – began to appear, especially in southern and eastern England, their grounds often laid out in schematic geometric designs influenced by the Italian Renaissance. The growing prosperity resulting from Tudor trade also increased the wealth of the merchant classes. In Staffordshire, the Leveson family, rich Wolverhampton wool merchants, bought the site of the medieval priory of Trentham. They continued to prosper and built a new house at Trentham in 1630. It was similarly a Shrewsbury merchant, Adam Ottley, who built Pitchford Hall in Shropshire (Fig. 6.5), its timbered style reflecting the wealthy town houses of the age, many of which still stand in Shrewsbury. Another fine timbered town house is Ledbury Park in Herefordshire. Although built within the town of Ledbury in the late 16th century by the Hall family, the park at its rear gives it every semblance of being a remote country house.

Fine timber-framed Tudor manor houses, whether large or small, displayed the fact that their owners were able to afford the timber for such features as close

studding. Among them, Huddington Court in Worcestershire, a small late 15th-century manor house held by the Winter family who were deeply involved in the Gunpowder Plot early in the 17th century, and the more elaborate Mere Hall in the same county, date mostly from around 1560. In Herefordshire, the mainly Jacobean Luntley Court has been described as 'an uncommonly charming house'[2] and as 'the *beau ideal* of a timber-framed manor house'.[3]

Throughout the Welsh borders and the West Midlands, houses like these are jewels in the landscape. The most elaborate timber framing of the period is found in the border counties, Little Moreton Hall in Cheshire having been described as the finest example of a timber-framed moated manor house in that county. Built between 1450 and 1580, its top-heavy appearance, formed by its now-reeling Elizabethan long gallery, gives it an air of deceptive fragility, for it has stood for over 400 years. Its elaborate timbered patterning is echoed in other Cheshire houses, such as Gawsworth Hall near Macclesfield, and in Derbyshire by Somersal Hall. The grand Italianate garden designs of the grandest palaces were seldom adopted at this level of the social hierarchy and Tudor knot gardens and herb gardens filled their courtyards with more intimate flowers and greenery.

Houses were continually rebuilt or improved in the styles of the day to portray the status and wealth of their owners. Few expressed the ambitions of their owners more than Hardwick Hall in Derbyshire, built in 1597 by Bess, Countess of Shrewsbury, which incorporated nearly 1,500 panes of blown glass (Fig. 6.6). Bess became the second richest woman in England after the death of her fourth husband, and intended the house to be a palace fit for a royal dynasty, an ambition that was never realised. Expressions of status were also extended to the grounds of country houses, with landscaping styles changing almost as often as that of the buildings themselves.

Brick was being used for some important buildings in the 15th century, mainly in the eastern counties, but improved techniques of brick making in the Tudor period extended the geographical spread to Middlesex, Hertfordshire and Cambridgeshire. Beyond this, brick houses like Plaish Hall in Shropshire were exceptional. It was not until Elizabethan and Stuart times that the use of brick became more general: Sudbury Hall in Derbyshire, with its diamond-patterned brick, remains one of England's finest Stuart mansions. It was begun by Mary

Vernon in 1613 but only completed after the Restoration of 1660 and is one of the most individual of late 17th-century houses.

In the early 17th century, Inigo Jones introduced an Italian Renaissance style into England, which entailed the symmetry and regular fenestration that he introduced in his plans for the Banqueting Hall in London's Whitehall. But his style was too new to be assimilated into most domestic architecture and it failed to replace the still-popular late Jacobean style that had developed from Elizabethan architecture, as seen at Aston Hall, Birmingham (*see* Fig. 6.23). The days of English Palladianism were yet to come.

Towards the end of the 17th century, the practice of 'strict settlement', in which the old estates had been entailed to prevent their fragmentation, was breaking up, and richer landowners were acquiring the ability to consolidate both their estates and their political power. The Crown was selling hereditary titles and ostentation was not only a display of power and wealth but also an expression of political views. The baroque style of architecture, with its curves and florid opulence, provided this. Houses newly built or simply remodelled could also be set amidst elaborate gardens which might include *parterres de broderie* and turf lawns around the house, with *bosquets* or ornamental woods beyond, and canals reflecting the Dutch influence. Flowers were used sparingly, like jewels set in velvet. The symmetry of house and garden is illustrated, for many such houses, in the engravings of Kip, Knyff and others, as at Hampton Court in Herefordshire, or Chatsworth in Derbyshire (Fig. 6.7). The west front of Chatsworth, a house that had, like Hardwick Hall, been built by Elizabeth Shrewsbury, was entirely remodelled in baroque style. The scheme was instigated by William Cavendish, 1st Duke of Devonshire, an opponent of the reigning monarch James II and of Catholicism, but was not finished for many years, due to repeated differences between Cavendish and his craftsmen. Eventually completed by his wife after his death, it was described by Defoe as 'a most glorious and magnificent house'.

The two most flamboyant English baroque houses were both designed by Sir John Vanbrugh, but lie well outside our region – Castle Howard in Yorkshire, and Blenheim Palace at Woodstock in Oxfordshire, built between 1705 and 1722 for John Churchill, 1st Duke of Marlborough. Unfortunately, most of the elaborate gardens designed for such houses, involving laboriously sculpted parterres and elaborate designs cut into lawns and even groves, have been swept away. The

OPPOSITE PAGE:

Fig. 6.6 A remarkable change: Hardwick Hall, Derbyshire, built to express the ambitions of Bess of Hardwick in 1597. Pevsner, not unimpressed, writes of its hardness, 'its uncompromising, unnatural, graceless, and indomitable self-assertiveness'.

Chatsworth   180 foot Front

Fig. 6.7 Baroque flamboyance with elaborate garden settings towards the end of the 17th century: Knyff's view of Chatsworth c. 1700 (The Devonshire Collection, Chatsworth).

symmetry provided by long avenues and French canals, with the addition of fountains and other water features, became too much for later tastes and often it is only through pictures, plans or archaeology that such gardens can be reconstructed. Those of Charlecote in Warwickshire, for instance, a house built for the Lucy family in 1558, are only shown in a picture of 1696 (Fig. 6.8) and on later historical maps.

Landowners, however much a showcase of power they created in their country house, expected to spend much of their time in London, strengthening their power base at court or in central government. But their movement around the country would help to bring an element of 'town culture' into what were still relatively isolated rural areas.

Fig. 6.8 The formal gardens at **Charlecote** *destroyed by Brown to make his new 'natural' park.*

THE AGE OF ELEGANCE

It was the 18th century, the 'Age of Elegance', which really witnessed the pinnacle of the country house ideal. The Whigs, supporters of the Revolutionary Settlement of 1688 that curtailed the power of the Crown, and of the Hanoverian succession, a measure of religious tolerance, and a foreign policy geared to peace,[4] came to power early in the century and brought a sense of security to estate owners, especially as agriculture was becoming more prosperous. Landowners dominated local and national politics and expressed their power and ideologies in both architecture and landscaping. Palladianism was the new architectural fashion, one of symmetry, grace and proportion with little extraneous ornament (characteristics already introduced to the 'formal houses' of Inigo Jones). A rectangular central block could be connected to side pavilions by lower galleries and colonnades, sometimes creating an impression of austere severity, although the first influence of the style was expressed in ordered internal house plans. This was, in part, a reaction to the grandiose architecture of the later Stuarts, for the Whigs deliberately chose to return to a more rational and less complicated style.

Palladianism claimed to be a more faithful interpretation of ancient architecture than the baroque style favoured by the previous Tory administration, based upon 'natural', perhaps God-given, rules of architectural design,[5] and supposedly expressing 'the divine harmony that lay behind the external world'.[6] The seeds of Palladianism had been planted much earlier, however, in Classical designs such as those of Robert Hooke at Ragley Hall in Warwickshire, originally built in 1678 but now dominated by a massive portico added by Wyatt in 1780. It made use of Greek and Roman styles – Corinthian, Doric, Ionic and Tuscan – allegedly rediscovered in Italy in the 16th century. Tabley House at Knutsford in Cheshire, completed in 1767 for the Leicester family who had lived at Tabley for over 700 years, is a particularly fine Palladian mansion. Another mansion, designed by Sanderson Miller, also on Palladian principles, was completed in 1760 at Hagley near Kidderminster (Fig. 6.9), for George Lyttelton, later the 1st Lord Lyttleton, a Tory who obtained considerable finances from his court jobs as Secretary to the Prince of Wales, then, successively, Lord of the Treasury,

Cofferer to the Royal Household and Chancellor of the Exchequer. It was planned with a private sector to the east grouped around one staircase and a public sector to the west grouped around another staircase, these linked by the hall and saloon (a room often used for dancing), as in the style of the earlier formal houses.

Throughout this period, houses were either built anew or remodelled to fit the current taste. Lyme Park in Cheshire, the family home of the Leghs since the 14th century, was given a new imposing frontage by Giacomo Leoni in the 1720s that, with

Fig. 6.9 Palladian elegance and symmetry: Hagley Hall, West Midlands.

its vast Ionic portico, has been described as 'one of the boldest achievements of Palladian architecture in this country'.[7] It stands within a 570ha medieval deer park. After 1750, a further shift in taste to a neoclassical style culminated in a Greek revival at the end of the century. A fine example of a neoclassical house is Kedleston Hall in Derbyshire, built between 1759 and 1765 for the Curzon family and little altered since.

The grounds of such houses, too, were to be provided with classical temples and the Palladian geometry transferred to the garden buildings and parkland. As the main reception rooms of the houses migrated from the first to the ground floor, the vistas onto which they looked had to be redesigned to allow them to be properly appreciated from this new lower level. This gave rise to a proliferation of groves as the chief ornaments of the garden and a complexity of paths; wildernesses were threaded with paths and studded with temples and sculptures of the kind familiar to any English country gentleman who had visited an Italian villa estate during his Grand Tour of the Continent. At Hagley, the 18th-century garden architecture included not only a 'Prince of Wales' column, an obelisk and a Temple of Theseus, but also a mock ruined castle nestling at the foot of the Clent Hills (Fig. 6.10). This, built in 1745, may have been the first deliberately built ruin erected in England. The idea that ruins could be incorporated into a design to provide atmosphere and improve the view – to create the picturesque *landskips* so admired at the time – quickly gained ground. Grottos were another introduction, involving the construction of cave-like chambers decorated with shells, fossils and coloured or unusual stones. Even the home farm could become ornamental and a *ferme ornée*, as a *landskip* in its own right, formed part of William Shenstone's design begun in 1743 at The Leasowes near Halesowen

Fig. 6.10 Eighteenth-century 'ruins': Hagley 'castle', from the Clents.

(now a golf club). The complicated styles that had dominated earlier geometric garden design were, however, beginning to be simplified at this time, as in the work of Charles Bridgeman, with more attention being paid to the landscape at increasing distances from the house. Old elaborate designs were to be 'naturalised' and William Kent, one of the new garden designers, attracted the praise of Horace Walpole:

> He leaped the fence and saw that all nature was a garden. He felt the delicious contrast of hill and valley changing imperceptibly into each other, tasted the beauty of the gentle swell, or concave scoop, and remarked how loose groves crowned an easy eminence with happy ornament.[8]

Some of the finance necessary to maintain these houses was 'old' money, invested in land and ancient estates that had been inherited down the generations and often assiduously augmented by careful marriages. Wealth could, moreover, attract even greater riches by placing its fortunate possessors in line for high office in court or government, as in the case of the Lyttletons at Hagley. Some professions also offered opportunities to those who scaled their heights, while other gains came from fortune in war or trade. Berrington Hall, near Leominster in Herefordshire, was built for Thomas Harley, the son of the 3rd Earl of Oxford, an ex-banker and former Lord Mayor of London who had held a lucrative government contract to pay and clothe the British forces in America. The new house, designed by Henry Holland and finished in 1781, is a plain but elegant rectangular neoclassical building with its roof hidden behind a balustrade and, at its entrance, a pedimented Ionic portico reached by a sweep of shallow steps (Fig. 6.11). It is set above the wide valley of a tributary of the River Lugg with views west and south to the Black Mountains and Brecon Beacons.

William Anson, who bought Shugborough in Staffordshire in 1624, was a Staffordshire lawyer, but much of the finance for the remodelling of the house in 1745 by his grandson Thomas came from the capture of a Spanish trans-Pacific galleon and its £400,000 cargo by Admiral George Anson, Thomas' younger brother, during his circumnavigation of the globe in 1740–4.[9] Some have even claimed that the galleon and its treasure were worth £800,000 – more than £50 million in early 21st-century terms – of which Anson obtained a three-eighths share.[10] The house at Shugborough was again extended in 1794–1806, to the

Fig. 6.11 New money: Berrington Hall, Herefordshire.

designs of Samuel Wyatt, by Thomas's great-nephew who became the 1st Viscount in 1806. The park was also enlarged at this time, with the removal of what remained of the village and the establishment of a model farm. The re-designed house is unusual in that the Ionic portico built by Wyatt stretches across the whole width of the central block; most of the slate exterior covering of the house has subsequently been replaced by stucco.

Elsewhere in the region, it was Clive of India who commissioned Sir William Chambers to remodel Walcot Hall at Lydbury North in Shropshire in 1736, while Eye Manor, in Herefordshire, was built for Ferdinando Gorges, a Barbados trader, in about 1680, on the proceeds of the slave and sugar trade.[11] Industry, too, was providing 'new' money, especially in the 18th and 19th centuries. At Cromford, overlooking the Derwent, it was the engineer Richard Arkwright's son, another Richard, who started to build Willersley Castle in 1789 with money from the family cotton business. In the event, this first building was burnt out before it was finished, to be replaced by a 'great plain house' bearing the same name. At Trentham, the Levesons had become marquises of Stafford by the late 18th century, with extensive midland estates, but their wealth was augmented by marriage that brought them additional estates in the Scottish Highlands, and from the coal and iron that lay beneath their Staffordshire and Shropshire properties: by 1883, they owned more land in Britain than any other aristocratic family.[12] Further to the west, Apley Park and its estates in Stockton, Shropshire, was bought in 1867 by William Orme Foster, a vastly rich Coalbrookdale ironmaster who had also inherited his father's and uncle's fortunes. Minor industrialists, too, were acquiring a new standing in society and were anxious to establish themselves as minor gentry; like their predecessors they frequently appear to have equated social status with the ownership of land, thus perpetuating the 'existing myths about the relative importance of landed as against commercial wealth'.[13] The barriers between the old aristocracy and new wealth were nevertheless breaking down as 'polite society' absorbed an ever-growing middle class.

Fig. 6.12 Berrington Park, Herefordshire, a 'Capability' Brown landscape.

THE NEW GARDENERS

The settings of country houses were now to change dramatically from the elaborate geometrical gardens of earlier times. Thomas Harley, when he first visited the Berrington estate in Herefordshire, had been accompanied by Lancelot 'Capability' Brown, whose designs were to provide a complete break with earlier formality and who in 1780 went on to create a 5.7ha lake in the grounds (Fig. 6.12). Brown's new approach was also to carry landscape planning out into the further countryside. Plainer, grander landscape settings for Palladian houses had already been devised by Bridgeman, and symmetry abandoned in the designs of William Kent, but it was Brown who altogether shunned linear planting and the long-admired avenue in favour of woodland with curvilinear edges, scattered clumps of trees and fine isolated specimens (often retained from the earlier landscape), sinuous lakes and serpentine carriage drives. Geometric formal gardens were to be swept away and the pastoral park carried right up to the lawns of the house, with animals kept out by the use of a concealed ditch known as a ha-ha. The largest lake created by Brown is to be found at Chillington, near Codsall Wood in Staffordshire, while at Moccas in Herefordshire his restoration of a deer park with probable medieval origins allowed it to become one of the finest in the county, noted too for its ancient oak pollards.

Now the landscape was to look 'natural', to express the 'genius of the place'. Moreover, the shelter-belts and woodland plantings could provide privacy, keeping the rest of the world at bay. Increasingly, entire settlements might be moved to create such seclusion. The planting of trees accentuated the impression of power in the land. 'Avenues, ridings, belts, clumps and screens were arranged to emphasize the apparent as well as the actual extent and unity of an estate', and planting was also seen as a patriotic duty, providing much-needed timber for the shipyards.[14] Brown's first parkland design was at Croome in Worcestershire, commissioned by the 6th Earl of Coventry in 1751. Here he replaced decaying elaborate Dutch gardens with rolling meadows, a lake and no fewer than 4.8km of shrubbery walks; he is even said to have designed the Palladian house although Sanderson Miller may have contributed to the initial design. At Charlecote, beside the Warwickshire Avon, Brown also replaced elaborate gardens with more natural parkland. He filled up ponds, and altered slopes to create 'a natural, easy and corresponding level with the house on every side',[15] dammed a brook to create a cascade and used a ha-ha which made 'the browsing deer appear to tiptoe on the very edge of the cedar lawn'.[16] At Chatsworth, he 'naturalised' the 1st Duke's formal gardens (Fig. 6.13) and at Warwick he created a new park

Fig. 6.13 Chatsworth, Derbyshire, standing within Brown's parkland: the earlier gardens have been swept away.

on the south side of the Avon to make a fitting vista from the castle for its owner, Lord Brooke. Entertainment of friends and family on a grand scale was very much a part of the country house ideal. By the mid-18th century, guests would expect to walk around a garden or drive around a park, and the creation of a suitable circuit thus provided another reason for replacing the axial planning and avenues of an earlier period.

Some, however, found Brown's landscapes 'boring' and of 'bland simplicity'. Although Humphry Repton promoted himself a successor to Brown, he took greater care to integrate the park into the wider landscape, using shelter belts to allow selected views from the house and park, making a property appear more extensive than it really was. He has, indeed, been regarded as 'the inventor of the English park'. He firmly believed that signs of ownership should be spread throughout an entire estate by paying attention to other buildings or the addition of ornamental features such as an obelisk – the public image of a place. Two houses that received Repton's attention are Tatton Park near Knutsford in Cheshire and Attingham Park in Shropshire. Tatton Park is a house of neoclassical design commissioned by the Egerton family who had held the estate for some 200 years. Provided with a grand portico set between side wings designed by Samuel Wyatt and built in stages from 1780 to 1813, it was set amidst 400ha of parkland in 'one of the most splendid historic estates in Europe'. Its grounds were to be landscaped by Repton, who would present his clients with illustrated details of his proposals in a 'Red Book', many of which survive.

Attingham Park was the name given to Tern Hall, 6km to the east of Shrewsbury, when it was inherited in 1783 by Noel Hill, 1st Baron Berwick, and transformed into a classical mansion. A new façade was added to the early 18th-century Queen Anne house and given cohesion by the addition of a central pedimented portico with four tall columns, its classical grandeur somewhat alien to the Shropshire landscape. Repton moved the location of the entrance drive at Attingham and reinforced the planting of the park with shelter-belts, although his designs for weirs and watercourses were not always adopted – a large lake designed for Beaudesert in Staffordshire was never made. Repton followed a 'softer' approach than Brown, even allowing flowers and fountains close to the house.

Repton's views brought him into contact with two Herefordshire landowners: Uvedale Price and Richard Payne Knight, the first holding an estate at Foxley in the south of the county, the second, a seat at Downton in the north (Fig. 6.14). At Downton, Knight, an ironmaster, had built his 'castle' between 1774 and 1778 and was to promote the preferences of the Revd William Gilpin for variety, surprise and interesting detail in a landscape – elements which included roughness and ruggedness, gnarled ancient trees and ivy-clad

Fig. 6.14 Downton, Herefordshire, the Picturesque ideal: the house and lands of Richard Payne Knight.

ruins, always incorporating a foreground, middle ground and far distance, as in a picture. At Downton, the River Teme flows in a narrow, precipitous gorge ideally disposed for Repton's aims and which allowed him to augment the natural attraction of the place in ways that would increase interest: 'large fragments of stone were irregularly thrown amongst the briars and weeds, to imitate the foreground of a picture'.[17]

Knight and Price were particularly against 'clumping and belting' within bare spacious lawns that were brought right up to the 'poor square edifice [of the house] exposed alone'. They called for a garden of 'neat gravel walks, mown turf, and flowering plants and shrubs' around the house or, if the latter had been abandoned, 'neglected paths, rugged lanes, and wild uncultivated thickets'.[18] Hanging terraces of Italian gardens were thought suitable for a house on an eminence and Price, in particular, welcomed the addition of flowers, especially the rose, which in due course 'was the flower that was to conquer the nineteenth-century garden'.[19]

Price's theories were put into practice at Hawkstone, near Marchamley in Shropshire, by Sir Rowland and Sir Richard Hill, the former having been Lord Mayor of London in 1759. An escarpment overlooking a valley was brought into the landscape, to accord with the rough and rugged view of Nature held by Knight. In its day, this was one of the most celebrated of the 'sublime' landscapes.[20] Here there was already a ruined medieval castle (the 'Red Castle') perched on a rock. Features included more than 6km of walks, a shell-encrusted grotto, a vineyard laid out with fortifications and turrets, walls and bastions, an Elysian hill, an 'Awful Precipice', a Gothic greenhouse, a Chinese temple, a Moorish tent, a menagerie and a hermitage. Such houses were meant for visiting and some, indeed, were almost the 'theme parks' of the day – at Hawkstone, it is claimed that there was an attendant dressed as a druid while a 'hermit' would come out of his cave as visitors approached waving two bloody stumps instead of arms and crying '*Memento mori*'.[21] Although described as a place of 'terrific grandeur' by Dr Johnson, its taste was perhaps being questioned when he concluded that 'the house was magnificent compared with the rank of the owner'.[22]

Such an impression might well have appealed to the Victorians who developed their liking for exotic images much further. A new era of plant collecting ushered a passion for the display of exotic plants, with the result that both houses and gardens became ever more theatrical. Gothic turrets and castellated towers were to arise in the countryside. Chateau Impney near Droitwich in Worcestershire (Fig. 6.15) was built by a Parisian architect between 1869 and 1875 as a Louis XIII chateau to please the French wife of the salt manufacturer John Corbett. In Staffordshire, John Talbot, the 15th Earl of Shrewsbury, transformed the ruined medieval castle of Alton into an extravaganza of a battlemented house replete with towers and turrets, as its new name, Alton Towers, was to suggest, 'one of the wonder houses of the kingdom', set amidst grounds 'unexcelled for beauty'.[23] Within the grounds are follies that include Grecian and Gothic temples, a three-storeyed pagoda and an edifice of boulders known as 'the Druid's Sideboard'. Eaton Hall in Cheshire was to be remodelled by the Duke of Westminster in the 1870s with the addition of a tall Gothic tower and associated chapel, and in the same county Peckforton Castle was built in

Fig. 6.15 Victorian exotica: the French-style 'chateau' built by the salt manufacturer John Corbett at Chateau Impney, Worcestershire.

1844 as an unusually good Victorian reproduction of a medieval castle. Such
nostalgia for a bygone age had been growing since the early 19th century and
already, in about 1812, Robert Smirke had designed a new baronial-style 'castle'
at Eastnor Park in Herefordshire for Lord Somers, complete with towers,
battlements and a baronial hall. The Gothic, Tudor or Elizabethan styles:

> *conjured up images of an old-style English gentleman, dispensing hospitality
> in a great hall, with fires blazing in the great arched fireplaces, smoke rising
> from innumerable chimney-stacks, comfortable groups gossiping in ingles
> and oriels, and generous sheltering roofs over all.*[24]

During the 19th century, estates continued to change hands. Some old landed
families were ruined, sometimes due to extravagance and sometimes for political
reasons: 'A much commoner cause of trouble ... was the widespread assumption
among genteel landowners at every level that estates could be endlessly milked
for levels of expenditure considered necessary to maintain their place in society
but unrelated to the income the land could yield'.[25] In Shropshire, the Craven
and Apley Park estates were broken up and the latter sold in its entirety in 1867.
There was, however, no shortage of
newly rich industrialists or
commercial men eager to purchase
and they had money from their
business fortunes to invest.

*Fig. 6.16 A new 'Elizabethan'
style: late Victorian splendour at
Madresfield, Worcestershire.*

   Little expresses this 'romantic
nostalgia' more forcefully than the rise
of the Arts and Crafts movement of
the late 19th century with its attempts
to return to a 'medieval' value of
craftsmanship. At Madresfield in
Worcestershire (Fig. 6.16), where a
brick-built Tudor mansion had already
been enlarged in the late 16th and late
18th centuries, the 5th Earl
Beauchamp and his brother, the 6th
Earl, used a largely inherited fortune to
create a new Elizabethan style
reconstruction after 1865. Much of the
interior decor reflects the Arts and
Crafts style much favoured at the turn
of the 20th century, with the former
entrance hall converted into an 'open
hall' complete with a minstrel gallery that incorporates a cast-iron balustrade, a
heavily decorated chapel and a library designed by C R Ashbee, a leading
designer in the movement. With timber framing reminiscent of a medieval hall,
Wightwick Manor, near Wolverhampton, was another new house that was
entirely decorated and furnished in the style of William Morris and the Pre-
Raphaelite Movement. Built between 1887 and 1893 and little altered, it is a rare
survival of its type. Other country houses were simply enlarged to house the
suites of apartments and armies of servants felt to be essential for the
entertainment of guests. Often such accretions detracted from the earlier
symmetry. Grand house-parties in the mid-19th century might fill such a house
for a week and in addition to the house servants there was a need for gardeners
and gamekeepers – at Witley Court, in Worcestershire, it took 25 full-time
gamekeepers to maintain a stock of partridges, pheasants and deer. In the
countryside, woods were maintained for shooting and coverts were planted
among the fields to provide shelter for game birds.

Ornamental parks came to be oases of pastoral rurality in the landscape, even if their imparkment occasionally meant the desertion of a former village or the closure of roads. In Shropshire, for example, settlements were moved at Bitterley and Upton Cressett, while in Staffordshire others were relocated at Enville (to make way for a new walled garden), Shugborough and Great Sandon. Roads were similarly diverted at Morville, Little Bragginton and Alberbury in Shropshire, at Madresfield in Worcestershire and at Studley in Warwickshire, where removal of a hamlet and associated road closure is said to have drawn upon all future owners of Studley Castle a curse of bankruptcy. Settlement displacement was, however, often accompanied by the construction of better estate housing (*see* below).

Today, the parks of these country houses often preserve mini-landscapes of fine pastures dotted with specimen trees. The latter are sometimes ancient pollards, but are often mature exotic species introduced in the heyday of the ornamental park: avenues of Wellingtonia at Oakley Park, Shropshire; Cedars of Lebanon at Kingsland House, Shropshire and Rowton Castle, Cheshire; Britain's finest *Ginkgo biloba* at Whitfield House, Herefordshire; a magnificent fern-leafed beech, *Fagus sylvatica*, in Kyre Park, Worcestershire. Indeed, the West Midlands has been described as the 'parkiest' of all the regions in England and Wales.[26]

The influence of these great houses was felt much more deeply and further afield than their own private parks, for large proportions of the countryside formed part of gentry estates and contributed to their income (*see* Chapter 5). Industrial resources on an estate could also be exploited. Woodland was felled to supply the growing ironworking industry, as in the Ironbridge region, but here demand eventually led, by the 16th century, to the planting of coppiced woodland to ensure supplies. The owners would often build furnaces and forges that were then leased to specialist ironmasters. Downton, in Herefordshire, had iron and timber resources: Bringewood Forge, owned by the Knight family, was producing 450 tonnes of iron goods a year in 1717, and by 1794 there was a charcoal furnace with a finery and three chaferies;[27] the Knight family also held other furnaces at Bouldon, Willey and Charlcotte in Shropshire, at Flaxley (as occupiers) in Gloucestershire and at Doddington in Cheshire. At Attingham, near Shrewsbury, an ironworks in 1717 was producing 300 tonnes of iron goods per annum from the Tern Forge on the river within the present park. By 1712 the Boevey family at Flaxley in Gloucestershire were also the owners of charcoal-fired blast furnaces on their estate and in 1794 the plant there consisted of a charcoal furnace, two fineries and a chafery.[28]

Most of the iron furnaces recorded at this time were in the hands of the big estate owners, although industry enabled some industrialists to become big landowners in their turn. The Foleys of Stourbridge, profiting from the opportunities of the Civil Wars, were leasing charcoal-fired iron furnaces from the 1630s through the 18th century to build up an unprecedented business empire; they held furnaces as far afield as Gloucestershire (Bishopswood, Blakeney, Newent, Flaxley and Longhope in Dean), Herefordshire (Linton, St Weonards), Shropshire (Willey), Staffordshire (Meir Heath, Madeley) and Derbyshire (Foxbrooke). It was Thomas Foley who bought the substantial house at Witley Court in Worcestershire in 1655. Landowners were also active in furthering and improving communications in the 18th and 19th centuries. The Trent and Mersey canal passed through the estate of Josiah Wedgwood at Etruria in Staffordshire, and the waterway was indeed widened to form an ornamental feature for the mansion, while at Tixall in the same county the canal was formed into a lake below the lawns of Tixall Hall.[29]

One of the most impressive mansion houses in Worcestershire has to be Witley Court (Fig. 6.17), although it remains only as a shell after a disastrous fire in 1937 (after it had been sold by the Dudleys in 1920). Here a Jacobean house that had belonged to the industrialist Foley family was purchased in 1837 by William

Humble Ward (later 1st Earl of Dudley) who had been forced to abandon his former home at Himley Hall in Staffordshire after it had been rendered 'uninhabitable' by the foundation of the nearby Oak Farm Iron Works in 1836. The house at Great Witley was considered too modest by Dudley, who commissioned a breath-taking new design by Samuel Dawkes in about 1860. The replacement house was clad in Bath stone and a giant portico of seven bays was built to overlook the garden, ending in a pavilion with large pilasters and columns – 'a Victorian version of Blenheim or Versailles in the Worcestershire countryside'.[30] The garden was equally impressive, laid out according to the ideas of 'Capability' Brown in the earlier 18th century but redesigned by Nesfield in the mid-19th century with two enormous classical fountains, one depicting Perseus on a horse, prancing in baroque abandon 8m above the water. To allow

Fig. 6.17 Witley Court, Worcestershire, *showing the shell of the burnt-out house and the restored Perseus fountain.*

the fountains to be played twice a week, 18,000 litres of water had to be pumped (by a 40-horse-power beam engine coupled to two Cornish boilers) from a nearby pool to a reservoir 1km away. The garden and the fountains have recently been restored by English Heritage.

Victorian gardens were to become more and more exotic as new plants were introduced – dahlias, new roses, fuschias, camellias, chrysanthemums, tree paeonies, hydrangeas and rhododendrons all became available to add their colour to an already overflowing palate. This trend has been described as the 'Display Garden ... the taste of whose owners quite frequently bore no relation whatever to their wealth'.[31] New ideas, too, streamed in: there were early 19th-century gardeners like John Loudon ever ready 'to disseminate new and important information on all topics connected with horticulture, and to raise the intellect and the character of those engaged in this art',[32] not only to the wealthy but also to the urban middle class through works like his *The Suburban Gardener and Villa Companion*. The accoutrements of the garden might now include rustic huts, arches, or cascades; the lawn mower, invented in 1830 and patented in 1832, allowed lawns to be more easily maintained and the availability of cheap coal allowed glasshouses to be heated to protect the less hardy newcomers introduced from subtropical and tropical lands. When William Hooker was appointed Director of Kew in 1844 he had Decimus Barton design a Palm House, while eight years earlier Paxton had built the Great Stove glasshouse at Chatsworth, the precursor of the Crystal Palace in which the first banana to ripen in England was sown.

A garden recently restored by the National Trust at Biddulph in Staffordshire shows the exuberance of the High Victorian era. When James Bateman moved here in 1840, he designed separate enclosed areas for groups of plants from different parts of the world, offsetting them with suitable architectural features: today a gilded water buffalo looks out over the Chinese garden where stretches of the 'Great Wall of China' and a temple provide a setting for tree paeonies and other exotic plants (Fig. 6.18); the Near East is evoked by a pyramid of yew flanked by Egyptian sphinxes. In 1883, William Robinson produced his *The English Flower Garden*, a book that advocated the cultivation of introduced species as 'wild flowers'. Although producing jumbled mixtures in innumerable beds, this did lead on to the naturalising of narcissi and daffodils in grass, a quintessential feature of many of today's 'natural' gardens. When Gertrude Jekyll added the subtle colour grouping of her designs, the foundation of the 'English garden' was complete.

Fig. 6.18 Restored Victorian gardens at Biddulph, Staffordshire.

THE END OF AN ERA

Country houses, if their owners were financially successful, had rarely remained unaltered through the ages. Baddesley Clinton in north-west Warwickshire, the particularly attractive part-15th-century moated manor house of the Ferrers family (Fig. 6.19), only escaped modernisation because the family, staunch Catholics, were repeatedly fined heavily for adhering to their faith. New generations, and new owners, were elsewhere keen to adopt the latest architectural styles to exhibit their status and perceived importance. The great peril facing large houses was fire, a danger increased by the presence of wooden panelling and the vast number of candles used for lighting before the days of gas and electricity. Even after the introduction of electric lighting, the list of great houses destroyed in this way in our region is long – it includes Stoke Edith in Herefordshire, gutted by fire in 1927, the timber-framed mansion of Park Hall near Oswestry, burnt in 1918, and the Moorish Gothic 'Castle' designed by 'Capability' Brown in 1756 at Tong and burnt down in 1913. Cheshire losses included Carden Hall in 1912, Oulton Park in 1926 and Alderley Park in 1931. Some, however, were rebuilt or restored, like Hagley Hall in Worcestershire, which had been damaged in 1926 in a fire caused by a defective flue.

Fig. 6.19 Baddesley Clinton, Warwickshire, an almost unaltered part-15th-century moated manor house in the Warwickshire Arden.

Unchallenged privilege and access to ample supplies of deferential labour to service large estates and households were the lifelines of the country house. By the later 19th century all this had come under serious threat. After the 1850s more people lived in the towns than the countryside, and although the impact of this was slow at first, finding adequate supplies of the right sort of servant became increasingly problematical. This was exacerbated by the agricultural depression that began to bite in the 1870s. Rising taxes added to the burden of falling rents and incomes. By the beginning of the 20th century, the majority of large country houses were ageing buildings requiring substantial investment. In Staffordshire, most of Trentham was pulled down in 1911, further blighted by the growing industrialisation of its surroundings; its demolition by the Duke of Sutherland was not due to any lack of wealth 'but because of the stinking steam of pollution which rose from his lake'.[33] The First World War was the final blow to the accepted order. Hundreds of thousands of men were lost in the trenches, affecting both the management and the day-to-day operation of these labour-intensive estates. Furthermore, the war had created expectations of a return to homes 'fit for heroes' and a further loosening of the deferential bonds that made the country house tick. The old distinctions within society could never be reinstated.

While fire may have been responsible for the demise of houses such as Witley Court, others were simply too large and cumbersome for their owners to maintain. In Worcestershire, for example, the late 19th-century agricultural depression with its resulting fall in rents, augmented by rising taxes, death duties and the after-effects of war, hastened the decline of the aristocratic and gentry families, most of whom had in any case never counted among the top ranks of the peerage. Of the 44 houses listed in *Burke's Landed Gentry* for 1871, 31 had changed hands by 1937.[34]

Many owners had possessed more than one country house and the time had come to rationalise their possessions. However, there was little market for large greedy houses that offered limited returns. The Marquess of Anglesey, whose main seat was at Plas Newydd in Anglesey, was unable to sell Beaudesert Hall in Staffordshire (Fig. 6.20) when he offered it for sale in 1932 despite its possession of an estate of 813ha and the fact that it had only recently been renovated. The original Tudor house had undergone several heavy-handed alterations after it had been damaged by fire in 1909, but in spite of the money spent it was to be sold eventually for demolition. Its fine Waterloo staircase found a new home at Carrick Hill in South Australia, leaving only the shell of its former banqueting hall and a few other ruins standing among derelict gardens (Fig. 6.21); its lands were later given, in lieu of death duties, to the King George V Memorial Trust for

Fig. 6.20 View of former hall at Beaudesert, Staffordshire, before demolition.

Fig. 6.21 The ruined shell of Beaudesert Hall today – the remains of the banqueting hall.

recreational purposes, today housing guide and scout camps. Drayton Manor in Staffordshire, the impressive 'Jacobean' house of Sir Robert Peel, a wealthy 19th-century industrialist with interests in the weaving and calico industries, was another house lost at this time. Many of its contents were sold between 1871 and 1900 and again after 1925, followed by the disposal of its estates in 1926 and by the final demolition of the house soon afterwards. The site was later to house a zoo. At Tixall in Staffordshire, where the great house was demolished in 1927, a solitary gatehouse now stands incongruously isolated in a field (Fig. 6.22).

Industrial or urban plight affected other houses besides Trentham. Wedgwood's Etruria Hall stood within an industrial landscape of smoking pottery kilns by the end of the 18th century, abandoned by the family in favour of a new home in Barlaston. Sutton Scarsdale near Chesterfield in neighbouring Derbyshire, the great baroque mansion house built by the 4th Earl in 1724 and later occupied by the Arkwright family, remains now as an impressive shell among the detritus of the coal-mining industry – following its partial demolition, in 1920, three of its rooms were transported in their entirety to the Philadelphia Museum of Art. Aston Hall (Fig. 6.23), a splendid early 17th-century Jacobean mansion in the heart of Birmingham, was once set within a park stocked with herds of fallow and red deer. In 1864 it was purchased by the City Council, initiating a fine tradition of urban house rescue, and has since been maintained as a museum; by contrast, the nearby Great Barr Hall had to find a new use as a mental

Fig. 6.22 Tixall gatehouse, Staffordshire.

Fig. 6.23 Aston Hall, Birmingham.

institution. Today, too, Shugborough is leased to Staffordshire County Council and houses the county museum.

Sadly, in the 1950s and '60s many other fine houses found no such new use; at the peak of the crisis, in 1955, a country house was being demolished every two and a half days somewhere in Britain.[45] In Shropshire alone, of 90 country houses standing in the 1870s no fewer than 35 had entirely disappeared by 1952.[36] In a wave of post-War destruction, Herefordshire lost, amongst many others: Aramstone, a house dating from the 1730s and once described as 'the most important house of its date in the county';[37] Goodrich Court, an enormous fantasy house inspired by the ruins of the nearby castle built in the 19th century; Eywood at Titley and Harewood Park – the latter, already abandoned by World War II, was finally blown up by the SAS in 1952. Perhaps Herefordshire was seen as something of a backwater in the 1950s, for its losses were greater than those of many other counties. Shropshire's casualties around this time included Apley Castle near Wellington, Badger Hall, Onslow Hall, and Shavington at Moreton Say; Staffordshire's Teddesley Park. Many, like Teddesley, or Uvedale Price's wonderfully dignified Foxley in Herefordshire, had been damaged when requisitioned by the army in the Second World War. At Alton Towers, the conservatories had been machine-gunned from the grounds above by the troops on one particularly boisterous evening. Death duties crippled other families. A few large houses escaped the fate of demolition by becoming schools: like Tunstall, Moreton Hall, Lutwyche Hall, Apley Park and Pell Wall in Shropshire – although in the cases of Cheyney Court and Knill Court in Herefordshire this did not prevent them from subsequently being burnt down. In Worcestershire, Hewell Grange now houses a prison and Hindlip Hall is the headquarters of the West Mercia Police; in Cheshire, the Palladian Tabley House near Knutsford is used partly as a nursing home. What is left of the Earl of Shrewsbury's great Gothic house at Alton Towers now stands amidst one of the largest fun-fairs in Britain.

The large estates which had supported these houses were similarly broken up or lost substantial acreages, their owners sometimes moving overseas. It was said in 1954 that the former Southern Rhodesia (now Zimbabwe) 'seemed to be peopled entirely with Shropshire county families and Central European refugees'.[38] Much land was acquired by the National Trust: in Shropshire, 2,213ha of the Long Mynd were acquired with the lordship of the manor of Stretton-on-the Dale in 1965. Other estates, like Madresfield, were kept together only by being placed under trusts. Land has also gone to financial institutions such as pension funds and insurance companies but there has also been an increase in owner occupation by previously tenant farmers.

While in the 1950s and '60s many unwanted country houses were being turned over to institutional uses, their attraction and potential is now being recognised anew. Some have gained a fresh life as elegant apartments, as in the case of Westwood Park at Hampton Lovett in Worcestershire, or as hotels and conference centres. At Hawkstone in Herefordshire, a golf course now winds its way through the park but most of the follies remain unscathed. Chateau Impney in Worcestershire is now a hotel and Teddesley, today a mere shell, is to be rebuilt to its 17th-century design to serve a similar use. Castle Bromwich Hall, set amidst its fine restored gardens (Fig. 6.24), has been bought privately and may be restored to single-family ownership. The main saviour of the country house, however, has been the National Trust and today many that it holds can be visited by the public. All are maintained to a high standard and at Ticknall in Derbyshire, just outside our region, the National Trust has deliberately preserved Calke Abbey, a baroque mansion built at the beginning of the 18th century, in its state of late 19th-century decline. A number of country houses have enjoyed literary associations that have kept them in the public eye. Apley Park in Shropshire, formerly used as a school but now again a private home, is a claimant for P G Wodehouse's 'Blandings Castle', and more recently some others have provided the setting for films and BBC productions: in Cheshire, the 18th-century Tatton Park was used for the television series *Brideshead Revisited* (the film version is moving to Chatsworth) and Lyme Park is the 'Pemberley' of the film version of *Pride and Prejudice*.

Other changes have also taken place. Many small farms are no longer viable unless amalgamated with others, with the result that surplus farmhouses have become modest country homes for businessmen. Redundant farm buildings have similarly been converted into houses, but only a few entirely new mansions have been built in this region. Their time, however, is not entirely past: a new Georgian-style house was built near Halford in Warwickshire in the 1990s and Wootton Hall in Staffordshire is another new house built on classical lines. At Harewood, in Herefordshire, the Prince of Wales is rebuilding, in a classic design, the former hall. But new country houses need not necessarily look to the past for architectural inspiration: a radical and futuresque 'starfish' house has been designed as Grafton New Hall in Cheshire although at the time of writing it has not yet been built (or found a purchaser).

Fig. 6.24 Castle Bromwich garden restoration.

CHURCHES AND RURAL HOUSING: BUILDINGS FOR THE PEOPLE

With such a varied geological background, the region's vernacular architecture is rich and diverse. The church, for generations governing every major stage of life and ordering the pace and timetable of rural society, was the focus of every parish. The great cathedrals of Hereford, Worcester, Chester and Lichfield stood at the top of the hierarchy and the three spires of Lichfield Cathedral still form a soaring landmark visible for miles around (Fig. 6.25). To them has been added Coventry's new cathedral, built to replace the one destroyed in the Second World War. Most of the great abbey churches suffered with the demise of their parent houses, but on the edge of the region in the Severn valley, the church of Tewkesbury Abbey

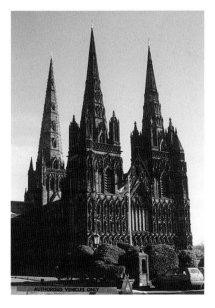

Fig. 6.25 Lichfield Cathedral.

was taken over by the town and its great Norman nave survives in splendour (Fig. 6.26). The church of Abbey Dore, in the Golden Valley of Herefordshire, was to lose its nave and only the crossing, transepts and chancel remained in use as a parish church (Fig. 6.27); at Leominster, the townspeople took over most of the abbey church but it was subsequently damaged by fire, so the monks' nave now stands to one side and leads nowhere.

The brightly coloured walls of the medieval churches were whitewashed over by the Puritans in an attempt to eradicate 'idolatrous' images and practices – the use of candles was likewise forbidden. Even in their newly acquired simplicity, however, the churches were – and still are – one of the delights of the countryside: from hidden gems like Herefordshire's Pudleston, with its chimney, or churches with detached bell towers like those at Richard's Castle and Pembridge, to the rococo white and sky-blue interior of the church rebuilt at Shobdon in 1752, the ornate baroque of St Michael's at Great Witley, Worcestershire, and the richly decorated Roman Catholic Pugin churches of the Churnet valley in Staffordshire. The latter included Alton Towers, where Pugin's was a finishing hand; St Giles in Cheadle, regarded as his masterpiece; and, further afield, St Alban's in Macclesfield: these are all worth seeking out.

While most early churches were ultimately to be rebuilt in stone, some timber-framed examples survive and are remarkably beautiful. The timber-framed churches of the borderland are well known, and those of Cheshire are a speciality of that county – the 14th-century churches of St James and St Paul at Marton

ABOVE: *Fig. 6.26 Tewkesbury Abbey* interior showing the Norman pillars of the nave.

Fig. 6.27 Abbey Dore church, Herefordshire. The ruins of the abbey's nave adjoin the surviving chancel of the church to the north-west.

and of St Oswald at Lower Peover are amongst the oldest, but others include Old St Werburgh's at Warburton, Chadkirk Chapel at Romiley, All Saints' at Siddington and St Luke's at Holmes Chapel.

With the rise of Nonconformity, a new breed of chapels arose, especially in industrial areas. At Hanley in Stoke-on-Trent, Bethesda Chapel is a fine example of a building that was the first New Connexion Chapel of an early break-away sect of Methodism, opened in 1798 but with a facade of 1859 (Fig. 6.28). Nonconformity was strongest in the industrial centres in the late 18th century but also spread throughout country regions in the 19th century (*see* Chapters 5 and 7). Many simple Nonconformist chapels, and some Anglican mission

Fig. 6.28 Bethesda Chapel, Hanley, Staffordshire.

churches, were erected to serve the squatter communities that were settling around the commons, especially in mining districts. The Anglican mission church at White Grit, on the border of Shropshire and Wales, was built for a community of lead miners. Rebuilt after a fire, it is a simple corrugated iron building (Fig. 6.29).

Of domestic dwellings, very few truly ancient houses survive and there is now no trace of the timber-framed longhouses that were still a recognised type of building in Worcestershire in the late medieval period. In that period, dwellings in the county were usually of cruck construction, open to the roof, and of one to five bays in length, the majority in the midland counties averaging two or three bays and nearly all of them of only one storey.[39] Most of the houses of substantial yeomen farmers were rebuilt in later centuries and have survived. Excluding Derbyshire, the English midlands has been seen as 'the home of black and white buildings'.[40] However, very few labourers' cottages are at all old.

Of the houses of the rural poor, Pitt, referring to Worcestershire at the beginning of the 19th century, commented:

> *The cottages, analogous to the farm buildings, are of different ages of construction ...; in the ancient villages and common field parishes, they often consist of timber and plaster walls covered with thatch, and are merely a shelter from the weather ...* [41]

Fig. 6.29 The mission church at White Grit, Shropshire, rebuilt after a fire.

Indeed, in the 16th and 17th centuries a 'cottage' was usually little more than a one-room structure of mud or weak timber with a roof of thatch. Heating and cooking were served by a fire on the bare earth floor whose smoke filtered out through the roof or holes in the walls (known as 'wind eyes'). There was absolutely no internal sanitation.[42] Many cottages were erected on the edges of the commons and wastes and the 1662 Act of Settlement attempted to prevent the poor from moving on to new situations with 'the most woods for them to burn and destroy', seeking to tie a man to the parish where he had been born. In 1663, the Worcestershire Quarter Sessions drew attention to the 'great number of cottages lately erected' that 'has caused this county to abound with poor more than any county we know of'.[43]

Most of today's 'cottages' were in fact the homes of yeomen farmers and were much more substantial dwellings than the wretched mud and stick hovels on the village wastes. On the lowland plains, timber, preferably freshly cut green oak, was still readily available for building in the 17th century. Cruck framing was an earlier form of arched construction widespread across the region but restricted the roof space available. Dairy Farm at Weobley in Herefordshire is a cruck-built open hall farmhouse of 15th- or early 16th-century date. The 'base-cruck' found in Herefordshire and Worcestershire is not a true cruck for it ended at the collar beam and could also be raised on a wall – it was usually reserved for buildings of quality associated with wide spans. The cruck frame was generally to be replaced by 'box frame' and 'post-and-truss' construction. In the former, the roof is a simple 'lid' resting on the wall-plate, but in the latter the roof consists of a series of transverse frames or cross-frames that include roof trusses with tie-beam and posts, the frames linked by means of wall-plates.[44] This method of building can support a heavy roof, the weight taken by the purlins, and is characteristic of the border region where the roofs are of heavy sandstone slabs, derived either from the Old Red Sandstone of Herefordshire, the Ordovician and Silurian rocks of the Welsh borderlands, or the sandstones of the Coal Measures. It also lent itself better to jettying, which increased the area of the upper floor, especially in towns where space was scarce, by allowing it to project out from the line of the ground floor.

Close studding (narrow panels between closely-spaced vertical timbers or studs) is also more characteristic of the western part of the region. This is found in some of the richer houses by the 16th century but required too much valuable timber when supplies were diminishing, so that most 17th-century timber framing is lighter and used in a square-panelled frame. Inside, timber posts would support horizontal beams tied together with wooden pegs. The panels were filled with wattles of oak rivings or hazel withies that were liberally daubed with a mixture of clay, manure, straw and animal hair, finished with a coat of limewash plaster to cut down draughts – the so-called 'wattle and daub' that has survived adequately to the present day. In many regions, the timbering was traditionally left to weather to a natural shade of silver-grey, but in the north midlands and along the Welsh border a blacker shade was often obtained by soaking cattle blood, paint or pitch into the timbers. The antiquity of this fashion is open to question for the style was copied widely in Victorian times – even Little Moreton Hall was not treated in this way until then and, like many others, is now being returned, by the National Trust, to its original state. Among the close-studded buildings, Huddington Court in Worcestershire and Lower Brockhampton Manor in Herefordshire (see Fig. 6.4) are fine examples of the manor-house class (see above). The latter has fine carved bargeboards, carrying a design of a trailing vine, intended to protect the projecting roof timbers of the house and gatehouse.

Timber framing, usually with square panels, is found across the whole region, for ample woodland was generally present. Roofs might be of thatch or tiles. Not only the wealthier yeomen's farms but also small houses and farmhouses have used this method of construction. In the Welsh borderland, more elaborate timber patterning was common, typically smaller more restrained versions of the

Fig. 6.3 Weobley town, Herefordshire.

ornate kind found in the mid-16th-century Little Moreton Hall or the 16th- or 17th-century Chorley Hall on Alderley Edge in Cheshire. The use of flamboyant criss-crosses, curves, zigzags and quatrefoils set into the panels has been termed a 'magpie' style. This is not to everyone's liking and has been described by one author as 'a somewhat tasteless exuberance consistent with the flamboyance of the late Tudor, Elizabethan and early Stuart ages in which so many of the larger houses were built'.[45] It is doubtful if many would agree. The 'black and white' villages of Herefordshire are gems in the rural landscape. From the small market town of Leominster (where the Old Town Hall was built in 1633, incorporating a patterned design), a 60km trail has been laid out that takes in Dilwyn, where timber-framed houses are grouped around a village green; Eardisley, where the houses line the village street; Weobley, a small town with a wealth of timber-framing; Pembridge, where almost every building is of this kind and cottages and inns cluster around an early 16th-century market hall; and Eardisland, beside the tranquil River Arrow. Weobley and Pembridge were indeed boroughs in the Middle Ages, both receiving their charters in the 13th century.

Weobley (Fig. 6.30) was still a rotten borough in 1646, granting its holder access to Parliament. It grew up at the foot of a motte-and-bailey castle that was probably built by the de Lacys at the end of the 11th century, but nothing remains of any later stonework. The town stands aside from any present-day main road with superlative timber-framed buildings, some of which date from the 14th century (even the reticent Pevsner was led to describe it as 'uncommonly rich in early timber-framed houses'), each side of the main Broad Street and a fine part-Norman church at the northern end of the town (*see* Fig. 4.5b). A particularly interesting house on the outskirts of the town has been painted in the rich deep rose popular in Tudor times. In the 16th century, the wealth of the town was augmented by the manufacture of gloves and the brewing of ale. In Worcestershire, Ombersley and Abbots Morton are equally fine villages with an abundance of timber-framed houses (such as the Old Rectory at Abbot's Morton). Isolated black and white farms nestle among the hedgerows and fields of most of the midland plain.

ABOVE: *Fig. 6.31 Dormston church* with *its timbered bell tower, central Worcestershire*.

ABOVE RIGHT: *Fig. 6.32 A timbered dovecote at Himbleton* in central *Worcestershire*.

Timber framing was not confined to houses. As noted above, it was not infrequently used in churches as well, and there are some especially splendid examples in the borderland. It is also found in the bell-towers of churches such as Pirton, Warndon, Kington and Dormston in mid-Worcestershire (Fig. 6.31), or Morton Bagot in the Warwickshire Arden – places that were never rich enough to 'spoil' their churches by over-restoration. Timber-framed barns are common across the region but even tiny dovecotes are built in this way at Huddington, Himbleton (Fig. 6.32) and Wichenford in Worcestershire, and elsewhere. Some of the midland's grander 'tithe barns', used to store manorial produce especially on church estates, were also timber framed; some were six bays or more in length. These include a cruck-framed barn on Church Farm at King's Bromley in Staffordshire, while that at Leigh Court in Worcestershire is the largest true cruck building extant. Built in about 1300, perhaps by the Abbot of Pershore, it is 42m long and 10.2m wide internally. Others in our region include a barn on Rectory Farm at Longdon in Worcestershire that served another early Pershore estate. The walls of the cruck-framed barn at Dean's Hall Farm at Brewood in Staffordshire, like many others, have now been rebuilt in brick. Such large barns can be expensive to maintain and that at Church Farm, Dosthill, Staffordshire, has now been converted into dwellings. At Leigh Court, however, the great barn is maintained in its original form by English Heritage.

The clays of the plain regions were much used to make brick and tiles. At first, the use of brick was confined to chimneys and door arches and only later used for whole buildings. To begin with, the bricks and tiles were made close to the point at which they were required (often leaving patches of red-coloured clay in the fields) and until the mid-16th century their use was practically confined to churches and wealthier houses. The bricks themselves were small and often weathered into a warm orange colour. A diamond pattern could be reproduced in walling by the use of over-fired bricks whose ends had turned blue in the kiln – a pattern much admired in Tudor times. In the 18th century, bricks were made in temporary kilns, often set up on village greens, and clay was dug and baked by the roadside before brick taxes were introduced after 1784. Houses of brick were not uncommon by the 18th century, ousting timber as the most popular material for walling, and some farmhouses were of three storeys.

Since the clays used were obtained locally, the colour of the finished bricks depended very much upon the type of clays from which they were made. This helped the houses and farm buildings to fit into the natural landscape and sit comfortably within their surroundings. On the Cheshire plain many are of a dusky red-brown, near Lichfield in Staffordshire they are a pale, washed-out dusty red, and in Worcestershire often dark red in colour; roofs are generally tiled. Different bonding patterns could also be used to lend variety. The square frames of timber-framed houses were also often filled in with brick, especially in the towns but also in some country regions from the 17th century. A decorative herring-bone brick infill, easier to fit into the panels, was often chosen. As methods of production became mechanised, and methods of transport greatly improved, brick became almost ubiquitous for houses everywhere. Power-driven grinding and mixing machines replaced the old hand-operated pugmills in about 1850 and extended the range of clays that could be used. With roofing now commonly of imported Welsh slate, brick houses spread throughout urban and rural districts all over the country.

Although cob, made from unbaked earth, was used in poorer houses in south Warwickshire (a cob-walled barn stands close to the church at Tredington) it was not a common building material in this part of the country. While timber-framed barns were the norm in the midlands during the 17th and 18th centuries, 19th-century 'model' farms were invariably built of brick – well laid out around farmyards to conform to up-to-date farming practice. The best layout was considered to have the stables and granaries, cart shed and byres on the east and west sides and a large barn on the north side to provide shelter for a south-facing yard. The building of open sheds and yards was an innovation of the 18th century.[46] Usually confined to great estates like those of the Marquis of Stafford at Shugborough in Staffordshire, most purpose-built model farms were located in the more profitable areas of eastern England while small farmers managed by adding extra stables and pigsties, cart sheds and dairies to their existing buildings.

Where stone was readily quarried it was widely used for housing, but with the exception of parts of southern England, its widespread use for smaller houses only stems from the beginning of the 17th century. The different kinds of stone available have helped to shape the nature and appearance of rural housing and, hence, the visual character of regional landscapes. The solid gritstone houses of the Dark Peak cling to the sides of the barren moorlands within their defiant patches of improved in-bye land (Fig. 6.33). The stone was also used in the cottages of textile workers in growing towns like Macclesfield and Bollington. Roofs are invariably of stone slabs derived from the brownish sandstone strata found immediately beneath the gritstone or from similar formations in the Coal Measures. They are heavy and keep the water out well so that the pitch is often low; eaves hardly overhang at all and the slab chimneys are situated at the ends of the roof. In the White Peak, the lighter grey-white Carboniferous Limestone is used everywhere for houses, farm buildings and field walls. Villages such as Tissington attract almost as many tourists as the mellow honey-coloured villages of the Cotswolds outside our region to the south. The pale-coloured Liassic limestones of the Jurassic belt, which outcrop as bands within the

Fig. 6.33 A gritstone farmhouse near Hathersage, Derbyshire.

clays in Worcestershire and Warwickshire in the south-east of the region, have also been used for building but produce a much less durable construction material. Limestone, too, has been used along Wenlock Edge – here a pale grey, almost lemon-grey, Silurian Limestone and roofs are normally of stone taken from the Hoar Edge area west of Much Wenlock.

The Old Red Sandstones of the border region have been much used for building although, like the New Red Sandstones of the later Triassic beds, they tend to spall and crumble badly when exposed to the weather except for isolated samples that are of far better quality. The use of this stone is virtually confined to Herefordshire, south Shropshire, Worcestershire and parts of Gloucestershire west of the Severn – the western parts of our region. The sandstones of the Ross region of Herefordshire have also been used for houses, such as the unusually-shaped mid-17th-century Newhouse at Goodrich with three protruding wings, but sandstone farmhouses and cottages are common across Herefordshire and Shropshire, especially on the hill farms of the Welsh border, and are often roofed with small clay tiles. In the valleys and on the hillsides below the Black Mountains, 16th- and 17th-century farmhouses often have wide, double-storeyed porches to protect them against the weather and their cowsheds and barns were frequently built for shelter on the downhill side. Sometimes the barn, used to house cattle and hold the winter feed, was built into the hillside as a 'bank barn' that allowed access at two levels – the cattle below and the stored hay above. This a type that first appears in the uplands of western Britain in the 17th century and in a true bank barn the upper floor could be used for threshing.[47]

Timber buildings could be moved and re-erected, or the timbers of older houses reused. This is often revealed by peg holes that are no longer part of the construction, although the suggestion that these were previously ship's timbers is generally erroneous. Not only were timbers reused but older houses have been found now converted into barns, as at Upper Spernall in Warwickshire. At Aston Eyre in Shropshire, a medieval hall is now a barn and another medieval hall house survives at Wellsbrook Farm near Peterstow in Herefordshire. Stone from abandoned buildings was soon 'robbed' to build others and it seems likely that this was the cause of the destruction of the Montford's castle at Beaudesert in Warwickshire, which still stood at the time of Leland's travels in the 16th century but whose stone was later carried away to be used in the houses of Henley-in-Arden below. Occasionally, more unusual materials were used in house building – a house of blocks of furnace slag exists in the Forest of Dean and one with iron lintels, window frames, doorsteps and chimney pots survives close to Coalbrookdale in Shropshire.[48]

House plans can also vary across the region – the longhouse, in which animals were quartered at one end under the same roof as the living quarters, separated by a cross passage, is today mainly a feature of south-western England but was once more widespread in the midland region. This linear plan was better suited to small upland farms rearing cattle and to buildings on sloping ground where the byre could be on the downhill side to permit adequate drainage. Some have survived in the Black Mountains area of Herefordshire, as at Black Daren in Llanveynoe, where a house of cruck construction with stone walls probably dates from the 15th century, and at Cwarelau near Newton.[49] A derivative of the longhouse was the linear farm, in which the byre was contiguous with the living quarters but with its own entrance, merely sharing the same roof line. These are not uncommon in the southern Pennines in Derbyshire and in the adjoining areas of Cheshire and Staffordshire. In most midland farmhouses, however, animals were quartered separately by the 15th century.

Medieval houses generally had an open hall but additional cross-wings could subsequently be added at each end, one containing the parlour with solar above for the family and the other the service rooms, including the buttery and pantry. Some timber-framed farmhouses from Derbyshire southwards maintained the medieval concept of a hall range with a cross-wing or wings, and in Herefordshire and Worcestershire one type had an axial stack serving the hall and parlour, as at Tardebigge Farm in Stoke Prior and Keys Farm in Bentley. Most farmhouses, however, were smaller and simpler, often with just a few rooms set in a linear plan but lacking the longhouse byre and with additions such as projecting pantries and wash-houses. Towards the end of the 18th century, square double-pile houses began to replace earlier elongated plans, with a ground floor of parlours and a kitchen, chambers above and often, too, attics. As with grand houses, Georgian design favoured symmetry and if a new house could not be built then a new façade might be added incorporating a new fenestration scheme.

An addition to the settlement pattern sometimes occurred as landowners rebuilt villages to more modern standards of design, some deliberately 'picturesque' in quality. At Ilam, in Staffordshire, a new village was begun by Jesse Watts Russell in the 1820s after he had made a fortune in industry. It stands below the spectacular mansion he also rebuilt around its original core; even the church was reconstructed and the village is dominated by a stone imitation of an Eleanor Cross, raised in memory of Russell's wife. Joseph Paxton, the Duke of Devonshire's head gardener, similarly created a new village at Edensor while re-shaping the park at Chatsworth (Fig. 6.34). The designs of estate houses were culled from pattern books of the time and ranged in style from Gothic, Renaissance and Tudor to Georgian, Italianate and Swiss 'chalet'. They produce 'a self-consciously picturesque and romantic' effect, at Edensor said to express the 6th Duke of Devonshire's 'taste, good feeling and liberal disposition towards those in humbled circumstances'.[50]

At Eastnor in Herefordshire, a complete village of picturesque cottages, including a thatched post office, was built by the Somers family to complement the new 'castle' built around 1812 (*see* above). A drinking fountain was provided on the village green and the school and stores were built to fit the overall scheme. Another estate village in Herefordshire was constructed at Brampton Bryan, while at Quatford in Shropshire all the cottages have barge boards and lattice-work porches and were sited below a mock castle; at Quat, near by, further stone and half-timbered cottages were situated along the roadside. Towards the end of the 19th century many of the more progressive estates were rebuilding substandard cottages for their tenants. In contrast, the cottages erected by squatters around the region's commons were simple buildings that

Fig. 6.34 Edensor, Derbyshire, a model village close to Chatsworth.

often used local stone, but few survive in anything like their original condition (Fig. 6.35).

History can thus be read in the buildings that survive today, records of the social and economic vicissitudes of the ages. Houses have always reflected the social standing of their inhabitants and building styles have been, indeed, deliberately manipulated to reflect wealth and status. This has not been confined to the houses of the gentry, for many farmers were moderately wealthy yeomen. In towns, merchants were often the wealthiest members of society. What we rarely see, however, are the meaner dwellings of the poor: many of today's rural 'cottages' were originally small farmhouses and humbler dwellings have usually failed to survive.

Fig. 6.35 A settlement below Titterstone Clee, Shropshire, *that probably began as a quarryman's cottage.*

NOTES

1   Excerpt from Thomas Elmham's *Metrical Life of King Henry V*, trans Thompson 1964, 223.
2   Pevsner 1963, 112.
3   Reid 1980, 45.
4   Williamson 1995, 15–16.
5   Ibid, 42.
6   Reed 1987, 166.
7   Fedden & Joekes 1973, 140.
8   Walpole, quoted in Fleming & Gore 1979, 98.
9   Fedden & Joekes 1973, 180.
10 Bettey 1993, 113.
11 Reid 1980, 24.
12 Taylor 1998, 122.
13 Williamson 1995, 113.
14 Daniels 1988, 45.
15 Brown quoted in Beevers & Meir 1994, 28.
16 Alice Fairfax-Lucy, *Charlecote and the Lucys*, 1990, quoted in ibid, 29.
17 Loudon 1969, 354.
18 Payne Knight 1806, quoted in Fleming & Gore 1979, 160–1.
19 Fleming & Gore 1979, 161.
20 Milln 2003, WMRRF, 7.
21 Tinniswood 1989, 75.
22 Quoted in Rowley 2001, 175.
23 Mee 1937, 22–5.
24 Girouard 1978, 272–3.

25 *VCH Shropshire IV* 1989, 209.
26 Milln 2003.
27 Riden 1993, 56.
28 Ibid, 39–40.
29 Bettey 1993, 106.
30 Palliser 1976, 195.
31 Fleming & Gore 1979, 171.
32 Ibid, 174.
33 Harris 1998, 2.
34 Cannadine 1982, 37.
35 Harris 1998, 5.
36 *VCH Shropshire IV* 1989, 254, citing Thompson 1963, 342.
37 Reid 1980, 4.
38 Newspaper reports quoted in *VCH Shropshire IV* 1989, 255.
39 Field 1965; Dyer 1994, 139.
40 Penoyre & Penoyre 1984, 95; *see* Roberts & Wrathmell 2002, 26, fig 1.12.
41 Pitt 1813, 21–2.
42 Woodforde 1969, 9, 14.
43 Dorothy M George, quoted in ibid, 12.
44 Brunskill 1994, 40–7.
45 Penoyre & Penoyre 1978, 99.
46 Wade Martins 1995, 85.
47 Ibid 1995, 72.
48 Laws 1992, 91.
49 Brown 1985, 91.
50 Bettey 1993, 112.

7

Industry, the 'Industrial Revolution' and Urbanisation

Industry had been present in the West Midlands long before the Industrial Revolution. Most medieval towns had their local crafts and industries based upon local agricultural and livestock products such as tanning and leather working, and the woollen industry of the region was a major source of wealth in the early Middle Ages. The making of gloves was a feature of the economy of Stratford-upon-Avon, Bewdley, Worcester, Nantwich, Chester, Hereford and many other country towns in the 16th century. Bewdley was also the centre of the Worcestershire woollen cap-making trade from the 16th to the 18th century, a craft also found in north-east Warwickshire at the time. Brewing was carried out in many parts of the region. The industries of a market centre like Leominster in Herefordshire in the 18th century were not untypical for a rural market town: leatherwork was the main craft, with some weavers and flax dressers, a few braziers and tinmen. But industry was also widely scattered across the rural countryside, developing wherever natural resources were available.

Major technological improvements were already underway in the 18th century, especially those involving water power, but more dramatic changes were to take place at the end of the century. The technological innovations funded and led by a number of entrepreneurial families transformed the character and location of many industries, and manufacturing processes were increasingly organised on a factory basis. The shift to a population willing to sell its labour to employers rather than relying on producing goods within its own households was one of the most visible facets of the so-called 'Industrial Revolution', although it did not happen across all industries at the same time. Some of its earliest beginnings were in the silk industry of Cheshire and the cotton industry of Derbyshire. It was at Ironbridge in Shropshire that technological invention pre-eminently allowed the region to become known as 'the cradle of the Industrial Revolution', but the Black Country also made claims to some of the earliest technological achievements. Such developments led inevitably to regional concentrations of industry, and in turn to growing urbanisation and the beginnings of today's 'consumer society'. But technological innovation was not entirely the rapid 'starburst' often assumed; frequently it drew upon earlier inventions, not all of them British.[1] The silk industry, for instance, was boosted in the 18th century by the introduction of Piedmontese throwing machines from Italy. It was the earlier industry, too, that laid the regional foundations for subsequent development. In spite of the rise of manufacturing in the 19th century in the rapidly growing industrial towns, outworking continued to play an important role, involving perhaps as much as 12 per cent of the British workforce as late as 1850.

TEXTILES

The medieval woollen industry had flourished in all the region's sheep-rearing districts. The swift streams along the edge of the Pennines around Macclesfield and Congleton were used to drive fulling mills. In the south-eastern Peak there was a fulling mill at Hartington by the 14th century and three on the Derwent by 1555. In Cheshire, linen cloth was woven from flax grown along the damp lowlands of the Dee valley, and the retting or softening of hemp and flax was an important activity around Kidderminster in Worcestershire and in parts of the Warwickshire Arden. For a time in the 16th century there was even a legal requirement to cultivate hemp (*Cannabis* sp.) as the raw material for making rope. Hemp was also widely grown for the manufacture of nets and, in Arden and elsewhere, many farms still have fields near the house known as the 'hemp pleck' and ponds formerly used for retting the fibres.

Some regional specialisation in textile production was already beginning to take place before the Industrial Revolution: Worcester broad-cloths were noted until the end of the 16th century. Shrewsbury in Shropshire was described by Defoe in the 18th century as:

> … *a beautiful, large, pleasant, populous, and rich town; full of gentry and yet full of trade too; for here too, is a great manufacture, as well of flannel, as also of white broadcloth, which enriches all the country round it.*[2]

Macclesfield, by the early 17th century, was known for its buttons made from padded wool or horn and embroidered with silk, linen thread or horsehair. Silk was first hand-thrown in east Cheshire, with weavers operating at Stockport, Congleton (which was also important for lace making) and Macclesfield, and later at Leek in Staffordshire. As silkworms could not be bred commercially in England, raw silk was mainly imported from Italy, although by the later 18th century increasing amounts were being brought in from Bengal and China. The silk mills pre-date Arkwright's cotton mills by a generation and have, therefore, a claim to being the true precursors of the industrial and economic system that became known as the 'Industrial Revolution'. By 1765, Macclesfield had seven major silk-throwing firms and east Cheshire had about one-third of the total silk mill capacity of England, the three main centres being Macclesfield, Congleton and Bollington. The mills were built along the banks of the rivers Bollin, Dane and Dean, whose water flows were altered and improved through the constructions of weirs and diversionary channels. Water-powered mills were subsequently also built along small tributaries that were dammed to provide an adequate water supply. In the 19th century, the last generation of mills became steam powered and were located close to canals and railways.[3] Many of the mill buildings remain, although now converted to other uses (Fig. 7.1).

Fig. 7.1 A Macclesfield mill building.

At the other end of the region, Coventry was noted for its woollen cloth production in medieval times, the finished material exported to Flanders and, through Bristol, to Portugal and towns around the Baltic. The monopoly of its guilds, however, strangled the market in the 16th century and thereby stimulated rural industry. Towns also came into competition with rural workers because the graziers who controlled the source of wool were often clothiers as well. But the making of caps and hats remained important in north-east Warwickshire, centred until the 17th century on Coventry and later spreading to Atherstone, Nuneaton and Rugby. At the beginning of the 18th century, silk manufacture also began at Coventry (Defoe comments upon the black ribbon trade in the 1720s). Kidderminster in Worcestershire, where linsey-woolseys had been produced as wall- and bed-hangings, similarly became a centre for the manufacture of silken fabrics at that time, although carpet manufacture took over by the middle of the 19th century. By 1838, 2,020 carpet looms were working there, and the industry had by then spread to Bewdley and Stourport.[4]

Some of the earliest factories established in the region (and, indeed, in the country) were the water-powered silk mills of west Derbyshire, which supplied the midland hosiery industry. They were much reliant on pitifully low wages and child labour – children as young as seven worked 13-hour days, crawling around moving machines to gather dropped material; work for more adult labourers continued through the night by candlelight. The production of cotton textiles was not important in Derbyshire before the late 18th century but was employing 3,000 people in factories by 1789 (including family members) and cotton was also being spun on hand-machines or wheels in the north-west of the county.[5] With the design of new machines, sometimes perfecting techniques introduced by others, cotton could be produced in quantity. These innovations included Richard Arkwright's spinning frame that adapted, more successfully, machines designed originally by Paul and Wyatt in 1738. In 1770 Strutt and Arkwright constructed the first cotton mill at Cromford, its exterior fortress-like design intended to protect it from hostile workers such as the cotton hand spinners (who had been partly responsible for driving him from his native Lancashire). Subsequently mills were built in the Peak at Bakewell, Cressbrook, Wirksworth, Ashbourne, Milford, Glossop, Belper and elsewhere and steam engines were powering some of them by 1790.[6]

Fig. 7.2 Cressbrook Mill, Derbyshire.

Working conditions in many of the mills were appalling – pauper children, employed in large numbers, could be beaten, starved and overworked – in contrast to the greatly improved conditions provided by William Newton at his new mill at Cressbrook, built in 1815 (Fig. 7.2). In 1747 Dutch swivel looms were installed at Cheadle, in Staffordshire, for the manufacture of tape, and in the early 19th century 2–3,000 people were employed in this occupation in the area. Steam power was only introduced generally towards the middle of the 19th century, but by that time the midlands were losing ground to other districts like Lancashire.[7] That region, close to its cotton importing port of Liverpool, was much better placed for development.

Surviving mill buildings, often converted now to new uses, remain the most immediately visible legacy of the textile industry's development, but the systems that managed the water supply – leats, aquaducts, dams and reservoirs – to keep the wheels of the earlier mills turning are often noteworthy elements in the landscape.

EXTRACTIVE INDUSTRIES AND POTTERY MANUFACTURE

Extractive industries, some established by late Iron Age and Roman times, had continued to expand. The Droitwich and Nantwich brine-producing areas continued to thrive and to be served by cart- and packhorse routes trading salt across and beyond the region. In Worcestershire, Droitwich retained a monopoly in salt production in the Middle Ages and also limited its output to ensure high prices. The Stoke Prior Works opened near the town in 1828 when salt deposits were discovered alongside the Worcester and Birmingham Canal; the railway came later. John Corbett (of Chateau Impney) had four brine pits and employed 5,600 workers producing 3,000 tonnes of salt per annum (and used 50 canal boats and 400 railway vans). A village with a school was built for the workers. However, the works was subsequently demolished and only parts of the village remain.

In Cheshire, the beds of rock salt were located in a trial boring at Marbury near Northwich in 1670 and by the early 18th century this was being raised and transported to the coalfields for refining. The area around Northwich and Winsford took over from Nantwich in importance, especially with the improvement of the Weaver navigation in 1732 (a role shared with Runcorn). A chemical industry developed, based upon salt and the production of alkalis, plus the specialised manufacture of soap in Lever's soapworks at Port Sunlight on the Wirral. Subsequently, salt extraction would cause much subsidence and the appearance of water-filled 'flashes', like those now used as a nature reserve at Sandbach (Fig. 7.3) where the saline waters support a unique assemblage of vegetation.

Peat provided a source of domestic fuel in moorland areas like the High Peak where wood was scarce. It was cut in vast quantities over the moorlands and the large cuts have left permanent

Fig. 7.3 A mere formed by former salt extraction in Cheshire: Sandbach Nature Reserve.

marks on the landscape. Before technological change, peat had also provided the fuel for lead smelting and iron smithing in the Peak District (*see* below), probably converted into charcoal before use.

Lead (and silver) continued to be mined in the White Peak area of Derbyshire and the south Shropshire hills. These had been an important source of revenue on royal estates at the time of Domesday Book (*see* Chapters 3 and 4). The mines were worked by small-scale operators who enjoyed free tenure in the 14th and 15th centuries, men doing the mining, while women and children washed and cleansed the ore above ground. This was sold on to smelters and merchants in Chesterfield or Derby. Gradually, gentry landowners took over ownership of many mines, paying wages to the miners and building up private fortunes for themselves: the Hainders of Haddon owned mines around Wirksworth in the

17th century. The earliest extraction followed the surface veins by opencast rakes (*see* Fig. 7.25) but later shallow shafts were dug. These became deeper when gunpowder became available in the 17th century and shafts could be driven into the solid limestone. These had to be drained by levels known locally as soughs. By the mid-18th century, the Derbyshire lead mines were producing 5–6,000 tonnes of lead per year.[8] The early smelters had been located on the hilltops where peat-fuelled, wind-assisted 'bole hills' had been constructed, but in the White Peak exhaustion of reserves, combined with the loss of land to enclosures, led to the diminishing use of peat, perhaps in the 1700s and early 1800s.[9] The hilltop smelters were to be replaced by slag-hearths and slag-mills driven by water by the end of the 16th century. These were still wasteful of ore and gave way to the reverbatory furnace introduced by Welsh miners in 1747 – the first of which was established at Ashover near Matlock.

Fig. 7.4 Ecton copper mine, Staffordshire.

Copper and lead were mined around Llanymynech in Shropshire, where they had been extracted from prehistoric and Roman times onwards. Copper was being taken from the Peckforton Hills and Alderley Edge in Cheshire in the 17th century, from Ecton in the Staffordshire Peak District, and in small quantities from Shropshire in the 18th and 19th centuries. At Ecton, a hilltop barn is a conversion of an original Boulton and Watt engine house, serving a mine that was 396m deep in 1788 (Fig. 7.4). In the mid-19th century, the Alderley Edge mines in Cheshire were sending thousands of tonnes of copper ore to smelters at St Helens and Swansea but the trade was to be killed by foreign competition later in the century, the area becoming a beauty spot and desirable residential district.

The Derbyshire lead-mining industry was in decline by the mid-18th century and miners were being forced to ever-greater depths to seek adequate ore, although steam-powered pumps became available in the 19th century to aid drainage. By the 19th century, only lower grades of ore remained and the industry faced growing competition from abroad. By 1811, the Ladywash mine at Eyam had reached a depth of 275m and drainage had become a problem – soughs or adits were created to drain water from the mines.[10] In the Stiperstones district of Shropshire lead mining reached its peak in the mid-19th century when the Snailbeach mine was one of the foremost national producers of lead and possibly the richest mine in Europe.[11]

Here the lead mines closed only in 1919, although the shallow workings above water level and the waste tips continued to provide barytes, used, ground, in paints and cosmetics, until the mid-1950s, and spar for use as pebble dash on buildings into the 1970s. The mine buildings still stand, surrounded by the detritus of spoil and lead-working (Fig. 7.5). The ore was first smelted at Pontesford but a new reverberatory smelter was constructed on the hillside near the mine in the mid-19th century; the railways that

Fig. 7.5 Snailbeach lead mine, Shropshire.

Fig. 7.6 Millstone quarry, Yarncliff, Padley Gorge, Derbyshire.

Fig. 7.7 Cement works near Castleton.

served the complex are also preserved. There were many other lead mines in this part of the borderland and the remains of pumping engine houses dot the landscape below the ridges. The miners' cottage settlements gave rise to new communities around the edges of the hill commons.

As the mining of ores declined, many Derbyshire miners moved over to quarrying. Across the region, quarries had for long been active wherever suitable stone occurred; alabaster, or gypsum, was being worked in the Tutbury area of Staffordshire by the late 12th century. Millstone Grit was in demand for the grindstones that gave it its name and these were produced in parts of the Dark Peak. In Padley Gorge at Yarncliff and at Stanage in Hathersage millstones were being worked by the mid-15th century. At Padley, numbers of millstones still lie close to the quarry from which they came (Fig. 7.6). There are small-scale quarries throughout the Peak District and towards the end of the 18th century the development of the fashionable new spa of Buxton encouraged the mining of Derbyshire marbles and fluorspars, especially Blue John from the caves of the Castleton area. Limestone was burnt in kilns in Derbyshire, north Staffordshire and Shropshire. In the White Peak, lime had been burnt and mixed with 'wood, peat, or cone', to produce fertiliser since the end of the 15th century[12] and there were fourteen kilns at 'the Dove Hole' near Chapel-en-le-Frith in 1650; at Stoney Middleton limestone burning was a main source of employment in 1788.[13] In Shropshire, at Llanymynech, limestone was brought down by tram-roads to the 18th- and 19th-century Montgomery Canal, to be boated to waterside kilns at Belan and elsewhere. Much of the lime thus produced was to be used on the newly enclosed Welsh hill lands.

Dramatic quarries on an enormous scale have been left behind. Some of the largest were developed on the grits and limestones of the Peak District, the limestone much used for cement, and today large quarries and clay pits are still a feature of the landscape near Hope and elsewhere; some of the largest limestone quarries lie to the south-east and north-east of Buxton. Today, in the White Peak, the limestone is still the basis of a number of huge cement works whose buildings dominate the local landscape, as near Castleton in the Peak (Fig. 7.7). Limestone was also required by the ironmasters by the 1680s. On the North Staffordshire Coalfield, limestone was quarried at Caldon Low and brought to the Stoke area after 1777 by railway and canal. In the Black Country, artificial caverns had been produced by the 1720s at Castle Hill, Dudley, and the Wren's Nest, the latter described in the mid-19th century as 'completely honeycombed with quarries'.[14] These awesome workings survive and those at Dudley later became animal pits in Dudley Zoo. In Shropshire the basalt of the Clees was quarried after 1863; the industry employed as many as 2,000 workers and almost destroyed the hillfort on Titterstone Clee (Fig. 7.8). Some of the hardest roadstone in the country, known as 'Rowley Rag', has been quarried at Rowley Regis near Dudley. Huge quarries, too, ate into the hard old rocks of the Malvern ridge and many other places that had stone suitable to be used as setts for paving.

Clay was another midland resource and the manufacture of pottery was a long-established industry in the region. The Malvern area of Worcestershire had been associated with pottery production since Roman times; medieval pottery and tile manufacture was established at Worcester in the 15th century, china

Fig. 7.8 Titterstone Hill quarries, Shropshire.

production at Newent in Dean, using local clays, in the 16th century, and at Yardley near Birmingham in the 18th; brownwares were produced at Coleford, Gloucestershire, in the 19th century.

The reason why certain industries developed in particular places was often the result of individual preferences as much as the availability of raw material. The establishment of china manufacture at Worcester in the early 18th century (the Royal Worcester Porcelain Factory was founded in 1749) is an example of this. While clay from Cornwall was easily transported up the Severn (as was the case with Bristol, the home of other major porcelain factories), it was more the fact that Dr John Wall, an excellent chemist, was a local resident, attached to the city with his own network of friends and family. His innovations led the way to Worcester becoming a centre for printing on porcelain. Derbyshire had an early pottery industry in the Duffield area by Norman times and Belper was a centre of production in the 18th century, but the Derbyshire pottery industry was mostly established outside our region to the east and south. Pottery was being made at Stoke-on-Trent by at least the 14th century and by the time of Robert Plot's visit to Staffordshire in about 1680 the Burslem area had become the main centre of pottery manufacture in the county. The potter Josiah Wedgwood (1730–95) moved his factory from Burslem to a new site he called Etruria in 1769, building a village for his workers and a large house for himself close to the Grand Trunk Canal (then under construction). Here he introduced the use of steam engines, acquired royal patronage and improved transport communications with turnpike roads and a branch canal from the Grand Trunk to Froghall, closer to the Caldon limestone quarries. He also introduced an 'assembly-line' approach into the pottery industry, which was to influence much of later factory design. His epitaph in Stoke church notes how he 'converted a rude and inconsiderable manufactory into an elegant art and an important part of national commerce' – although this is an exaggeration of the facts for there were other notable potters in the area.[15] Other local manufacturers, especially Josiah Spode, were to produce bone china, particularly at Longton. One of the first coke-fired furnaces had been introduced at Springwood, north of Chesterton, in 1768–9, at about the same time as those in the Black Country were being built. At Cheddleton, there were two flint-grinding mills that supplied the north Staffordshire pottery industry, the ground flint transported by canal to the Potteries.

Later, brick making, another industry based on local clays, was carried out in many parts of the region, especially on the East Warwickshire Coalfield around Coventry and elsewhere in eastern Arden, and on the North Staffordshire Coalfield. The western parts of the South Staffordshire Coalfield specialised in the production of 'Staffordshire blue bricks' around 1900.

WOODLAND INDUSTRY

Woodland provided fuel for a number of early industries. Glass manufacture was carried out in several wooded districts and was already established to the north-east of the Cannock Chase district by the 13th and 14th century – the Abbots Bromley and Wolseley area was one of the three main regions in England for glass production in the Middle Ages, providing glass for major churches lying far distant from the region such as York Minster and Tatteshall (Lincolnshire).[16] Silica, here obtained from sand and the small quartzite pebbles scattered over the area, and alkali from bracken ash and lime (from wood ash) were the main requirements, and considerable quantities of wood were required to fuel the furnaces. By the 1580s, glassmakers from Lorraine (descendants of craftsmen who had migrated to France from Bohemia sometime during the 14th century) had settled here and in the Eccleshall area but were rarely welcome because of the depredations they made in timber resources. In the 17th century, the glassworkers moved to the Amblecote and Stourbridge area on the Staffordshire/Worcestershire boundary, where a particularly fine clay found near Amblecote and Lye was suitable for moulding the pots in which the glass was made. Here they became famous for the production of coloured window glass.

In the 18th century, the industry also flourished in the Stour valley and at Dudley, Birmingham and Smethwick. The glass industry was partly responsible for the introduction of the chemical industry into the area in the 18th century. James Keir established his works at Tipton to supply alkali, potash, soda soap and red lead to the glass industry and in Birmingham, in 1741, Samuel Garbutt and James Roebuck were supplying sulphuric acid to the Birmingham brass makers. Wolverhampton became a centre for Mander's chemicals and dyes needed for the japanning industry. Glass was also made at St Weonards, in Herefordshire, in the 19th century.

The woodlands of the Wyre forest were, like those of Dean (see below), a source of charcoal for centuries; in the 12th and 13th centuries their produce was in great demand for the iron trades of Dudley and Halesowen and for the Droitwich saltworks. By the 16th and 17th century, iron furnaces were active at Mawley, Cleobury, Furnace Mill and elsewhere in Wyre, the demand for charcoal peaking in the early 18th century with the expansion of the iron industry in Birmingham and the Black Country. The Severn Gorge area had depended heavily upon Wyre's charcoal in the 16th and 17th centuries and charcoal was also needed by the glassblowers of Stourbridge and Bromsgrove and by the Teme Valley hop industry. Although Wyre was disafforested somewhere between 1615 and 1700 the usefulness of its timber ensured the survival of the woodland, managed by coppicing – the cutting down of trees periodically so that new shoots might grow. The sites of the charcoal burner's hearths can sometimes be located and the colliers would have camped close by in temporary 'wigwams' made of poles and sacks during the burn.

Other resources gathered from the forest included oak bark for tanning leather, used in the leather industries of Bewdley, Walsall (a centre of saddlery) and Worcester (noted for its glove making). Tanning had a voracious appetite – 25 tonnes of bark were required to tan 100 hides. Bark collection was a seasonal activity carried out, often by women, from late April to mid-June when the rising sap made the bark a rich source of tannin. After seasoning on racks for six to eight weeks, the bark strips were hauled out on horse-drawn wagons to where they would await grinding before being placed in the tanning pits. Baskets (locally known as skeps or scuttles) were made from oak poles split into thin laths, with coppiced hazel poles forming the rims. Skeps were used across the midlands by fruit pickers and farmers as well as by bark collectors and colliers, the latter using the baskets to load up the trucks from the work face. At one time, coracles had been made in a similar way. Birch twigs and heather from the forest were used to make besoms, the birch cleared out from the coppices periodically. Whisks made of green stripped birch twigs were used by the Kidderminster carpet manufacturers, although softer heather was preferred in the Stourbridge glass houses.[17] Even the bracken was used for packing the fruit from the Wyre orchards that was destined for the Birmingham and even Scottish markets.

Unusually, the woodlands of Cannock Chase were decimated by 16th- and 17th-century charcoal burning, enclosure and tree felling. Between 1589 and 1610, Paget lands had been leased to Sir Fulke Greville who had destroyed much of the woodland for iron making. Even the holly, necessary as winter fodder for the graziers, was lost. The Bunter pebble beds which underlie much of the area were soon impoverished by the removal of the trees and by grazing; the forest was unable to regenerate on the high plateau, being replaced by man-made heath suitable only for the grazing of sheep. In 1686, Robert Plot wrote of the Chase:

> ... now the woods are most destroyed, and the wind and sun admitted in so plentiful a manner between the Coppices, which at due distance now only crown the summits of some few hills, such as Gentle Shaw, Stile Cop ... the plains or Hays below in great part being covered only with the purple odiferous 'ling'.[18]

Fig. 7.9 Old coppiced tree in Padley Gorge, Derbyshire.

The extent of the great heath at the end of the 18th century was estimated at 'forty square miles, or upwards of twenty-five thousand acres' (100 sq km).[19] The underlying pebble beds have also been worked for sand and gravel. Today the planting of coniferous woodland has replaced most of the woodland that survived (*see* Fig. 5.37c). Only a small area near Brocton remains as 'ancient woodland', with its old wood-pasture pollarded oaks in various stages of decay.

The lead miners of the White Peak have also been blamed for the destruction of woodland in the 17th and 18th centuries when timber props were needed for the mines but here, as in Coalbrookdale, there is evidence of coppicing. Coppiced wood was, in particular, used to produce the white coal (dried wood) needed for ore smelting. Old overgrown coppiced trees can still be seen in many woods (Fig. 7.9), although this form of management is once again common in woods managed for wildlife.

IRONWORKING

One of the heaviest users of wood was the region's iron industry. Iron was mined and worked across the region on a small scale throughout medieval and post-medieval times but in Staffordshire the industry tended to migrate from the northern part of the county to the south over the centuries. In the late 12th and 13th centuries, the industry was already established along the

Staffordshire/Cheshire border and in Staffordshire in the Churnet valley around Cheadle (later to become a centre for copper and brass working), on Cannock Chase, and on the North and South Staffordshire coalfields. The name Biddulph means 'the place of the mine' and it may have been iron that was being mined here before the Norman Conquest – there was certainly an old iron mine 'called in English le Brodedelph' at Cheadle by the late 12th century.[20] Bloomeries used for smelting the iron have been identified in the Churnet valley and there was ample wood for the making of charcoal in the valley and the neighbouring district. In the 16th century, charcoal-fired blast furnaces took over from simple bloomeries but their location was still dependent upon nearby woodlands for supplies of fuel. The earliest in this region may also have been the first outside the Surrey-Sussex Weald (where they were first established in 1496), introduced as the 'new Firnes' by Sir William Paget, 1st Baron Paget of Beaudesert, on his estate on Cannock Chase by 1561 – indeed, there were two by that date, plus two forges, with another forge at Abbots Bromley.[21] Charcoal from the Chase was used in the furnaces to produce pig iron and at the forges for producing bar iron from the pig. Slag heaps can still be seen along Rising Brook Valley between Cannock and Rugeley and there was a furnace, too, at Slitting Mill, built about 1625, producing rod iron to be transported elsewhere to make nails.

Vast quantities of cord wood (wood cut into suitable lengths) were required and coppices were enclosed to provide it. The forges required water power to operate the various hammers that were needed to refine the pig iron, which was otherwise too brittle for most uses. The new charcoal-fired furnaces spread after the mid-17th century, still located in districts with plentiful supplies of woodland. By the mid-17th century, south Shropshire and south Staffordshire had concentrations of charcoal-fired blast furnaces (Fig. 7.10), and there were others across southern Cheshire, north Staffordshire and south Derbyshire. In Cheshire, the industry provided forged rods for nail and chain making, with forges at Church Lawton and Cranage, for example, using haematite ores from Furness in Cumbria. The changeover in the salt industry to the use of iron instead of lead pans for evaporation stimulated production in mid-Cheshire, although iron was also sent to the metal-working areas of the Black Country. The greatest concentration of charcoal-fired blast furnaces was, however, in the Forest of Dean and the neighbouring districts of the Wye valley and south Herefordshire.[22]

Nowhere in the region achieved the importance attained by the Forest of Dean, which came to dominate the trade in iron. Iron had been worked in the Forest of Dean in prehistoric and Roman times and in 1086 Gloucester paid, to the Crown, a rent of 36 loads and 100 rods of iron from Dean. The woodland provided charcoal for iron furnaces and forges throughout the medieval period, producing about one-sixth of the country's iron in the late 13th century. The inhabitants of the area held traditional rights to dig for iron ore, coal or stone. These were rights they guarded jealously, with the miners holding their own courts to settle disputes from the 17th century[23] – a freeminer was defined as a man born and living within the hundred of St Briavels who had worked there a year and a day in a coal or iron mine. They also enjoyed 'the sole privilege of carrying ore and coal' and were limited to only four horses for this purpose. These restrictive rights of exclusion and protectionism became a source of contention, and miners were increasingly tempted to lease their holdings to outsiders, especially gentlemen of quality. Rival ironmasters, in any case, paid little heed to the customs of the freeminers and commoners, with ensuing riots, but by the 18th century iron production was largely in the hands of the Foley partnership, based in the Black Country. Only in 1838 did the freeminers admit that they held such rights by royal sufference, thus weakening their position and opening up the way for 'regulating the opening and working of mines and quarries in the Forest of Dean'.[24]

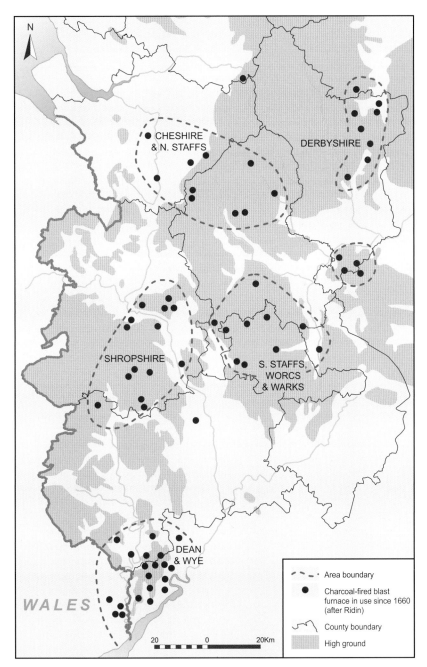

Fig. 7.10 Charcoal-fired blast furnaces in use in the region since 1660 (after Riden 1993).

Iron mining began as opencast workings in shallow deposits, known locally as 'scowles', as at Dean Pool in the west of the forest, with deeper deposits reached by bell pits. When the resources of one pit became exhausted, another was simply opened up alongside. There are areas where the disturbed ground produced by mining can still be seen. Charcoal-fired blast furnaces had replaced bloomeries by the 17th century and the Forest of Dean was pre-eminent in the region. Most furnaces were associated with water-powered forges, perhaps making this the greatest concentration of ironworks in the country (Fig. 7.10). Woodland for the charcoal and iron-smelting industries was generally managed as coppice with standards. The woods had been devastated by kings who needed cash, especially during the Civil Wars, and, allegedly, by some 17th-century ironworkers like Sir John Winter of Lydney who bought virtually the whole Forest for £106,000 and immediately started felling and enclosure. He is said to have stripped the forest bare to feed his charcoal blast furnaces but this aroused such local opposition that his grant was subsequently withdrawn.[25]

The Foley family from Dudley was to dominate iron production in Dean throughout the 17th and 18th centuries, having first established forges in the Stourbridge district of Worcestershire. In Dean, Paul Foley purchased some furnaces for demolition and by 1717 he had concentrated production on six blast furnaces. Most continued to rely upon charcoal rather than coke for fuel before the construction of the Cinderford Ironworks by the Crawshay family in 1795 (the last ironworks to close in 1894). Guns Mill, operating from 1705–32 and mortgaged to Thomas Foley, remains the best preserved of the Dean charcoal-fired furnaces and one of most impressive of its kind in England. Thomas supplied iron cannons and their ballistics in the Civil Wars and married Anne Browne, the daughter of George Browne, the greatest gun manufacturer in the country, with whom he formed a partnership to cast guns at Bedgebury in Kent in the second half of the 17th century. The Foley family owned or leased early blast furnaces not only in Dean but also in Shropshire, Cheshire and north Staffordshire (in the area around Stoke-on-Trent), and, for a time, in Derbyshire.

After 1838, royal consent was granted for outsiders to open mines and, consequently, new iron mines were opened up below earlier workings at Clearwell and Westbury-Brook. New collieries were also established across the area and in 1841 there were 104 collieries and 20 iron mines, although most furnaces continued to draw iron ore from outside the region.[26] In 1856, 221 coal workings within the forest were producing 467,799 tonnes a year, the two largest collieries, those of Parkend and Lightmoor, producing more than 87,000 tonnes each. By 1898, production had risen to over 1 million tonnes.[27] Industrial activity reached a peak before the First World War and at that time iron production was at its greatest, coal mining was flourishing and a network of railway lines ran through the forest. The towns of Coleford, Cinderford and Lydney expanded and, with them, a maze of outlying villages. Industry declined later in the 20th century – the railways were closed, iron mining ceased and the last major coal pit closed in 1965.

The woodland of Dean had been better appreciated as a source of timber for the navy in the 17th century and there was much conifer planting in the 18th century. The Admiralty ordered the replenishment of timber supplies by the planting of both conifers and oaks in the early 19th century – ironically just as wooden ships were about to be replaced by iron steamships. The Forestry Commission was responsible for further conifer plantations after the First World War, but in 1938 Dean became a National Forest Park and an attempt has since been made to maintain a balance between conifers and broad-leaved trees (Fig. 7.11). Today woodland has regrown over many of the old industrial workings and at the New Fancy colliery one can stand on top of

Fig. 7.11 View over the Forest of Dean.

a part-levelled spoil heap and look out over the forest for miles around. Some sites have been preserved as industrial museums, including a new Dean Heritage Centre at Soudley located in a former water-powered forge and iron foundry known as Camp Mill (Fig. 7.12). At Clearwell, the ancient caverns extended by iron mining are also open to the public and still produce natural ochres used to colour paints and glazes for pottery (some may even have been used to paint the ceiling of the Sistine chapel in Rome in the 16th century).

Fig. 7.12 Dean Heritage Centre, Soudley.

Charcoal, too, fuelled the early iron industry of the Ironbridge and Coalbrookdale district in Shropshire and woodland was abundant along the valley of the Severn where the river flows through the gorge (*see* Fig. 4.31). The medieval abbeys of Buildwas and Wenlock had carried out small-scale iron working in bloomeries and it was local woods that supplied the charcoal for the increasingly important 17th-century iron furnaces that lay between Wombridge on the north and Bringewood (Herefordshire) in the south-west (*see* Fig. 7.10). The first steel-producing cementation furnace in England was recently discovered on the Upper Forge site at Coalbrookdale, operating from the 1620s.[28] The woods were managed with care and many new coppices were created from the 16th century

Fig. 7.13 Abraham Darby's iron bridge, Coalbrookdale, Shropshire.

onwards to provide timber for the industry. It was only the development of specialist industrial techniques in the 18th century, using coke for smelting, which led coal to replace charcoal as the main source of fuel. It was this technological break-through of using coke for smelting, the development of techniques for the recycling of water and the use of steam, that revolutionised the iron industry in the mid- to late 18th century. At Coalbrookdale, Abraham Darby began to use coke in 1709, although the advantages of this were not appreciated until his son developed the process in the 1750s and began to supply coke-blast iron to the principal forges in the midlands. Abraham Derby I is probably best remembered as the builder of the world's first cast-iron bridge, constructed across the Severn at Ironbridge in 1777–81 (Fig. 7.13). By the 18th century, the landscape of Coalbrookdale had been transformed, with the dammed ponds that served the furnaces and forges crammed into the narrow valley, hemmed in by coppice woodland (Fig. 7.14). Tramways, with horse-drawn wagons

running on iron or wooden rails, linked the sites, the mines and the river, carrying coal, clay and other heavy goods. The early ones were often re-routed to avoid the growing spoil heaps and brickyards before they gradually gave way to railways after the 1860s, although some continued in use into the 20th century.[29]

A little to the south of Coalbrookdale, at Willey, John Wilkinson, who pioneered a technique for boring larger iron guns, developed the world's first coal-cutting machines and in 1776 first applied the Boulton and Watt steam engine to his ironworks at his New Willey Furnace. This liberated iron making from its former dependence upon water power, and he also built the first iron boat at Willey Wharf in 1787. A feature of mid-18th-century development was the integration of mining and iron production by ironmasters and miners. New companies were established, like the Madeley Wood Company at Ironbridge that built iron furnaces at Bedlam beside the Severn or the partnership of colliers who built an ironworks at

Fig. 7.14 The industrial landscape of the Severn Gorge Ironbridge/ Coalbrookdale region.

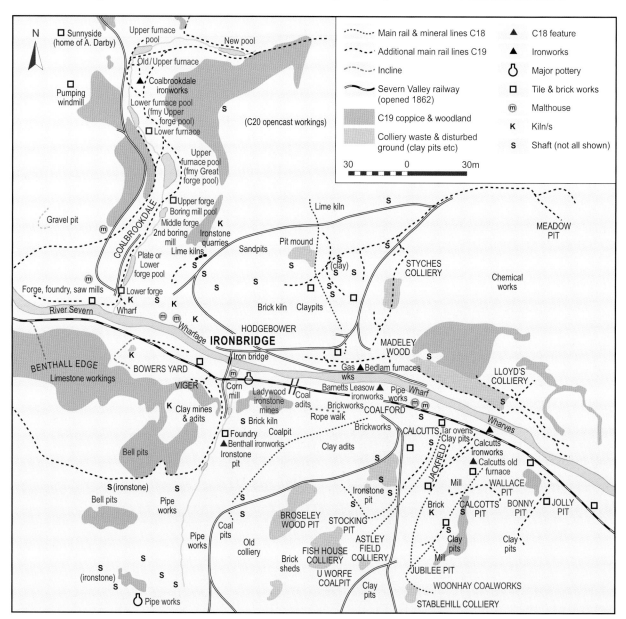

Lightmoor in the same area. Limestone was taken from Benthall Edge for the blast furnaces of Coalbrookdale and the sites of the quarries are clearly visible within the woodland; several limekilns survive on Ironbridge Wharfage. Ironworking also began to move northwards as mining moved to the deeper seams of the Shropshire Coalfield. This concentration of industry was augmented by the growth of the 16th- to 17th-century brick and clay-pipe industry based upon the use of local clays, which turned, in the 18th and 19th centuries, to the production of fine ceramics and porcelain, tiles and bricks. There were also innovations in coal-mining methods in the area: the longwall method of mining coal was first developed on the Coalbrookdale coalfield, probably pioneered at Madeley Wood. Steam engines were being used to drain a mine in Madeley by 1719 and winding engines were dominant features of the landscape by the end of the 18th century.[30] In the 20th century, coal was also being used to generate electricity and the large cooling towers of Buildwas power station, opened in 1932 but now gas fired, still dominate views over the Severn (Fig. 7.15).

Fig. 7.15 Buildwas power station cooling towers.

It was this development of industry, mainly in the 19th century, which led to the gradual urbanisation of the Ironbridge district and an increasingly 'busy' industrial landscape (Fig. 7.14). In the early part of the century an increased density of worker housing clustered around the old centres such as Broseley Wood or the riverside settlements of Coalford and Calcutts. To the south of the river, the coal seams had since the 16th century been worked by adits, and later bell pits, and Calcutts was soon to be overwhelmed by the spread of land-hungry brick and tile works.[31] Jackfield was a poor settlement with lodging houses, alehouses and brothels, where a domestic pottery industry led to the construction of small kilns attached to cottages; these stood amidst a landscape of ironstone mines, ironworks, brickworks, pottery kilns, clay-pipe manufactories and a tar distillery:[32]

> *not all the world, but a very poor bit of the fag end of it … made up of old pit shafts, pit mounds, rubbish heaps, brick ends, broken drain and roof and paving tiles, dilapidated houses, sloughy lanes and miry roads.*[33]

Settlements also spread along the north bank of the Severn. A new industrial village was established at Coalport, at a point of transport interchange, and it was soon to have its own china works. There were wharves, malthouses and inns along the river

Fig. 7.16 Bedlam furnaces, Madeley Wood, Ironbridge. Built on the riverside by the Madeley Wood Company in 1757–8, but the fortunes of the company's iron trade were wildly erratic: the location of the furnaces distant from productive mines led to the abandonment of the Bedlam foundry in 1803 and the removal of the ironworks to Blists Hill in 1832.

to the west of the new iron bridge, a more built-up area with a market square closer to the bridge and deliberately planned clusters of houses that swelled the old nuclei along the slopes of the Gorge and the Dale, including larger villas set within gardens that were often later subdivided for further development. Several mine-owners and ironmasters, including Abraham Darby, had their houses overlooking the upper parts of Coalbrookdale. Ironbridge itself was to become the commercial centre for the Gorge.

Diminishing resources and difficulties of access were factors in the demise of industry in the Ironbridge district in the 20th century, but its contribution to the country's industrial growth has given the area World Heritage status. Many industrial buildings remain (Fig. 7.16) and the features associated with former mining and limestone extraction are now preserved, still within a woodland setting.

Blast furnaces, producing cast iron, came relatively late to the Black Country: the first recorded furnace was at West Bromwich in 1561 or 1562. Most of the output from the furnaces was converted into wrought iron and treated in the finery of a forge where the iron would be heated with charcoal and blasted with air to oxidise impurities, then hammered to consolidate the bloom. Water-driven hammers were soon in use and, at a nearby chafery, tilt hammers would continue to work the iron. The use of the water-powered tilt hammer to expel slag, and of the slitting mill in the later 16th century to mechanise the process of cutting rod iron, had increased the importance of ironworking centres along the south-western edge of the Birmingham plateau. Iron furnaces, forges and slitting mills were established along the River Stour and its tributary the Smestow Brook. Richard Foley was one of the first to erect a slitting mill in the midlands, at Hyde near Stourbridge in 1628, but another was built at Bustleholme Mill between West Bromwich and Wednesbury in the same year by Sir Edward Peyto, and others quickly followed at Wilden near Kidderminster and in the Wolverley district.[34] In such a mill, which was driven by water power, rods of iron, already drawn down to a suitable size under a tilt hammer and then rolled into strip, could be cut (or slit) mechanically into convenient lengths to supply the nailmakers who worked across the northern Worcestershire and south Staffordshire countryside until machine production gradually took over in the 19th century (*see* below). Bromsgrove was a nailing centre in the 18th and 19th centuries although overshadowed by Halesowen, Lye and Stourbridge in the Black Country.

As at Ironbridge, the early iron industry of the Black Country had relied upon charcoal for smelting, but by the first decade of the 17th century this was becoming difficult to obtain in sufficient quantities. As supplies of charcoal decreased, it was Dud Dudley, the illegitimate son of the Earl of Dudley, who experimented with 'pit-cole' as a substitute for charcoal to fuel the blast furnaces on Pensnett Chase, although he probably met with little success and never brought his ideas into commercial use.[35] His forges and fineries at Pensnett and Cradley were ruined by floods in 1622; in the 1630s his forges around Dudley and his new furnace at Himley were destroyed by the established ironmasters who still used charcoal, then finally the Civil Wars broke out and shattered his prospects – he was a Royalist in a district strongly sympathetic to the

Parliamentarians. At the same time, he faced the enmity of the ironmasters of Dean and Bristol, and was finally forced to give up iron making altogether. Yet his efforts resulted in the town of Dudley becoming the centre of the iron trade, employing, according to Yarranton, more people than anywhere else in north Worcestershire around 1677.[36] Dudley claimed that there were 20,000 smiths working within 10 miles (16km) of Dudley castle and he himself had four forges. Iron from the Forest of Dean was being brought up to Dudley and Stourbridge in the 17th century, much of it turned into bar iron for a wide variety of purposes. At about the same time, the Foleys were establishing their ironworks on the south-western edge of the South Staffordshire Coalfield at Stourbridge, still using Dudley's techniques in 1686, and they had forges on Maer Heath.

It was not until about 1709, when Abraham Darby succeeded in turning coal into coke, that this became a realistic source of fuel, but even he enjoyed little commercial success in his own lifetime. He successfully applied the coking process in Staffordshire in about 1750. He, too, was a native of the Black Country, having been born at the Wren's Nest near Dudley. There were other technical advances in the area: Thomas Newcomen's steam engine erected near Dudley in 1712 was the first workable engine in the world to have a piston and cylinder to operate the pumps needed for deeper mining.[37] Such new developments put the Black Country in a particularly strong position. Wilkinson opened up the Bilston district, erecting his first blast furnace in the region at Bradley in around 1758 (Fig. 7.17). In the Wolverley area, the Foley Forge and ironworks belonging to the Foley family were working at Cookley by the end of the 17th century, located beside the Stour (another inhabitant of Cookley perfected the patent tinning process). The Foley family's iron-founding business was centred on Stourbridge to the north and in the mid-17th century the family held the furnaces at Grange, Cradley and Hales. In 1655, Thomas Foley had purchased the estate at Great Witley in Worcestershire with his profits from the iron cannon trade, and his grandson, who had been created Baron Foley of Kidderminster in 1711, carried out extensive improvements to the mansion house and park (*see* Chapter 6).

An offshoot of the south Staffordshire ironworking industry was the production of edge tools and these were being manufactured throughout the north

Fig. 7.17 Watercolour of Bradley ironworks near Bilston 1836 by Robert Noyes.

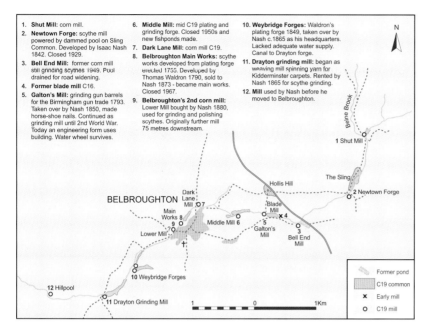

1. **Shut Mill:** corn mill.
2. **Newtown Forge:** scythe mill powered by dammed pool on Sling Common. Developed by Isaac Nash 1842. Closed 1929.
3. **Bell End Mill:** former corn mill still grinding scythes 1949. Pool drained for road widening.
4. **Former blade mill** C16.
5. **Galton's Mill:** grinding gun barrels for the Birmingham gun trade 1793. Taken over by Nash 1850, made horse-shoe nails. Continued as grinding mill until 2nd World War. Today an engineering form uses building. Water wheel survives.
6. **Middle Mill:** mid C19 plating and grinding forge. Closed 1950s and new fishponds made.
7. **Dark Lane Mill:** corn mill C19.
8. **Belbroughton Main Works:** scythe works developed from plating forge erected 1755. Developed by Thomas Waldron 1790, sold to Nash 1873 - became main works. Closed 1967.
9. **Belbroughton's 2nd corn mill:** Lower Mill bought by Nash 1880, used for grinding and polishing scythes. Originally further mill 75 metres downstream.
10. **Weybridge Forges:** Waldron's plating forge 1849, taken over by Nash c.1865 as his headquarters. Lacked adequate water supply. Canal to Drayton forge.
11. **Drayton grinding mill:** began as weaving mill spinning yarn for Kidderminster carpets. Rented by Nash 1865 for scythe grinding.
12. **Mill** used by Nash before he moved to Belbroughton.

Fig. 7.18 The landscape of the Belbroughton scythe industry.

Worcestershire part of the South Staffordshire Coalfield by the beginning of the 17th century. Scythe making was established along the Belne Brook in the Belbroughton area where it survived until the 20th century; other centres for this industry were Wolverley, Cradley and Hartlebury, with nearly 400 smiths engaged in scythe making in 1841. The Belne Brook falls 150m in the 6.4km between its source and Drayton, flowing in a deeply incised valley that could easily be dammed. A blade mill had been operating in Belbroughton near Bell Hall by the 16th century, using the waters of the brook to harden sword blades, but by the 18th century water power was being used to plate the scythes that had been hand-forged by the smiths of Belbroughton and Clent (Fig. 7.18).

The industry owed much to Thomas Waldron who established his works here in about 1790, producing scythes for the American market until the American Civil War, and to Isaac Nash who purchased most of the mills in the valley in the later 19th century. In 1842, Nash developed Newtown Forge. In about 1850 he purchased Samuel Galton's Mill, which had ground gun barrels for a Birmingham firm in the Napoleonic Wars. In 1865 he rented a former weaving mill at Drayton at Chaddesley Corbett that was spinning yarn for the Kidderminster carpet trade and turned it over to scythe grinding (possibly returning the mill to an earlier usage). At about the same time, he took over the two Weybridge forges, one of which may have been an earlier gun mill but had been used as a plating forge by Waldron – Lower Weybridge became Nash's headquarters. In 1873 he purchased Waldron's Main Works in the heart of the village as his main mill – powered by the largest water-wheel in the county – and in 1880 he added the Belbroughton Corn Mills at either end of the village to his empire, using the Lower Mill for grinding and polishing scythes. Belbroughton specialised in the production of 'Crown' scythes, a welded product made with the finest steel imported from Sweden, the blade finally sharpened using grindstones of local sandstone. Today many of the mill buildings still stand along the brook: in 1949 Bell End Mill was still grinding scythes and Lower Weybridge was in use as a water-driven plating forge, but they are now converted to other uses (Fig. 7.19); however, the dams and leats of many of the mill pools can be traced on the ground.

The Napoleonic Wars had been a great stimulus to the iron industry: by 1805, the 31 Staffordshire furnaces were producing about one-fifth of the total pig iron production of England and Wales,[38] most of them in the triangle formed by Bilston, Wednesbury and Dudley with a minor group between Brierley Hill and Dudley Wood to the south-west. The greatest expansion occurred in the first quarter of the 19th century and by 1830 there were 123 blast furnaces in operation in the Black Country. The demand for iron canal and road bridges, and the requirement for steam-engine cylinders, led to the dramatic development of iron founding in the area. Heavy castings were made at the Boulton and Watt Soho foundry, the Eagle Foundry at Birmingham, and by the Horsley Iron Company at Tipton; malleable iron for small metal containers was made at West Bromwich and elsewhere, while cast-iron goods of a wide variety were produced throughout the Black Country. In 1856, at the time of the region's greatest prosperity, the Bessemer acid converter process made the production of cheap steel a practicable proposition and a rival to the lower-grade wrought iron; the Earl of Dudley's old-established iron-making plant at Round Oak, Brierley Hill, was converted into a steelworks.

A feature of the region was the continuing specialisation of individual centres that had already become established before the Industrial Revolution. Wolverhampton was a centre of lock making by the late 17th century, later to be joined by Willenhall; Walsall was producing items associated with horsemanship such as leather saddles and horse furniture: spurs, bridles and stirrups; edge tools were produced along the south-western edge of the Birmingham plateau; nail making was carried out at Dudley, Halesowen and Lye and chain making at Netherton, Cradley and Lye (Fig. 7.20). As industrialisation spread, the countryside changed: one has to imagine 'more and more a strung-out web of iron-working villages, market-towns next door to collieries, heaths and wastes gradually and very slowly being covered by the cottages of nailers and other persons carrying on industrial occupations in rural surroundings'[39] until an amorphous mass of settlement and industry, in which houses and factories and mines lay closely intermingled, had produced the notoriously polluted 'Black Country'. Outworking continued throughout the 19th century and even into the early 20th: chains were hand-forged by the wives

Fig. 7.19 Nash Works: *a former scythe mill in Belbroughton.*

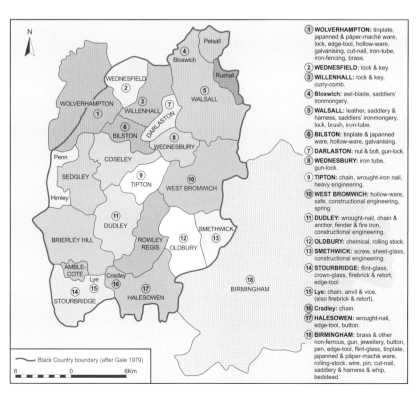

Fig. 7.20 Nineteenth-century specialisation: *local trades in the industrial centres of the Black Country and Birmingham. The boundary of the Black Country follows Gale 1979 with 1965 borough and parish boundaries. By 1931 vehicle manufacture and allied trades were established in Wolverhampton and the south-east part of the region (Birmingham, Halesowen, Oldbury and Smethwick); the jewellery and plate industry in Birmingham and Smethwick; and cutlery and small tools were produced in Wolverhampton and across the south part of the region (Stourbridge, Amblecote, Dudley, Rowley Regis, Halesowen, Oldbury and Birmingham).*

1. **WOLVERHAMPTON**: tinplate, japanned & pâper-maché ware, lock, edge-tool, hollow-ware, galvanising, cut-nail, iron-tube, iron-fencing, brass.
2. **WEDNESFIELD**: lock & key.
3. **WILLENHALL**: lock & key, curry-comb.
4. **Bloxwich**: awl-blade, saddlers' ironmongery.
5. **WALSALL**: leather, saddlery & harness, saddlers' ironmongery, lock, brush, iron-tube.
6. **BILSTON**: tinplate & japanned ware, hollow-ware, galvanising.
7. **DARLASTON**: nut & bolt, gun-lock.
8. **WEDNESBURY**: iron tube, gun-lock.
9. **TIPTON**: chain, wrought-iron nail, heavy engineering.
10. **WEST BROMWICH**: hollow-ware, safe, constructional engineering, spring.
11. **DUDLEY**: wrought-nail, chain & anchor, fender & fire iron, constructional engineering.
12. **OLDBURY**: chemical, rolling stock.
13. **SMETHWICK**: screw, sheet-glass, constructional engineering.
14. **STOURBRIDGE**: flint-glass, crown-glass, firebrick & retort, edge-tool.
15. **Lye**: chain, anvil & vice, (also firebrick & retort).
16. **Cradley**: chain.
17. **HALESOWEN**: wrought-nail, edge-tool, button.
18. **BIRMINGHAM**: brass & other non-ferrous, gun, jewellery, button, pen, edge-tool, flint-glass, tinplate, japanned & pâper-maché ware, rolling-stock, wire, pin, cut-nail, saddlery & harness & whip, bedstead.

Black Country boundary (after Gale 1979)

6   0   6Km

and children of chainmakers in sheds attached to their homes in Cradley Heath but, apart from in Dudley, nail making was pushed out by new industries into north Worcestershire, especially around Bromsgrove.

By the 19th century, although it was the Black Country that dominated the iron trade, the iron industry had not entirely forsaken the northern part of Staffordshire area. In the 18th century, there were ironworks at Consall and Oakamoor and slag from an early blast furnace and even earlier bloomeries has recently been found at Oakamoor. Copper and brass works were also established in the valley at Oakamoor and Froghall, working Ecton copper. In 1851 Bolton and Sons of Birmingham developed the Oakamoor site into one of the biggest plants in the country and it numbered amongst its products the first transatlantic telegraph cable. The works were demolished in 1963. At Biddulph, grassed-over mountains of slag are all that remain of Robert Heath's ironworks where there were once four blast furnaces and a forge.

COAL MINING

The lessening of the dependence upon water power by the development of the steam engine opened up new locations for industry. The region was fortunate to have ample coal for coking, ironstone, limestone for flux and the refractory clays and sands needed to build and repair the furnaces – but industrial development particularly favoured an increase in the production of coal (Fig. 7.22). Before the Industrial Revolution, coal had been extracted over a wide area, often by the use of simple bell pits and was initially mainly for domestic consumption. Coal had been mined in the midland region at an early date wherever seams were closer to the surface. There were bell pits around Titterstone Clee in Shropshire as early as 1235. This form of mining was operating until the 17th century and the pits, surrounded by their spoil heaps, are still visible on the lower slopes near Doddington (Fig. 7.21).[40] A wind furnace was smelting iron ore on the Clees in the 16th century and coal, iron, limestone and basalt were all being extracted. Coal was being dug in the South and North Staffordshire coalfields by the 13th century and in Dean and Wyre throughout the Middle Ages. In Cheshire, the East Cheshire Coalfield that extends southwards from Stockport into the Pennines behind Buxton developed rapidly in the 17th century to meet the increasing demand for coal for salt boiling and domestic use, but it was the Wirral Coalfield that became important in the late 1750s when the Ness colliery became one of the largest in the county. Coal was being mined in the Ironbridge district of Shropshire by the mid-16th century and areas of later bell pits survive.[41] Here, before the improvement of drainage methods (the horse gin followed by the steam engine), coal mining was a seasonal activity carried out in the summer months when the water-table was lower, while iron production was concentrated in the autumn and winter when there was more available water to power the bellows of the forges. Many colliers were at first part-time miners, combining this with farming and other industrial occupations such as clay-pipe or pottery making in the Ironbridge Gorge and nail making in the Black Country and north Worcestershire where colonies of nailers were established around patches of waste and common. As late as the 19th century, miners at Wildboarclough, Wincle and Lyme Handley in the Pennines combined coal mining with work in farming.

It was major development in industries such as pottery manufacture and ironworking, and the demand for fuel to drive the newly developed steam engines, which stimulated coal production in the mid-18th century. Mining spread widely wherever there were seams, and as mines became deeper they became more reliant upon the new engines to pump out water and to sink the new shafts. The two coalfield districts that rose to pre-eminence after the Industrial Revolution were the North Staffordshire and South Staffordshire

Fig. 7.21 Clee Hill, Shropshire: bell-pits near Doddington.

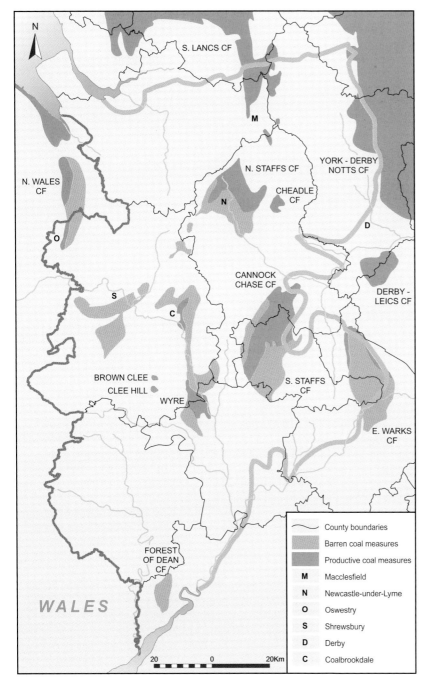

Fig. 7.22 Midland coalfields (CF):
N Staffs or Potteries CF: coal and clay for 19th-century pottery industry.
Extension of S Lancs CF: Goyt Moss Colliery, 19th century, closed 1880s.
Oswestry CF: S extension of N Wales CF: coal for lime burning and ceramic manufacture.
Shrewsbury CF: coal used locally for lime burning and brick making.
Coalbrookdale: coal for ironworks especially 18th–19th centuries; exported by river, canal and rail; coal and clay for brick making, roof tiles, pottery and china industries. Coal used later for electricity generation.
Clee Hill: worked since the 13th century for lime burning, brick making, local ironworks.
Wyre Forest: mainly 19th-century mining, taken out on Severn Valley Railway; ceased mining 1973.
S Staffs and Cannock Chase CFs: Cannock Chase developed end of the 19th century; coal sent to Black Country.
S Staffs: thick coal, iron, marls and limestone for 19th-century iron industry; decline after 1900 with move to concealed field early in the 20th century.
E Warks CF: worked since 13th century but steeply dipping seams; coal sent to Black Country and Birmingham; 20th-century development.

Legend:
- County boundaries
- Barren coal measures
- Productive coal measures
- **M** Macclesfield
- **N** Newcastle-under-Lyme
- **O** Oswestry
- **S** Shrewsbury
- **D** Derby
- **C** Coalbrookdale

coalfields. After 1800 the north-eastern sector of the latter between Wolverhampton and Walsall was opened up, followed after 1850 by the Cannock Chase Coalfield and areas to the south-east around Oldbury and West Bromwich. By the 1870s, shafts were being sunk at Sandwell and Hampstead into the 'thick coal' at depths of as much as 550m. Gradually pit banks spread across the fields and commons of the Black Country, adding to the pervasive industrial scene (Fig. 7.23).

The Cannock Chase was another coalfield where coal mining took over from charcoal production. Small industries such as coal mining, ironworking, charcoal

Fig. 7.23 Staffordshire Colliery *from* Cyclopaedia of Useful Arts and Manufactures, *ed. Charles Tomlinson,* c.*1880s (engraving) by William Henry Prior (1812–82): 'Pit head, Staffordshire'.*

burning and quarrying had developed here by the end of the 13th century and a significant glass industry had been established near Rugeley in medieval times (*see* above). Coal was already being mined in the south of the region near Pelsall and Bloxwich in the 17th century and there was also a local iron industry. Here seams were close to the surface, as they were in the vicinity of Beaudesert and Brereton, and pits were small. Celia Fiennes, the 17th-century traveller and diarist, commented how, on Lord Paget's estate, in the 'Coale pitts where they were digging, they draw up the coale in baskets with a little wheele or windless like a well, its very good'.[42] Sir William Paget had developed iron making and coal mining on the Chase on a large scale in the latter half of the 16th century.

Transport of the coal to the Black Country was facilitated in later years by the construction of tramways and canals, especially the Wyrley–Essington Canal that opened in 1792, but it was only after the approaching exhaustion of the best and most accessible South Staffordshire seams after 1850 that the Cannock Chase Coalfield was really developed. By 1800, the coalfield was prospering: the large landowners like Lord Gower at Brereton were investing heavily in new pits. By 1875, collieries had spread to the northern part of the coalfield to the east of Cannock and in 1891 the area was producing as much coal as that of the South Staffordshire Coalfield. Mining communities established settlements across the region – straggling street villages with long lines of terraced housing, described by an observer at the end of the 19th century who noted that:

> 'They possess so little that is attractive, … they are ill-built and ill-kept; their very architecture is depressing; they present nothing to elevate or refine, either in the nature of the industry, or in the environments of the people's daily life'. Socially, the life of these villages was often barren; they possessed few amenities; the welfare of the mining communities was sacrificed in the search for coal.[43]

There were blast furnaces for a time near Walsall and Pelsall but the area was not rich in ironstone or coking coal and apart from the light metal industries that were already established in the southern part of the district and in Cannock most of the towns and villages remained single-industry settlements. In the mid-20th century, the winding gear and waste tips of collieries were a common sight

(Fig. 7.24). In the 20th century, seams in the south and east were becoming exhausted and a new deep pit was sunk at Lea Hall near Rugeley in 1960. Throughout this development, the heaths and commons of the district were continuously invaded by settlement and only the heartland of Cannock Chase survived (*see* Fig. 5.37c).

The 19th century was the heyday of coal mining, at least for mine owners. As in the Coalbrookdale and Ironbridge district, ironmasters worked hand in hand with the coal producers and virtually every iron furnace had its own coal and ironstone mines: by 1830 the ironmasters were said to control the south Staffordshire coal trade.[44] By the mid-19th century, however, the hewers of coal were often hired as a team by the much-detested 'butty', who negotiated prices and wages on a short-term basis and drew a substantial proportion of the miners' profits. This and other restrictions led eventually to strikes and riots, although these protests were seldom as well organised in Staffordshire as in the north-east of England. An iron and steel boom in the early 1870s stimulated production and the new canal network aided transport. Some abandoned pits were reopened and on the South Staffordshire Coalfield a new colliery at Hamstead was begun in 1875 and eventually reached the 'thick coal' at a depth of 550m. Deeper collieries were also sunk in north-east Warwickshire, tapping the concealed areas of the coalfield: Kingsbury Colliery was sunk in 1894, a new large-diameter shaft constructed at Baddesley in 1896, and deeper workings made at existing collieries such as those of Haunchwood and Griff.

Fig. 7.24 A pit bank of the Walsall Wood colliery *beside the Rushall Canal at Brownhills, Walsall – by the late 1950s an air of dereliction and abandonment already pervades the scene.*

The development of the lesser coalfields is no less interesting than that of the major ones. The Wyre Forest lies on infertile coal measure rocks, and workable seams extend in a narrow outcrop southwards from the Coalbrookdale Coalfield, widening towards Bewdley and Mamble (*see* Fig. 7.22). At first, the coal was merely raked from the beds of rivers and streams or dug from surface outcrops and there is a reference to coal being dug in the reign of Richard II, when coal from Abberley was sold to Worcester Cathedral. Later, bell pits would be dug or drifts (or adits) driven into hillsides, as at Chorley and Gladder Brook. As surface seams were worked out, shafts were sunk to greater depths but the mines were usually small and worked as a seasonal activity by local farmers or smallholders, a tradition common in other coalfield areas. Work was hampered by poor ventilation and drainage and a lack of transport facilities. Coal mining was better organised by the late 19th century once the steam engine allowed deeper mining, and collieries had been opened up across the whole area from Bayton to Abberley. There were over 40 recorded collieries in the Wyre Coalfield in addition to the many small excavations along the outcrops. Much of the coal was carried on the Severn Valley railway. The largest pit was Alveley Colliery, which only opened in 1939; in the 1950s it employed 1,250 men, but mining ended there in 1969. The last pit, Hunthouse Colliery, closed in 1973, although the coal has by no means been exhausted.

BIRMINGHAM AND COVENTRY

Although it lacked much in the way of natural resources of its own, Birmingham had become by the 16th century a centre for metal working (in iron, brass, copper alloy and pewter), leather tanning, bone working, hemp and flax retting, and brick, tile and pottery manufacture, with the Bull Ring at the hub of these activities. Sword manufacture was a major industry by the 17th century and in 1786 an order was placed for 10,000 cavalry swords for the East India Company.[45] It was a natural progression for the city to later excel in gun manufacture.

Although Birmingham has been called 'the city of 1,000 trades' it is the metal trades that have brought it most fame. When James Watt went into partnership with Matthew Boulton their factory at Handsworth began to build steam engines improved by a cylinder invented by John Wilkinson. But Matthew Boulton was also innovative in the 'toy' trade at his Fothergill Manufactory at Soho – 'toys' were polished iron and lighter steel wares produced for many different purposes, including buckles, purse mounts, brooches, bracelets, watch chains, key rings and swivels – with many processes carried out in small independent workshops brought together under one roof. It is claimed that prior to the French Revolution half of Birmingham was dependent on the light steel toy trade.[46] In particular, the trades of brass, copper, plating, gun making (expanding with the increased demand for firearms during the Crimean and Napoleonic wars), button, watch and jewellery making were carried out in a multiplicity of small workshops depending upon skill and adaptability for their success. This has long been a characteristic of Birmingham industry, and remains so to this day. Even locks, nails, chains and nuts-and-bolts continued to be made in backyard workshops well into the second half of the 19th century – a few even survived into the 20th.

Today, Birmingham's gun and jewellery quarters have been restored and are still productive, although barely a shadow of their former selves. The jewellery industry has left a highly distinctive landscape. It surged in importance after the middle of the 19th century and was an intensely subdivided trade carried out in family workshops. The industry came to be concentrated in the newly built streets around St Paul's church and from there migrated north and westwards, first to the main Birmingham–West Bromwich road before finally settling in the Vyse Street and Warstone Lane district. Characterised by small firms and few large factories, the area is densely packed with workshops. The earliest formed part of the manufacturers' houses, giving the quarter a strong domestic feel. Later workshops were set to the rear of showrooms forming a distinctive pattern that is concealed from the street and only fully appreciated from the air. Jostling hugger-mugger, one with another, these workshops make Birmingham's Jewellery Quarter one of the best-preserved light-industrial areas in existence, clearly reflecting the industry's development from the late 18th century to the present day.

By the mid-19th century, the cycle industry was developing in Coventry and Birmingham, carrying with it a large number of ancillary trades such as the manufacture of gear cases and lamps by Lucas & Co. Car manufacture was added and the first motor car was produced by the Daimler Company at Coventry in 1896. At Coventry, car firms went on to include Humber, combining British workmanship with French engineering, and later Swift, Rover and Singer. The motor trade was employing over 10,000 by the middle of the 20th century in Coventry alone.

RURAL INDUSTRY

Apart from the extraction of mineral ores, rural industry was mostly connected with farming and woodland management. The woods were managed mainly as coppice with standards and a main use was to supply charcoal for the iron industry, established in many parts of the region and especially in Dean. In Staffordshire, wood fed the glass furnaces of Eccleshall and Cannock Chase until its use for this purpose was banned in the early 17th century. In Herefordshire, woodland also produced wood for hoops (used for binding barrels for the West Indian sugar trade), hop poles and pit props, and limekilns are frequently recorded in the 19th century in woodland. As we have seen, peat was dug on a large scale on the moorlands of the Peak District to be used as both domestic and industrial fuel. The resulting landscape results in a distinctive broken surface, where light-coloured grasslands have replaced the dark blanket-mires on exposed mineral soils.[47] Where the cut peat was hauled by sled, or carried on packhorses or carts, dense networks of tracks may survive, as in the upper Goyt valley.[48]

There were, however, pockets of industry that were not connected with agriculture, moorland or woodland. Indeed, many of today's apparently rural villages were sustained by occupations other than just agriculture; nor did rural industry across the region cease entirely with the Industrial Revolution. Even in the least industrialised county, Herefordshire, there were, in the 19th century, forges at Downton and Whitchurch and pottery and tiles were made at Deerfold. In west Warwickshire needle making in the Arrow valley was a home-based occupation until the middle of the 19th century, machinery being used only for the finishing processes. In north Worcestershire and the Black Country, rural outworking also played an important role in the production of chains and nails, as we have already seen.

Industry also gave rise to new settlements in the post-medieval period. Especially in mining districts, the poor were encroaching on the margins of the hill commons, which were gradually reduced in extent as cottagers enclosed an acre or two for their homes. Such 'squatting' was to increase in amount through the succeeding centuries, often carried out by miners who combined mining with smallholding. Near Ironbridge, Broseley's commons had disappeared by about 1600 as immigrant coal miners, considered by the dispossessed locals as 'lewd persons, the scums and dregs of many counties', moved in and built primitive cottages at Broseley Wood.[49] Pockets of cottage encroachments were also noted in the 17th century around the skirts of Needwood in Staffordshire and around the Clees and other commons in Shropshire. Where squatter settlements survive they often convey a confusing landscape with small cottages, built of poor materials, constantly extended with little outshuts and extra room bays, and set within irregular small holdings, flimsily enclosed among the fragments of common or waste land (*see* Fig. 5.21).

There are many rural areas in which former industrial development has left a considerable impression upon the landscape. While urban areas still contain many former industrial buildings, some of them preserved as museums, there are often relics of industry scattered in countryside locations, sometimes half-hidden in woods and undergrowth. On Stanton Moor in Derbyshire, for instance, quarries, paved ways, stone-lined tanks and broken buildings are all that remain of former stone quarries on the gritstone. Further south, in the White Peak, dumps of soil in the fields represent the debris of former lead mines (Fig. 7.25). Other relics of this industry are prominent in south Shropshire, such as the mounds on the hillside left by the White Grit mine near Shelve or the complex of features at Snailbeach (*see* Fig. 7.5). Ponds and leats are found along most of the rivers and streams of the region, some formerly associated with simple corn mills but others with mills that powered forges, or carried out the processes of slitting, fulling or needle finishing.

Fig. 7.25 The surface remains of lead mining: Tideslow/Moss Rake, Derbyshire.

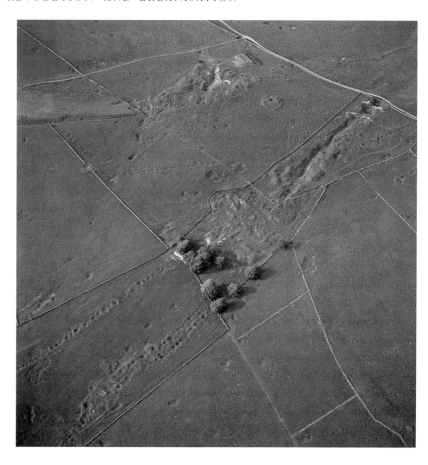

Fig. 7.26 A packhorse trail over the Dark Peak. L J Wood: The Roaches near Leek c. 1840.

TRANSPORT

Although travellers like Defoe and Fiennes dreaded having to cross the Dark Peak, ancient packhorse trails made their way over the desolate moorlands (Fig. 7.26), with stones set up as waymarkers in prominent locations or at junctions. Packhorses were a major means of transferring industrial goods throughout the region until the 18th century. River transport, too, was important and the Severn-Avon, Weaver and Trent systems provided arteries into the region. Transport was to play as important a part in the Industrial Revolution as any other technological advancement, 'both a cause and consequence of industrial and commercial growth'.[50] Turnpike roads were being opened by the early 18th century and river transport was invaluable. Improvement of navigation on the Weaver began in 1730. Along with timber and pottery, the Trent carried coal from Derbyshire, iron products from Staffordshire and cheese from Cheshire to coastal ports. The Severn was navigable from Shrewsbury and, in times of flood, from Welshpool. The main commodity carried was soft clod coal from the Ironbridge district, much of it for the Droitwich saltworks, but in the early 18th century pig iron was also brought up-river from the Forest of Dean to supply midland forges. Later, as supplies dwindled, the pig iron was replaced by unprocessed ore imported from overseas and unloaded at Bristol.

Again, packhorses carried finished iron goods from Manchester, Stourbridge, Dudley and the Stour ironworks to Bridgnorth or Wribbenhall near Bewdley. Transport down-river was by 'trow' and barge. Trows were distinctive local vessels that carried 40 to 80 tons and were some 18m or more long with a main and top mast and square sails. Most were locally built. Bewdley, a Severn port (Fig. 7.27), was the natural outlet for many of Wyre's products and for agricultural produce from the surrounding district, including cider, wool, leather, cheese and hops. Goods were brought in by packhorse and transferred to the trows. Leather goods

*Fig. 7.27 **The River Severn at the former port of Bewdley**. Steps, still present, led down from the sandstone quays to the river and goods such as wool, wood and coal were conveyed in the flat-bottomed Severn trows. Ships of 60 tons could sail up-river as far as the port.*

from the Black Country and the east midlands, wool from Staffordshire and Shropshire, earthenwares from the Potteries, glass, nails and iron goods from Stourbridge, were carried to Bristol. Many of the products were destined for the American colonies, and until the period of canal and railway construction Bewdley/Wribbenhall remained the chief port for the West Midlands and the Black Country, but when the Staffordshire and Worcester Canal reached Stourport in the later 18th century the new port rapidly captured much of its trade.

Although roads were being improved in the 18th century (*see* Chapter 5), it was the canal that was to permit the carriage of heavy industrial goods relatively cheaply over long distances. The network was developed in the 18th century when road communications in the region were still generally poor. Greatest enthusiasm was first shown in the Potteries, which had to obtain china and stone clay from the South-West by coasting vessels landing at Chester or navigating along the Mersey.

Here their loads were transferred to packhorses and wagons that brought back finished pots to Liverpool. Others carried pots to Bewdley and Bridgnorth to be sent down the Severn to Bristol. Although Josiah Wedgwood at first had reservations about its usefulness, a canal to link the Trent and Mersey systems, beginning in Derbyshire at the confluence of the Derwent and Trent, was built by James Brindley. Inaugurated at Brownhills in 1766, it opened as the Grand Trunk Canal in 1777 (later to be known as the Trent and Mersey), some years after Brindley's death. It effectively linked Liverpool with Hull via Cheshire and Staffordshire, and Brindley's Staffordshire and Worcestershire Canal (1766–72), which left the Grand Trunk at Great Haywood, near Stafford, provided a link to the Severn at Stourport and hence by river to Bristol (Fig. 7.28). The Grand Trunk was further linked to London and the South-East by a canal completed in 1790 from Fradley near Lichfield to Coventry and then by another canal to the Thames at Oxford. Thomas Pennant and others noted the immediate effects upon the districts served by the canals: tiles and slate replaced thatch for roofing, manure was carried to barren fields, poverty was alleviated and the rich prospered.[51] In the mid-1780s, plans for further canals across Cheshire resulted in the Ellesmere Canal to Chester (1796) and thence into Montgomeryshire (1805). The Macclesfield Canal was not opened until 1831 and was too late to avoid competition from the railways.

The engineering required to make the canals was prodigious and bands of navvies had to be employed to carry out the work. The difficulties of constructing canals over the steep edges of the Birmingham and south

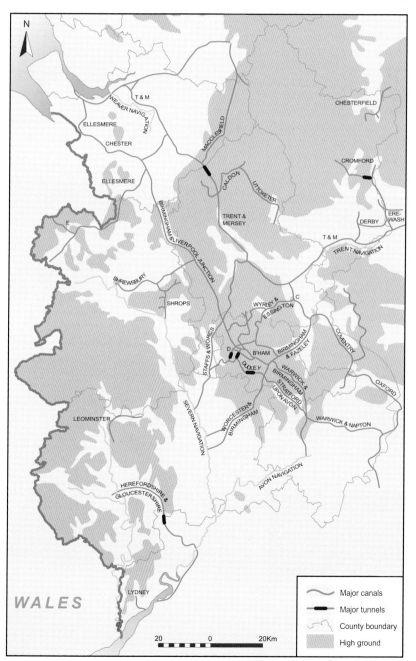

Fig. 7.28 The midland canal network
(C: Coventry; D: Dudley; E: Ellesmere; T & M: Trent and Mersey canals). Although rivers were used for navigation, goods had to be carried overland by cart and packhorse before the first canals were built in the second half of the 18th century. For the first time, it then became possible to transport heavy bulky goods for long distances – a spur to the region's industrial development. Although the canals were to be supplanted by the railways in the 19th century, the most important lines carried commercial traffic for nearly 200 years – far longer than most of the railways or the turnpike roads.

Staffordshire plateau and the provision of sufficient water for the canals had both to be surmounted. The plateau, in particular, had to be reached by flights of locks and the canals supplied with adequate water. The Stourbridge Canal needed 20 locks to rise from Stourton to Pensnett Chase and was then forced to wind around Brierley Hill to Black Delph in the West Midlands before climbing through another nine locks to join the Dudley Canal. The Birmingham Canal at first wound around Coseley Hill until, in 1837, a tunnel was cut through the hill. The longest single flight of locks in the British Isles – some 30 in number – plus a 530m tunnel, was needed to carry the Birmingham and Worcester Canal down the steep descent from the Birmingham plateau to the Severn plain at Tardebigge (Fig. 7.29). The water was provided by reservoirs and the line was finally opened in 1815.

Sometimes canals and navigable rivers ran at different levels and a means had to be found to link them for the haulage of goods: at Ironbridge two branches of the Shropshire Canal terminated at least 100m above the Severn. The western branch ran to Brierly Hill just above Coalbrookdale, and here goods were wound down 36m-deep vertical shafts, while the eastern branch terminated above Coalport on the Severn. Here, the Hay and Windmill inclined planes were built. The Hay plane dropped some 19m in 320m, and an ingenious system of counterbalancing was used to carry boats down to a lower canal and the river, not always without mishap:

> … on the chain snapping we have known a canal boat with five tons of iron pigs on board gain such velocity that on coming in contact with the water in the lower canal it has broken away from the iron chains which held it to the carriage, bounded into the air, clearing two other boats moored on the side, together with the embankment, and alighted in the Severn, close to the ferry-boat, into which it pitched some of the iron pigs it contained.[52]

The canal has now been restored, with its canal basins at the top and bottom. Reservoirs to hold water to feed the canals included Cofton, Lower and Upper Bittell, King's Norton and Rotton Park near Birmingham, with others elsewhere in the region. The creation of the early reservoirs on the upper Arrow to the south of Birmingham met considerable opposition from mill owners downstream who feared the loss of an adequate flow to drive their wheels.

To access the Black Country, a 2,900m tunnel was cut through the Sedgley–Rowley ridge near Dudley on the Birmingham and Stourbridge Canal

Fig. 7.29 Tardebigge locks, Worcestershire.

OPPOSITE PAGE:

Fig. 7.30 Monsal Dale railway viaduct, Derbyshire.

by 1792, linking Birmingham to the Staffordshire–Worcestershire Canal and the River Severn. It had branches that included a private side tunnel of 1,122m to Lord Dudley's workings at Wren's Nest completed in 1837 and another to Castle Mill quarries. The Lapal tunnel, some 3,470m long, was the fourth largest in England and took the Netherton–Selly Oak extension of the Dudley Canal under the same ridge further to the south. It took four hours to 'leg' through the tunnel until the introduction of a steam pumping engine in 1841 created a current to help boats through. The Netherton tunnel, 2,768m long, was the third to cut through the central ridge of the South Staffordshire Coalfield; opening in 1858 it provided a short cut to the mines of the Stour valley and was the last canal tunnel to be built in the country. In the 19th century, the courses of many canals were thus improved and shortened and new cuts were made to the growing colliery districts. By the mid-19th century, 'The Birmingham Canal Navigations had become the hub of the national canal system', with factories clustering along the canal sides, often with their own wharves.[53] Coal, iron and limestone were carried by canal in horse-pulled narrow boats and trade was opened up with Bristol, Liverpool and Hull. Canal building also effected further urban development: where Brindley's Staffordshire and Worcestershire Canal reached the Severn a new town developed at Stourport when the basin there was opened in 1771. The town that grew up was regarded, according to a local paper, as 'the resort of people of fashion', but it soon became an industrial centre with its own iron and carpet works. The canal heritage is today finally appreciated for its contribution to the region's landscape and culture and as a leisure resource: in Birmingham, Gas Street Basin has been restored and new developments congregate around Brindley Place, including the new National Indoor Arena.

By the mid-19th century, railways were competing with the canals as the most important means of transport. Wooden and iron tramways had been used to carry raw materials in horse-drawn wagons from mines since the 18th century but their courses were irregular, far from level and often transient. A particularly dense network served the coal mines and ironworks of the Ironbridge region. By the middle of the 19th century, however, the railway networks, under a number of separate companies, were under construction. Some of the new rail companies actually bought up the canal companies, either to promote rail–water interchange or discourage it where the lines were not their own. The first railway of national importance was the Grand Junction Railway linking Birmingham with Merseyside. It opened in 1837 and the following year it was extended south to the Birmingham–London line. Local lines were added in the second half of the century until the region was covered with a network that provided cheaper and quicker freight carriage than the canals and more comfortable and faster travel for passengers than the turnpikes. In turn, the railways stimulated local road transport offering access 'to the rails'.

In the towns, industry followed the railways as it had the canals, and a long tongue of industrial development stretched out from central Birmingham south-eastwards along the Warwick Canal and the Birmingham–Oxford Railway towards Tyseley, including the Birmingham Small Arms Company established at Small Heath in 1861. Subsequent development, largely after 1910, saw the almost complete industrialisation of the Tame valley to the north-east of the city, along the Birmingham–Derby railway line. Large factories here included the tyre and rubber works of Fort Dunlop, situated between the railway and the Fazeley Canal. Railways carved through the countryside added a new feature to the communication network and opened up new areas for 'out-of-town' living – the Alderley Edge district of Cheshire and the Malvern foothills of Worcestershire, for instance, became desirable places for the middle classes.

In places, the railways contributed engineering spectacles of their own. The Monsal Dale Viaduct in Derbyshire (Fig. 7.30), built in 1863 to carry the former Midland Railway's main line from London to Manchester, was detested by John

Fig. 7.31 Curzon Street Station, Birmingham.

Ruskin who complained that 'The valley is gone and the Gods with it', but it is today regarded with affection and is preserved as a feature of historic and architectural interest. Metropolitan pride in this new form of transport is expressed in Birmingham by the austerely elegant Ionic arches of Curzon Street Station (Fig. 7.31) built in 1838 at the terminus of the London and Birmingham Railway, a counterpoint to the now-demolished Doric Euston Arch that once adorned the other end of the line. In Cheshire, Crewe developed as a major rail junction and railway engineering became the mainstay of the town's economy, especially after the re-grouping of railway companies in 1923.[54]

NINETEENTH-CENTURY WORKING AND LIVING CONDITIONS

The living conditions of the labouring classes in the 19th-century West Midlands were as difficult for the rural worker as for those in the rapidly growing industrial areas. The 'improvements' introduced by the enclosure movement, driven by the pressure to produce more food and to produce greater profits for landowners, robbed many living around commons and greens of their patches of free grazing – cottagers and squatters often faced absolute ruin and were forced to hire themselves out for ridiculously low wages at 'hiring fairs'. Under the terms of 'Settlement Laws', they were often forbidden to leave their own village without a certificate guaranteeing that their parish would accept responsibility should they become chargeable to rates. If driven to poaching to avoid starvation they were liable, as we have seen, to imprisonment, whipping, hard labour, transportation or death:

> *You have sold the labouring man, squire*
> *Body and soul to shame,*
> *To pay for your seat in the House, squire*
> *And to pay for the feed of your game.*
>
> *You made him a poacher yourself, squire,*
> *When you'd give neither work nor meat,*
> *And your barley-fed hares robbed the garden*
> *At our starving children's feet.*[55]

With the development of industry in the region's towns, the rural poor were drawn in from the countryside in ever increasing numbers. Industrialisation brought social revolution: 'The bondage of summer hirings and virtual serfdom broke down to be replaced by a strange free bondage. A bondage that gave the worker an illusion of freedom, yet, in reality he was no better and perhaps worse off than his agricultural counterpart'.[56] In a part of the country where many of the inhabitants were closely bound within their working environment of mining and manufacture there developed a strong regional character expressed in manner, habit and language that is still present in some measure today. The Black Country dialect is distinct; local fables and verse abound, often based upon a peculiarly acid humour and a fighting spirit perpetuated in the late survival of blood-sports such as bull-baiting and cock-fighting, and the rearing of bulldogs, bull terriers and whippets (the poor man's greyhound). This aspect is discussed further in Chapter 8.

Yet if working conditions in mills, factories and mines were arduous and frequently life-threatening, the break-up of the rural social hierarchy did in fact provide a certain freedom for individual thought and action. In Europe, the latter part of the 18th century had witnessed the French Revolution, and in England many, like William Wordsworth, William Blake and Joseph Priestley, recognised in these events a common cause for freedom, at least until events in France grew increasingly violent. Joseph Priestley came to Birmingham in 1791 as a Unitarian minister and spoke for many fellow radicals determined to overthrow 'the old building of error and superstition'. Conditions for the working classes worsened in the economic slump that followed the end of the Napoleonic Wars, and the newly introduced Corn Laws, which raised the price of English wheat, increased their hardship. When profits fell in the coal mining and iron industries, the wages of the coal miners and ironworkers would be reduced. But an articulate working class was beginning to demand greater rights. The Luddites were active in the midlands and the north of England from about 1811, especially focusing their attention upon the cotton mills in which once-prosperous weavers found themselves working long hours for very low pay; they destroyed machinery and burned factories. A wholesale strike of Black Country miners and ironworkers broke out in 1815 in protest against drastically reduced wages: 'between three and four thousand men marched into Wolverhampton with bludgeons and sticks, bent on riot and depredation'.[57] One of the worst riots by the colliers was at Clinker Hill, near Wellington in Shropshire, in 1821 where some of the Yeoman cavalry, who had been called out to quell the riot, were injured by stones and clinkers hurled at them; several protesters were killed. Other riots broke out in the Potteries. By the middle of the century a Chartist movement was demanding a 'People's Charter' of rights granting household suffrage, salaried members of Parliament, the abolition of a property qualification, ballots and triennial elections. A meeting in Birmingham in 1838 drew 10,000 delegates from across the country but further meetings in July 1839 culminated in riots when special constables, militia and dragoons, bolstered by a new military police brought in by train, had to dispel crowds gathered in the Bull Ring, where further worse disturbances were to occur. There were other serious riots and some of those taken after these rebellions were transported or sentenced to hard labour. The growth of the Trade Union movement after the 1860s did much to benefit workers when economic conditions were reasonably good.

Such social conflict and the gradual political emancipation of working people in the 19th and early 20th centuries have left few indelible marks on the face of the West Midlands landscape. Private interaction with the physical world – the landscape of the imagination – forms the subject of the next chapter. More public displays of self-help may be found in individual buildings such as working men's institutes or the cottages of squatters that we have already encountered. Quieter relics of the Chartist movement survive in the midland landscape: at Great Dodford near Bromsgrove in north Worcestershire is a village laid out by Chartists as an urban 'back-to-the-land' movement in 1848, when land bought by Fergus O'Connor for this purpose was divided into 40 plots, each with a

Fig. 7.32 Chartist's cottage, Great Dodford near Bromsgrove, Worcestershire, recently renovated by the National Trust.

cottage, the first of which was occupied on 2 July 1849. Many of the original uniformly planned cottages remain, each with its plot of land (Figs 7.32 and 7.33). There were other small Chartist settlements at Snigs End in Staunton and Lowbands in Redmarley D'Abitot on the west side of the Severn close to the Worcestershire–Gloucestershire border.

But for most, the reality was very different. Although houses were rapidly built in the growing towns for the labouring classes, they were often of very poor quality and offered squalid living conditions. There were no building regulations in the first part of the 19th century and sanitation had barely improved since medieval times. In Birmingham, almost a quarter of the population in the mid-

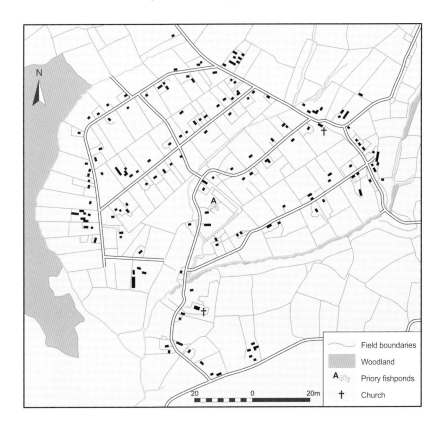

Fig. 7.33 Dodford Chartist settlement, Bromsgrove, Worcestershire. A small Augustinian priory had been founded here 1184–91, later annexed to Halesowen Abbey.

	Field boundaries
	Woodland
A	Priory fishponds
†	Church

19th century lived in courts, either in the notorious 'back-to-backs' or 'tunnel-backs'. A covered entrance led to a courtyard bounded on three sides by houses and on the fourth by a high wall, with many families sharing a few privies.[58] Streets were virtually open sewers and cholera outbreaks were frequent. Conditions in the Black Country in the 19th century were notoriously harsh:

> *This was a black country by day and a red country by night. 'For when darkness falls, the smoke changes to flame, and the dark sky overhead is lit up with the glare of a myriad of fiery furnaces. Then, as the silence of night settles down, the incessant din of heavy machinery becomes more perceptible in its rumbling monotony. Mighty engines spin, and whirl, and writhe with the clanking of chains, the thud of ponderous arms, and the groan of heavy wheels …And ever and anon … the jaws of some fiery furnace gape wide apart'.[59]*
> (Fig. 7.34)

The descriptions in Brett Young's novel *Far Forest* of the mean lives of many of the chainmakers living around 'Mawne Heath' near Cradley are hardly exaggerations. Terrible injuries were sustained in the coal mines and hardly a week passed without some fatality or injury caused by the fall of coal of rock or by the dangerous gases that could cause poisoning, suffocation or explosion. Children were employed in the mines and were not exempt. The landscape was one of desolation – in 1837 men returning home from work lost their way in a dense fog near Netherton and fell into a coal pit; a four-year-old boy fell to his death when a cover over an old pit gave way at the Old Buffery Works at Dudley the following year.[60] Thomas Tancred describes the conurbation in 1843:

> *The traveller appears never to get out of an interminable village, composed of cottages and very ordinary houses. In some directions he may travel for miles, and never be out of sight of numerous two-storied houses; so that the area covered by bricks and mortar must be immense. These houses, for the most part, are not arranged in continuous streets but are interspersed with blazing*

Fig. 7.34 N A Chapman: Homer Hill Colliery: *the view from Two Lanes End.*

furnaces, heaps of burning coal in process of coking, piles of ironstone calcining, forges, pit-banks, and engine chimneys; the country being besides intersected with canals, crossing each other at different levels; and the small remaining patches of the surface soil occupied with irregular fields of grass or corn, intermingled with heaps of the refuse of mines or of slag from the blast furnaces. Sometimes the road passes between mounds of refuse from the pits, like a deep cutting on a railway; at others it runs like a causeway, raised some feet above the fields on either side, which have subsided by the excavation of the minerals beneath … The whole country might be compared to a vast rabbit warren. It is a matter of every day occurrence for houses to fall down, or a row of buildings inhabited by numerous families to assume a very irregular outline … caused by the sinking of the ground into old workings.[61]

Houses were still collapsing due to mining subsidence at Clayhanger on the Cannock Chase Coalfield in the 1940s.

Despite the popular view that associates the Industrial Revolution exclusively with factories, outwork had been an important source of funds for rural folk. Needles were made by the poor in the villages around Redditch and in the Arrow valley of the Worcestershire–Warwickshire border in the 19th century, although by that date water-driven corn mills were being converted for the finishing processes. Outworkers purchased rods of iron from middlemen to fashion the needles in their homes and it was not until local mills were converted in the 18th and early 19th centuries that the poor lost this means of livelihood. With the enclosure of the commons at this time, the poor also lost their rights of common pasture and many were forced into semi-urban slums, such as the settlement of Wapping, in Studley, to work in the new factories. Many rural workers around the periphery of industrial towns were engaged in some form of outwork: the metal parts of locks were made in the villages around Wolverhampton (such as Brewood, Pendeford and Coven) and then brought to the town to be cased in wood. Nail making employed thousands in the villages around Birmingham and the Black Country in the 18th century, extending out to the Bromsgrove area and beyond. For nails and chains, as for needles, rods of iron were collected from middlemen – factors in the midlands often called 'foggers' – and the products fashioned in small workshops and outhouses attached to dwellings. With chain making, from a hundredweight of iron (112 pounds; 51kg) they were expected to return 104 pounds (47kg) of chain and were fined a penny for each pound short.[62] The growing production of nails by machine caused a progressive fall in the rates paid to hand-workers and led to bitter strikes in the middle of the 19th century. In the 1890s, a former secretary of the defunct nailmakers' union said:

Nailmaking is one of the worst trades in the kingdom. There are scores of men in this parish [Bromsgrove] who are not earning nine shillings a week for seventy, eighty, or ninety hours work, and out of these earnings have to pay from one shilling to eighteen pence a week for firing, and about sixpence for keeping their tools in order.[63]

Worse, the nails were often paid for with tokens (sometimes referred to as 'tommy notes') that had to be used in the fogger's own shop or tavern (bacon might cost 10 pence per pound here although it was available elsewhere for 6 pence). Although the nailmakers were renowned for 'whining', in 1842 thousands of strikers collected in Rowley Regis in order to march to Dudley to confront the dealers with their wage claims and had to be dispersed by troops sent in from Birmingham. In Bromsgrove, there were bread riots in 1809, and strikes in 1828, 1842 and 1852. A later strike, in 1862, led to a song that expressed their utter dejection, but the wage increase led to only a temporary respite.

You Nailmakers all that day remember well,
In the last strike of which this tale I tell,
How cold and hungry we that heavy day,
To Bromsgrove town did take out toilsome way.

And these Nailforgers miserable souls,
Will not forget the givers of the coals,
Nail Masters are hard-heated files,
The way we took was thirteen miles.

Oh the slaves abroad in the sugar canes,
Find plenty to help and pity their pains,
But the slaves at home in the mine and fire,
Find plenty to pity but none to admire.[64]

The handworking of chains and nails could only flourish if wages were minimal and was eventually to become another trade that eventually had to compete with machine-made goods.

Another movement that we have already seen gaining ground in the 18th and 19th centuries was Nonconformity. Puritanism had long had a following in urban centres – in the Civil Wars the smiths of Walsall are said to have refused to supply swords to the Royalist followers while Birmingham supplied 15,000 swords to the leaders of the Parliamentary forces.[65] Nonconformity involved the people and preached equality; it became especially popular in the industrial and mining areas and the Quakers were one of the first sects to meet openly. John Wesley, the founder of Methodism, visited Staffordshire first in 1738. By the middle of the century Wednesbury had become a centre in the Black Country, although the first chapel was built in Tipton in 1755. By 1766 there was a chapel in the Potteries and Wesley himself noted in his Journal in March 1794 'I preached in the new meetinghouse at Hanley Green; but this was far too small to hold the congregation. Indeed this country is all on fire, and the flame is still spreading from village to village'.[66] Methodism was brought to the Ironbridge area by John Fletcher, the vicar of Madeley, in the late 18th century and there was a great revival in 1821 that brought Primitive Methodists to the area. Primitive Methodism began as an offshoot in the Potteries where a group of Wesleyans began to hold open air meetings at Mow Cop (Fig. 7.35), high on the gritstone ridge on the Staffordshire/Cheshire border to the north of Stoke – a sham ruin crowning the hilltop had been built in 1754 as an eye-catcher to be seen from Rode Hall on the Cheshire plain below. On the centenary of the first assembly, more than 70,000 people gathered on the hill.

Fig. 7.35 Mow Cop, *to the north of Kidsgrove on the Cheshire/Staffordshire border.*

Further Nonconformist sects formed, among them the Baptists, Presbyterians, Congregationalists and Unitarians. Their chapels and meetinghouses appeared both in the towns and in the countryside. The Revivalist sects were implemental in the moral reform of industrial society – they not only condemned alcohol but also campaigned against cruel sports such as bull-baiting and cock-fighting. By the mid-19th century, chapel-goers outnumbered Anglicans and Catholics in the urban areas of the region, although the later part of the century saw a massive programme of church building throughout England.

METROPOLITAN PRIDE

New buildings were erected in town centres in the 19th century as Victorian philanthropism and civic pride, fed by the prosperity of trade and industry, began to take hold. In noting the buildings of the industrial conurbations, Pevsner in 1974 described the 'Five Towns' of the Potteries as 'an urban tragedy' without a centre, never mind a civic centre, apart perhaps from Longton, but others places were more admirably provided. Of these, Birmingham, a much-maligned city, is outstanding. Narrowly escaping the proposed destruction of the 1960s, fine Victorian buildings line Colmore Row and form a fitting setting for the 18th-century church (now the Cathedral of St Philip designed by Thomas Archer (Fig. 7.36)). The Town Hall, with its bold façade of Corinthian columns begun in 1832, said to be based upon the temple of Castor and Pollux at Rome, has similarly escaped (Fig. 7.37) and with the classical-style Council House designed by Yeoville Thomason provides a noble surround to Chamberlain and Victoria Squares (Fig. 7.38). Here there is a memorial erected in 1876 to Joseph Chamberlain. Chamberlain had been elected councillor for St Paul's Ward in 1869 and mayor in 1873; he had founded the University of Birmingham in 1900. Sadly, the university's original headquarters, Mason College in Edmund Street, an ornate brick building begun in 1875 and founded by Sir Josiah Mason at his own expense as a Scientific College, have now given way to the modern architecture of the Reference Library. A new shopping street, Corporation

BELOW: *Fig. 7.36 Birmingham Cathedral square.*

BELOW RIGHT: *Fig. 7.37 Birmingham Town Hall.*

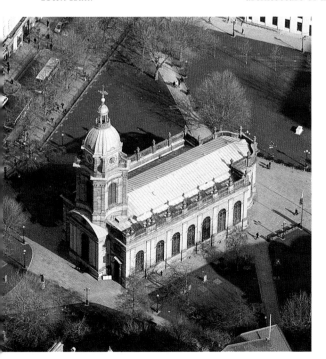

Street, was also designed by Joseph Chamberlain with, at its lower end, Aston Webb's Victorian Law Courts (now augmented by a new building across the road), and, in Steelhouse Lane, the great brick General Hospital. The new university had expanded to a new and additional site in Edgbaston by 1909, its buildings, also designed by Aston Webb, dominated by the tall Tuscan campanile of the Chamberlain tower (Fig. 7.39), affectionately known today as 'Joe'. Further civic developments have maintained Birmingham's civic centre. An extension along Broad Street has the 20th-century Hall of Memory and Baskerville House, and the modern Symphony Hall complex opens onto Centenary Square. On the eastern side of the centre, St Martin's church in the old Bull Ring is today framed between sections of an up-to-the-minute new shopping centre (Fig. 7.40).

Philanthropy was not limited to the building of civic centres. New schools and hospitals were being established in all major towns, including provision for the mentally ill and destitute, and were often funded by private contributions. A few philanthropic industrialists were anxious to improve the lot of their workers: as early as the 1760s Josiah Wedgwood was providing housing for his workers at Etruria that was of a considerably advanced standard for its day, with terraces of four-roomed cottages, every few dwellings sharing a well and a pump. Other cotton industrialists, such as Richard Arkwright and Sir Robert Peel, also built model houses for their mill workers. At Ironville, just beyond the eastern edge of the region, terraces were constructed for workers in the ironworks there; at Port Sunlight on the Wirral, W H Lever built a model community named after his best-selling brand of soap. In Birmingham, Cadbury's Bournville represents one of the best developments of its day.

ABOVE LEFT: *Fig. 7.38 Council House, Birmingham.*

ABOVE: *Fig. 7.39 Birmingham University Tower, Edgbaston: fondly nicknamed 'Joe' after Joseph Chamberlain.*

Fig. 7.40 New Bull Ring shopping Centre, Birmingham, with St Martin's church in juxtaposition to the new buildings.

197

The founders of the chocolate industry, Cadbury, Fry in Bristol and Rowntree in York, were all members of the Society of Friends (Quakers) and the production of chocolate was itself partially philanthropic. They shared a concern about children drinking alcoholic drinks in order to avoid unclean water – cocoa offered a cheap and palatable alternative. John Cadbury advertised cocoa as 'a most nutritious beverage for breakfast' in 1824, when he was engaged in breaking up roasted beans at Bull Street in Birmingham. He was a Street Commissioner and Overseer of the Poor, had taken up the campaign to replace chimney-sweep 'climbing boys' with mechanical cleaners and was also looking at ways of reducing atmospheric pollution in the city. When his sons, George and Richard, relocated their cocoa factory to Bournville in 1878, the factory soon became renowned for its chocolate. George purchased land near to the factory in 1895 in order to build a model village, primarily to alleviate:

> *… the evils which arise from the insanitary and insufficient housing accommodation supplied to large numbers of the working classes, and of securing to workers in factories some of the advantages of outdoor village life, with opportunities for the natural and healthful occupation of cultivating the soil.*[67]

The first houses had been built by 1900 and were managed by the Bournville Village Trust. The domestic architecture was much influenced by the late 19th-century Arts and Crafts movement and houses were nostalgically grouped around a 'village green', close to schools, and this is still a much sought after family area to this day (Fig. 7.41). The Cadbury family also gave large tracts of open land on the Lickey Hills for the enjoyment of Birmingham people.

The movement to provide cities with public parks and gardens was another alliance between landowning wealth and urban corporations, and in Victoria's reign (1837–1901) private benefactors allied with the corporations to provide new areas for public enjoyment. By the middle of the 19th century, public subscriptions were being launched in Manchester and elsewhere, and Birmingham was to follow in establishing baths and walks by public subscription. The first public parks had been in London, a development of the royal parks, although in Birmingham the grounds of the Holtes' old manor at Duddeston were opened as Vauxhall Gardens

Fig. 7.41 Bournville: the 'Village Green'.

for public enjoyment in 1758 and was also used for major events such as galas, firework displays and balloon ascents – the midland equivalent of the Tivoli Gardens. The country's first public arboretum was laid out at Derby in 1840 by J C Loudon on land belonging to Joseph Strutt. It was modelled on the only other (private) arboretum in England at Chatsworth, but had no funding for maintenance and was forced to charge for admission on five days of the week.[68] Other landowners, such as Charles Adderley and Lord Calthorpe, gave land in Birmingham – in 1856 and 1857 respectively. Louisa Anne Ryland, a noted philanthropist who lived at Barford Hill House in the Avon valley, gave Cannon Hill Park (Fig. 7.42) to the people of Birmingham in 1873, first landscaping its grounds at her own expense and providing boating and swimming pools; she also gave Small Heath Park and built several new hospitals. Queen Victoria had opened a park at the Holtes' new family seat at Aston Hall in 1858 and in 1864 this was acquired by Birmingham Corporation to become the city's largest municipal park, with a stage, aquarium, skating rink and cycling track. The Birmingham Football Association also met a few years later in Aston Lower Grounds.[69]

Victorian prosperity also led to the expansion of many of the region's industrial towns as the middle classes moved out from town centres. Maintained as a private estate, Birmingham's Calthorpe estate in Edgbaston has managed to retain its elegance (Fig. 7.43) and other Victorian suburbs are to be found in most of the region's larger towns. Many went through a period of depression after the Second World War when the size and high maintenance costs of their houses brought them into disfavour for a time, but even the smaller Victorian terrace houses now have an appeal of their own.

The provision of clean water was another step towards improving the health of city dwellers that had a dramatic effect upon the countryside. When Birmingham Corporation gained control over water supplies to the town in 1875 it was in a position to carry out suggestions put forward some years earlier by Robert Rawlinson that water might be brought from mid-Wales from the rivers Elan and Claerwen. The Corporation took a decision that was formidable in its conception and far-sightedness, despite the costs involved – £6,600,000.

Fig. 7.42 Cannon Hill Park, Birmingham.

Fig. 7.43 Edgbaston Victorian houses, Birmingham.

It bought 180sq km of land to the west of Rhayader, dammed rivers to create reservoirs, and built an aqueduct and tunnel 118km long to Frankley in Birmingham. By 1905, 55 million litres a day were supplying all of Birmingham's needs. In 1858 the upper Churnet was dammed to create Tittesworth reservoir to provide water for Stoke. The northern towns similarly turned to the Dark Peak for their supplies. Here, high rainfall, narrow valleys and impermeable strata provided suitable conditions for reservoirs to be constructed and these were made along the Etherow in Longdendale between 1848 and 1875, in the upper Kinder valley in 1911, and in the Goyt and Derwent valleys in the 1930s (the Kinder and Goyt reservoirs serving the

Fig. 7.44 Fernilee reservoir in the Goyt valley, Derbyshire.

Stockport area). Whole communities were sometimes sacrificed: when Fernilee reservoir was built (Fig. 7.44), Norman Price described watching 'the dazed Goyt folk' leaving the valley in 1953:

> *The waters bayed up to the sturdy lichened walls of the empty stone farmhouses in the deep of the valley. Then, slowly, the defeated rural men strapped their ancient bedsteads on to hay wagons, fumblingly fastened tin trunks on to their milk carts, and turned away up the lane that led through the deserted village of Fernilee, and all those little windswept streets they would never see again, except as a fading memory.*[70]

The Errwood reservoir, the southernmost reservoir in the valley, was added in the 1960s. The Sheffield urban area was also greedy for water and on the Derwent, which rises on the Howden Moors, great masonry dams (Fig. 7.45) were constructed in 1912 and 1916, using stone brought by rail from Grindleford some 13.7km away, followed by a third dam, the Ladybower, opened in 1945, that exploited the new techniques then available for building improved earthen dams. The construction of the Ladybower reservoir in the 1940s, on land sold by the Duke of Norfolk, led to the drowning not only of valley farmhouses and Derwent Hall but the two villages of Derwent and Ashopton. For a time, the steeple of Derwent church stood above the surface of the water. The Blithfield reservoir in Staffordshire opened in 1953 within an area of former parkland, and the Tittesworth Reservoir was extended in 1959–62.

Fig. 7.45 The Derwent dam in Derwent Dale, west of Sheffield.

201

SUBSEQUENT DEVELOPMENTS

The last hundred years have seen massive changes in the industrial map of Britain. Towards the end of the 19th century, both iron and coal supplies were dwindling and ironworks were closing. The last (and newest) Cheshire colliery, at Poynton, closed in 1935. The coal industry was nationalised in 1946 and the National Coal Board established the following year, with its headquarters at Himley Hall in Staffordshire, bought from the Earl of Dudley. At first there was a demand for coal to supply gasworks, and coal mining became concentrated on the deeper mines of the concealed coalfields. A new modern colliery was sunk at Lea Hall near Rugeley in 1960 to supply an electricity generating station on the same site; on the East Warwickshire Coalfield, output was declining by 1964 in spite of high productivity, but a new shaft was opened at Daw Mill in 1965 and the colliery is still working. Wolstanton colliery in north Staffordshire became the deepest mine in Britain and took over the workings of the nearby Chatterley Whitfield colliery in 1974. But oil and electricity began to take over in the 1960s, and in 1967 North Sea gas started to replace gas made from coal. Steel output increased at Bilston, Brierley Hill and Shelton as works were modernised after the end of the Second World War, but the industry could not survive the collapse of the British steel industry in the 1970s and significant midland production has ceased. The tiny metal trade shops were similarly swept away. In the Potteries, the production of ceramics has similarly declined. Today the Black Country region is no longer 'black' with the smoke from steam engines and their chimneys, furnaces and other fires, the scene punctuated at night by the red glare from the furnaces.

Heavy industry has instead given way to light engineering throughout the midland region, and manufacturing has been largely replaced by assembly and service industries. This builds upon the early traditions of places such as the Soho factory at Handsworth, but is now carried out in modern premises. Electricity, having replaced steam as the main source of power, has also given greater flexibility to industrial location. Small electricity supply companies run by private enterprise and municipalities were amalgamated when the national electricity grid was established in 1926; the English Electric Company was based in Stafford by 1932, Peel-Connor and British Houston at Coventry. The two World Wars gave considerable impetus to the new car and bicycle firms of Birmingham, Coventry and Wolverhampton that were able to produce army vehicles in quantity. Munitions were also in great demand – during the Second World War hostels were provided to house extra workers and factories were turned over to the production of aeroplane parts, shells and other vital supplies.

Many of the engineering companies could adapt to post-war demands by continuing to supply cars, motorcycles, washing machines and cameras; aluminium works were established near Birmingham and at Wolverhampton between the wars. The innovative production of plastic goods was based in Tyseley after 1933 and new synthetic fibres such as rayon were produced at Coventry where the silk industry still lingered. Subsequently, big multinational companies have replaced the traditional small firms – in 1926 ICI represented the amalgamation of four great companies that had themselves incorporated dozens of small firms – although the change-over has been far from rapid. Between the wars, great car firms such as Rootes and Standard at Coventry were employing thousands of workers and the reorganisation of the Longbridge car plant had brought in new layouts with 10km of assembly line by 1930 (Fig. 7.46); many parts and accessories, however, were still bought in from numerous smaller firms. Machine tool firms flourished and the Birmingham and Black Country conurbation could claim the benefit of a skilled workforce. Today, large car assembly plants like those of the former MG/Rover at Longbridge, Land Rover near Elmdon, or Jaguar at Castle Bromwich dominate the surrounding urban fringe landscape but face an uncertain future.

The West Midlands has remained one of Britain's main manufacturing regions although changes continue. Between 1900 and 1990, 80 per cent of UK patents were taken out in Birmingham. The motor trade is still a major employer in the Birmingham–Wolverhampton area. Although Fort Dunlop in Birmingham no longer makes tyres – after a period of steady decline the company sold out in 1983 to the Japanese who closed the factory – the production of car components remains a major industry in the area. Telford has also been successful as a new manufacturing centre. Birmingham is England's 'Second City' after London and is also the second most important media centre of the country. Today, industrial location is not influenced by the old canal or rail networks but by motorways. Since the 1960s, these have been driven across the countryside to serve major conurbations and Birmingham, with its notorious and tortuous 'Spaghetti Junction', lies at the focus of the midland motorway system (Fig. 7.47). As the M56, M6, M1 and M42 became increasingly congested, Britain's first toll motorway was opened in 2003 as the 'Birmingham Relief Road' to link the M42 with the M6.

Industry has always attracted immigrants to the region – glass blowers from Lorraine were introduced by the Tyzack family to Bishop's Wood at Eccleshall in Staffordshire in about 1585; German miners were manufacturing copper and brass in Staffordshire in the 1680s; French immigrants formed part of the labour force of the Bilston enamelware industry in the 18th and 19th centuries.[71] The surge in industrial growth after the mid-19th century not only sucked in the rural poor and those from outlying rural towns in the midland region but also attracted huge numbers of migrants from elsewhere in Britain and beyond. A small Jewish community, largely drawn from Eastern Europe, had become established in Birmingham by 1800 and an Italian community by 1914. But greatly outnumbering all others before the middle of the 19th century were Irish immigrants settling in the town or visiting it for seasonal work, their numbers augmented following the potato famine. By 1861, nearly 11,500 Irish lived in the

Fig. 7.46 **View from the Lickeys over Longbridge.** *The former MG/Rover plant can be seen on the right of the picture with the tall buildings of central Birmingham in the distance.*

Fig. 7.47 'Spaghetti Junction': the motorway interchange near Birmingham.

worst housing conditions Birmingham had to offer, with several families occupying every room, from cellar to garret, in the inner city slums. Many came from Connaught, were unskilled and spoke only Gaelic. It is not perhaps surprising, therefore, that violent riots broke out in 1875, fired by religious intolerance, urban violence, drunkenness and the vexed issue of Home Rule. By the middle of the 20th century, Birmingham needed all the immigrant workers it could get to man its depleted council workforce after the Second World War – in the early 1950s around one-third of transport workers in the city were Irish and hospitals were manned by Irish nurses. Increasingly, West Indians from the Caribbean and people from India and Pakistan were recruited to the workforce. This was not a new situation – Chinese workers had arrived during the First World War to work in the factories. Further immigration from the Indian subcontinent and Africa (some following the division between India and Pakistan in 1947, others after the troubles in Uganda during the 1970s) has helped to establish a considerable Muslim community in the city and present political uncertainties have brought in refugees from the Middle East. Synagogues and mosques stand side-by-side with Christian churches and chapels of many different denominations as testament to the present rich cultural fabric of the city (Fig. 7.48).

Other conurbations have shared in this influx and the general increase in the region's urban populations. A comparison between the various editions of the one-inch Ordnance Survey maps shows immediately how the towns have spread outwards, how centres have coalesced, villages been absorbed and ribbons of interwar housing have stretched out along roads (Fig. 7.49). Between the two World Wars, housing improvements led to the construction of municipal housing on a grand scale: between 1920 and 1946, of the nearly 100,000 houses built in Birmingham, half were so-called 'council houses' and whole new suburbs, vast seas of redbrick houses, developed, as at Kingstanding to the north of the city (Fig. 7.50). In the 1960s, high-rise council buildings began to re-house those made homeless by inner-city slum clearance. Found both within the inner cities and around their margins, they were

Fig. 7.48 The Central Birmingham mosque.

Fig. 7.49 Urban development in the midland conurbations.

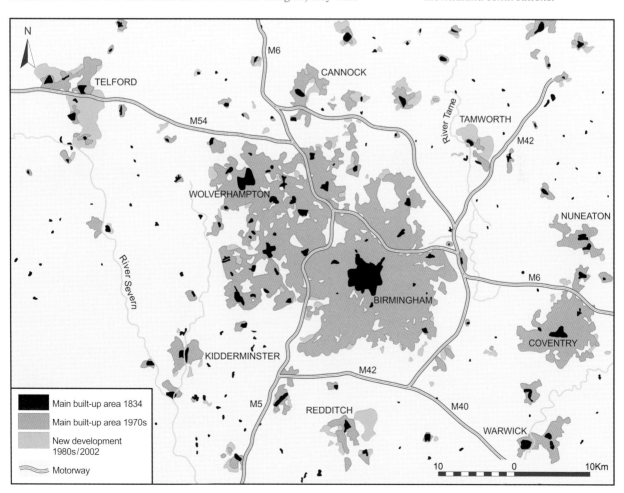

Main built-up area 1834

Main built-up area 1970s

New development 1980s/2002

Motorway

Fig. 7.50 The spread of interwar municipal housing: Kingstanding, Birmingham.

constructed wherever land was readily available. Today, private housing is still pressing hard upon the urban fringe although there has been considerable redevelopment, too, of so-called 'brown-field sites' – former derelict land within the conurbations. Indeed, the expanses of derelict land that were once so characteristic of industrial areas such as the Black Country – where nearly 3,600ha of quarries, mines, spoilbanks and tips still existed in 1948[72] – have all but disappeared under redevelopment.

Most recently, the expansion of the motorway network and the corresponding dominance of road transport have offered new incentives for settlement and industrial location along the most accessible routes – most modern industrial buildings, including warehouses, are now found in defined 'factory estates' close to major roads and motorways. New towns were established at Redditch and Telford in the 1960s and both have been outstandingly successful in attracting new industry. Telford was to replace the sprawl of the old 19th-century towns of Wellington, Oakengates, Dawley, Madeley and Ironbridge. As in other coalfield conurbations, competition between centres had prevented any of these emerging as the acknowledged urban centre of the district. Redditch is planned around the car, with a generous system of interlinking roads, but provision has also been made for pedestrian thoroughfares separated from the traffic. Planning applications for 'new dormitory green villages', hypermarkets and industrial complexes are continuously proposed – some are successful, and help to expand the built-up area to the very edge of the 'green belt'. The idea of 'green belts' to preserve lungs of countryside around and between conurbations developed in the 1930s – London and Birmingham were among the first urban centres to designate such zones – but these have been consistently under threat. Some have indeed suggested 'green wedges' that would permit development of 'linear towns' along major motorways, but these have so far been resisted. Sports facilities, especially golf courses and riding stables, now increasingly spill out into the 'urban fringe' and beyond, merging with smallholdings and farms.

As the countryside changes its character, with fewer people directly employed on the land or in rural pursuits, the links between town and country may grow stronger. The problems raised by commuting and the consequent increase in traffic cannot be easily absorbed by the country's infrastructure but the smaller towns of the region are being seen as increasingly attractive places to live, providing the amenities of a town close to the countryside. As populations age, many are free to 'relocate' in such surroundings. To meet the challenge, however, the region's conurbations are also expanding their role as cultural centres. The Royal Ballet has moved to Birmingham; the Corporation has developed a new sports and cultural centre in the heart of the city at the Indoor Arena. The city has also made a feature of its 19th-century canal landscape, and of its historic jewellery and gun-making quarters. Other cities have developed similar amenities and the relics of 19th-century industry are now as likely to offer the settings for industrial heritage centres as 'fill-gap' industrial enterprises. The Gladstone Pottery Museum at Stoke, the various Ironbridge complexes, and the Dean Heritage Centre at Soudley are just a few instances of such developments. These are, however, matched by up-to-date facilities for sport and the arts.

Considering the impact that 19th-century industry had upon this region its landscape legacy is perhaps surprisingly slight. Colliery pit mounds have been 'restored' into ineffectual hillocks, areas of mining spoil cleansed and returned to non-industrial usage. Isolated industrial buildings survive but are usually now to be found in quite foreign milieux, reused for all manner of purposes. A few survive in museum settings. Many, but by no means all, the canals still thread their way through town and countryside, often today quiet rural byways (Fig. 7.51), and main-line railways, of course, remain in use (Fig. 7.52). But the communications network is now dominated by the motorways that began to be built in the middle of the 20th century, drawing industry to more accessible

Fig. 7.51 A quiet rural canal in Worcestershire.

locations and attracting house-building ever further from place of work. The Ironbridge area has a rich concentration of earlier industrial features and has justly been given the status of a World Heritage Site, but elsewhere the legacy seems to be more a matter of urban sprawl than true industrial landscapes – a measure, indeed, of continued economic success.

Fig. 7.52 An iron horse: an iconographic symbol of former Black Country manufacture; one of many set up beside the Birmingham–Wolverhampton railway line.

NOTES

1   Symonds 2003.
2   Furbank *et al.* 1991, 206: Defoe, Letter VII.
3   Crosby 1996, 102–3.
4   *VCH Worcestershire II* 1906, 298.
5   Pilkington 1789, 51.
6   *VCH Derbyshire II* 1907, 372–4; Childs 1987, 96.
7   Rowlands 1987, 240.
8   *VCH Derbyshire II* 1907, 331–3.
9   Rotherham *et al.* 2005, 107.
10 *VCH Derbyshire II* 1907, 341.
11 Watson & Musson 1993, 107.
12 *VCH Derbyshire II* 1907, 322 quoting Fitzherbert, *Surveying*, cap. xxxviii.
13 *VCH Derbyshire II* 1907, 322.
14 Anon 1868, 35, cited in *VCH Staffordshire II* 1967, 196–7.
15 Greenslade & Stuart 1984, 88.
16 Welch 1997.
17 Rolt 1949, 226–9.
18 Plot 1686, quoted in Countryside Commission 1994, 29.
19 Pitt 1796, 108.
20 Palliser 1976, 78.
21 Welch 2000, 18–20.
22 Riden 1993, 34–53.
23 Smith & Ralph 1972, 71.
24 *VCH Gloucestershire II* 1907, 222–32.
25 Smith & Ralph 1972, 71.
26 *VCH Gloucestershire II* 1907, 232.
27 Ibid, 233.
28 Belford 2003; Belford & Ross 2004.
29 Alfrey & Clark 1993, 70–4.
30 Trinder 1996, 109.
31 Alfrey & Clark 1993, 130–68.
32 *VCH Shropshire X* 1998, 264, citing Trinder 1981, 41, 65.
33 H P Dunnill 1870, *Ironbridge Quarterly*, 1984, quoted in Alfrey & Clark 1993, 140.
34 King 1999, 62–4, 71–3.
35 Ibid, 61–2.
36 *VCH Worcestershire II* 1906, 268.
37 Gale 1979, 27.
38 Rowlands 1987, 236–46.

39 Court 1938, 22.
40 Watson & Musson 1993, 108.
41 Alfrey & Clark 1993, 42.
42 Morris 1995, 148.
43 Wise 1950, 282, quoting an anonymous observer at the end of the 19th century.
44 Rowlands 1987, 247.
45 *VCH Warwickshire II* 1965, 195.
46 Ibid, 199.
47 Rotherham *et al.* 2005, 108.
48 Barnatt & Smith 1997, 87.
49 Quoted in Stamper 1989, 33.
50 Crosby 1996, 91.
51 Hadfield 1985, 35.
52 J Randall, *History of Madeley*, 1880, 94, quoted in Hadfield 1985, 158–9.
53 Wise & Johnson 1950, 186.
54 Crosby 1996, 124.
55 Charles Kingsley, *The Bad Squire*, 19th century, reproduced in Raven 1977, 36.
56 Ibid, 31–2.
57 Ibid, 47.
58 Upton 1993, 135
59 Johnson & Wise 1950, 235, quoting a description illustrated by a painting, *Blast Furnaces at Cradley in the 1870s*.
60 Goode 1994, 20–2.
61 Tancred 1843, quoted in Johnson & Wise 1950, 241.
62 Palmer 1996, 90.
63 Ibid, 91–2, citing Sherard 1896, 167.
64 'The Nailmakers' Strike' from the collection of the late Mark Washington Fletcher, quoted in Raven 1977, 80–1.
65 Court 1938, 46.
66 Wesley's Journal, quoted in Greenslade & Stuart 1984, 59.
67 George Cadbury, quoted in Upton 1993, 157.
68 Lasdun 1991, 157–9.
69 Upton 1993, 44–5, 170–1.
70 Norman Price, *The Derbyshire Dales*, 1953, quoted in Talbot & Whiteman 1997, 119.
71 Raven 1977, 8.
72 West Midlands Group 1948, 172–3.

8

The Countryside in Literature and Legend

LANDSCAPE AND LEGEND

To properly understand the landscape of the West Midlands we need to see it not just through our own eyes but through those of its past inhabitants. Some impressions have passed into folk legend; others have found expression in poetry, folk song and literature. Together these provide a fascinating insight into how Midlanders and others have felt about the region, ideas that help to bind us to our English homeland or provide newcomers with a sense of our region.

Many unusual natural features of the landscape have attracted legendary associations with the Devil, especially prominent small hills or holes leading underground. Like many before them, the pagan Anglo-Saxons believed that the gods could be reached in a 'nether world' through pits and watery places. After the adoption of Christianity these invariably became associated with the Devil, dragons or other evil monsters. The mythical Grendel and his dam, the monsters of the poem *Beowulf* that devoured human beings, inhabited a 'lake ... overhung with groves of rime-crusted trees whose roots darken the water', in an 'unvisited land among wolf-haunted hills, windswept crags, and perilous fen-tracks, where mountain waterfalls disappear into mist and are lost underground'.[1] The poem is set in Denmark but the poet is likely to have composed his epic in the midland Mercian court and there is much here that may have been influenced by a familiarity with the Peak District. Features referred to as 'Grendel's pit' or 'Grendel's mere' appear in the boundary clauses of pre-Conquest charters describing landmarks along estate boundaries and at least two are recorded in this region – at Abbots Morton, just below the ridgeway separating Worcestershire from Warwickshire, and on the boundary of Oldswinford in the north of the county.[2] Other pits on the boundaries of Cleeve Prior and Church Honeybourne were associated with a *thyrs*, a 'giant'.[3]

The gods and monsters of pagan Britain were usually subsumed into the Devil under the dominance of the medieval Church and it was he who was set to spoil all that was good. Folklore describes the Cobbler's Mound near Shobdon as a huge shovelful of earth thrown down by the Devil when his plan to bury the fine church of Shobdon was thwarted by a local cobbler. A coda to this story explains the dismantling of the church in the mid-18th century as an effort by the villagers to deter any further attempts by the Devil (although the reality is that this was the initiative of the local landowner, Richard Bateman of Shobdon Hall). It is interesting that it was Shobdon church that was the subject of this story, for the first church here was heavily decorated with motifs of the medieval Herefordshire School of church architecture, many of which were misunderstood in later centuries. The chancel arch and other features were re-erected as a landscape feature by the owner of Shobdon Park (Fig. 8.1). A similar story explains the Wrekin in Shropshire, not far distant, as a mound of earth left by a

Fig. 8.1 Shobdon Arches, Herefordshire: the Norman chancel arch and medieval carvings from the old priory church, re-erected as a folly by Batemans in the mid-18th century.

giant who wished to flood Shrewsbury by damming the Severn to drown all its inhabitants in revenge for their ill-will shown to his son. As before, the giant was thwarted by a local cobbler. Another legend claims that the Devil with Jack o' Kent, a medieval mythical figure who had sold his soul in exchange for supernatural powers, was trying to dam the weir at Orcop Hill in Herefordshire in order to make a fishpond (or build a bridge across the Monnow) when he dropped, at cock-crow, the stones on Garway Hill to form the White Rocks. A story of the same kind accounts for the origin of the Seven Sisters at Symonds Yat.

Other hills that allegedly represent sacks of earth dropped by the Devil after the intervention of humans include two conical hills known as Pyon Hill and Butthouse Knapp (locally known as Robin Hood's Butt) near King's and Canon Pyon in Herefordshire.[4]

It has also been said that if the Shropshire ridge of the Stiperstones should sink into the ground then all England would be ruined. Consequently, the Devil attempted to stamp them out but, failing, he sat periodically in his chair on the summit, waiting for a new opportunity. One day he discovered that Hell's Gutter was letting air into Hell and, in an attempt to block up the crack, he gathered rock that was being laid as a causeway by giants between Ireland and Scotland. He tried to carry the rocks in a leather apron but, tired out, he resorted to his chair; in his impatient rage his apron strings broke and the rocks were scattered over the hillside (Fig. 8.2). The place is said to still attract mists and cloud when the Devil comes back to his chair. Mary Webb, in *The Golden Arrow*, reflects local superstitions about 22 December when all the ghosts of the county were thought to congregate at the Devil's Chair:

Fig. 8.2 The rocky summit of the Stiperstones, Shropshire.

For miles around in the plains, the valleys, the mountain dwellings it was feared. It drew the thunder, people said. Storms broke round it suddenly out of a clear sky. No one cared to cross the range after dark – when the black grouse laughed sardonically and the cry of a passing curlew shivered like broken glass …Whenever rain or driving sleet or mist made a grey shechinah there, people said, 'There's harm brewing.' 'He is in his chair.' Not that they talked of it much; they simply felt it, as sheep feel the coming of snow.[5]

The Malvern Hills also have their legends. A monk at Little Malvern Priory, below the Malvern Hills, is said to have fallen in love with a local woman, thus breaking his vow of chastity. As penance, he was made to crawl up Raggedstone Hill on his hands and knees each day. In torment, just before dying, he uttered a curse: 'May all upon whom the shadow of this stone falls untimely die'. The 'cursèd ragged stone' (the poem possibly a 19th-century creation) inspired several poems after the First World War, blaming the curse for untimely death.

Certain lesser landscape features play a prominent role in mythology and legend. Holes were as strange as or stranger than hills. In the Peak District of Derbyshire, a pothole in the district is Eldon Hole, described by Defoe as

a frightful chasme, or opening in the earth, or rather in the rock, … this opening goes directly down perpendicular into the earth, and perhaps to the center … it has no bottom, that is to say, none that can yet be heard of.[6]

It was said to be the Devil's bolt-hole to Hell. Two highwaymen are said to have forced their victim to walk over the edge here. Pits and holes have been associated with buried treasure and at the ruined Bronsil Castle near Eastnor the croak of a raven at midnight is said to be heard close to the spot where Lord Beauchamp buried his treasure before going on a crusade. It is, however, a jackdaw that guards the treasure hidden at Penyard Castle near Ross-on-Wye. A whole village is said to have disappeared into a swamp at Pembridge and a stone cast down a well was believed to be striking the top of its church spire deep below.[7]

Stones and springs were natural phenomena associated with pre-Christian religion and they were constantly the subject of edicts issued by the early Christian church forbidding supernatural belief and worship.[8] Wells and springs, often associated with healing properties, were taken over and sanctified by Christian saints. There are many so-called 'holy wells', like St Anne's Well at Aconbury in Herefordshire, the Holy Well dedicated to St Edith of Polesworth near Church Eaton in Staffordshire, its waters thought to alleviate afflictions of the eyes, or that dedicated to St Bertelin at Ilam in Staffordshire. At Clent in Worcestershire, legend claims that the Mercian boy-king, Kenelm, was murdered at the instigation of his sister in about 821. His head rolled into nearby bushes, to be discovered by a red cow, and he was subsequently regarded as a saint. A spring is said to have gushed forth at the site of his murder. This lay beneath the present church but a new site close by still, allegedly, has healing powers (Fig. 8.3). The spring at Stoke St Milborough in Shropshire is said to have been found

Fig. 8.3 St Kenelm's well, Clent: *the rags are hung up by those seeking healing from the spring waters.*

miraculously by St Mildburh (Mildburg) when she was fleeing from her enemies. Rivers, often the sites of votive offerings in prehistory, remained greedy for life. The Wye was said to require a victim annually, the bodies of the drowned rising on the ninth day. Stones were thought to move around under certain circumstances – the Whetstone on Hergest Ridge above Kington in Herefordshire is reputed to go down to the Buck Brook to drink when it hears the morning cock crow. Other stones, led by a black dog, were driven across the River Lugg watermeadows by a mighty wind in 1642, while King Arthur is said to be buried below Arthur's Stone near Dorstone (the capstone of a Neolithic burial mound).

The forest lay at the heart of medieval experience; hunting nurtured the skills required in the defence of the realm and was very much part of knightly practice (Fig. 8.4). It appears frequently, therefore, in medieval folklore and literature (*see* the tanner of Tamworth above, Chapter 4, and *Sir Gawain* below), sometimes as the haunt of outlaws, in others as a place sought out by hermits. Saints were often associated with lonely remote places and it was claimed that both the priories of Little and Great Malvern developed on the sites of hermitages within the area that was to become Malvern Forest. St Dubricus, or Dyfrig, a late 5th-century saint, is said to have founded a monastery in a well-wooded area of Herefordshire abounding in fish that was to become known as Moccas ('promontory, moor or place of pigs') on account of the auspicious presence of a white sow and her piglets. But Moccoss was previously the name of a Celtic god, the Holy Boar, and the association may have arisen through 'cross-referral between pre-Christian, Celtic traditions and early Christian hagiology'.[9]

Among the less saintly characters associated with woodland, Edric the Wild, a Saxon nobleman who opposed the Normans in the border country, is said to have become lost in Clun Forest while following a white hart, but there he found and married a fairy bride. She forbad him to question her occasional wanderings but on one occasion, tired after hunting, he did this and thereby lost her. He forfeited his estates because of subsequent neglect while obsessively seeking for her. The legend of the wild hunt – the 'Black Horseman' and 'the death-pack' – that is an omen of war or death is not uncommon in hilly districts. It is heard at night before a tragic event and is referred to in Mary Webb's novel, *Gone to Earth*, where the pack rode out across the Stiperstones, betokening the death of the ill-used Hazel Woodus. In other forest districts, the huntsmen were 'black and huge and loathsome', accompanied by black, wide-eyed hounds. On the Lickey Hills, near Birmingham, the Devil and his chief huntsman, Harry-ca-nab, mounted on white bulls, would hunt the wild boar by night near Bromsgrove with a pack of hounds that the Devil kept at Halesowen. The night sky was also haunted by the Seven Whistlers, which some claimed to be the Devil's hounds; others thought them to be six birds of fate in search of the seventh, and if they found it the world would surely end. Lickey lay at the northern end of the Forest of Feckenham and on the eastern margin of the forest a black dog haunted the site of the abbey of Bordesley after its dissolution.

Fig. 8.4 Deer in the Wyre Forest, Worcestershire, *once the object of the royal hunt. A rare white buck can be seen in the photograph but it is no longer in the forest.*

Individual trees, usually the old and venerable, play a part in folklore. The mythical Yggdrasill was the giant ash-tree of Norse legend that united the underworld, middle-earth and the heavens. The yew-tree possessed a special place and its connection with death and resurrection was apparently recognised by the Christian church, possibly because it had already been accepted into Roman Christianity. Giant yews are very much a feature of borderland churchyards, as at Church Preen (Fig. 8.5), Ashford Carbonel, Clun, Acton Scott, Norbury, Uppington and Claverley in Shropshire, and some, like the hollow tree at Much Marcle in Herefordshire (*see* Fig. 3.5), are likely to pre-date the churches beside which they stand. At Claverley the tree overshadows a Romano-British burial site and at Hope Bagot, below Brown Clee in Shropshire, an enormous yew stands over a 'holy' well in the churchyard.

Fig. 8.5 Ancient yew, Church Preen, Shropshire.

By the medieval period, a midland school of poets had given rise to *Sir Gawain and the Green Knight* and *Perle*, two great poems that show by their language and metre a source in the West Midlands,[10] and *Sir Gawain* in particular includes many Cheshire dialect words. But both poems also incorporate folktale motifs – the 'beheading contest' and the 'exchange of winnings' – found in earlier Celtic folklore, together with later Arthurian imagery. The location of the barrow known as the 'green chapel' that was protected by the green knight, or of his castle wherein Gawain was tested and tempted, remains unknown. But the medieval forest described in this poem of *c*. 1400 could easily have been one of the great forests of Cheshire. Its location has, indeed, been seen as the Forest of Delamere,[11] which was encountered by Gawain as he journeyed on from 'the wilderness of Wirral' before finding the moated castle within the forest that was inhabited by the green knight and his wife:

> *By a mount in the morning*
> *merrily he was riding*
> *into a forest that was*
> *deep and fearsomely wild,*
> *with high hills at each hand,*
> *and hoar woods beneath*
> *of huge aged oaks by*
> *the hundred together;*
> *the hazel and the hawthorn*
> *were huddled and tangled*
> *with rough ragged moss*
> *around them trailing,*
> *with many birds bleakly on*
> *the bare twigs sitting*
> *that piteously piped there for*
> *pain of the cold.*[12]

Fig. 8.6 A Green Man carving.

Green men are not uncommon in the region's churches and are usually found in a Christian context, often with tendrils of foliage issuing from the mouth. This 17th-century carving appears on the corner post of the gatehouse at Stokesey Castle, Shropshire.

There have been obvious suggestions of an affinity of the green knight with the so-called 'Green Man', who figures prominently in many of the border churches decorated by the 12th-century Herefordshire School of sculptors (Fig. 8.6). This figure, noted for the green tendrils issuing from his mouth (usually oak or vine), has been linked with the world-wide notion of the death of the king that was popularised by Sir James Frazer in his *Golden Bough*, and also identified as the later 'Jack in the Green', the 'spirit of the tree', that represented the annually renewed spirit of vegetation. Jack was a figure that was popular in the 19th century but is also a character in many mumming plays. In truth, the symbolism of the Green Man is not understood. This was a popular figure in 12th-century France, one of many adopted by the Herefordshire School, but probably had its origins in 1st-century Roman art, carried as leaf masks from earlier temple buildings to Trier Cathedral in Germany in the 6th century and thus incorporated into Christianity. (Others have suggested an Indian origin.) In the 13th century, the green-man carvings in France became more naturalistic, incorporating a wide range of native plants. This is seen, too, at Southwell Minster in Nottinghamshire, where one of the plants depicted is the hawthorn. However, the green men of the Welsh borderland are usually of the 'stiff-leaf' type or heavily stylised, like that on a 12th-century pillar capital at Garway St Michael, or on the door jamb and the capitals of a 12th-century window in the church of Kilpeck St Mary and David. There are further examples – with fruiting vine leaves – on 12th-century capitals in the priory church of St Peter and Paul, Leominster, where another sits as a corbel high above the north nave that was originally the external wall of the old monastic church. Others are found on the capitals of the cathedrals at Lichfield and Hereford (the latter with oak leaves and a split tongue emerging from a closed mouth), at Much Marcle St Bartholomew (here *c.* 1230, with vine branches and grapes growing in profusion from his mouth) and at Nantwich St Mary. Green men can also be found on the misericords of Coventry Holy Trinity, Chester Cathedral and Ludlow St Laurence. Many others are known but are perhaps most common within this region in Herefordshire. Basford has argued that the foliate head frequently portrayed a demonic character, reiterating the views of an 8th-century theologian, Rabanus Maurus, that 'the leaves represented the sins of the flesh or lustful and wicked men doomed to eternal damnation'.[13] Others have been less critical, and Canon Albert Radcliffe has suggested a second alternative: that 'he was the representative of pagan and natural human nature, witnessing to Christ, and thereby redeemed and brought into the service of the gospel'.[14]

LITERARY LANDSCAPES: CHANGING ATTITUDES

The landscapes of the West Midland region inspired and formed the setting for literature from a very early date, even though the early church had discouraged any preoccupation with nature. The medieval poet William Langland was born at either Ledbury or Cleobury Mortimer and his *Piers Ploughman* was inspired by the Malvern Hills on a May morning in the 14th century when he allegedly fell asleep at Prime's Well:

> *In a summer season, when soft was the sun,*
> *I enshrouded me well in a shepherd's garb,*
> *And robed as a hermit, unholy of works,*
> *Went wide through the world, all wonders to hear.*
> *And on a May morning, on Malvern hills,*
> *Strange fancies befel me, and fairy-like dreams*[15]

Christian mystical poets in the 17th century rejected the caution of the early and medieval church and were beginning to see the natural world as an expression of God's glory. Among them was Thomas Traherne, a shoemaker's son born in or near Hereford in about 1636, who became a priest: '... in the remotest Borders the causes of peace delight me, and the Beauties of the Earth when seen were made to entertain me ...'.[16]

Although William Shakespeare and Michael Drayton did not set out to make the countryside a prime feature of their verse, they have become inextricably linked with Warwickshire's 'Forest of Arden'. In Drayton's *Poly-Olbion* 'mighty Arden' extended from the Severn into Warwickshire:

> *Muse first of* Arden *tell, whose footsteps yet are found*
> *In her rough wood-lands more than any other ground*
> *That mighty* Arden *held even in her height of pride;*
> *Her one hand touching* Trent, *the other* Severne's *side.*[17]

Shakespeare's *As You Like It* evoked the image of the hunting forest where the Duke and his courtiers found:

> *... tongues in trees, books in the running brooks,*
> *Sermons in stones, and good in everything.*[18]

Landscapes cannot be detached from the people who inhabit them and they have been viewed in diverse ways at different periods and by different kinds of people. Attitudes to landscape were changing, for instance, in the 18th century. Until then, landscape had played a mere incidental role in literature, and the interests of those wealthy and leisured enough to indulge in visits to more exotic or 'educational' places were satisfied more by travels to the home of 'classical values' in Greece and Rome: the 'Grand Tour' became an aim of the educated. Wars with the Continent brought these travels to an end and led people to seek meaningful landscapes closer to home.

At the start of the 18th century, 'wild' places were ones to be avoided. Describing a Peakland moor (Fig. 8.7), Defoe wrote, following a visit in 1712:

> *Upon the top of that mountain begins a vast extended moor or waste, which,*
> *for fifteen or sixteen miles together due north, presents you with neither hedge,*
> *house or tree, but a waste and houling wilderness ...'.*[19]

Fig. 8.7 Axe Moor, the Dark Peak.

It was not until travellers began to appreciate 'sublime' and 'romantic' landscapes (*see* below), that such attitudes were to change. Owners of grand houses had laid out their grounds to conform to the new ideals of the century and these also led to a new enthusiasm for painting and literature. When Horace Walpole visited Hagley Park, on the northern border of Worcestershire, he described it as one of the most magnificent and enchanting parks in the country:

> *It is a hill of three miles, but broke into all manner of beauty; such lawns, such woods, rills, cascades, and a thickness of verdure quite to the summit of the hill, and commanding such a vale of towns, and meadows, and woods extending quite to the Black Mountains in Wales, that I quite forgot my favourite Thames ...*[20]

The 18th century was to produce a crop of 'ploughman poets' who revelled in the pastoral idyll, among them James Thomson. Thomson came from the Scottish borders but his *The Seasons* contains an allusion inserted into 'Spring' after his visit to Hagley Park in Worcestershire in 1743. He was used to praising the estates of his patrons, and he described it in rather 'flowery' language, using his words as the artists of the day used their paints:

> *Meantime you gain the Height, from whose fair Brow*
> *The bursting Prospect spreads immense around;*
> *And snatch'd o'er Hill and Dale, and Wood and Lawn,*
> *And verdant Field, and darkening Heath between,*
> *And Villages embosom'd soft in Trees,*
> *And spiry Towns by surging Columns mark'd*
> *Of household Smoak, your Eye excursive roams:*
> *Wide-stretching from the Hall, in whose kind Haunt*
> *The Hospitable Genius lingers still*
> *To Where the broken Landskip, by Degrees,*
> *Ascending, roughens into Hills;*
> *O'er which the Cambrian mountains, like far Clouds*
> *That skirt the blue Horizon, dusky, rise.*[21]

The longing to discover a Golden Age harmony that overlooked the realities of pastoral life, a re-creation of Milton's Eden, may be apparent here but Thomson helped to arouse an interest in British scenery. After the middle of the 18th century, interest in the georgic pastoral diminishes and wilder landscapes began to attract, despite their 'horrid grandeur'. Both painting and literature began to seek a more 'romantic' image. But it was some time before the preoccupation with the landscape as a perceived *landskip*, understood by the educated and initiated, was to come to fruition in the 'Picturesque' movement, as expressed in the paintings of Claude and Dughet. By the end of the century, this more specialised attitude had developed, in which landscapes were appreciated by reference to painting and a search for 'that kind of beauty which would look well in a picture'.[22] These were landscapes to be enjoyed by the initiated: 'a person conversant with the writings of Theocritus and Virgil will relish pastoral scenery more than one unacquainted with such poetry'.[23] The preferred landscapes were heavily influenced by images from Italian scenery, a love of ruins and of neglect – a contrived landscape rather than the world of reality. Later in the century, the more dedicated travellers seeking the 'Picturesque' view would use a Claude glass, a specially designed convex mirror, to reflect a miniaturised landscape.

Two of the main propagandists of the Picturesque movement who transferred their ideals into reality held estates in rural Herefordshire – Richard Payne Knight at Downton in the north of the county and Uvedale Price at Foxley in the south – and both attempted to adapt the best features of the natural landscape to meet their ideal. At Foxley, Price completed a belt of encircling woodland to give the compositional coherence he craved and, at Downton (*see* Fig. 6.14), Knight chose to enhance the landscape by a preference for native tree species in a way that would have found favour with today's conservationists. The results of his designs are depicted in the paintings of Thomas Hearne and others. But Knight was a poet as well as a designer and in his treatise in verse, *The Landscape*, published in 1794, he fully embraced the 'Picturesque' ideal:

> *Bless'd too is he, who, 'midst his tufted trees,*
> *Some ruin'd castle's lofty Tower sees;*
> *Imbosom'd high upon the mountain's brow.*[24]

and

> *How best to bid the verdant Landscape rise,*
> *To please the fancy, and delight the eyes;*
> *Its various parts in harmony to join*
> *With art clandestine, and conceal'd design;*[25]

His preference for native trees is expressed in the following stanza:

> *Choose, therefore, trees which nature's hand has sown*
> *In proper soils, and climates of their own;*
> *Or such as, by experience long approved,*
> *are found adopted by the climes they loved.*[26]

Yet improvement was to be utilitarian as well as decorative, in the spirit of the age's 'improvers':

> *But let not still o'erbearing pride of taste*
> *Turn fertile districts to a forest's waste:*
> *Still let utility improvement and guide,*
> *And just congruity in all preside:*
> *While shaggy hills are left to rude neglect,*
> *Let the rich plains with wavy corn be deck'd;*
> *And while rough thickets shade the lonely glen,*
> *Let culture smile upon the haunts of men;*
> *And the rich meadow and the fertile field*
> *The annual tribute of their harvest yield.*[27]

These ideals were expressed in the landscape parks of the country landowner but remained the province of the rich and the intellectual.

On a more practical level, various commissions were being set up throughout the late 18th and early 19th centuries to examine the state of the country's farming. In general, the 'Age of Improvement' favoured the good husbandry practised by those with the money to run landed estates and carry out schemes for land improvement. Fine woods, managed for their timber, were appreciated, or the newly evolving methods of improving the growth of grass on flooded water meadows (*see* Chapter 5).

> *Walked by Benthal hall to a steep over the river called Benthal Edge. It is a*
> *very fine woody bank which rises very steep from the Severn; you look down*
> *an immense declivity on a beautiful winding valley two miles over, cut into*
> *rich enclosures, and broken by tufts of wood, the steep on which you stand*
> *waving from the right line exhibits the noblest slopes of hanging wood …*[28]

*The hedge rows, through a large portion of the fertile parts of the county, are
well stored with elm timber, the largest, finest, and, I believe, best in the
kingdom, growing lengthy, fine, and large, and being generally sound and
hearty, free from shakes and flaws;* [29]

Many were highly appreciative of the landscape but with an obviously greater
appreciation when the man-made scene expressed the results of good
husbandry and, in their view, visual enhancement. On the view from Mordiford,
overlooking the confluence of the rivers Lugg and Wye in the south of the
county, John Duncumb in his *General View of the Agriculture of the County of
Hereford* in 1805 noted:

*Looking from this point towards the east, an immense expanse of woodland is
seen, as far as the eye can reach, with a white cottage and a cultivated acre
occasionally intervening. Deep and winding roads intersect the whole with a
narrow track, and a bleak and barren common which appears 'far from the
busy haunts of man', completes the cheerless scene.*

*The admirer of nature unadorned, will contemplate this prospect with
pleasure; and it may remind him of many parts of America; but the contrast
afforded from the same spot by reversing his position, will surely excite more
agreeable sensations.*

*Towards the west, the most fertile meadows are enlivened by cattle grazing
on the banks of rivers occasionally seen in beautiful reaches and in rocky
channels; towards the south-west is the extensive park and residence of the
Duke of Norfolk; towards the north-west, the elegant mansion of Longworth,
and between them, the beautiful grove of Rotherwas. Still further are seen the
cathedrals and spires of the provincial metropolis, backed at a considerable
distance by the mountains of Wales.* [30]

There was a stirring of both national and regional consciousness in the 19th
century that found expression in literature and poetry, although some of the
earlier works tended to be coloured by Victorian escapism and sentimentality.
Elizabeth Barrett Browning was brought up at Upper Colwall at the foot of the
Malvern Hills and her poem *Aurora Leigh* conjures up the view over
Herefordshire from the hills (Fig. 8.8):

Hills, vales, woods, netted in a silver mist,
Farms, granges, doubled-up among the hills;
And cattle grazing in the watered vales,
And cottage chimneys smoking from the woods,
And cottage gardens smelling everywhere,
Confused with smell of orchards. [31]

Fig. 8.8 Mist below the Malverns.

The 'Romantics' cast away the contrived landscapes as seen through a Claude glass with a passionate concern for 'true' nature, that was itself seen to have a vital formative influence on man. Wordsworth saw the landscape as cherishable because of the way it expressed the efforts and aspirations of man. He was a poet of the Lake District but one poem written in his later years that was influenced by a visit to Derbyshire is that of a maid called Lucy:

> *She dwelt among the untrodden ways*
> *Beside the springs of Dove,*
> *A maid whom there were none to praise,*
> *And very few to love.*[32]

Further changes in attitudes to the landscape developed with 19th-century radicalism and the birth of socialism, as new emphasis was placed upon 'the common man'. However, landscape itself was only appreciated if permeated with culture: 'the works of nature are admirable only as the poor life of man has illustrated them'.[33] Thomas Hardy, too, claimed that 'a beautiful scene in nature is unimportant compared with the wear of a foot on a threshold'.[34] The focus changes from the stylised landscape of the Picturesque, admired for a set of aesthetic, encoded values to the landscape expressing a different philosophical attitude – the veneration of 'the working man'.[35]

John Clare and William Cobbett were more sympathetic to the landscape of the ordinary man. John Clare was a poet of the commonplace rather than of the landed estate, but he was not a poet of this region and it is to 19th-century authors like George Eliot that we must turn for an awareness of the change that was taking place here in the 19th century. George Eliot was the pen-name of Mary Ann Evans. She was born in Warwickshire at Arbury Farm (now South Farm) near Nuneaton and was the daughter of a Derbyshire carpenter and wheelwright. She used the Derbyshire background for her novel *Adam Bede*, supposedly basing the main figure upon a characterisation of her father. Her father was later the agent for the Arbury estate in Warwickshire, and she brought her experience of peasant and provincial city life into her novels. Her 'Cheveral Manor', the 'castellated house of grey-tinted stone' in *Scenes of Clerical Life* (1858), was inspired by her familiarity with Arbury Hall; her home village, Chilvers Coton, became 'Shepperton' in the same novel, and Nuneaton became 'Milbly' in *Janet's Repentance* (1857). Arbury Mill near her later home, Griff House, inspired *The Mill on the Floss* (1860). There is nostalgia for the midland landscape of her childhood in *Middlemarch*:

> *The pool in the corner where the grasses were dank and the trees leaned*
> *whisperingly; the great oak shadowing a bare place in mid-pasture; the high*
> *bank where the ash-trees grew; the sudden slope of the old marl-pit making a*
> *red background for the burdock; the huddled roofs and ricks of the homestead*
> *without a traceable way of approach; the grey gate and fences against the*
> *depths of the bordering wood; and the stray hovel, its old, old thatch full of*
> *mossy hills and valleys with wondrous modulations of light and shadow such*
> *as we travel far to see in later life, and see larger, but not more beautiful. These*
> *are the things that make the gamut of joy in landscape to midland-bred souls*
> *– the things they toddled among, or perhaps learned by heart standing*
> *between their father's knees while he drove leisurely.*[36]

Her places were far removed from the idealised 'picturesque' and imbued with a concern for reform and greater sharing of resources: she was familiar with the rick burning that accompanied the Reform bills. Another 19th-century author who looked back nostalgically upon a midland childhood was Mrs Elizabeth Gaskell. She remembered in her novels her childhood visits to rural Cheshire – to the small town of Knutsford and her grandfather's farm at Sandlebridge, renamed 'Hope Farm' in *Cousin Phillis* – contrasting this with the awful lives of Manchester workers 'crammed into dark tenements and stinking cellars, deprived of the light itself'.[37] At the end of the century, Henry James in his *English Hours* described the English midlands as 'the core and centre of the English world; midmost England, unmitigated England … the genius of pastoral Britain'.[38]

Other early 20th-century writers were equally involved in the life of the countryside, capturing a rapidly disappearing remoteness and parochialism that saw the lives of country folk played out within a narrow confined world largely unknown to town dwellers. In Shropshire, Mary Webb, in her novels that include *Gone to Earth* and *Precious Bane* (published in 1917 and 1924), sets her characters within the landscape of the south Shropshire hills (Fig. 8.9). Here are intimate enclosed landscapes of remote valleys separated by green hills with patches of ancient woodland where human emotions are played out against the changing natural panoply of the weather and the seasons. In *Gone to Earth*, Hazel Woodus is driven by imagined signs intermingled with her own half-understood instincts to her meeting with Jack Reddin in the woods below the Mountain. But the scene is one of quiet foreboding:

> *The hedges were full of white 'archangel' and purple vetch. When she came to the beginning of Hunter's Spinney she felt frightened; the woods were so far-reaching, so deep with shadow; the trees made so sad a rumour, and swayed with such forlorn abandon. In the dusky places the hyacinths, broken but not yet faded, made a purple carpet, solemn as a pall. Woodruff shone whitely by the path and besieged her with scent. Early wild-roses stood here and there, weighed down with their own beauty, set with rare carmine and tints of shells and snow, too frail to face the thunderstorm that even now advanced with*

Fig. 8.9 The Stiperstones – the atmospheric setting for Mary Webb's novel Gone to Earth.

unhurrying pomp far away beyond the horizon. She hurried along, leaving the beaten track, creeping under the broad skirts of the beeches and over the white prostrate larch-boles where the resin ran slowly like the dark blood of creatures beautiful, defeated, dying. She began to climb, holding to the grey, shining boles of mountain ash-trees. The bracken, waist-high at first, was like small hoops at the top of the wood, where the tiny golden tormentil made a carpet and the yellow pimpernel was closing her eager eyes.

Hazel came out on the bare hill-top where gnarled may-trees, dropping spent blossom, were pink-tinted as if the colours of the sunsets they had known had run into their whiteness. Hazel sat down on the hill-top and saw the sleek farm-horses far below feeding with their shadows, swifts flying with their shadows, and hills eyeing theirs stilly. So with all life the shadow lingers – incurious, mute, yet in the end victorious, whelming all. As Hazel sat there her own shadow lay darkly behind her, growing larger than herself as the sun slipped lower.[39]

Although novelists were naturally more concerned with people and the human condition, the enjoyment of nature was a recurrent thread through the writings of the late 19th and early 20th century – not the contrived landscapes of the Picturesque, nor even the orderly, well-managed landscapes of agricultural improvement, but nature for its own sake: blossom and birdsong, sunlight and dappled shade – the roots of the modern conservation movement.

LANDSCAPE AND REGIONAL IDENTITY

There is a large body of literature directly related to perceptions of local landscapes. The West Midland region encompasses many different kinds of countryside, as we have seen, with extensive upland areas such as the Peak District and Pennine fringe, the south Shropshire hills and the south Staffordshire and Birmingham plateau; isolated upland massifs like the Malverns and the Clees; and the lowland plains of Cheshire, north Shropshire and central Staffordshire, central and eastern Herefordshire and central Worcestershire. Each district had its own iconographic associations, expressed in literature, art, music and mythology. The region as a whole also tends to straddle the north–south (of England) divide although its iconographic associations seem to lean most strongly towards the former.

Even the Victoria County History of Derbyshire notes the rebellious nature of the folk of the northern uplands when confronted with, for instance, the Roman invasion[40], but the same could be said for resistance to the campaigns of William the Conqueror or much of the baronial opposition to medieval kings. It was the Derbyshire miners, too, who, realising the value of lead for shot in the troubled times of the 17th-century Civil Wars, demanded rights from King Charles I that freed them from certain tithes that had traditionally been levied from them in the past. Even in the world of 19th-century religion, the industrial regions tended to be Nonconformist in their views, rejecting the rigid conformity of the established church and propounding views that recognised greater equality between men. Early Nonconformist meetings were often held out in the open, free from the constraints of urban formality, and their chapels were frequently built on the moorland fringe (*see* Chapter 6). Politically, free-thinking and radicalism flourished in these regions.[41]

This independence of thought has been associated with character traits such as stoicism, self-reliance, strength and perseverance – key elements in a northern perception of northern England, which presented its people as hardier and less deferential than their southern equivalents, with the south a softer, more effete place:

OPPOSITE PAGE:
Fig. 8.10 Peveril Castle, Derbyshire,
the setting for Scott's Peveril of the Peak.

Such notions long pre-dated industrialisation and were based in part on the strength of pastoral traditions in the rural north, which encouraged greater independence, individuality and reliance on the family group than was common in the village communities of more southern districts. They also reflected northern discomfort at political power that favoured the landowning, privileged classes of southern England.[42]

Some of this independence of spirit was inevitably to be expressed as 'lawlessness'. There was also, undoubtedly, a somewhat wild underclass, as in any region that was relatively remote and with country districts far from the rules of law and order. Exmoor may have had its Doone family, but Shropshire had its 'Edric the Wild', and bands of tinkers are said to have 'hung out' in Peak Cavern in Derbyshire. This insalubrious place was known as early as Domesday Book as *Pechesers*, 'Peak's arse' (as water syphons through one part of the cavern it does emit a somewhat vulgar sound). Here the 'beggar king', Cock Lorell, who had traditionally supped with the Devil, is said to have dwelt, to be commemorated in Ben Jonson's ballad written in 1621 as 'the early Tudor prototype of the rogue hero'.[43] From the mid-17th century, ropemakers lived and worked in squalid conditions within the cavern mouth. The ropes were in great demand in the lead mines, although reputedly also for the gallows – highway robbery was rife in the neighbourhood and for many centuries travellers were afraid to journey through the wild northern parts of Derbyshire. Other Derbyshire caves were also associated with brigands. High above the Dove in Dovedale are two caves studded with dark tufts of yew, one of which was used as a refuge by a local brigand called Reynard; and a genuine murder occurred at Thor's Cave in Manifold valley in 1874 when a young woman was pushed into a pit by an attacker who also sent an American tourist, who went to her aid, to a lingering death in the same place.[44]

The castle above Peak Cavern (Fig. 8.10) also witnessed rebellion and intrigue. This was immortalised in Sir Walter Scott's novel *Peveril of the Peak* whose ancestor, allegedly the bastard son of William the Conqueror, 'chose his nest upon the principles on which an eagle selects her eyry, and built it in such a fashion as if he had intended it ... for the sole purpose of puzzling posterity'. This was the 'Gothic fortress, which, hanging over the mouth of the Devil's Cavern ...', gave 'the name of Castleton to the adjacent village'. The great fief lay adjacent to 'wastes and forests' and the castle well illustrated the 'high descent and lofty pretensions' of its owners.[45] From its almost inaccessible location, William Peveril had administered Peak Forest. The family was involved in later intrigue, for William Peveril IV was accused in the 12th century of poisoning Ranulf, the Earl of Chester; his estates were forfeited and taken over by Henry II. When the king's son rebelled against him, Peveril Castle was probably refortified with its additional 12m-square great tower. In 1215 the castle was in the hands of the barons who were opposed to 'Bad King John' but in Scott's novel, William Peveril is a Royalist confronting Parliamentarian supporters.

Among the upper classes, warfare and rebellion continued to attract followers to different camps: in Staffordshire, in the 14th century, supporters of earls such as Thomas, Earl of Lancaster, based at Tutbury, were in conflict with those loyal to king – the Bassetts, de Somerys and the Audleys. Political ambitions were played out in an arena of local rivalries that often led to bloodshed, and 'wayward' younger sons, in particular, are found at the midst of local skirmishes.[46] There were three or four loose gangs and 'confederacies' in 14th-century Staffordshire and John, a younger son of the Cotterells, pillaged across Derbyshire and Staffordshire, while family connections ensured that such perpetrators were usually acquitted of crime. Cheshire men could raid with impunity because, as Cheshire was a Palatine county (ie Cheshire men enjoyed royal privileges within their own territory), they risked no forfeiture for crimes committed outside their

own borders. Family feuds (as between the Swynnertons, followers of Edward II, and the Staffords, followers of the Earl of Lancaster) were expressed in activities such as gang warfare, robbery and horse-stealing, while John de Somery, lord of Dudley castle, was said to dominate the county 'more than a king', thriving in a climate of bribery and extortion.[47]

In the 15th century such feuds might lead to local warfare and in the second year of Henry V's reign 1,000 men, the followers of Hugh Erdeswyk of Sandon and his brother Robert, were involved for three days in keeping 'the field arrayed as for war' near Newcastle-under-Lyme against their foe, Sir John Blount, forcing the king to come to Lichfield to deal with complaints.[48] Such behaviour was not restricted, however, to the upper classes and ordinary men and women were not always prepared to accept the role of 'underdog'. Historical documentation usually records more about the concerns of the upper classes than those of the common man but this itself reveals much about the interests of the age. Urban communities rarely got a 'good press' and in the 1530s the inhabitants of Walsall were described as 'light persons suddenly moved to affray and insurrection'.[49]

Much of the independent spirit was conveyed to the industrial era, when ideas of hard, physical labour became attached to the male, working-class worker as a symbol of manliness and, as such, they became associated with the industrial areas of the region such as the industrial north and the Black Country.[50] The industrial working of coal, iron ore, limestone and clay demanded a powerful and unyielding physique, manual strength and dexterity.[51] The miner, his skills in great demand, was seen as the 'top-dog' of the workers' hierarchy, quick to defend his patch – Staffordshire bull terriers and all! The Dudley miners, in particular, had 'all of them the reputation of bold spirited men'.[52]

Folk song frequently emanates from working-class culture and aptly captures much of this outlook on life. Of Black Country songs it has been commented:

> As the rural songs disappeared the industrial revolution gave birth to a new music. A hybrid music that lived and breathed and sweated in the same way as its makers. A music suited to noise, dirt and inhumanity. Frequently poor in poetry and music it was rich in life.[53]

Industrial strife also found an outlet in this medium – the Luddites were active in the midlands and the north from about 1811; miners and ironworkers, in particular, were ready to riot against the Corn Laws a few years later. Local riots broke out from time to time, as at Clinker Hill (*see* Chapter 7), and another riot led by colliers at Dudley was only calmed by the intervention of Lord Dudley Ward:

> Tip'on lads they did us join,
> And we formed a strong combine.
>
> We marchen into town
> Resolved to pull the housen down.[54]

Life was often brutal and harsh, and leisure likewise: bull baiting, cock fighting and dog fighting were favourite pastimes, as shown in the ballad 'Perrys Croft Bull Bait', which describes an event that took place in the Black Country some time between the 1790s and the 1840s. The dogs – often Staffordshire bull terriers – were set on the bull, which would be chained to a stake, and encouraged to tear at the animal's nose:

> At last they set six dogs at him
> At which Bedlam begun
> The dogs all yelled, the crowd all roar;
> To see such rippin' fun.

Dog after dog went sailin' up
Like birds into the air,
An wen they drapt they fairly howl to
Like cripples at a fair.

The bull breaks free and:

Right through the crowd he rushed away
An gored em az he run,
Which made the rascals cuss and swear
For they da' call that fun.[55]

John Lacey describes the festivities that took place at 'a rabbling kind of wake'
held near Bromsgrove in 1778, a district where the poor who had settled around
the edges of the waste lived mainly by nailing:

The third Sunday in July a Wake (a rabbling kind of Wake) at Sythemoor
[Sidemoor] and also at a small village called Catshill about two miles north
of the town where Bull baiting, bowling, Wrestling, Cockfighting, and other
such Disagreeable and cruel sports are used, to the disgrace of humanity,
scandle of Christianity and shame of our officers who suffer such shameful
things to be done in their parish.[56]

Dickens was concerned with the social problems of 19th-century England.
He denounced the squalor of industrial landscapes and in his novel *The Old
Curiosity Shop* he writes with experience of what he saw on a journey to
Wolverhampton (Fig. 8.11):

On mounds of ashes by the wayside, sheltered only by a few rough boards, or
rotten pent-house roofs, strange engines spun and writhed like tortured
creatures; clanking their iron chains, shrieking in their rapid whirl from time
to time as though in torment unendurable, and making the ground tremble
with their agonies. Dismantled houses here and there appeared, tottering to
the earth, propped up by fragments of others that had fallen down, unroofed,

Fig. 8.11 A view of the Black Country
with smoke rising from the industrial factories
around Wolverhampton in the Midlands.

windowless, blackened, desolate, but yet inhabited. Men, women, children, wan in looks and ragged in attire, tended the engines, fed their tributary fires, begged upon the road, or scowled [peeped] half-naked from the doorless houses. Then came more of the wrathful monsters, whose like they almost seemed to be in their wildness and their untamed air, screeching and turning round and round again; and still, before, behind, and to the right and left, was the same interminable perspective of brick towers, never ceasing in their black vomit, blasting all things living or inanimate, shutting out the face of day, and closing in on all these horrors with a dense dark cloud.

But night-time in this dreadful spot! – night, when the smoke was changed to fire; when every chimney spirted up its flame; and places, that had been dark vaults all day, now shone red-hot, with figures moving to and from within their blazing jaws, and calling to one another with hoarse cries – night, when the noise of every strange machine was aggravated by the darkness; when the people near them looked wilder and more savage; when bands of unemployed labourers paraded in the roads, or clustered by torchlight round their leaders, who told them in stern language of their wrongs, and urged them on to frightful cries and threats; when maddened men, armed with sword and firebrand, spurning the tears and prayers of women who would restrain them, rushed forth on errands of terror and destruction, to work no ruin half as surely as their own … [57]

Of the terrible pollution that killed all vegetation around and seriously damaged health, he described in his *Pickwick Papers* a journey that took him through Birmingham:

The straggling cottages by the road-side, the dingy hue of every object visible, the murky atmosphere, the paths of cinders and brick-dust, the deep-red glow of furnace fires in the distance, the volumes of dense smoke issuing heavily forth from high toppling chimneys, blackening and obscuring everything around; the glare of distant lights, the ponderous wagons which toiled along the road, laden with clashing rods of iron, or piled with heavy goods – all betokened their rapid approach to the great working town of Birmingham. [58]

But Dickens retained a belief in the common man and in *The Old Curiosity Shop* describes how Nell and her grandfather were sheltered by a workman beside his furnace. [59]

In the growing industrial regions, the landscape itself was a hard unpleasant environment even in the 20th century. Arnold Bennett grew up in the Potteries, a region with which he enjoyed something of a love-hate relationship, and he wrote his first Staffordshire novel in 1898. In his third novel, *Anna of the Five Towns*, he describes how his landscapes had been soiled by industry:

Five contiguous towns – Turnhill, Bursley, Hanbridge, Knype, and Longshaw – united by a single winding thoroughfare some eight miles in length, have inundated the valley like a succession of great lakes … They are mean and forbidding of aspect – sombre, hard-featured, uncouth; and the vaporous poison of their ovens and chimneys has soiled and shrivelled the surrounding country till there is no village lane within a league but what offers a gaunt and ludicrous travesty of rural charms. Nothing could be more prosaic than the huddled, red-brown streets; nothing more seemingly remote from romance. [60]

The harshness of the Black Country has inspired other, later, novelists. The chainmakers' environment and the culture it gave rise to is described by Brett Young in his novel *Far Forest*. He describes the chainmaker's workshop that stood behind his equally mean house:

The interior of this building received no daylight save that which the upper half of the door (which was open) and one unglazed window admitted. Its walls, furred with carbon like the throat of a chimney, and its low roof, festooned with funereal trappings of sooty cobweb, absorbed all the light that entered. The only active illumination within this black cavern proceeded from the gleed on the 'hearth', which glowed in the draught of the treadle-bellows, and displayed, with each fierce pulsation, a single high-light: the white torso of Aeron Hadley.[61]

The chainmakers lived on Mawne Heath 'on the Staffordshire side of the River Stour':

… a sunless, treeless waste, within a crescent of mournful hills from whose summits a canopy of eternal smoke was suspended above a slagged desert, its dead surface only variegated by conglomerations of brick surrounding the forges and pit-heads and brick-yards and furnaces in which the smoke was brewed; by mounds on which the mineral and metallic waste of these had been tipped, as on gigantic middens; by drowned clay-pits and sullen canals whose surface appropriately reflected an apocalyptic sky.[62]

Fig. 8.12 Wyre forest close-up.

Yet less than 24km away lay a different world: the Wyre Forest, Brett Young's 'Werewood' (Fig. 8.12). In its hidden depths a sparse population hardly ever ventured far beyond its confines, the seasons providing a timeless backdrop to their lives:

In Werewood the passage of time is so leisurely as to be barely perceived. The first quality of the forest itself is its timelessness. The growth of its close-ringed oaks is so gradual that the span of one human generation adds little to their girth or stature. Men are born and live and die among them without marking much difference. It is only they who change. And the current of their own lives flows through them smoothly and imperceptibly, draining away like the limpid waters of the Gladden Brook, unhurried, unchecked, unvaried, except by sharp tempest or changes of season so gradual as not to be noticed.[63]

When she [Jenny Hadley] first, and timidly, explored it, the bracken was barely tarnished; the oaks stood in dark leaf. Soon the leaves began to loosen with frost, and fell, whispering. The fern-fronds flamed, then faded to brittle gold under pallid November skies whose searching light beat down through an inky filigree of bared branches onto the forest's russet floor. The dead leaves lay heaped in the hollows thigh-deep, or drifted in ditches; when the wind rose they rustled dryly along the edge of the wood. In the heart of it every path was spanned in the early morning with gossamer that sparkled in the light that glistened from sodden leaves, illumining, too, grotesque forms of night-born fungi – ashen white, or pale amber or scarlet blotched with ivory – sinister shapes compared with those of the milk-white mushrooms that studded the kindlier green of meadow and orchard. Now the smell of Werewood grew damp, its deep mould releasing the summer heat in which slow-worms and adders had been born.[64]

Brett Young's novels, written in the first half of the 20th century, illustrate other social tensions within the region. In his *The House under the Water*, he compares the more tender concept of lowland England with the harshness of the Welsh hills, but in others he contrasts, in his view, the vulgarity of the 'new rich' Black Country entrepreneurs and industrialists with the sensitivity of the landed gentry to which he, like so many before him, aspired to belong.[65] This was not a new feeling, for the rigid hierarchy of early 19th-century England, so eloquently described in Jane Austen's *Emma*, had little time for social upstarts, as expressed by the dreadful Mrs Elton: 'They came from Birmingham, which is not a place to promise much, you know, Mr. Weston. One has not great hopes from Birmingham'.[66] This, despite the fact that Birmingham had been the meeting place of the Lunar Society, a gathering of some of the most learned scientific and intellectual men of the time, since the mid-1760s, and Austen must have been well aware of this conflict between knowledge and ignorance!

Brett Young is only one of many authors who show a strong awareness of regional consciousness and the feeling of belonging to a special part of this country. With increasing mobility, horizons have undoubtedly been widened but this sense of 'belonging' has by no means disappeared. Another modern writer who captures the life of people confined within a relatively small area is Bruce Chatwin who writes in *On the Black Hill* of the communities straddling the border between Wales and England. He also contrasts the harshness of the Welsh outlook expressed in the character of Amos Jones with the 'softness' of his English wife, Mary.

The harshness of the uplands underlies much of the writing of the Brontë sisters who lived at Haworth in Yorkshire and used the dark moorland settings for many of their novels. But the moors spread across into Derbyshire and it is North Lees Hall, near Hathersage, which may have inspired the setting, if not the exact model, for Thornfield Hall in Charlotte's *Jane Eyre*:

... the grey and battlemented hall was the principal object in the vale below me; its woods and dark rookery rose against the west. I lingered till the sun went down amongst the trees, and sank crimson and clear behind them ...[67]

Here Jane would fall in love with Mr Rochester, whose demented wife was confined to the attics of the old building, and would leave him until a fire released him from his vows – the countryside, with its spreading moors and menacing ridges, again providing the kind of dramatic setting that mirrored the atmosphere of the turbulent lives of the novel's characters.

It would be easy to fill this entire book with local literary quotations, for most people feel a special affection for places they feel are 'home'. This feeling was to be deepened by the outbreak of two World Wars in the first half of the 20th century. Many poems became increasingly nostalgic, written by travellers or in times of old age or war:

... I had a song, too, on my road,
But mine was in my eyes;
For Malvern Hills were with me all the way,[68]

This was the same Worcestershire landscape that inspired Edward Elgar to compose much of his music. The 'blue remembered hills' of A E Housman, 'the land of lost content', were those of Shropshire, prominent landmarks seen from his native north Worcestershire (Fig. 8.13), itself commemorated in the oft-quoted lines:

In summertime on Bredon
The bells they sound so clear;
Round both the shires they ring them
In steeples far and near,
A happy noise to hear.[69]

Fig. 8.13 The Shropshire hills.

Alison Uttley was also inspired by her childhood in Derbyshire: a farmer's daughter, she was brought up on a small farm, Castle Top Farm near Cromford. In *The Country Child* she writes of childhood fears of the Dark Wood and the fields above through which Susan had to walk to school, and the agony of having to pass an old rugged oak:

... she took in deep breaths in readiness for the next ordeal, an immense rugged
oak tree which waited at the cross-road, where her path cut across two others
... Once, two years ago, when she was seven, a pair of eyes had looked at her
from behind the tree, and once a dead white cow had lain there, swollen and
stiff, brought to be buried in the wood.[70]

Hills and uplands have long attracted admiration, and sometimes fear, and have drawn artists, writers and poets to explore their changing moods. They have also been seen as symbols of a landscape that has withstood man's attempts to change it, and that has become a repository of memories and events of long ago. Many regions have their own notable artists, like Joseph Wright and George Turner who painted Derbyshire scenes in the 18th and 19th centuries and modern-day artists like Dave Prentice, who captures the changing seasonal vistas of the Malverns (Fig. 8.14). Margery Lea describes a Shropshire hill in verse:

There is a ring of beeches on the hill
Lifting to the quiet evening sky
Layered tracery of green and grey,
Voicing reed-like in the hill-wind's sigh
Tales of long ago and far away.
Beneath them lies the valley wide and still.

Fig. 8.14 **Autumn in Malvern,** *1992, by*
D Prentice (watercolour).

There is forgetfulness within this ring,
Where memory's steeped in calm and thought is stilled.
For they the secrets of old earth enfold
Within their shadowed forms whose crowns are filled
With lustre of the west and evening gold,
And in the listening silence seem to sing.[71]

Ernest Challenger's 'Vox Populi' expresses a more uncomfortable mood:

O, I care not to go through the long fields haunted
    when the night draws downward and the hills lean close,
For every rock's shade holds the ghost of a sorrow,
    as the wide trees whisper and the stealthy wind blows.[72]

Rivers, too, from 'The meandering, wandering Wye'[73] to 'The Severn sweeping smooth and broad',[74] evoke images of the midland countryside. The Revd Robert Francis Kilvert wrote evocatively in his *Diary* (1870–9) of the district between Clyro in Radnorshire and Staunton on Wye in Herefordshire. Describing the view from his bedroom window in early September, he writes:

Out of the great white fog sea rises an island ridge of trees above Wye Cliff and one great solitary fir stands up alone like an isolated rock and stems the tide of the rolling mist. The sun has risen cloudless and the fog sea gleams brilliant and dazzling, and shining like silver. Now the sea of mist has swallowed up the island ridge of trees and the great solitary fir. Everything is swamped and gone down in the bright rolling flood which tosses and heaves and seems to dash itself in spray against the mountain sides.[75]

On another earlier occasion, he had been wandering about Clyro churchyard among the graves in early Spring:

> *Here it was very quiet and peaceful, nothing to disturb the stillness but the subdued village voices and the cawing of the rooks nesting and brooding in the tops of the high trees in the Castle clump ...* [76]

An earlier, 17th-century writer, was Izaac Walton, whose *The Complete Angler* was published in 1653. It delights in the sport and delights of the river, here the Dove in Beresford Dale where Walton stayed with a local estate owner and poet Charles Cotton at Beresford Hall.

It was not only hills and valleys, however, which stirred the emotions, for forests, too, were strongly associated with local identity ever since Michael Drayton and Shakespeare. The myth of the wide unbroken forest was so strong that many people accept it without question and few paintings perpetuate this better than Frederick Henry Henshaw's *A Forest Glade, Arden, Warwickshire,* exhibited in 1845 (Fig. 8.15). Here are the huge forest trees of the legendary Arden. There are some enormous old trees in the Arden area, like 'the Domesday Oak' at Ullenhall, but they are today isolated specimens, and even in early medieval times patches of woodland were interspersed with fields, farmsteads and hamlets. English woods had ceased to be the gloomy dark counterparts of Germanic myth. Leonard Clark's Dean was a much-loved place, too dear to recall without anguish:

> *In this lost forest sleep hovers night and day;*
> *I sit alone and hear*
> *Only a rustling bird or stir*
> *Of foraging insect through the shade;* [77]

Artists of the West Midland rural scene must also include Benjamin William Leader, whose wonderfully muddy Worcestershire scene *February Fill Dyke,* hangs in Birmingham Art Gallery.

Today's writers have continued to be inspired by their familiarity with the region. The late J R R Tolkien carries his knowledge of midland industrial landscapes into his mythical world of the Middle-Earth. In his *Silmarillion,* his dwarves were the underground engineers and craftsmen of the Industrial Revolution, but the battle between good and evil in *The Lord of the Rings* took place 'in a ravaged nightmare of an industrial landscape'. [78] His childhood near Sarehole Mill and Moseley Bog in Birmingham is said to have inspired *The Hobbit* and the two Edgbaston towers his twin Towers of Gondor in *The Lord of the Rings.* One of these is the 'Gothick' Perrot's Folly, a 29.3m-tall tower built in 1758 in what was then open country, which provided views over the city (Fig. 8.16); the other is a mid-19th-century waterworks building designed by

Fig. 8.15 **A Forest Glade, Arden, Warwickshire** *by Frederick Henry Henshaw.*

ABOVE: ***Fig. 8.16 Perrot's Folly,***
Edgbaston – *Tolkien's tower?*

ABOVE RIGHT: ***Fig. 8.17 Waterworks Tower,***
Edgbaston.

John Henry Chamberlain and William Martin (Fig. 8.17). Moseley Bog is formed on what was once a supplementary storage pool for the mill and is still an oasis of 'semi-wilderness' within the city, but it becomes the 'Old Forest' where

> … *the trees do not like strangers. They watch you. They are usually content merely to watch you, as long as daylight lasts, and don't do much. Occasionally the most unfriendly ones may drop a branch, or stick a root out, or grasp at you with a long trailer.*[79]

Tolkien was professor of English at the University of Oxford and his deep knowledge of Old English and Scandinavian mythology lends his work a richness unrivalled by many other authors trying to recreate magical situations and figures, but his descriptions of legendary destruction owed much to his familiarity with poisoned industrial landscapes.

TRAVELLERS AND TOURISM

Not surprisingly, the attitudes of travellers also changed over the centuries. Usually educated men and women, they showed a preference for the houses and estates of the gentry, and preferred towns that were obviously thriving. They tended to list the chief 'curiosities' of some shire; John Leland in his antiquarian tour through England between 1535 and 1543 noted over 30 castles in Herefordshire with others over the border. However, these early travellers could also be perceptive about the nature of the countryside. Noting the difference between the Warwickshire Arden and Feldon, Leland remarks:

*... the grownd in Arden is muche enclosyd, plentifull of gres, but no great
plenty of corne. The othar part of Warwyk-shire that lyethe on the lefte hond
or ripe of Avon river, muche to the southe, is for the moste parte champion,
somewhat barren of wood, but very plentifull of corne.*[80]

Travelling northwards through Herefordshire from the county town towards
Dinmore he passed 'by enclosyd grownde, not very hilly, plentifull of all good
corne and pasture and metely well woodyd a 4 miles'.[81]

For the early travellers, it was the towns, the churches and the country seats of
the gentry that were the main attractions, for an 'eye for the countryside' was yet
to be fostered. Ogilby's *Britannia*, a series of linear road maps, appeared in 1675,
and it gives glimpses of the countryside bordering the main routes and, in
particular, indicates enclosed and unenclosed ground. Celia Fiennes, on her
journeys, also admired the country seats of the gentry. Travelling through
Derbyshire in 1697, she acclaimed the Duke of Devonshire's house at Chatsworth
and the Earl of Rutland's Haddon Hall but did not admire the countryside:

*All Derbyshire is full of steep hills, and nothing but the peakes of hills as thick
one by another is seen in most of the County which are very steepe which
makes travelling tedious, and the miles long, you see neither hedge nor tree but
only low drye stone walls round some ground, else its only hills and dales as
thick as you can imagine, but tho' the surface of the earth looks barren yet those
hills are impregnated with rich Marbles Stones Metals Iron and Copper and
Coale mines in their bowells, from whence we may see the wisdom and
benignitye of our greate Creator to make up the defficiency of a place by an
equivolent as also the diversity of the Creation which encreaseth its Beauty.*[82]

The Dark Peak (near Eldon Hole) was even worse: '... the Country hereabout is
so full of moore or quagmires and such precipices that one that is a stranger
cannot travell without a Guide, and some of them are put to a loss sometymes'.[83]
In common with the tastes of her time, she obviously preferred a controlled man-
made landscape, such as the view of Staffordshire from 'a high hill below which
the River Trent rann and turn'd its silver streame forward and backward into Ss
which looked very pleasant circling about the fine meadows in their flourishing
tyme bedecked with hay almost ripe and flowers'.[84]

Daniel Defoe began his tours of Great Britain in 1705 as the political emissary
of a leading politician, Robert Harley, and went on to publish his *A Tour Through
the Whole Island of Great Britain* in three volumes between 1724 and 1726.
London was the centre of his world and like Fiennes he liked to see, above all,
the spectacle of plenty, 'the plenty that nature offers and almost thrusts into
mankind's hands, and the plenty which arises from the creativity and mutual
dependence of human beings'.[85] He was enthusiastic about pre-industrial
capitalism and the riches it promised, notwithstanding the use of child labour,
and, like Fiennes, gloried in the great country houses he saw: Chatsworth in
Derbyshire he describes as 'indeed a most glorious and magnificent house'.

But attitudes were changing as travellers began to appreciate the English
landscape. Arthur Young was an agricultural journalist and later secretary to the
Board of Agriculture. When he visited Coalbrookdale in Shropshire in 1776 he
noted the 'the furnaces, forges, etc. with the vast bellows that give those roaring
blasts, which make the whole edifice horribly sublime' (Fig. 8.18) and also
commented how

*These iron works are in a very flourishing situation, rising rather the
contrary. Colebrook Dale itself is a very romantic spot, it is a winding glen
between two immense hills which break into various forms, and all thickly
covered with wood, forming the most beautiful sheets of hanging wood. Indeed*

Fig. 8.18 **Coalbrookdale at Night**, *1801,*
by Philip James (Jacques) de Loutherbourg
(1740–1812) (oil on canvas).

too beautiful to be much in unison with that variety of horrors art has spread
at the bottom: the noise of the forges, mills, & c. with all their vast machinery,
the flames bursting from the furnaces with the burning of the coal and the
smoak of the lime kilns, are altogether sublime … [86]

It is, perhaps, difficult to judge Young's feelings for the new industrial landscape
but others, too, were moved to wonder at the scenes they saw here, still then
something of a novelty. Henry Skrine, a popular travel writer expressed his
reactions when he visited Coalbrookdale in 1798:

> *By day, the busy scene in this neighbourhood, and the vast quantity of craft*
> *with which the river is busy, add not a little to the interest in view; while by*
> *night the numerous fires arising from the works on the opposite hills, and*
> *along the several channels of the two valleys, aided by the clangour of forges in*
> *every direction, affect the mind of one unpractised in such scenes with an*
> *indescribable sensation of wonder, and transport in fancy the classic observer*
> *to the workshop of Vulcan or an epitome of infernal regions.* [87]

Eventually, for most, industrial scenes such as this would become increasingly
abhorrent.

By the end of the 18th century there were more and more travellers seeking
out the 'Picturesque', their Claude glass to hand. William Marshall, who wrote a
history of landscape painting in 1795, likened these to 'the big-game hunter …
boasting of their encounters with savage landscapes, "capturing" wild scenes,
and "fixing" them as pictorial trophies in order to sell them or hang them up in
frames on their drawing-room walls'. [88] William Gilpin, who published his
journals of his tours around Britain in the late 18th century, indeed encouraged
travellers 'to pursue the beauties of nature' rather than 'a trivial animal'. [89] Gilpin
was one of the first to admire the landscape for its own sake and for its rich

variety: 'From whatever cause it proceeds, certain I believe it is, that this country exceeds most countries in the *variety* of its picturesque beauties'.[90]

One of the most popular of the 'Picturesque' tours was that of the Wye valley, popularised by Gilpin in 1782 (after a tour made in 1770) and Wordsworth in the 1790s. Thomas Gray, too, had made the river voyage from Ross to Chepstow a few weeks before Gilpin and described it as 'a succession of nameless wonders'. Gilpin agreed: 'the whole is such a display of picturesque scenery that it is beyond any commendation'.[91] To him, the river scenery, viewed from the relaxed conditions offered by boat travel, had four grand parts, and the association with art is clearly apparent: 'the *area*, which is the river itself; the *two side-screens*, which are the opposite banks, and mark the perspective; and the *front-screen*, which points out the winding of the river'; the views 'though composed only of these *simple parts*, are yet *infinitely varied*'.[92]

Most visitors started at Ross, where the churchyard commanded the prospect of a broad, horse-shoe sweep of the river, travelling past the ruins of Goodrich Castle into the gorge of the Wye. Cottages were perched within the wood-covered hills and an iron forge worked beside the New Weir, but these were 'harmonious appendages' to a landscape 'sublimely steep and wild'. As today, Symonds Yat Rock 'gave the tourist a thrilling taste of the Picturesque modulating swiftly into the Sublime'. From here, the River Wye runs northwards in a huge meander between wooded hills (Fig. 8.19) and peregrine falcons still nest on the crags of Coldwell Rocks. The tour continued on to Monmouth and thence to the chief architectural glory of the valley – the ruined Tintern Abbey, a romantic place of 'secular pilgrimages', its atmosphere captured by Turner in his *Interior of Tintern Abbey*, painted in 1794:

> *Approaching this sublime and sequestered spot, the enthusiastic lover of simplicity in art and nature, the admirer of the picturesque and beautiful, the antiquary and the moralist will feel the effect, as it were, of enchantment, and become lost almost in a pleasing melancholy.*[93]

One of the most neglected garden landscapes of the Picturesque style, Piercefield, still overlooks the Wye on the Welsh side to the south of Tintern. The tour ended at Chepstow where the great stone castle of the Osberns stood guard over a strategic crossing point of the river. This was amongst the first of Britain's stone-built strongholds and continued in use until 1690. A massive and mighty medieval fortress, it still provides a fitting climax to a tour of the Wye. The Forest of Dean shared some of this popularity and John Byng, touring in 1781, made a special detour to ride through the Forest from Mitcheldean to a mile or so above Coleford in order to experience the 'awful grandeur' of the place, the evening sky obscured by 'noble waving woods, hill above hill'.[94]

Fig. 8.19 The River Wye from Symonds Yat.

More practically minded 19th-century travellers began to take a growing interest in the 'improvement' of rural farming. In his *Rural Rides*, William Cobbett describes the land around Bollitree in Herefordshire in 1821: 'The land is very rich, the pastures the finest, I ever saw, the trees of all kinds, surpassing upon an average, any that I have before seen in England'.[95] He goes on to praise the orchards that produced such fine cider and perry, criticising the gentry for preferring wine and spirits, and enjoyed meeting the farmers at Hereford market. A few years later, in 1826, he was equally enamoured of 'the finest meadows of which it is possible to form an idea' found along the Severn, and the vale pastures grazed by sheep and cattle, the latter 'the Hereford, white face and dark red body, certainly the finest and most beautiful of all horn cattle'. Worcester was 'one of the cleanest, neatest, and handsomest towns I ever saw', despite its cathedral being 'a poor thing'.[96] It was still an invitation to stay on a country estate that brought him to the midlands in 1826, a region that lay beyond his normal travels. He stayed with Sir Thomas Winnington at Stanford Park beside the Teme but he was no sycophant to the rich:

> *Of all the mean, all the cowardly reptiles, that ever crawled on the face of the earth, the* English land-owners *are the most mean, and the most cowardly: for, while they support the churches, in their several parishes, while they see the population drawn away from their parishes, to the Wens, while they are taxed to keep the people in the Wens, and while they see their own Parsons pocket the tithes, and the glebe-rents, and suffer the parsonage-houses to fall down; while they see all this, they, without uttering a word in the way of complaint, suffer themselves and their neighbours to be taxed, to build new churches for the monopolizers and tax-eaters in those Wens! Never was there in this world, a set of reptiles so base as this. Of course, all they want is the income, and, the less the parsonage-house costs, the larger the spending income. But, in the meanwhile, here is a destruction of public property; and also, from a diversion of the income of the livings, a great injustice, to the middle and the working classes.*[97]

Here he echoes the rising consciousness of the 19th-century labourer. His concern for the common man is also shown in his admiration of the relative prosperity of the country people living near Worcester. Glove-making brought in a goodly income here but it was the family pig that provided security. Cobbett's views reflect the growing social conscience of mid-19th-century England.

After the Industrial Revolution, travellers found it increasingly difficult to ignore or circumvent the growing towns. At the risk of including yet one other description of the Black Country, the following are the comments of John Britton who journeyed through the midlands in 1850:

> *From Birmingham to Wolverhampton, a distance of thirteen miles* [21km], *the country was curious and amusing though not very pleasing to the eyes, ears or taste. For part of it seemed a sort of pandemonium on earth – a region of smoke and fire filling the whole area between earth and heaven amongst which certain figures of human shape – if shape they had – were seen occasionally to glide from one cauldron of curling flame to another. The eye could not descry any form of colour indicative of country, or of the hues and aspect of nature, or anything human or divine. Although nearly mid-day in Summer, the sun and sky were obscure and discoloured. Something like horses, men, women and children occasionally seemed to move in the midst of the black and yellow smoke and flashes of fire, but were again lost in obscurity …The surface of the earth is covered and loaded with its own entrails, which afford employment and livelihood for thousands of the human race.*[98]

ACCESS TO THE COUNTRYSIDE

The 'common folk' were by no means slaves to the changing order. In the 19th century a new movement was gaining strength among them. Already, in the late 18th century, some altruistic employers had seen it as their duty to improve the lives of their workers as the Industrial Revolution got underway. In Coalbrookdale, in Shropshire, where changing techniques in the iron industry had marked the beginning of the Industrial Revolution, Richard Reynolds in the late 18th century established the 'Workmen's' or 'Sabbath Walks' on the slopes of Lincoln Hill on the eastern slopes of the dale. These were for his workers' enjoyment and relaxation although he also wished to discourage them from frequenting public houses on Sundays. Walks were laid out, with shrubs and fir trees, 'and adorned ... with temples and other ornamental buildings with iron pillars, rustic seats and other accommodation'.[99] In the second half of the 19th century Octavia Hill was one of the most effectual people striving to promote enjoyment of the countryside as a social benefit, especially for the urban poor. John Ruskin, too, in 1871 set up the Guild of St George to purchase land for the benefit of the people, but he and Hill were frequently in bitter conflict. Other groups active in the field at this time included the Commons Preservation Society and the Lake District Defence Society, and their combined interest resulted in the establishment of the National Trust. This was founded in 1895, embodying social and moral objectives, to preserve selected land and properties 'of beauty or historic interest ... for the benefit of the nation'.[100]

But ordinary folk were also beginning to assert their own 'rights' to the countryside, rights that they saw as heavily abraded by the enclosure of the commons. Although the open moorlands of the Peak District still lay open, they were now regarded as private grouse moors and access was forbidden. Landowners wielded immense power and there were many in late 19th-century Britain who, although unable to join this small section of society, were rich enough to rent shooting rights and so identify themselves with the gentry. The workers in the industrial conurbations around saw the moorlands as 'forbidden land' and bitterly resented the situation, seeing the open moors as their means of at least temporary escape from the crowded industrial slums of the towns. By the beginning of the 20th century, walking had become a national pastime. Yet in 1935, although the moorlands of the Peak District covered some 557sq km, there were only 12 footpaths that exceeded 3km in length.[101] Rallies were organised and one spring Sunday in 1932, 400 men and women took part in a mass trespass over Kinder Scout in order to demonstrate 'for the rights of ordinary people to walk on land stolen from them in earlier times'.[102] The ringleaders were sent to prison, but the movement was irrepressible and two other mass trespasses followed. The Ramblers' Association was founded in 1935.

With improvements in transport, more and more townspeople were able to rediscover the countryside. Trams carried people from town centres to the more rural outskirts and, in Birmingham, the Lickey Hills became a favourite destination. As early as 1868, the American consul in Birmingham had noted the recreational opportunity of the continuous tract of hilly land that stretched from Wychbury Hill near Hagley, through Walton Hill in the Clents to Beacon and Bilbery Hills in the Lickeys; '... for use of ornament they [the hills] are beautiful and valuable features of the Green Border Land of the Black Country, and thousands of all ages luxuriate on these heathered heights in summer' (Fig. 8.20).[103] In Birmingham, the commons that surrounded the city on its southern side had been enclosed in 1831, as the Lickey Hills were taken in, but after the Open Spaces Acts of 1877 and 1881 local authorities were able to secure open land for public enjoyment. The Birmingham Association for the Preservation of Open Spaces bought Rednal Hill with the help of the Cadbury and Plymouth families; Birmingham Corporation leased Bilberry Hill in 1889 to protect it from

Fig. 8.20 The Clent Hills, Worcestershire.

quarrying, and additional gifts of land including Beacon Hill were made by the Cadburys. When the Plymouth estate broke up in 1919, Birmingham Corporation bought Cofton Hill and woodland at Barnt Green, thus securing the Lickey Hills for public enjoyment. Farmland around Lowhill Farm was opened up for public access in 1936 as Cofton Park. Subsequent measures such as the defensive 'green belts' around conurbations helped to slow down the loss of rural land around towns. These measures have since been augmented by Parliamentary Acts to establish National Parks, Areas of Outstanding Natural Beauty and Countryside Parks, in which the promotion of public enjoyment is a major aim.

CONSERVATION OF THE COUNTRYSIDE

Under the National Parks and Access to the Countryside Act of 1949, National Parks were set up with conservation and the promotion of public enjoyment as guiding, if sometimes conflicting, aims. A major objective was to protect remaining regions of 'semi-wilderness' and the first National Park to be established was in this region – the Peak District, set up in 1951 and covering an area of 1,400sq km in the Southern Pennines. After 1956 a further tier of Areas of Outstanding Natural Beauty (AONBs), which tended to be of lesser extent in the agricultural lowlands, was added and, beneath these, much smaller 'Countryside Parks'. Cannock Chase, the Wye Valley, the Malverns and the South Shropshire Hills are now recognised as AONBs. The Countryside Act of 1968 introduced new elements in countryside policy, among them an awareness that conservation and recreation problems had to be addressed outside the statutory designated areas. Consequently, the Countryside Commission was established to oversee conservation issues and general 'countryside management'; it worked closely with the Nature Conservancy Council (now English Nature), also established in 1949, and in 1999 it was re-named the Countryside Agency. Other measures to protect the countryside included the setting up of nature reserves, Environmentally Sensitive Areas (which include the Wyre Forest), and thousands of Sites of Special Scientific Interest, 'the gems of the countryside, the last stand for Britain's wild life'.

To these conservation measures may be added the work of numerous private bodies such as the National Trust, the Royal Society for the Protection of Birds and the county wildlife trusts, and of government-sponsored bodies such as English Heritage, which has a special concern for historical sites and monuments. English Nature maintains the National Nature Reserves, which are found throughout the region. After generations of drainage to acquire additional land for agriculture the value of wetlands is again being appreciated, primarily now as wildlife and plant reserves. Along the Shropshire–Cheshire border, under the auspices of English Nature, water levels are being raised at places like Wem, Fenn's, Whixall, Bettisfield and Wybunbury Mosses, all classified as National Nature Reserves, to provide habitats for mire species – some of these sites only narrowly escaped complete destruction by intensive peat extraction. Aqualate Mere in Staffordshire is fed by a number of steams and is fringed by reed swamp, alder and willow carr, damp grassland and fen communities, supporting a rich population of fish and breeding birds.

Other reserves include woodlands such as the mixed woods of Downton Gorge in Herefordshire, woods mainly of sessile oak, ash, lime, wych elm and birch that provide a home for otters and polecats, or the ash woods of the Derbyshire dales, the oldest also containing wych elm and small-leaved lime. Reserves have also been established in Monk's, Cressbrook, Lathkill, Biggin and Long Dales, and on south-facing slopes the lime-rich grasslands are particularly flower-rich and the home to many rare plants. The Wyre Forest and Chaddesley Woods in Worcestershire and Lady Park Wood and Highbury Wood on the Wales–Gloucestershire border are other woodland reserves while the Stiperstones in Shropshire is a moorland reserve with high-altitude upland heath. Many other reserves are maintained on a voluntary basis by county groups (Fig. 8.21).

Alongside measures to conserve existing environmental resources attempts are now being made, largely through the impetus of the Countryside Agency, to increase the acreages of England's woodland and a new 'national forest' stretching from Staffordshire to Leicestershire incorporates what is left of the ancient forest of Needwood. In addition, the planting of woodland as 'community forests' around some urban conurbations is being encouraged, as in the 'Forest of Mercia' that has been designated across the Cannock Chase coalfield around Cannock, Brownhills and Aldridge, with its most extensive blocks to lie south-east of Hilton Park to the north of Wednesfield and Bloxwich; the 'Mersey Forest' will extend southwards into Cheshire.

To increase public access to the countryside, long-distance footpaths have been established, like the Offa's Dyke Path that runs from Chepstow on the Severn estuary to Prestatyn on the north Welsh coast via the border hills of Herefordshire and Shropshire. The Pennine Way, the first long-distance path to

Fig. 8.21 Trench Wood, Worcestershire, *a local nature reserve.*

Fig. 8.22 A view near Kinder Scout in the Dark Peak.

be completed, in 1965, is a hard exposed route that runs along the Pennine chain from near Macclesfield to the Cheviots on the Scottish border. It runs through some of the emptiest hills in England and the first part, beginning at Edale and Kinder Scout (Fig. 8.22), falls within our region. The Heart of England Way was initially the result of voluntary initiative: local rambling clubs mapped out a long-distance route of 160km (100 miles) linking the Gloucestershire Cotswolds with Cannock Chase in Staffordshire. County and local district authorities have opened other long walks, such as the Worcestershire Way that runs from Kinver to the Malverns, offering views over the Teme valley to the west, or the North Worcestershire Path that follows the high land to the south of Birmingham. In Staffordshire, the South Staffordshire Way runs northwards from Kinver; the Mortimer Trail runs through south Shropshire and north Herefordshire from Ludlow to Kington and takes in the new Mortimer Forest and the hillforts of Croft Ambrey and Wapley (Fig. 8.23), linking with other routes that include the Shropshire Way and the Marches Way. Apart from these selected routes, right of way is restricted to legally recognised old byways, footpaths, bridleways and concessionary ways. The claim to 'a right to roam' over open uncultivated ground has come nearer fulfilment with the passing of the Countryside and Rights of Way Act in 2000, but what land is involved is still subject to discussion.

In the past, the government-funded Countryside Agency (formerly the Countryside Commission) dealt with rural social matters while English Nature was more concerned with the physical environment. Now, these are to unite with the Rural Development Service in a single agency, 'Natural England', with conservation much to the fore. The countryside responsibilities of the government's old Department of the Environment have been transferred to a new Department for Environment, Food and Rural Affairs (Defra), which also fosters conservation through the management of voluntary farming schemes such as Countryside Stewardship. With the problems of over-production still facing Britain's farmers, schemes designed to foster long-term sustainable farming allied to the conservation of traditional landscapes will play an increasing part in Government policy. Funding has been made available through Countryside Stewardship for, among other things, the preservation of previously unprotected old herb-rich grasslands and orchards, with extra grants available for carrying out such traditional practices as hedge-laying according to local style and the rebuilding of stone walls provided that additional public access is encouraged. The Environmentally Sensitive Areas scheme encouraged the preservation and management of those features most applicable to specific regions. The new Environmental Stewardship scheme will continue this work. We face a dilemma: society demands more housing, continuing economic development and good communications, but there is also a deep desire to preserve both traditional landscapes and our last vestiges of 'semi-wilderness'. The twin aims of maintaining biodiversity and the visual diversity of the landscape go hand in hand, but they can only be successfully achieved if the evolution of the landscape is truly understood.

NOTES

1   *Beowulf*, trans Wright 1970, 59.

2   Hooke 1990, 43–4, 164–5.

3   Ibid, 155–7, 382–3.

4   Palmer 2002, 10, 27.

5   Mary Webb, *The Golden Arrow*, 1916,
    quoted in Countryside Commission
    1993, 32.

6   Furbank *et al.* 1991, 251.

7   Palmer 2002, 11–13.

8   Hooke forthcoming.

9   Harding & Wall 2000, 16.

10 Tolkien 1979, 1.

11 Lacy 1988, 262, citing Erik S Kooper,
    University of Utrecht.

12 Anon, *Sir Gawain and the Green Knight*,
    trans J R R Tolkien, ed. Tolkien 1979, 33.

13 Basford 1998, 12.

14 Preface to Hicks 2000.

15 From William Langland, *Piers the
    Ploughman* 'The Field of Folk', trans
    Bradley-Birt 1934, 190.

16 Thomas Traherne, *Third Century*, quoted
    in Drabble 1979, 36.

17 Michael Drayton, *Poly-Olbion*, The
    Thirteenth Song.

18 William Shakespeare, *As You Like It*, Act 2,
    Scene 1.

19 Furbank *et al.* 1991, 251.

20 Walpole, quoted in Drabble 1979, 59.

21 J Thomson, *The Seasons: Spring*, 1746, after
    a visit in 1743; *see* Cohen 1970, 71–2.

22 Gilpin 1798.

23 Payne Knight 1805, 150.

24 Payne Knight, *The Landscape: A Didactic
    Poem*, 1794, Book II, 284–6.

25 Ibid, Book I, 1–8, discussed in Wall 1994.

26 Ibid, 1795, Book III, 37–40.

27 Ibid 1795, Book II, 200–9.

28 Young 1932, 150.

29 Pitt 1813, 185.

30 Duncumb 1805, 94–5.

31 Elizabeth Barrett Browning, *Aurora Leigh,
    'The Sweetness of England'*, 1856,
    reproduced in Coppin 1993, 53.

32 William Wordsworth, *Lucy*.

33 George Marsh 1860, *Christian Examiner*, 68,
    33–62, quoted in Lowenthal 1999, 140.

34 Lucas 1988, 87.

35 Discussed in Andrews 1989, 40–1.

36 George Eliot, *Middlemarch*, 1871–2, ch 12.

37 Elizabeth Gaskell, *Cousin Phillis*, 1863–4;
    Drabble 1979, 85.

38 Quoted in Drabble 1979, 80.

39 Mary Webb, *Gone to Earth*, 1917, ch 25.

40 *VCH Derbyshire I* 1905, 92.

41 Marshall 1986, 9.

42 Tebbutt 2005, 142.

43 'Song' from *The Gypsies Metamorphos'd* by
    Ben Jonson 1621: Herford Percy &
    Simpson 1941, 601–3; Riggs 1989, 271.

44 Ford 1999, 42–3.

45 Sir Walter Scott, *Peveril of the Peak*, ch 1.

46 Hunt 1997 and forthcoming.

47 *VCH Staffordshire I* 1908, 232.

48 Ibid, 240.

49 *VCH Staffordshire 17* 1976, 145.

50 Jewell 1994, 211–12.

51 Fletcher 1977.

52 Thomas Habington's *Survey of Worcestershire* 1895–9, I, 195, ed Amphlett, nd, quoted in Currie & Lewis 1994, 424.

53 Raven 1977, 3.

54 Ibid, 50, quoting verses from *The Brave Dudley Boys*, collected 1840s.

55 Ibid, 117–18, quoting verses from *Perry's Croft Bull Bait*, probably early 19th century.

56 Mobley 1977, 11.

57 Charles Dickens, *The Old Curiosity Shop*, 1840–1, ch 45.

58 Charles Dickens, *Pickwick Papers*, 1837, ch 50.

59 Charles Dickens, *The Old Curiosity Shop*, 1840–1, ch 44.

60 Arnold Bennett, *Anna of the Five Towns*, 1902, ch 1.

61 Francis Brett Young, *Far Forest*, 1936, Part I, ch 2, i.

62 Ibid.

63 Ibid, Part I, ch. 5, ii.

64 Ibid, Part I, ch. 3, ii.

65 Cannadine 1982.

66 Jane Austen, *Emma*, Vol II, ch 18.

67 Charlotte Brontë, *Jane Eyre*, ch 12.

68 Lascelles Abercrombie, 'Ryton Firs', from *Twelve Idylls*, 1928, quoted in Coppin 1993, 86.

69 A E Housman *c.* 1895, *A Shropshire Lad* XXI: Bredon Hill.

70 Alison Uttley, *The Country Child*, 1931, ch 1.

71 Margery Lea, 'On a Hill in Shropshire', from *These Days*, quoted in Coppin 1993, 33.

72 Ernest K Challenger, 'Vox Populi', in Fowler Wright, nd, 53–5.

73 Donald Hughes 1934, 'The Wye', quoted in Coppin 1993, 73.

74 Andrew Young, 'At Arley', quoted in ibid, 80.

75 *Kilvert's Diary*, 14 September 1874, in Plomer 1938, Vol 3, 80–1.

76 Ibid, Vol 1: 24 March 1871.

77 Leonard Clark, *The Forest*, from *English Morning*, 1953, reproduced in Coppin 1993, 103.

78 Drabble 1979, 230–1.

79 J R R Tolkien, *Lord of the Rings*, Book One, ch VI.

80 *Leland's Itinerary*, Part V, fo 61a,b, reproduced in Toulmin Smith 1964, Vol 2, 47.

81 Ibid, 71: Part V, fo 76b.

82 Morris 1995, 104.

83 Ibid, 110; cf. Furbank *et al.* 1991, 251: Defoe, Letter VIII.

84 Ibid, 28.

85 Furbank *et al.* 1991, x.

86 Young 1932, 152.

87 Skrine 1798, in Trinder 1988, 62.

88 Andrews 1989, 67.

89 Ibid, 68.

90 Gilpin 1786, *Lakes* i, 5.

91 Thomas Gray, Letter 24 August 1770; Gilpin, Letter 3 July 1770; quoted in Andrews 1989, 89.

92 Gilpin, quoted in Andrews 1989, 89.

93 Samuel Ireland, quoted in Andrews 1989, 97.

94 John Byng, *The Torrington Diaries* (ed C Bruyn Andrews), quoted in Carroll 1994, 113.

95 Cobbett, 'Journal: From Gloucester, to Bollitree in Herefordshire …', 1821, reproduced in Morris 1992, 24.

96 Ibid, 178–9: Cobbett, 'Ride from Malmesbury, in Wiltshire, through Gloucestershire, Herefordshire, and Worcestershire', 1826.

97 Ibid, 183: Cobbett, 'Ride from Ryall, in Worcestershire, to Burghclere, in Hampshire', 1826.

98 John Britton, quoted in Blunden & Turner 1985, 21–2.

99 Plymley 1793 (Br Mus Add MSS. 21018), quoted in Trinder 1973, 363; Hooke 1998b, 6.

100 Waterson 1994, 52.

101 Shoard 1987, 113.

102 Rothman 1982, quoted in Shoard 1987, 114.

103 Burritt, quoted in Williams 1984, 1–3.

Bibliography

Ainsworth, S and Wilmott, A 2005. *Chester Amphitheatre: From Gladiators to Gardens*. London: English Heritage

Alfrey, J and Clark, C 1993. *The Landscape of Industry: Patterns of Change in the Ironbridge Gorge*. London: Routledge

Andrews, M 1989. *The Search for the Picturesque*. California: Stanford University Press

Anon. 1868. *Dudley, Illustrated by Photographs*. London: W H Laxton

Aston, M 1993. *Monasteries*. London: Batsford

Baker, N 2003. 'The archaeology of pre-Conquest towns', West Midlands Regional Research Framework for Archaeology, Seminar 4, www.arch-ant.bham.ac.uk/wmrrfa/index.htm

Barnatt, J 1996. 'Barrows in the Peak District: a review and interpretation of extant sites and past excavations', *in* Barnatt, J and Collis, J (eds) *Barrows in the Peak District: Recent Research*. Sheffield: Sheffield Academic Press, 3–94

Barnatt, J 1998. 'Monuments in the landscape: thoughts from the Peak', *in* Gibson, A and Simpson, D (eds) *Prehistoric Ritual and Religion*. Stroud: Alan Sutton, 92–105

Barnatt, J and Smith, K 1997. *Book of the Peak District: Landscapes through Time*. London: Batsford/English Heritage

Barnatt, J and Smith, K 2004. *The Peak District: Landscapes through Time* (new edn). Bollington, Macclesfield: Windgather Press

Basford, K 1978. *The Green Man*. Repr 1998, Woodbridge: Brewer

Bassett, S 1992. 'Church and diocese in the West Midlands: the transition from British to Anglo-Saxon control', *in* Blair, J and Sharpe, R (eds) *Pastoral Care Before the Parish*. Leicester: Leicester University Press, 13–40

Beale, J 1656. *Herefordshire Orchards, a Pattern for All England* (1724 edn). Dublin: George Grierson

Beevers, J and Meir, J 1994. 'Charlecote', *in* Fryer, H (ed.) *Lancelot (Capability) Brown, Warwickshire Commissions*. Warwick: Warwickshire Gardens Trust, 27–30

Belford, P 2003. 'Forging ahead in Coalbrookdale: historical archaeology at the Upper Forge'. *Industrial Archaeology Review* **25.1**, 59–62

Belford, P and Ross, R A 2004. 'Industry and domesticity: exploring historical archaeology in the Ironbridge Gorge'. *Post-medieval Archaeology* **38.2**, 215–25

Bettey, J H 1993. *Estates and the English Countryside*. London: Batsford

Blair, J 1985. 'Secular minster churches in Domesday Book', *in* Sawyer, P (ed.) *Domesday Book, A Reassessment*. London: Edward Arnold, 104–42 (in fig captions)

Blair, J 1988. 'Minster churches in the landscape', *in* Hooke, D (ed.) *Anglo-Saxon Settlements*. Oxford: Blackwell, 35–58

Blunden, J and Turner, G 1985. *Critical Countryside*. London: BBC

Bond, J 2004. *Monastic Landscapes*. Stroud: Tempus

Bonser, K J 1970. *The Drover. Who They Were and How They Went: An Epic of the English Countryside*. London: Macmillan

Bowden, M 2000. *British Camp or Herefordshire Beacon* (unpubl English Heritage Report)

Bradley-Birt, F B 1934. *A Worcestershire Anthology*. Kidderminster: G T Cheshire and Sons

Brayley, E W and Britton J, 1801–15. *The Beauties of England and Wales*, 25 vols. London: Vernor and Hood

Brian, A 1993. 'Lammas meadows'. *Landscape History* **15**, 57–69

Brown, R J 1985. *English Farmhouses*. London: Hamlyn

Brunskill, R W 1994. *Timber Building in Britain* (2nd edn). London: Gollancz

Bruyn Andrews, C (ed.) 1934–8. *John Byng, the Torrington Diaries*. London: Eyre and Spottiswoode

Cannadine, D 1982. *This Little World: The Value of the Novels of Francis Brett Young as a guide to the state of midland Society, 1870–1925* (Worcestershire Historical Society Occasional Publications **4**). Wednesbury: Worcestershire Historical Society

Cantor, L 1982. 'Forests, chases, parks and warrens', *in* Cantor, L (ed.) *The English Medieval Landscape*. London: Croom Helm, 56–85

Capelli, C, Redhead, N, Abernethy, J K, Gratrix, F, Wilson, J F, Moen, T, Hervig, T, Richards, M, Stumpf, M P H, Underhill, P A, Bradshaw, P, Shaha, A, Thomas, M G, Bradman, N and Goldstein, D B, 2003. 'A Y chromosome census of the British Isles'. *Current Biology* **13**, 979–84

Carroll, D 1994. *A Literary Tour of Gloucestershire and Bristol*. Stroud: Alan Sutton

Childs, J 1987. *A History of Derbyshire*. Chichester: Phillimore

Chitty, L F 1963. 'The Clun–Clee ridgeway. A prehistoric trackway across south Shropshire', *in* Foster, I L and Alcock, L (eds) *Culture and Environment: Essays in Honour of Sir Cyril Fox*. London: Routledge and Kegan Paul, 171–92

Cleverdon, F 1995. 'Survey and excavation in the Manifold valley'. *Staffordshire Archaeol Stud* **5**, 30–6

Coates, R 2004. 'The Lyme'. *J English Place-Name Soc* **36**, 39–50

Cohen, R 1970. *The Unfolding of the Seasons*. Baltimore: John Hopkins Press

Coplestone-Crow, B 1989. *Herefordshire Place-Names* (BAR Brit Ser **214**). Oxford: British Archaeol Reps

Coppin, J 1993. *Between the Severn and the Wye*. Moreton-in-Marsh: Windrush Press

Countryside Commission 1993. *The Shropshire Hills Landscape* (CCP 407). Cheltenham: Countryside Commission

Countryside Commission 1994. *The Cannock Chase Landscape* (TCCP 469). Cheltenham: Countryside Commission

Countryside Commission and English Nature 1997. *The Character of England: Landscape, Wildlife and Natural Features*. Cheltenham and Peterborough: Countryside Commission and English Nature

Court, W H B 1938. *The Rise of the Midland Industries 1600–1838*. London: Oxford University Press

Crosby, A 1996. *A History of Cheshire*. Chichester: Phillimore

Cunliffe, B 2000. *The Danebury Environs Programme: The Prehistory of a Wessex Landscape, 1* (Engl Heritage and Oxford Univ Comm Archaeol Monogr **48**). Oxford: Oxford Univ Comm Archaeol

Currie, C R J and Lewis, C P 1994. *English County Histories: A Guide*. Stroud: Alan Sutton

Daniels, S 1988. 'The political iconography of woodland in later Georgian England', *in* Cosgrove, D and Daniels, S (eds) *The Iconography of Landscape*. Cambridge: Cambridge University Press, 43–82

Daniels, S and Watkins, C 1994. *The Picturesque Landscape: Visions of Georgian Herefordshire*. Nottingham: University Nottingham Department of Geography

Darby, H C 1977. *Domesday England*. Cambridge: Cambridge University Press

Darby, H C and Maxwell, I S (eds) 1962. *The Domesday Geography of Northern England*. Cambridge: Cambridge University Press

Darby, H C and Terrett, I B (eds) 1978. *The Domesday Geography of Midland England* (2nd edn). Cambridge: Cambridge University Press

Dark, P 2000. *The Environment of Britain in the First Millennium AD*. London: Duckworth

Drabble, M 1979. *A Writer's Britain: Landscape in Literature*. London: Thames and Hudson

Dugdale, Sir W 1656. *History of Warwickshire II*

Duncumb, J 1805. *General View of the Agriculture of the County of Hereford*. London: Richard Phillips

Dyer, C 1994. *Everyday Life in Medieval England*. London: Hambledon Press

Evans, J G with Rhys, J (ed.) 1893. *The Text of the Book of Llan Dâv. Reproduced from the Gwysaney Manuscript*. Oxford. Facsimile edn 1979, Aberystwyth: National Library of Wales

Fairfax-Lucy, A 1990. *Charlecote and the Lucys: The Chronicle of an English Family*. London: Gollancz

Faith, R 1994. 'Tidenham, Gloucestershire, and the history of the manor in England'. *Landscape History* **16**, 39–51

Fedden, R and Joekes, R 1973. *The National Trust Guide*. London: Jonathan Cape

Field, R K 1965. 'Worcestershire peasant buildings, household goods and farming equipment in the later middle ages'. *Medieval Archaeology* **9**, 105–45

Fleming, L and Gore, A 1979. *The English Garden*. London: Spring Books

Fletcher, J 1977. 'Introduction' to Raven, J *The Urban and Industrial Songs of the Black Country*. Wolverhampton: Broadside

Ford, D J 1999. *The Land of the Dove*. Leek: Churnet Valley Books

Fowler Wright, S (ed.) nd. *Contemporary Poetry of Shropshire, Worcestershire, Herefordshire, and Monmouthshire*. London: Fowler Wright

Fuller, R M 1987. 'The changing extent and conservation interest of lowland grassland in England and Wales: a review of grassland surveys 1930–1984'. *Biol Conservation* **40**, 218–300

Furbank, P N, Owens, W R and Coulson, A J (eds) 1991. *Daniel Defoe, A Tour Through the Whole Island of Great Britain*. New Haven and London: Yale University Press

Gale, W K V 1979. *The Black Country Iron Industry*. London: Metals Society

Gelling, M 1990. *The Place-Names of Shropshire, Part 1*. Cambridge: English Place-Name Society

Gelling, M 1992. *The West Midlands in the Early Middle Ages*. Leicester: Leicester University Press

Get Mapping.com 2001. *England: The Photographic Atlas*. London: Harper Collins

Gilpin, W 1786. *Observations Relative Chiefly to Picturesque Beauty, Made in the Year 1772, on Several Parts of England; Particularly the Mountains, and Lakes of Cumberland, and Westmoreland*. Repr 1996, Poole: Woodstock Books

Gilpin, W 1798. *Observations on the Western Parts of England, Relative Chiefly to Picturesque Beauty*. London: Cadell and Davies

Girouard, M 1978. *Life in the English Country House*. New Haven and London: Yale University Press

Goode, D J 1994. *Black Country Life 1830–1880*. Upton upon Severn: Images Publishing

Green, M 1993. *Celtic Myths*. London: British Museum Press

Greenslade, M W and Stuart, D G 1984. *A History of Staffordshire* (2nd edn). Chichester: Phillimore

Habington, T 1895–9. *A Survey of Worcestershire*, ed Amphlett, T, 2 vols. Worcestershire Hist Soc **2**. Oxford: Worcestershire Historical Society

Hadfield, C 1985. *The Canals of the West Midlands* (3 edn). Newton Abbot: David and Charles

Harding, P T and Wall, T 2000. 'Rationale and background', *in* Harding, P T and Wall, T (eds) *Moccas: An English Deer Park*. Peterborough: English Nature, 11–17

Harris, J 1998. *No Voice from the Hall*. London: Murray

Harrison, C 1999. 'Fire on the Chase: rural riots in sixteenth-century Staffordshire', *in* Morgan, P and Phillips, A D M (eds) *Staffordshire Histories: Essays in Honour of Michael Greenslade*. Keele: Staffs Rec Soc and Univ Keele Centre for Local Hist, 97–126

Hay, D 1977. 'Poaching and the game laws on Cannock Chase', *in* Hay, D, Linebaugh, P, Rule, J G, Thompson, E P and Winslow, C (eds) *Albion's Fatal Tree*. Harmondsworth: Penguin, 189–254

Herford Percy, C H, Simpson, P and Simpson, E (eds) 1941. *Ben Jonson, Vol VII*, Part ii: 'Masques at Court, 1605–1631'. Oxford: Clarendon Press

Hicks, C 2000. *The Green Man: A Field Guide*. Helhoughton: Compassbooks

Higham, N J 1993. *The Origins of Cheshire*. Manchester: Manchester University Press

Hill, D and Worthington, M 2003. *Offa's Dyke: History and Guide*. Stroud: Tempus

Hodges, R 1991. *Wall-to-Wall History: The Story of Roystone Grange*. London: Duckworth

Holly, D 1962. 'Derbyshire', *in* Darby, H C and Maxwell, I D (eds) *The Domesday Geography of Northern England*. Cambridge: Cambridge University Press, 278–329

Hooke, D 1980. 'The hinterland and routeways of Anglo-Saxon Worcester: the charter evidence', *in* Carver, M O H (ed.) *Medieval Worcester, Trans Worcestershire Archaeol Soc* **3**, ser 7, 39–49

Hooke, D 1981a. *Anglo-Saxon Landscapes of the West Midlands: The Charter Evidence* (BAR Brit Ser **95**). Oxford: British Archaeol Rep

Hooke, D 1981b. 'The Droitwich salt industry: an examination of the West Midland charter evidence'. *Anglo-Saxon Studies in Archaeology and History* **2** (BAR Brit Ser **92**), 12–69. Oxford: British Archaeol Rep

Hooke, D 1983. *The Landscape of Anglo-Saxon Staffordshire: The Charter Evidence*. Keele: Dep Adult Education, Keele University

Hooke, D 1985a. *The Anglo-Saxon Landscape: The Kingdom of the Hwicce*. Manchester: Manchester University Press

Hooke, D 1985b. 'Village development in the West Midlands', *in* Hooke, D (ed.) *Medieval Villages: A Review of Current Work* (Oxford Univ Comm Archaeol Monogr **5**), 125–54. Oxford: Oxford Univ Comm Archaeol

Hooke, D 1988. 'The Warwickshire Arden: the evolution and future of an historic landscape'. *Landscape Hist* **10**, 51–9

Hooke, D 1989. 'Pre-Conquest woodland: its distribution and usage'. *Agric Hist Rev* **37**, 113–29

Hooke, D 1990. *Worcestershire Anglo-Saxon Charter-Bounds*. Woodbridge: Boydell Press

Hooke, D 1996. 'Reconstructing Anglo-Saxon landscapes in Warwickshire'. *Trans Birmingham Warwickshire Archaeol Soc* **100**, 99–116

Hooke, D 1998a. *The Landscape of Anglo-Saxon England*. London: Leicester University Press

Hooke, D 1998b. 'The historic land use and cultural landscape of the Ironbridge and Coalbrookdale area', unpublished report for the Severn Gorge Countryside Trust

Hooke, D 1998c. 'Medieval forests and parks in southern and central England', *in* Watkins, C (ed.) *European Woods and Forests. Studies in Cultural History*. Wallingford: CAB International, 1–32

Hooke, D 1999. *Warwickshire Anglo-Saxon Charter-Bounds*. Woodbridge: Boydell Press

Hooke, D 2002. 'Landscape studies', *in* Ecclestone, M, Gardiner, K S, Holbrook, N and Smith, A (eds) *The Land of the Dobunni: A Series of Papers Relating to the Transformation of the Pagan, Pre-Roman, Tribal Lands, into Christian, Anglo-Saxon Gloucestershire and Somerset*. From the Symposia of 2001 and 2002. Comm Archaeol Gloucestershire and Counc Brit Archaeol – South-West, 68–76

Hooke, D forthcoming. *Trees in Early Medieval England: Landscape, Literature and Legend*

Horn, P 1987. *Labouring Life in the Victorian Countryside*. Abingdon: Fraser Stewart

Hunt, J 1997. 'Families at war: Royalists and Montfortians in the West Midlands'. *Midland Hist* **22**, 1–34

Hunt, J forthcoming. 'Law, disorder and county society in early 14th-century Staffordshire'

Hutton, R 1996. *The Stations of the Sun*. Oxford: Oxford University Press

Jackson, M 1988. *Castles of Shropshire*. Shrewsbury: Shropshire Libraries

Jewell, H M 1994. *The North–South Divide: The Origins of Northern Consciousness in England*. Manchester: Manchester University Press

Johnson, B L C and Wise, M J 1950. 'The Black Country 1800–1950', *in* Kinvig, R H, Smith, J G and Wise, M J (eds) *Birmingham and its Regional Setting, a Scientific Survey*. Birmingham: Br Assoc for the Advancement of Science, 229–48

King, P 1999. 'The development of the iron industry in south Staffordshire in the 17th century: history and myth'. *Staffordshire Archaeol Hist Soc Trans* **38**, 59–76

Kirby, K 2005. 'Was the wildwood closed forest or savannah – does it matter?'. Paper presented at Sheffield Hallam University conference *Crisis and Continuum in the Shaping of Landscapes*, 31 March–2 April 2005

Lacy, N J (ed.) 1988. *The Arthurian Encyclopedia*. Woodbridge: Boydell Press

Lake, J 1989. *Historic Farm Buildings*. London: Blandford

Lasdun, S 1991. *The English Park*. London: Andre Deutsch

Laws, B 1992. *Old English Farmhouses*. London: Collins and Brown

Lilley, K D 2002. *Urban Life in the Middle Ages 1000–1450*. Basingstoke: Palgrave

Lloyd, D 1993. *A History of Worcestershire*. Chichester: Phillimore

Losco-Bradley, S and Kinsley, S 2002. *Catholme. An Anglo-Saxon Settlement on the Trent Gravels in Staffordshire* (Nottingham Studies in Archaeology **3**). Nottingham: Univ Nottingham Dep Archaeol

Loudon, J C 1969. *The Landscape Gardening and Landscape Architecture of the Late Humphry Repton Esq.* (1840). New edn, Farnborough, Hants: Gregg International Publishers

Lowenthal, D 1999. 'From landscapes of the future to landscapes of the past'. *Norsk Geografisk Tidsskrift* (*Norwegian Journal of Geography*) **53**, 139–44

Lowry B, and Wilks M, 2002. *The Mercian Maquis*. Little Logaston Woonton Almeley: Logaston Press

Lucas, J 1988. 'Places and dwellings: Wordsworth, Clare and the anti–picturesque', *in* Cosgrove, D and Daniels, S (eds) *The Iconography of Landscape*. Cambridge: Cambridge University Press, 83–97

Magilton, J forthcoming. 'A Romano-Celtic temple and settlement at Grimstock Hill, Coleshill, Warwickshire'. *Trans Birmingham Warwickshire Archaeol Soc*

Marshall, J D 1986. 'Why study regions (2); some historical considerations'. *J Regional Local Stud* **6** (**1**), 1–12

Marshall, W, 1789. *The Rural Economy of Gloucestershire*, 2 vols

Mee, A 1937. *Staffordshire: Beauty and the Black Country*. London: Hodder and Stoughton

Milln, J 2003. 'Estate landscapes in the west midlands'. West Midlands Regional Research Framework for Archaeology, Seminar 7, www.arch-ant.bham.ac.uk/wmrrfa/index.htm

Mobley, P H 1977. *A Place Called Catshill. An Introduction to its History*. Private pub

Morris, C (ed.) 1992. *Selections from William Cobbett's* Illustrated Rural Rides 1821–1832. Waltham Abbey: Fraser Stewart

Morris, C (ed.) 1995. *The Illustrated Journeys of Celia Fiennes 1685–c. 1712*. Stroud: Alan Sutton

Murray, A 1813. *General View of the Agriculture of the County of Warwick*. London: Board of Agriculture Rep

Nash, T R 1725–1811. *Collections for the History and Antiquities of Worcestershire*

Palliser, D M 1976. *The Staffordshire Landscape*. London: Hodder and Stoughton

Palmer, R 1996. *The Sound of History: Songs and Social Comment*. London: Pimlico/Random House

Palmer, R 2002. *Herefordshire Folklore*. Little Logaston Woonton Almeley: Logaston Press

Payne Knight, R 1794. *The Landscape: A Didactic Poem* (2nd edn 1795)

Payne Knight, R 1805. *An Analytical Inquiry into the Principles of Taste* (3rd edn 1806)

Penoyre, J and Penoyre, J 1978. *Houses in the Landscape*. London: Faber and Faber; 1984 Faber Paperback

Percy, T 1996. *Reliques of Ancient Poetry, Vol II*. London: Routledge

Pevsner, N 1958. *The Buildings of England: Shropshire*. Harmondsworth: Penguin

Pevsner, N 1963. *The Buildings of England: Herefordshire*. Harmondsworth: Penguin

Phillips, A D M 2002. 'Soils, climate, and field systems', *in* Phillips, A D M and Phillips, C B (eds) *A New Historical Atlas of Cheshire*. Chester: Cheshire County Council, 52–3

Pilkington, J 1789. *View of Present State of Derbyshire, in Two Volumes, with an Account of its Most Remarkable Antiquities*

Pinkerton, J 1808. *A General Collection of the Best and Most Interesting Voyages in all Parts of the World, Vol VIII*

Pitt, W 1796. *General View of the Agriculture of Staffordshire* (2nd edn)

Pitt, W 1813. *General View of the Agriculture of the County of Worcester*. London: Sherwood, Neely, and Jones, Board of Agric Rep. Repr 1969, Newton Abbot: David and Charles

Plomer, W (ed.) 1938. *Kilvert's Diary. Selection from the Diary of the Rev Francis Kilvert*, 3 vols. London: Jonathan Cape

Plot, R 1686. *The Natural History of Staffordshire*

Price, N 1953. *The Derbyshire Dales*. London: Warne

Rackham, O 1986. *The History of the Countryside*. London: Dent

Rackham, O 1996. *Trees and Woodland in the British Landscape* (rev edn). London: Phoenix

Randall, J 1880. *History of Madeley: Including Ironbridge, Coalbrookdale, and Coalport*. Repr 1975, Shrewsbury: Salop County Library

Rattue, J 1995. *The Living Stream. Holy Wells in Historical Context*. Woodbridge: Boydell Press

Raven, J 1977. *The Urban and Industrial Songs of the Black Country and Birmingham*. Wolverhampton: Broadside

Reed, M 1987. *The Age of Exuberance 1500–1700*. London: Paladin

Reid, P 1980. *Burke's and Savills Guide to Country Houses, Vol II: Herefordshire, Shropshire, Warwickshire, Worcestershire*. London: Burke's Peerage

Richardson, R E and Musson C 2004. *Herefordshire Past and Present: An Aerial View*. Little Logaston Woonton Almeley: Logaston Press

Riden, P 1993. *A Gazetteer of Charcoal-fired Blast Furnaces in Great Britain in Use Since 1660*. Nottingham: Merton Priory Press

Riggs, D, 1989. *Ben Jonson: A Life*. Cambridge (Mass) and London: Harvard University Press

Rivet, A L F and Smith, C 1979. *The Place-Names of Roman Britain*. London: Batsford

Roberts, B K 1973. 'Field systems of the west midlands', *in* Baker, A R H and Butlin, R A (eds) *Studies of Field Systems in the British Isles*. Cambridge: Cambridge University Press, 188–231

Roberts, B K and Wrathmell, S 2000. *An Atlas of Rural Settlement in England*. London: English Heritage

Roberts, B K and Wrathmell, S 2002. *Region and Place. A Study of English Rural Settlement*. London: English Heritage

Rolt, L T C 1949. *Worcestershire*. London: Robert Hale

Romilly Allen, J 1906. 'Early Christian art', in *VCH Worcestershire II* 1906, 183

Rotherham, I D, Egan, D and Ardron, P A 2005. 'Fuel economy and the uplands: the effects of peat and turf utilisation on upland landscapes', *in* Whyte, I D and Winchester, A J L (eds) *Society, Landscape and Environment in Upland Britain* (Soc Landscape Studies Supp ser **2**). Birmingham: Soc for Landscape Studies, 99–109

Rothman, B 1982. *The 1932 Kinder Trespass*. Altrincham: Willow Publishing

Rowlands, M B 1987. *The West Midlands from AD 1000*. London: Longman

Rowley, T 1972. *The Shropshire Landscape*. London: Hodder and Stoughton

Rowley, T 2001. *The Welsh Border: Archaeology, History and Landscape*. Stroud: Tempus

Saunders, R 1959. *The Drovers' Highway*. London: Oldbourne

Saunders, V A 1978. 'Shropshire', *in* Darby H C and Terrett, I B (eds) *The Domesday Geography of Midland England* (2nd edn). Cambridge: Cambridge University Press, 115–62

Sheppard, J A 1979. *The Origins and Evolution of Field and Settlement Patterns in the Herefordshire Manor of Marden* (Dep Geography, Queen Mary College, London Univ, Occas Pap **15**). London: London Univ

Sherard, R H 1896. 'The white slaves of England, No 2. The nailmakers of Bromsgrove'. *Pearson's Magazine*

Shoard, M 1987. *This Land is Our Land*. London: Paladin

Shoesmith, R 1996. *Castles and Moated Sites of Herefordshire*. Little Logaston Woonton Almeley: Logaston Press

Skipp, V 1979. *The Centre of England*. London: Eyre Methuen

Skrine, H 1798. *Two Successive Tours through the Whole of Wales with Several of the English Counties*

Smith, B and Ralph, E 1972. *A History of Bristol and Gloucestershire*. Chichester: Phillimore

Stamper, P 1989. *'The Farmer Feeds Us All': A Short History of Shropshire Agriculture*. Shrewsbury: Shropshire Books

Stamper, P 2003. 'The post-medieval countryside'. West Midlands Regional Research Framework for Archaeology, Seminar 6, www.arch-ant.bham.ac.uk/wmrrfa/index.htm

Symonds, J 2003. 'Beyond the Industrial Revolution'. *Br Archaeol* **72**, 19–23

Talbot, R and Whiteman, R 1997. *The Peak District*. London: Weidenfeld and Nicolson

Tancred, T 1843. *Report of the Midland Mining Commission*

Tate, W E and Turner, M E 1978. *A Domesday of English Enclosure Acts and Awards*. Reading: Reading Univ Library

Taylor, C 1998. *Parks and Gardens of Britain: A Landscape History from the Air*. Edinburgh: Edinburgh Univ Press

Taylor, C 2004. 'Ravensdale Park, Derbyshire, and medieval deer coursing'. *Landscape History* **26**, 37–57

Tebbutt, M 2005. 'Gendering an upland landscape: masculinity and place identity in the Peak District, 1880s–1920s', *in* White, I D and Winchester, A J L *Society, Landscape and Environment in Upland Britain*. (Soc Landscape Studies Supp ser **2**). Birmingham: Soc Landscape Studies, 141–8

Thirsk, J 1987. *Agricultural Regions and Agrarian History in England, 1500–1750*. Basingstoke: Macmillan Education

Thompson, F M L 1963. *English Landed Society in the 19th Century*. London: Routledge and Kegan Paul

Thompson, M W 1964. 'Reclamation of waste ground for the Pleasance at Kenilworth Castle, Warwickshire'. *Medieval Archaeol* **8**, 222–3

Thurlby, M 1999. *The Herefordshire School of Romanesque Sculpture*. Little Logaston Woonton Almeley: Logaston Press

Tinniswood, A 1989. *A History of Country House Visiting: Five Centuries of Tourism and Taste*. Oxford: Basil Blackwell

Tolkien, C (ed.) 1979. *Sir Gawain and the Green Knight, Pearl, Sir Orfeo*, trans J R R Tolkien. London: Unwin

Toulmin Smith, L (ed.) 1964. *The Itinerary of John Leland in or about the Years 1535–1543*, Parts 1–5. London: Centaur

Trinder, B 1973. *The Industrial Revolution in Shropshire* (2nd edn 1981). Chichester: Phillimore

Trinder, B 1988. *'The Most Extraordinary District in the World' Ironbridge and Coalbrookdale* (2nd edn). Chichester: Phillimore

Trinder, B 1996. *The Industrial Archaeology of Shropshire*. Chichester: Phillimore

Trueman, A E 1938. *The Scenery of England and Wales*. London: Gollanz

Upton, C 1993. *A History of Birmingham*. Chichester: Phillimore

VCH Derbyshire I 1905. *A History of Derbyshire, Vol I*. London: Constable

VCH Derbyshire II 1907. *A History of Derbyshire, Vol II*. London: Constable

VCH Gloucestershire II 1907. *A History of Gloucestershire, Vol II*. London: Constable

VCH Herefordshire I 1908. *The Victoria History of the County of Hereford, Vol I*. London: Constable

VCH Shropshire IV 1989. *The Victoria History of Shropshire, Vol IV, Agriculture*. Oxford: Oxford Univ Press for Inst Hist Res

VCH Shropshire X 1998. *The Victoria History of Shropshire, Vol X*. Oxford: Oxford Univ Press for Inst Hist Res

VCH Staffordshire I 1908. *The Victoria History of Stafford, Vol I*. London: Constable

VCH Staffordshire II 1967. *A History of the County of Stafford, Vol II*. Oxford: Oxford Univ Press for Inst Hist Res

VCH Staffordshire VI 1979. *A History of the County of Stafford, Vol VI*. Oxford: Oxford Univ Press for Inst Hist Res

VCH Staffordshire 17 1976. *A History of the County of Stafford, Vol 17*. Oxford: Oxford Univ Press for Inst Hist Res

VCH Warwickshire II 1908. *A History of the County of Warwick, Vol II*. London: Constable. Repr 1965, London: Dawson for Inst Hist Res

VCH Worcestershire II 1906. *A History of Worcestershire, Vol II*. London: James Street

Vera, F W M 2000. *Grazing Ecology and Forest History*. Wallingford: CAB International

Wade Martins, S 1995. *Farms and Fields*. London: Batsford

Wager, S J 1998. *Woods, Wolds and Groves: The Woodland of Medieval Warwickshire* (BAR Brit Ser **269**). Oxford: Brit Archaeol Rep

Wall, T 1994. 'The verdant landscape: the practice and theory of Richard Payne Knight at Downton Vale', *in* Daniels, S and Watkins, C (eds) *The Picturesque Landscape: Visions of Georgian Herefordshire*. Nottingham: Univ Nottingham Dep Geography, 49–60

Warwick County Records iii 1937, ed. Ratcliffe, C and Johnson H C. Easter Quarter Sessions Records, 1655. Warwick: L Edgar Stephens

Waterson, M 1994. *The National Trust: The First Hundred Years*. London: National Trust and BBC Books

Watson, M and Musson, C 1993. *Shropshire from the Air*. Shrewsbury: Shropshire Books

Weale, M E, Weiss, D A, Jager, R F, Bradman, N and Thomas, M G 2002. 'Y chromosome evidence for Anglo-Saxon mass migration'. *Mol Biol Evol* **19** (**7**), 1008–21

Welch, C 1997. 'Glass-making in Wolseley, Staffordshire'. *Post-Medieval Archaeol* **31**, 1–60

Welch, C 2000. 'Elizabethan ironmaking and the woodlands of Cannock Chase and the Churnet valley, Staffordshire'. *Staffordshire Stud* **12**, 17–73

West, J 1962. *Village Records*. London: Macmillan

West, J and West, M 1985. *A History of Herefordshire*. Chichester: Phillimore

West Midland Group on Post-War Reconstruction and Planning 1948. *Conurbation: A Planning Survey of Birmingham and the Black Country*. London: Architectural Press

White, P 2003. *The Arrow Valley, Herefordshire: Archaeology, Landscape Change and Conservation* (Herefordshire Studies in Archaeol, Ser **2**). Hereford: Herefordshire County Council

White, R 2003. 'The west midlands in the fifth and sixth centuries'. West Midlands Regional Research Framework for Archaeology, Seminar 4, www.arch-ant.bham.ac.uk/wmrrfa/index.htm

White, R and Barker, P 2002. *Wroxeter: Life and Death of a Roman City*. Stroud: Tempus

Whitehead, D 2000. 'The de Fresnes, Vaughans and Cornewalls: 1160–1771', *in* Harding, P T and Wall, T (eds) *Moccas: An English Deer Park*. Peterborough: English Nature, 41–8

Wilkinson, G 1978. *Epitaph for the Elm*. London: Hutchinson

Williams, A F 1984. *Waseley Hill Country Park and its Neighbourhood* (Northfield Conservation Group Occas Pap **15**). Birmingham: Northfield Society

Williamson, T 1995. *Polite Landscapes: Gardens and Society in Eighteenth-century England*. Stroud: Alan Sutton

Williamson, T 1998. 'Questions of preservation and destruction', *in* Everson, P and Williamson, T (eds) *The Archaeology of Landscape: Studies Presented to Christopher Taylor*. Manchester: Manchester Univ Press, 1–24

Wise, M J 1950. 'The Cannock Chase region', *in* Kinvig, R H, Smith, J G and Wise, M J (eds) *Birmingham and its Regional Setting: A Scientific Survey*. Birmingham: Br Assoc for the Advancement of Science, 269–88

Wise, M J, and Johnson, B L C 1950. 'The changing regional pattern during the eighteenth century', *in* Kinvig, R H, Smith, J G and Wise, M J (eds) *Birmingham and its Regional Setting: A Scientific Survey*. Birmingham: Br Assoc for the Advancement of Science, 161–86

Woodforde, J 1969. *The Truth about Cottages*. London: Routledge and Kegan Paul

Wright, D (trans) 1957, 1970. *Beowulf*. 1957 Harmondsworth: Penguin; 1970 London: Panther

Yelling, J A 1977. *Common Field and Enclosure in England 1450–1850*. London: Macmillan

Young, A 1741–1820. *Tours in England and Wales; Selected from the 'Annals of Agriculture'*. Repr 1932, London: London School of Economics and Political Science

Index

Picture Credits

Author acknowledgements

I should like to thank the librarians at the University of Birmingham, the archaeological officers and many other friends who responded so readily to my queries, and those who helped to suggest and supply many of the illustrations – particularly David Prentice, who so willingly sent me slides of his paintings of the Malvern Hills, and Ron Moss, who suggested and supplied old photographs of the Black Country. A special thank you for permission to reproduce the extracts of various poems, including: Bob Clark, for permission to reproduce lines from Leonard Clark's poem 'The Forest'; Jon Raven, for permission to quote excerpts from a number of poems published in his book *Songs of the Black Country* (Broadside, 1977); Johnny Coppin, for his interest and advice. While every effort has been made to contact the copyright holders, the publishers would be happy to hear from anyone they have been unable to trace.

Aerial survey acknowledgements

New English Heritage aerial photographs were taken by Damian Grady, Peter Horne, David Macleod and Jane Stone. The Aerial Reconnaissance team would like to thank the following people for their help: a special note of thanks must go to the skills and patience of the pilots Mark Julian, Mick Webb and Marten White; the aircraft owners Anthony Crawshaw and David Sanders; the NMR cataloguing team Rose Ogle, Katy Groves, Catherine Runciman, Cinzia Bacilieri, Philip Daniels, Geoff Hall; Jon Proudman for all the publication scanning; Sarah Prince for laser copying thousands of aerial photographs to send to the authors; and Kate Bould for post reconnaissance administrative support in York.